THE HUMANITIES THROUGH THE ARTS

W9-BVB-117

Saint Peter's University Library
Withdrawn

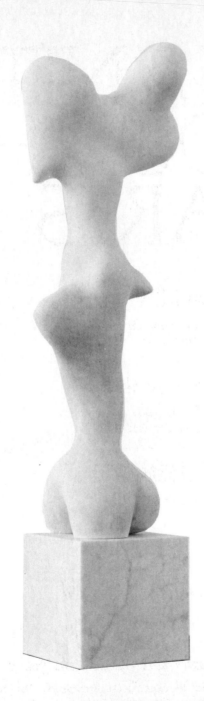

Jean Arp, *Growth*. 1938.
Marble, 39½ inches high.
Courtesy of the
Solomon R. Guggenheim Museum.

THE HUMANITIES THROUGH THE ARTS

F. David Martin

Professor of Philosophy
Bucknell University

Lee A. Jacobus

Professor of English
University of Connecticut

Third Edition

McGraw-Hill Book Company

New York   St. Louis   San Francisco   Auckland   Bogotá   Hamburg
Johannesburg   London   Madrid   Mexico   Montreal   New Delhi
Panama   Paris   São Paulo   Singapore   Sydney   Tokyo   Toronto

THE HUMANITIES THROUGH THE ARTS

Copyright © 1983, 1978, 1975 by McGraw-Hill, Inc. All rights reserved. Printed in the United States of America. Except as permitted under the United States Copyright Act of 1976, no part of this publication may be reproduced or distributed in any form or by any means, or stored in a data base or retrieval system, without the prior written permission of the publisher.

567890DOCDOC898765

ISBN 0-07-040639-1

This book was set in Trump Mediaeval by Black Dot, Inc. (ECU).
The editors were Kaye Pace and Barry Benjamin;
the designer was Joan E. O'Connor;
the production supervisor was Dominick Petrellese.
R. R. Donnelley & Sons Company was printer and binder.

Library of Congress Cataloging in Publication Data

Martin, F. David, date
    The humanities through the arts.

    Includes bibliographies and indexes.
    1. Arts—Psychology.   2. Art appreciation.
I. Jacobus, Lee A.   II. Title.
NX165.M37   1983   700'.1   82-15302
ISBN 0-07-040639-1   AACR2

JX
65
737
983
.9

WE DEDICATE THIS STUDY TO TEACHERS
AND STUDENTS OF THE HUMANITIES.

CONTENTS

PREFACE

The Humanities through the Arts is an exploratory approach to the humanities that focuses on the special role of the arts. The relation of the humanities to values—objects and events important to man—is emphasized; and a basic distinction is made between the role of artists and that of other humanists. Artists reveal values; the other humanists study or reflect upon values. This book provides a self-contained program for studying values as revealed in the arts and reflected upon in the other humanities.

Revelatory aesthetics, the basic theory that organizes the presentation of material in this study, offers a relatively uncomplicated basis for understanding and appreciating the arts. Our approach is one which should be especially welcome to the student, for whom an explicit concern about values is usually central to his or her education. Teachers, for their part, while respecting the usefulness of formal analysis, are aware of the limitations of separating art from the larger concerns of human values.

While most humanities texts study the arts chronologically within the frameworks of their social and stylistic environments, we have not organized our study historically, except incidentally. The book begins with a general introduction to the humanities, focusing on what they are and the basic importance of the arts to the other humanities. The next two chapters, devoted to definitions of art and varieties of critical approaches to the arts, establish a foundation for critical response. Then the various arts are explored individually in chapters on painting, sculpture, architecture, literature, drama, music, dance, film, and photography, with the relationships of subject matter, form, and content in each of these arts supplying the framework of the analyses.

The emphasis throughout the text is on participation and involvement with maximum understanding and thus maximum intensity of enjoyment—allowing each work of art to unfold its fullness. To help the reader sharpen his or her perceptive responses to the work of art, we have provided "perception keys," making this book unique among humanities texts. Concentrating on specific works of art, the perception keys include questions and suggestions designed to elicit more sensitive perception. The student is enabled to see immediately the extent or limit of his or her understanding of any given example. The perception keys also encourage both critical and creative activities by the student. Through genuine participation, the student is prevented from being a passive receptor of absolute value statements about the arts. The perception keys invite the student to question and test virtually all statements of interpretation and value—whether implicit or explicit—throughout the text as well as in the classroom and in his or her own general experience. Our analyses, which usually follow rather than precede the keys, are offered not as *the* way to perceive a given work of art, but rather as one possible way. We avoid dogmatic answers and explanations; our primary interest is in exciting our readers to perceive the splendid singularity of a work of art.

In the final chapter, the relationships of values in the arts to the other humanities—especially history, philosophy, and religion—are explored with the help of "conception keys." Similar in format to the perception keys, they involve the student in conceptual problems and explore the distinctions between perceiving and conceiving. Through its use of perception and conception keys, *The Humanities through the Arts* comes as close to being self-instructional as a humanities book can be.

In the second edition of *The Humanities through the Arts*, a chapter on drama was added. In this third edition—along with refinement of discussions and new material and analyses—a chapter on photography has been added. Photography is explored as an art independent of painting and film. This third edition, furthermore, has been more closely coordinated with the telecourse—"Humanities through the Arts"—based on our book. Produced by KOCE-TV (Channel 50) and Coast Community College District, consisting of thirty one-half hour programs, and hosted by Maya Angelou, the telecourse is now widely distributed in cassettes as well as being broadcast nationally by the Public Broadcasting Corporation.

We believe that the arts and the other humanities are a commonwealth, that they comment on and complement each other just as the sciences do. By deepening our understanding of the revelations and reflections about values that the humanities provide, we deepen the foundations for our value decisions. We also strengthen our powers to endure and to enjoy life; for the humanities, perhaps more than any other civilizing activity, satisfy our insistent zest for existence.

Acknowledgments

A book of this nature must always be indebted to far more people than can be properly credited. Yet some names must be mentioned. A number of anonymous reviewers read the manuscript at various stages, and for their help we are indeed grateful. Harrison Davis, of Brigham Young University, had some important suggestions and valuable criticisms which led to revisions that strengthened the book. The critical eye of such people as Selma Jeanne Cohen, editor of *Dance Perspectives*, led to changes and refinements which might not have been made otherwise. Conversations with numerous people involved in the humanities all led, in one way or another, to adjustments or insights that helped during the formulative phases of this book. Such people as Gerald Eager of the art department of Bucknell University; Deborah Jowitt, dance critic of the *Village Voice*; the dance critic Marica Segal; Martha Myers, chairman of the Department of Dance at Connecticut College; Joanna J. Jacobus, choreographer and dance teacher; Walter Wehner of the Music Faculty of the University of North Carolina at Greensboro; Marceau Myers, Dean of the Music Conservatory at Capitol University; William E. Parker, photographer, of the University of Connecticut; Alison Meersschaert, Cheryl Melhalik, and Kaye Pace of McGraw-Hill; and many more besides them, all made contributions of one kind or another which found their way into our book. Naturally, we also express gratitude to our students, whose insights and whose needs are reflected here. And we thank Mrs. Nancy Johnson, who scrupulously cared for the manuscript and the frequent overhauls it sustained. Finally, we thank the Bucknell University Press for permission to paraphrase and quote from *Art and the Religious Experience*, 1972, and the University Press of Kentucky for permission to paraphrase and quote from *Sculpture and Enlivened Space*, 1981, both by F. David Martin.

F. David Martin
Lee A. Jacobus

THE HUMANITIES THROUGH THE ARTS

THE HUMANITIES: AN INTRODUCTION

The Humanities and the Sciences

Not too many centuries ago the word "humanities" distinguished that which pertained to God from that which pertained to humans. Mathematics, the sciences, the arts, and philosophy were humanities: They had to do with humans. Theology and related studies were the subjects of divinity: They had to do with God. This distinction does not have the importance for most of us that it once did. Today we think of the humanities as those broad areas of human creativity and study that are distinct from mathematics and the "hard" sciences, mainly because in the humanities strictly objective or scientific standards are not usually dominant.

The separation between the sciences and the humanities is illustrated by the way in which values work differently in the two areas. Consider, for example, the drinking of liquor: a positive value for some people, a negative value for others. The biologist describes the physiological effects. The psychologist describes the psychological effects. The sociologist takes a poll tabulating people's value preferences concerning drinking. These scientists study values, but they are concerned with "what is" rather than "what ought to be." That is why they can apply strictly scientific standards to their investigations. If they make a value judgment, such as that liquor ought to be banned, they will tend—as scientists—to make it clear that their pronouncements are personal value judgments rather than scientific statements. With humanists, on the other hand, the sharp separation between the "is" and the "ought," between scientific statement and value judgment, is usually not so evident, primarily because the scientific method is not so basic to their work. Most scientists and humanists will agree that we must all make value judgments and that the sciences can often provide important information that helps us make sound decisions. For example, if biologists discovered that liquor shortens the life span significantly, this discovery would indeed be relevant to a value judgment about banning liquor. On the other hand, such consensus seems to be lacking with respect to the relevance of the humanities to value judgments. Scientists, more than humanists, probably would be dubious about an assertion that novels such as Dostoevski's *Brothers Karamazov* contribute important information for making sound value judgments about the banning of liquor.

The discoveries of the scientists—for example, the bomb and the pill—often have tremendous impact on the values of their society. Yet some scientists have declared that they merely make the discoveries and that others—presumably politicians—must decide how those discoveries are to be used. Perhaps it is this last statement that brings us closest to the importance of the humanities. If many scientists feel they cannot judge how their discoveries are to be used, then we must try to understand why they give that responsibility to others. This is not to say that scientists uniformly turn such decisions over to others, for many of them are humanists as well as scientists. But the fact remains that governments—from that of Hitler to that of Churchill and those of such nations as China, the Soviet Union, and the United States—have all made use of great scientific achievements without pausing to ask the "achievers" if they approved of the way their discoveries were being used. The questions are: Who decides how to use such discoveries? On what grounds should their judgments be based?

Studying the behavior of neutrinos or ion-exchange resins will not help get us closer to the answer. Such study is not related to the nature of humankind but to the nature of nature. What we need is a study that will get us closer to ourselves. It should be a study that explores the reaches of human feeling in relation to values—not only our own individual feelings and values, although that is first in importance, but also the feelings and values of others. We need a study that will increase our sensitivity to ourselves, others, and the values in our world. To be sensitive is to perceive with insight. To be sensitive is also to feel and believe that things make a difference. Furthermore, it involves an awareness of those aspects of values that cannot be measured by objective standards. To be sensitive is to respect the humanities because, among other reasons, they help develop our sensitivity to values, to what we as individuals place importance on. Values are strictly in the domain of the humanities because they are strictly relative to us and our condition.

There are numerous ways to approach the humanities. The way we have chosen here is the way of the arts. The arts clarify or reveal values. As we deepen our understanding of the arts, we necessarily deepen our understanding of values, for that is what the arts are about. We will study our experience with works of art as well as the values that others associate with those works. We will look at the "whys and whats" of art by examining why certain kinds of values are associated with certain kinds of art. And in the process of doing this we will also be educating ourselves about the nature of our own values.

Taste

This brings us to a crucial issue. Most people have already made up their minds about what art they like and what art they do not like. There are opera buffs who think opera in English is necessarily inferior to opera in Italian, French, or German. In fact, because we have so long listened to opera in foreign languages, the odds are that an American opera lover will find it difficult to accept any opera the words of which he or she can understand. People have various kinds of limitations about the arts. Some cannot look at a painting or sculpture of a nude figure without smirking. Some think any painting is magnificent as long as it has a dog in it, or a horse, or a sunset, or a rolling sea, or a battle, or—and this is an extreme but not impossible case—no recognizable figures at all. And we know people who will read any book that has automobile racing as part of its subject matter, that has a scientific angle to it, or that is about something they are already deeply interested in. By watching the local papers we can see how the taste of the mass public shifts. Movies, for example, survive or fail commercially on the basis of the number of people they can appeal to. Consequently, films change periodically in subject matter and style in order to "cash in" on current popular tastes; and the film, of course, is only one form of commercial art in our time.

Tastes change, and, as anyone who has lived in the Western world knows, they change with alarming rapidity. What this means is sometimes difficult to assess; but one thing it certainly means is that by playing on popular tastes, the arts can also play on our limitations. It means that commercially successful arts can play upon values in such a way as to give us what we think we want rather than what we really need with reference to insight. Also, we all have limitations as perceivers of art; most of us defend ourselves against stretching our limitations by assuming that we have developed our taste and that any effort to change it is "bad form." An old saying—"Matters of taste are not disputable"—can be credited with making many of us feel very righteous about our own "taste." What the saying means is that there is no accounting for what people like in the arts, for beauty is in the eye of the beholder. Thus, there is no use trying to do anything that might help someone change his or her mind about the arts. Or, to put it differently: There is no use in trying to educate anyone about the arts.

Obviously we do not feel that way about the arts ourselves. We believe that all of us can and should be educated about the arts and should learn to respond to as wide a variety of the arts as possible: from rock, to jazz, to string quartets; from Charlie Chaplin to Ingmar Bergman; from Lewis Carroll to T. S. Eliot; from primitive folk art to Picasso. "Taste," in other words, is a term we sometimes use to approve our limitations. And since we all have limitations, we must admit that the word sometimes comes in handy. But we also realize that we can do without the word in that narrow sense—and happily so if doing without it can help us discover something new and really exciting in the arts we might otherwise have missed.

Most of us use the word "taste" defensively for a good reason. Anyone who tampers with our taste is tampering with our deep feelings. Anyone who tries to change our responses to art is really trying to get inside our minds. If we fail to understand its purpose, this kind of education naturally arouses resistance in us—unlike the kinds of education that entail gathering facts or learning specific skills.

There are many facts involved in the study of the arts. We can verify the dates of Beethoven's birth and death and the dates of his important compositions. We can investigate the history of jazz and the claims of Jelly Roll Morton for having been its "inventor." We can decide who was or was not part of the Barbizon school of painting in nineteenth-century France, when Corot and Manet were painting. There are oceans of facts associated with every art. But our interest is not in facts alone.

What we mean by a study of the arts is something that penetrates beyond facts to the values that evoke our feelings—the way a succession of guitar chords can be electrifying or the way song lyrics can give you a chill. In other words, we want to go beyond the facts *about* a work of art and get to the fact of the work itself, to the values working in the work. This means we want to learn how to "come to" the work of art itself, to get as close as possible to what is there. This is the meaning of "education" in the sense that we have been using the term. The problem with taste and concepts like it is that they get in the way of our education. We all know some people we do not bother to talk to about the kind of music we like. We do not worry much about it, but we all think that what we like is pretty good and that other people could benefit from paying attention to it—maybe. And the "maybe" is usually connected with two things: whether or not we can get those other people to listen to what we think is good and then whether or not the experience these other people have is a full and fair one. That last point is crucial: Even though a person is exposed to a work of art, the experience may not "take" unless he or she perceives as much as possible of what is there. A failure of perception is precisely what happens to us when we experience a work of art we are told is good (presuming it actually is good) and we are unable to appreciate it. How many times have we all found ourselves liking something that, years or months before, we could not stand? And how often do we find ourselves now disliking what we previously judged a masterpiece?

Responses to art

Our responses to art usually involve processes so complex that they can never be fully tracked down or analyzed. They can only be hinted at when we talk about them. Let us begin by looking at a painting by David Alfaro Siquieros, a contemporary Mexican painter, called *Echo of a Scream* (Figure 1-1).

This is a highly emotional painting—in the sense that the work seems to demand a strong emotional response. What we see is the huge head of a baby crying, and then, as if issuing from its own mouth, the baby himself. What kinds of emotions do you find stirring in yourself as you look at this painting? What kinds of emotions would you expect your friends to be having when they look at it? You will not find, under any conditions, that the emotions you might be able to isolate—such as shock, pity for the child, irritation at a destructive, mechanical society, or any other nameable emotion—will sum up the painting or be equivalent to it. This is natural and desirable. If Siquieros could have gotten the same effect in words, he would not have needed to paint.

PERCEPTION KEY ECHO OF A SCREAM

1. Identify the objects in the painting.
2. What is the condition of the objects? What is their relationship to the baby?
3. What is the meaning of those strange round forms in the upper right corner?
4. How would your response differ if the angular lines were smoothed out?
5. How does Siquieros establish the relative importance of shapes in the composition?
6. Discuss the function of the distortions of natural shapes in the painting. Is awareness of these distortions crucial to a sensitive response to the painting?

FIGURE 1-1 David
Alfaro Siquieros, *Echo of
a Scream*. 1937. Duco on
wood, 48 by 36 inches.
Collection, The Museum
of Modern Art, New
York. Gift of Edward
M. M. Warburg.

Consider another work, very close in temperament to Siquieros'
painting: *Eternal City* by the American painter Peter Blume (Color
Plate 1).

PERCEPTION KEY ETERNAL CITY

1. What common ingredients do you find in the Blume and Siquieros
   paintings?
2. Do you have a similar reaction to each painting?

3. Is the effect of the distortions similar or different?
4. In terms of the objects and events represented in each painting, do you think the paintings are comparable? Give reasons.
5. Can you think of other works of art in other media—such as sculpture, architecture, literature, drama, music, dance, and film—that represent objects and events similar to those represented in *Eternal City?*
6. Of the other arts mentioned in the fifth question, which one or ones seem most capable of representing the objects and events of *Eternal City?* Will these other media, nevertheless, necessarily represent them differently? And if so, what significance may this have for our study of the arts?

Having attended carefully to the kinds of responses awakened by *Eternal City,* take note of some information about the painting that you may not have known. The date of this painting is the same as that of *Echo of a Scream:* 1937. *Eternal City* is a name reserved for only one city in the world: Rome. In 1937 the world was on the verge of an enormous war between the fascist nations of Italy and Germany and the democratic nations of Europe and America. In the center of the painting is the Roman forum, close to where Julius Caesar, the alleged tyrant, was murdered by Brutus. But here we see Fascist Black Shirts beating people. At the left is a figure of Christ and beneath him is a beggar woman—a cripple. Near her are ruins of classic Roman statuary. The enlarged and distorted head, wriggling out like a jack-in-the-box, is that of Mussolini: the man who invented the Black Shirts and fascism. Now look at the painting closely again. Do you now respond differently to the painting?

Before going on to the next painting, which is quite different in character, we should pause to make some observations about what we have done. With added knowledge about its cultural and political implications—what we shall call the background of the painting—your responses to *Eternal City* perhaps have changed significantly. Ideally they should have become more focused, intense, and certain. Why? The painting is surely the same physical object you looked at originally. Nothing has changed in that object. Therefore, something has changed because something has been added to *you:* information that the general viewer of the painting in 1937 would not only have had right at his or her fingertips but also probably would have responded to much more emotionally than we do now. Consider how a fascist or an Italian humanist and lover of Roman culture would have reacted to this painting in 1937. Obviously, the experience of this painting is not one thing or one system of things but an innumerable variety of things. Moreover, knowledge *about* a work of art can often help give you knowledge *of* the work of art, a deeper experience of that work. This is important as a basic principle, since it means that we can be educated about what works in a work of art, not just about the things that are external to a work, such as its historical background. It means we can learn to respond more sensitively than we do. It also means that painters such as Peter Blume sometimes produce works of art that we must know something about if we are to appreciate them fully. This is particularly true of literature, since most literature assumes that we can fit ourselves into the psychological framework of the characters and the sociological framework of their society as well as the cultural framework of the story. Therefore, there are times when we cannot respond very deeply to a work of art simply because we do not have the background knowledge the artist presupposes.

Picasso's *Guernica* (Figure 1-2) is one of the most famous paintings of the twentieth century. It was painted in 1937, like the other paintings. Its title comes from the name of an old Spanish town that was bombed during the Spanish Civil War—the first aerial bombing of noncombatant civilians in modern warfare. Examine this painting carefully.

PERCEPTION KEY GUERNICA

1. Distortion again is powerfully evident in this painting. Is its function similar to that of the distortion in Blume's or Siquieros' paintings?
2. Describe the objects in the painting. What is their relationship to each other?
3. Why the prominence of the light bulb?
4. What large geometrical shapes dominate the painting? Why are these shapes used? Are they basic to the overall organization of the painting? Do they have anything to do with the balance of the painting?
5. Because of reading habits in the West, we tend initially to focus on the left side of most paintings and then move to the right. Is this the case with your perception of *Guernica*? In the organization or form of *Guernica* is there a countermovement that, once our vision has reached the right side, pulls us back to the left? If so, what in the painting causes this countermovement? Do these left–right and right–left movements have anything to do with the balance of the painting?
6. The bull seems to be totally unaffected by the carnage. Do you think the bull may be some kind of symbol? For example, could the bull "stand for" the spirit of the Spanish people? Could the bull "stand for" General Franco, the man who ordered the bombing? Or could the bull "stand for" both? To answer these questions adequately do you need further background information or can you defend your answers by referring to what is in the painting, or do you need to do both?
7. Is there a clear distinction between the way the horse and the human beings are represented? What does your observation imply?
8. If you were not told, would you know that this painting was a representation of an air raid?
9. Is the subject matter—what the work is about— of this painting war? Death? Suffering? Can you relate the subject matter of *Guernica* to the subject matters of the other paintings we have just discussed? Are these subject matters the same? Could sculpture, architecture, literature,

FIGURE 1-2   Pablo Picasso, *Guernica*. 1937. Oil on canvas, 11 feet 6 inches by 25 feet 8 inches. © SPADEM, Paris/VAGA, New York, 1982.

drama, music, dance, and film have the same kind of subject matter as *Guernica?* Be as specific as possible.

10.   What kinds of responses does the painting evoke in you?

The next painting—(Color Plate 2)—was completed in 1936 by Piet Mondrian, a very influential Dutch painter.

PERCEPTION KEY COMPOSITION IN WHITE, BLACK AND RED

1.   If you were to comment on "distortion" in this painting, what would that imply about what the painting represents?
2.   What are the objects represented in the painting? Do they have anything to do with life outside the painting? What?
3.   How would your responses differ if all the black areas were repainted orange? Would the balance of the painting be distorted?
4.   Suppose the horizontal black line running across the width of the painting were raised nearer to the top. Would the balance of the painting be disturbed?
5.   Suppose the little black rectangle at the upper left-hand corner were enlarged. Would the balance of the painting be disturbed?
6.   Suppose the red rectangle were repainted green. Would the balance of the painting be disturbed?
7.   Is balance an especially important factor in this work? Explain.
8.   Suppose upon entering a room you noticed that the picture frame of the

Mondrian had been hung so that its horizontal and vertical lines were not parallel to the lines of the wall. Do you think you would have any need to straighten the frame? Suppose you found *Echo of a Scream* similarly awry. Would you have as strong a need to straighten its frame? Explain.

9. Do you need any historical background to appreciate Mondrian's painting? Is what we have said about world conditions in 1937 irrelevant to this painting? Soon after that date, Mondrian's country, Holland, partially destroyed itself by opening its dikes in an attempt to keep Hitler out. Does this fact influence the way you look at this painting?

Does the painting evoke strong responses in you? Do you have more difficulty articulating your responses to it than to the paintings by Siquieros, Blume, and Picasso? If so, how is this to be explained?

10. Is the painting by Mondrian more like music than the paintings by Siquieros, Blume, and Picasso? Explain.

Artistic Form

The Mondrian obviously is very different from the other paintings in subject matter and style. The responses you have when you look at it are probably quite different from those you had when you were viewing the other paintings, but why? You might reply that the Mondrian is pure form, nothing but a sensuous surface. Unlike the other paintings, no objects or events are represented. And yet this painting can be very exciting. Form—the interrelationships of lines, colors, light, textures, and shapes—can be very moving. Most of us have the capacity to respond to pure form, even in paintings that have a subject matter that distracts us from pure form. Thus, for most people, responding to *Eternal City* involves responding not just to a painter's interpretation of fascism taking hold in Italy but also to the shapes, colors, and proportions of things in the painting. This is certainly true of *Echo of a Scream;* if you look back at that painting, you will see that the distortions and placement of figures are calculated to help our responses become deeper than they would be if the crying baby and the destruction of war were represented without distortion. In the hands of a good painter (or any artist), form is a weapon for getting inside our minds without our necessarily being aware of it.

Every painter uses form, but every painter does not necessarily call attention to it the way Mondrian does. And since we often respond to form without even being conscious that it is affecting us, it is of the first importance that a painter make sure form is successful. Study the composition of *Eternal City*. Figure 1-3 is a tracing of the basic form.

In the "center stage" of the composition is the scene of Fascist Black Shirts brutalizing citizens: the government in its forum. To one side is Christ, not only removed but bricked off. Moreover, Christ is smaller and less important to the composition than Mussolini's head—the largest shape—close to the action and in control. The two

FIGURE 1-3 Line tracing of Blume's *Eternal City*.

shapes beneath Mussolini's head represent the smiling common people, the middle-class citizens who helped Mussolini gain power and who thought they would benefit from his government.

The form of any painting can be analyzed because any painting has to be organized: Parts have to be interrelated. Moreover, it is very helpful to look closely and think carefully about the form of individual paintings. This is particularly true of paintings one does not respond to immediately—to "difficult" or apparently uninteresting paintings. Often the analysis of form can get us into such paintings and open them up so that they become genuinely exciting.

PERCEPTION KEY ANALYSIS AND RESPONSE

Analyze the form of some paintings—*Echo of a Scream*, *Guernica*, or any other painting you see in this book. Do the same with works of art in other media. Do you find that after such analyses your responses to these works are more satisfactory?

Perception

We cannot respond properly to a work of art that we do not perceive properly. What is less obvious is what we referred to previously: the fact that we can often give our attention to a work of art and still not really perceive very much. The reason for this should be relatively clear from what we have already said: There are frequently things we do not know about the background of a work of art that would aid our perception of it. If we do not know that background, we may not be able to perceive what is there. Anyone who did not know who Christ was, what fascism was, and what Mussolini meant to the world would have a difficult time making much sense of *Eternal City*. But it is also true that anyone who could not perceive the form of Blume's painting might have a completely superficial response to it. Such a person could indeed know all about the background and understand the more or less symbolic statement being made by the painting, but that is only part of the painting. From seeing what Mondrian can do with lines and color, you can understand that the formal qualities of a painting are neither accidental nor unimportant. In Blume's painting, the form acts in such a way as to focus attention and organize our perceptions by establishing the relationships between the elements of the composition.

Form is basic to all the arts and to everything that is organized by humans (as well as everything organized by other forces). To perceive any work of art adequately, we must perceive form. Examine the following poem—"l(a"—by E. E. Cummings, a modern American. It is unusual in looks, just as it is unusual in its form and its effects upon most of us.

l(a

le
af
fa

ll

s)
one
l

iness

[Copyright © 1958 by E. E. Cummings. Reprinted from his volume, *Complete Poems 1913–1962*, by permission of Harcourt Brace Jovanovich, Inc.]

This poem looks at first like a strange kind of code, like an Egyptian hieroglyphic. But it is not a code—it is more like a Japanese haiku poem, a poem that sets a scene or paints a picture and then waits for us to "get it." And to "get it" requires sensitive perception.

PERCEPTION KEY "l(a"

1. Study the poem carefully until you begin to make out the words. What are they?
2. One part of the poem is a general term; the other is the name of an event. What is the relationship between them?

3. Is the shape of the poem important to the meaning of the poem?
4. Why are the words of the poem hard to perceive? Is that difficulty important to the poem?
5. Once you have perceived the words and imagery of the poem, is your response to it different?
6. Compare your analysis of the poem with ours, which follows.

In this poem there is a word interrupted by parentheses. The word is simply "l one l iness"—"loneliness"—a feeling which we have all experienced and which we can all bring to mind at will. Because of its isolating, biting power, we ordinarily do not like this feeling. Then, inside the parentheses, there is a phrase, "a leaf falls," which is a description of an event: a leaf falls. In poetry such a description is usually called an "image." In this poem the image "illustrates" the idea, or theme, of loneliness. The image reinforces the idea and gives us something we can all imagine to make us feel more deeply the idea of loneliness. But that is not all Cummings had done to help us get a deeper, more intense feeling from the poem. Notice the devices that symbolize or represent oneness, which in a way is what loneliness is. The poem begins with the letter "l," which in the typeface used in the original poem looks like the number "one." Even the parenthesis separating the "a" from the "l" helps accent the isolation of the "1." Then there is the "le," which is the singular article in French. The idea of one is repeated, doubled, in the "ll" figure. Then Cummings brazenly writes "one" and follows it by "l" and then the ultimate "iness." Furthermore, in the original edition the poem is number one of the collection. By now we should indeed have perceived what Cummings is getting at. But it takes very close looking at this poem to observe that much. And there is more to it even than this. As you look at the poem, you will notice that your eye follows a downward path that swirls in a pattern similar to the diagram in Figure 1-4.

This is merely following the parentheses and the consonants. If you follow the vowels as well, you will see that the curves become spirals, and the figure is indeed much like that of a leaf actually falling; this accounts for the long, thin look of the poem. Now, go back to the poem and reread it. Has your response changed? How?

Of course, most poems do not work in quite the way this poem does. Most poems do not rely on the way they look on the page, although this is one of the most important things to Cummings. But what most poets are concerned with is the way the images or verbal pictures fit into the totality of the poem, how they make us experience the whole poem more intensely. In Cummings' poem the single, falling, dying leaf—one out of so many—is virtually perfect for helping us understand loneliness from a dying person's point of view. People are like leaves in that they are countless when they are alive and together. But like leaves, they die singly. And when one person

FIGURE 1-4 Diagram of E. E. Cummings' "l(a)."

separates him- or herself from the community of friends, that person is as alone as the separate leaf.

Abstract Ideas and Concrete Images

Cummings' poem presents an abstract idea fused with a concrete image or word picture. It is concrete because what is described is a physical event: a falling leaf. Loneliness, on the other hand, is abstract. Take an abstract idea: love, hate, indecision, arrogance, jealousy, ambition, justice, civil rights, prejudice, the generation gap, revolution, coyness, insanity, or any other. Then link it with some physical object or event that you think illustrates the abstract idea. By "illustrate" is meant simply to make us feel that the object or event is bringing the abstract idea to life, to a life that is important to us: a value. If it doesn't make any difference to us, then it is not "working" right: fusion has failed. Of course, you need not follow Cummings' exact way of splitting the word and using parentheses for the event. You may use any way of lining the words up that you think is interesting. You may find that when you have really suited yourself with a satisfactory connection, you will have suited other people as well.

In *Paradise Lost*, usually thought to be a difficult poem, John Milton describes hell as a place with "Rocks, Caves, Lakes, Fens, Bogs, Dens, and shades of death." Now, neither you nor the poet knows precisely what a "shade of death" is although the idea is in Psalm 23, "the valley of the shadow of death." Milton gets away with it because he has linked this abstract idea to so many concrete images in this single line. He is talking about the *mood* of hell just as much as about the specific landscape, and we realize that he gives us so many topographic details in order to get us ready for the last detail—the abstract idea of shades of death—which in many ways is the most important.

Poetry worked in much the same way in seventeenth-century England as it does in twentieth-century America. The same principles are at work: the described objects or events are used as a means of bringing abstract ideas to life. In turn, the descriptions take on a wider and deeper significance—wider in the sense that the descriptions are connected with the larger scope of abstract ideas, deeper in the sense that because of these connections the descriptions elicit more sensitive responses from us.

The following poem is particularly telling for us because its theme is highly complex: the memory of an older culture (simplicity in this poem) and the consideration of a newer culture (complexity). It is an African poem by the Nigerian poet Gabriel Okara; and knowing that it is African, we can begin to appreciate the extreme complexity of Okara's feelings about the clash of the old and new cultures. He symbolizes the clash in terms of music, and he opposes two musical instruments: the drum and the piano. They stand for the African and the European cultures. But even beyond the musical images that abound in this poem, look closely at the images of nature, the pictures of the panther and leopard, and see how Okara imagines them.

PIANO AND DRUMS

When at break of day at a riverside
I hear jungle drums telegraphing
the mystic rhythm, urgent, raw
like bleeding flesh, speaking of
primal youth and the beginning,
I see the panther ready to pounce,
the leopard snarling about to leap
and the hunters crouch with spears poised;

And my blood ripples, turns torrent,
topples the years and at once I'm
in my mother's lap a suckling;
at once I'm walking simple
paths with no innovations,
rugged, fashioned with the naked
warmth of hurrying feet and groping hearts
in green leaves and wild flowers pulsing.

Then I hear a wailing piano
solo speaking of complex ways
in tear-furrowed concerto;
of far-away lands
and new horizons with
coaxing diminuendo, counterpoint,
crescendo. But lost in the labyrinth
of its complexities, it ends in the middle
of a phrase at a daggerpoint.

And I lost in the morning mist
of an age at a riverside keep
wandering in the mystic rhythm
of jungle drums and the concerto.

[From *The African Assertion*, Austin J. Shelton
(ed.), Odyssey, N.Y., 1968–originally in
Black Orpheus #6, 1959, p. 22.]

PERCEPTION KEY "PIANO AND DRUMS"

1. What are the objects of most importance in the poem? Do they have significance beyond their existence as observable or useful things?
2. What are the two conflicting forces in the poem? Why are they symbolized by the drum and the piano?
3. Why do you think Okara chose the drum and the piano to help reveal the clash between the old and new cultures?

Such a poem must speak directly to legions of the current generation of Africans. But consider some points in light of what we have said earlier. In order to perceive the kind of emotional struggle that Okara talks about and that is, in fact, the subject matter of the poem, we need to know something about Africa and the struggle new nations in Africa are having bringing their technology into line with that of more economically advanced nations. We also need to know something of the history of Africa and the fact that European nations, such as Britain in the case of Nigeria, once controlled much of Africa. Knowing these things, we know then that there is no thought of the "I" of the poem accepting the "complex ways" of the new culture wholeheartedly. The "I" does not think of the culture of the piano as manifestly superior to the culture of the drum. That is why the labyrinth of complexities ends at "a daggerpoint." The new culture is a mixed blessing.

We have argued that perception of a work of art is aided by background information and that sensitive perception must be aware of form at least implicitly. But we believe there is much more to sensitive perception. Somehow the form of a work of art clarifies or reveals values, and our response is intensified by our awareness of those revealed values. But how does the form do this? And how does this awareness come to us? In the next chapter we shall consider these questions, and in doing so we will also raise the question: What is a work of art? As in this chapter, the emphasis will be on painting, although only for the convenience of illustration. Once we have examined each of the arts, it will be clear, we hope, that the principles developed in these opening chapters are equally applicable to all the arts.

Summary

Unlike scientists, humanists generally do not use strictly objective standards. Artists reveal values; other humanists study values. Our approach to the humanities is through the arts. Our taste about works of art is connected with our deep feelings. Yet our taste can be continually improved. Background information about a work of art and increased sensitivity to its form intensifies our responses.

Chapter 1 Bibliography

Barthes, Roland. *Image, Music, Text.* New York: Hill and Wang, 1977.
Beardsley, Monroe C. *Aesthetics: Problems in the Philosophy of Criticism.* New York: Harcourt, Brace & World, 1958.
Dewey, John. *Art as Experience.* New York: Minton, Balch, 1934.
Edman, Irwin. *Arts and the Man.* New York: Vinco, 1946.

Guggenheimer, Richard. *Creative Vision*. New York: Harper, 1950.

Jacobus, Lee A., ed. *Aesthetics and the Arts*. New York: McGraw-Hill, 1968.

Jarrett, James L. *The Humanities and Humanistic Education*. Reading, Mass.: Addison-Wesley, 1973.

Langer, Susanne K., ed. *Reflections on Art*. New York: Oxford University Press, 1958.

———. *Problems of Art*. New York: Scribner's Sons, 1957.

Lipman, Matthew. *What Happens in Art?* New York: Appleton-Century-Crofts, 1967.

Maslow, Abraham. *New Knowledge in Human Values*. Chicago: Henry Regnery, 1959.

Rader, Melvin and Bertram Jessup. *Art and Human Values*. Englewood Cliffs, N.J.: Prentice-Hall, 1976.

Read, Herbert. *Art and Alienation*. New York: Viking, 1970.

———. *Education through Art*. London: Faber and Faber, 1943.

Santayana, George. *The Sense of Beauty*. New York: Dover, 1955.

Whitehead, Alfred North. *Adventures of Ideas*. New York: Macmillan, 1933.

WHAT IS A WORK OF ART?

Many ways of defining a "work of art" have been proposed. But no definition seems to be completely adequate, and none is universally accepted. Thus we shall not propose a definition here, but rather attempt to clarify some criteria or distinctions that can help us identify works of art. Since the term "work of art" implies the concept of making in two of its words—"work" and "art" (short for "artifice")—we frequently find it proposed that a work of art is something made by a person. Hence sunsets, beautiful trees, "found" natural objects such as lovely grained driftwood, "paintings" by insects or birds, and a host of other natural phenomena cannot be considered works of art. You may not wish to accept the proposal that a work of art is of human origin. However, if you do accept it, consider the "construction" shown in Figure 2-1, Jim Dine's *Shovel*.

FIGURE 2-1 Jim Dine, *Shovel*, 1962. Mixed media. Sonnabend Gallery. Photograph by Eric Pollitzer.

Shovel is part of a highly valuable collection of art and was first shown at a respectable art gallery in New York City. Furthermore, Dine is widely recognized as an important American artist. He did not make the shovel himself, however. Like most shovels, it was mass-produced. Dine mounted the shovel in front of a painted panel and presented this construction for serious consideration. Given these credentials, is it then a work of art?

We can hardly discredit it as a work of art simply because Dine did not make the shovel, since we often accept objects manufactured to specification by factories as genuine works of sculpture. Collages by Picasso and Braque, which include objects such as paper and nails mounted on a panel, are almost universally accepted as works of art, as is Kurt Schwitters' *Merz Konstruktion* (Figure 5-40). Museums have even accepted such objects as a signed urinal by Marcel Duchamp, one of the Dadaist artists of the early twentieth century, who in many ways anticipated the works of Dine, Warhol, Oldenburg, and others in the recent Pop Art movement. Thus, it is not the novelty of Jim Dine's use of a ready-made object that appeals to art collectors but, rather, apparently something about the way he presents the shovel.

Identifying Art Conceptually

Three of the most widely accepted criteria for determining whether or not something is a work of art are (1) that the object or event should be made by an artist, (2) that the object or event should be intended to be a work of art by its maker (thus apparently ruling out the shovel, which was intended to be a tool), and (3) that important or recognized "experts" agree that it is a work of art. Unfortunately, these considerations rely upon information that is not always ascertainable by perceiving the work in question. This creates difficulties. In many cases, for instance, we may confront an object like *Shovel* and not know whether Dine himself may possibly have constructed the shovel very carefully in imitation of the mass-produced object, thus satisfying the first criterion that the object be made by an artist; or whether Dine intended it to be a work of art; or whether experts agree that it is a work of art. In fact, Dine did not make this particular shovel; but since this fact cannot be established by ordinary perception, one has to be told. Obviously, we might have a long wait before getting the information needed to classify *Shovel* as a work of art.

PERCEPTION KEY IDENTIFYING A WORK OF ART

1. If Dine actually made the shovel in his construction by hand, would *Shovel* then be unquestionably a work of art?
2. Suppose Dine made the shovel himself, and it was absolutely perfect in the sense that it could not be readily distinguished from a mass-produced shovel. Would that kind of perfection make the piece any less a work of art?

3. Find people who hold opposing views about the question of whether or not *Shovel* is a work of art. Ask them to argue the point in detail, being particularly careful not to argue simply from personal opinion. Ask them to point out what it is about the object itself that qualifies it for or disqualifies it from being identified as a work of art.

Identifying Art Perceptually

Perception and conception are closely related: We are often led to see what we expect or want to see; we recognize an object because it conforms to our conception of it. The ways of identifying a work of art mentioned above depend very heavily on the conceptions of the artist and experts on art and perhaps not heavily enough on our perceptions of the work itself. Objects and events do have qualities that can be perceived without the help of artists or experts, although this is not to say that these specialists cannot be helpful. If we wish to consider the artistic qualities of objects or events, we can easily do so. Yet to do so implies an attitude or an approach. We are going to suggest an approach here that is simple and flexible and that depends on perception, although not so exclusively as to rule out important conceptual aspects. The distinctions of this approach will not lead us to a definition of art, but they will offer us a way to examine objects and events with reference to whether they possess artistically perceivable qualities. And in some cases at least, it should bring us to reasonable grounds for distinguishing certain things as art and others as nonart. We will consider three terms related primarily to the perceptual nature of the work of art:

1. Artistic form
2. Content
3. Subject matter

A fourth term relates primarily to what our perception of the work of art does to us:

4. Participation

Artistic Form

All objects and events have form. They are bounded by limits of time and space, and they have structural (large) and detailed (small) elements that bear distinguishable relationships to one another. Form is the interrelationships of part to part (structural detail) and part to whole (structure). To say something has *form* may mean no more than that some object or event is identifiable because it has some degree of perceptible unity. Thus, a single isolated tone played on a piano has form, although it is probably not very significant. To say that something has *artistic form*, however, usually implies that there is a strong degree of perceptible unity. Artistic form is one of the things we expect to find in a work of art as a way of distinguishing it from objects or events that are not works of art (and we do so no matter what the problems of definition may be).

"Artistic form" is a term that implies that the elements we perceive—lines, colors, and shapes, for example, in a painting—have been organized for the most profound effect possible. The word "organized" implies a structuring that is related to organic or living order. However, not all works of art have organic form in this sense—for instance, Mondrian's *Composition in White, Black and Red* (Color Plate 2). Not all works need it. Yet the idea of organicism also suggests unity: the way an object or event takes on a distinct quality because its elements function together in such a way that the object or event is an identity. All works of art have unity.

Nature provides the artist with innumberable models of unity: small pebbles, conglomerations of stone and mud and sand, flowers, trees, animals, humans, the heavens. However, our experience is usually characterized more by disunity than by unity. Consider, for instance, the order of your experiences during a typical day or even a segment of that day. Compare that order with the order most novelists give to the experiences of their characters. One impulse for reading novels is to experience the tight unity that artistic form usually imposes, a unity almost none of us come close to achieving in our daily lives. Much the same is true for music. Noises and random tones in everyday experience lack the order that most composers impose. Indeed, even nature's models of unity are usually far less strongly perceptible than the unity of most works of art. Consider, for example, birdsongs, which are clearly precursors of music. Even the song of the meadowlark, which is longer than most birdsongs, is fragmentary and incomplete. It is like a theme that is simply a statement and repetition, lacking development or contrast. Thus, the composer, finding the meadowlark's short theme monotonous when repeated again and again, enriches it by adding notes to those already sounded, by varying the basic melody or theme through alternation of rhythm, or changing the pitch of some of the notes to higher or lower positions on the musical scale, or by adding a completely different theme to set up a sense of contrast and tension with the initial theme. These developments help us understand the resources of the theme, and this, in turn, helps us grasp its identity. Its individuality comes forth more distinctively. Since strong, perceptible unity appears so infrequently in nature, we tend to value that unity highly when it appears, as it usually does, in art.

Artistic form, then, refers to a high degree of perceptible unity. That means the elements must work together tightly, establishing the singularity of the work. Works of art differ, of course, in the power of

SAINT PETER'S COLLEGE LIBRARY
JERSEY CITY, NEW JERSEY 07306

their unity. If that power is weak, then the question arises: Is this a work of art? Consider the Mondrian (Color Plate 2) with reference to its artistic form. If its structural details were not carefully proportioned to the overall structure of the painting itself, the tight balance that produces a strong unity of structure would be lost. Mondrian was so concerned with this problem that he worked out the areas of lines and rectangles almost mathematically to be sure they had a clear relationship to the total structural area.

Of course, disunity or establishing an "almost unity" can also be artistically useful at times. Some artists realize how strong the impulse toward unity is in those of us who have perceived many works of art. Consequently, some artists will aim for intense responses by playing against our need for, and expectation of, unity in works of art. This is particularly true in contemporary art. For some people, the contemporary attitude toward the loose organization of formal elements is something of a norm, and the highly unified work of art is thought of as old-fashioned. However, it seems that the effects achieved by a lesser degree of unity succeed only because we recognize them as departures from or variations upon well-known, highly organized forms.

Artistic form as distinct from nonartistic form, we have suggested, involves a high degree of perceptible unity. But how do we determine what is a "high degree"? And if we cannot be clear about this, how can this distinction be of much help in distinguishing works of art from things that are not works of art? Consider, for example, the following news photograph—taken on one of the main streets of Saigon in February 1968 by Eddie Adams, an Associated Press photographer—showing Brig. Gen. Nguyen Ngoc Loan, then South Vietnam's National Police Chief, killing a Vietcong captive (Figure 2-2).

Adams stated that his picture was an accident, that his hand moved the camera reflexively as he saw the General raise the revolver. The lens of the camera was set in such a way that the background was thrown out of focus. The blurring of the background helped bring out the drama of the foreground scene. Does this photograph have a high degree of perceptible unity? Is it a work of art? Certainly the skill and care of the photographer are evident. Not many amateur photographers would have had enough skill to catch such a fleeting event with such stark clarity. Even if an amateur had accomplished this, we would be inclined to believe that it was more luck than skill. Adams' care for the photograph is even more evident. He risked his life to get it. If this photograph had not been widely publicized and admired, we can imagine the dismay he would have felt. But do we admire this work the way we admire Siquieros' *Echo of a Scream* (Figure 1-1)? Do we experience these two works in the same basic way? If you think so, why is it that no one, as far as we know, has proposed that this photograph be hung in a museum of art as part of a permanent collection? Was it more appropriate to display this photograph, as was

FIGURE 2-2 Eddie Adams, *Execution in Saigon*, 1968. Wide World Photos.

the case, in newspapers and magazines? Such display served a useful purpose as news. Was this its only proper function?

Compare a painting of a somewhat similar subject—Goya's *May 3, 1808* (Color Plate 3).

PERCEPTION KEY GOYA'S PAINTING AND ADAMS' PHOTOGRAPH

1. Is the painting different from Adams' photograph in the way the details work together? Be specific.
2. Could any detail in the painting be changed, moved, or removed without weakening the unity of the structure, the total design? What about the photograph?
3. Is there anything that you could do to the painting that would increase the power of what it reveals—human barbarity?
4. Is it as easy to sustain your attention on the photograph as on the Goya?
5. Are there details in the photograph that distract your attention?
6. Do the buildings in the background of the photograph add to or subtract from the power of what is being represented here? Compare the looming architecture in the painting.
7. Do the shadows on the street add anything to the significance of the photograph? Compare the shadows on the ground in the painting.
8. Does it make any significant difference that the Vietcong prisoner's shirt is checkered? Compare the white shirt on the gesturing man in the painting. Would you have explicitly noticed the checkered shirt on the Vietcong prisoner if it had not been called to your attention? Did you particularly notice the white shirt in the painting before your attention was called to it?

9. Is the expression on the soldier's face, along the left side of the photograph, appropriate to the situation? Compare the facial expressions in the painting.
10. Would the theme of human barbarity be more emphatic if General Loan's arm were stiff—just on the point of firing—rather than just reflexing from the shot?
11. What are basic differences between seeing a real man being killed, a photograph of that event, and a painting of that event?

Goya chose the most terrible moment, that split second before the crash of the guns. There is no doubt that the executions will go on. The desolate mountain pushing down from the left blocks escape, while from the right the firing squad relentlessly hunches forward. The soldiers' thick legs—planted wide apart and strictly parallel—support like sturdy pillars the blind, pressing wall formed by their backs. These are men of a military machine. Their rifles, flashing in the bleak light of the ghastly lantern, thrust out as if they belonged to their bodies. It is unimaginable that any of these men would defy the command of their superiors. In the dead of night, the doomed are packed up against the mountain like animals being slaughtered. One man alone flings up his arms in a gesture of utter despair—or is it defiance? The uncertainty increases the intensity of our attention. Most of the rest bury their faces, while a few, with eyes staring out of their sockets, glance out at that which they cannot help seeing—the sprawling dead smeared in blood. Only the monk seems to be seeing beyond the moment.

With the photograph of the execution in Vietnam, despite its immediate and powerful attraction, sustained attention seems hardly necessary. It takes no more than a glance or two to grasp what is presented. *Undivided* attention, perhaps, is necessary to become aware of the significance of the event, but not *sustained* attention. In fact, to take careful notice of all the details—such as the patterns on the prisoner's shirt—does not add to our perception of the significance of the photograph. If anything, our awareness will be sharper and more productive if we avoid such detailed examination. Is such the case with the Goya? We believe not. Indeed, without sustained attention to the details of this work, most of what is revealed would be missed. For example, block out everything but the dark shadow at the bottom right. Note how differently that shadow appears when it is isolated. We must see the details individually and collectively, as they work together. Unless we are aware of their collaboration, we are not going to grasp fully the structure or total design.

We are suggesting that the Goya has a much higher degree of perceptible unity than Adams' photograph, that perhaps only the Goya has artistic form. We base these conclusions on what is given for us to perceive: the fact that the part-to-part (structural details) and the part-to-whole (structural) relationships are much stronger in the Goya.

Now, of course, you may disagree. No judgment about such matters is indisputable. Indeed, that is part of the fun of talking about whether something is or is not a work of art; we can learn how to perceive from each other.

Participation

Both the photograph and the Goya painting tend to grasp our attention. Initially for most of us, probably, the photograph has much more pulling power than the painting. Both are exhibited and preserved for us to perceive with undivided attention. But the term "participate" is much more accurately descriptive of what we are likely to be doing in our experience of the painting. With the painting, we must not only give but also sustain our undivided attention. If that happens, we lose our selfconsciousness, our sense of being separate, of standing apart from the painting. We participate. And only by means of participation can we come close to a full awareness of what the painting is all about. On the other hand, participation is not as obviously required for a full awareness of what the photograph is all about. This difference suggests another key distinction in helping to identify works of art: *participation*. Works of art are created, exhibited, and preserved for us to perceive with not only undivided but also *sustained* attention. Artists, critics, and philosophers of art or aestheticians generally are in agreement about this. Thus, if, in order to understand and appreciate it fully, a work requires our participation, we have an indication that the work is art. Therefore—unless our analyses have been incorrect, and you should satisfy yourself about this—the Goya would seem to be a work of art. Conversely, the photograph would seem not to be a work of art. Or at the very least, the photograph is not as obviously a work of art as the painting, and this is the case despite the fascinating impact of the photograph. Yet these are highly tentative judgments. We are far from being clear about why the Goya requires our participation and the photograph apparently does not. Until we are clear about these "whys," the grounds for these judgments remain shaky.

Goya's painting tends to draw us on until, ideally, we become aware of all the details and their interrelationships. For example, the long dark shadow at the bottom right underlines the line of the firing squad, and the line of the firing squad helps bring out the shadow. Moreover, this shadow is the darkest and most opaque part of the painting. It has a forbidding, blind, fateful quality that, in turn, reinforces the ominous appearance of the firing squad. On the other hand, the dark shadow on the street just below the forearm of General Loan takes us nowhere. It is just there. It might as well not be there. The photograph is full of such meaningless details. Thus our attempts to keep our attention on the photograph tend to be forced—which is to say that they will fail. Sustained attention or participation cannot be achieved by acts of will. The splendid singularity of what we are attending to must fascinate and control us to the point where we no longer need to will our attention.

We can make up our minds to give our undivided attention to something. But if that something lacks the pulling power that holds our attention, we cannot participate with it. A boring or disunified something will keep us aware of ourselves as separate from that something. Participation cannot be forced.

Adams' photograph does not seem to lend itself to participative experiences or even to repetitive experiences. Despite the intense interest it arouses at first, once we have seen it, we have no strong desire to see it again and again. If we were to see it again and again (try this yourself), we would probably find our viewings increasingly boring. No demands that require either our participation or repeated viewings are made upon us by the photograph. Conversely, the Goya tends to defy boredom from repetition. Of course, this is far more true of the actual painting than of even the best reproductions. Many experiences of the painting are necessary before we begin to come close to what it offers. The Goya keeps drawing us back to it. There is an inexhaustibility about the Goya that the photograph seems to lack. That is the basic reason why we appreciate having the Goya exhibited on a permanent basis.

Participation and Artistic Form

The participative experience—the undivided and sustained attention to an object or event that makes us lose our sense of separation from the object or event—is induced by strong or artistic form. Participation is not likely to develop with weak form because weak form tends to allow our attention to wander. Therefore, one of the indications of a strong form is the fact that participation occurs. Another indication of artistic form is the way it clearly identifies a whole or totality. In the case of the visual arts, a whole is a visual field or design framed by boundaries that separate that field from its surroundings. Both Adams' photograph and Goya's painting have visual designs, for both have forms that produce boundaries.

PERCEPTION KEY ADAMS' PHOTOGRAPH AND GOYA'S PAINTING

Does the photograph have a more sharply delineated boundary than the painting? Why?

No matter what wall these two pictures are placed against, the Goya probably stands out more distinctly and sharply from its background. Both works are helped by frames, but the photograph seems to need a frame more than the Goya. This is because the form of the Goya is much stronger and thus outlines itself more surely. No detail in the Goya fails to play a part in the total design. To take one further instance, notice how the lines of the soldiers' sabers and their straps reinforce the ruthless forward push of the firing squad. The photograph, on the other hand, has a weak form because a large number of details fail to cooperate with other details. For example, running down the right side of General Loan's body is a very erratic line. This line fails to tie in with anything else in the photograph. If this line were smoother, it would connect more closely with the lines formed by the Vietcong prisoner's body. The connection between killer and killed would be more vividly established. But as it is, and after several viewings, our eye tends to wander off the photograph. The unity of its form is so slack that the edges of the photograph seem to blur off into their surroundings. That is another way of saying that the form of the photograph fails to establish a clear-cut whole or identity.

Artistic form normally is a prerequisite if our attention is to be grasped and sustained. Artistic form makes our participation possible. Some aestheticians, such as Clive Bell and Roger Fry, even go so far as to claim that the presence of artistic form—what they usually call "significant form"—identifies a work of art. And by "significant form," in the case of painting, they mean the interrelationships of elements: line to line, line to color, color to color, color to shape, shape to shape, etc. The elements make up the artistic medium, the "stuff" the form organizes. Any reference of these elements and their interrelationships to objects or events should be basically irrelevant in our awareness.

According to the proponents of significant form, if we take notice of the executions as an important part of Goya's painting, then we are not perceiving properly. We are experiencing the painting not as a work of art but rather as an illustration telling a story, thus reducing a painting that is a work of art to a level of commercial communications. When the lines, colors, etc., pull together tightly, independently of any objects or events they may represent, there is a significant form. That is what we should perceive when we are perceiving a work of art, not some portrayal of some object or event. Anything that has a significant form is a work of art. If you ignore the objects and events represented in the Goya, significant form is evident. All the details jell together, creating a strong structure. Therefore, the Goya is a work of art. If you ignore the objects and events represented in the Adams photograph, significant form is not evident. The organization of the parts is too loose, creating a weak structure. Therefore, the photograph is not a work of art. "To appreciate a work of art," according to Clive Bell, "we need bring with us nothing from life, no knowledge of its ideas and affairs, no familiarity with its emotions."

Does this theory of how to identify a work of art satisfy you? Do you find that in ignoring the representation of objects and events in the

Goya much of what is important in that painting is left out? For example, does the line of the firing squad carry a forbidding quality partly because you recognize that this is a line of men in the process of killing other men? In turn, does that line's close relationship with the line of the long shadow at the bottom right depend to some degree upon that forbidding quality? If you think so, then it follows that the artistic form of this work legitimately and relevantly refers to objects and events. Somehow artistic form, at least in some cases, has a significance that goes beyond just the design formed by elements such as lines and colors. Artistic form somehow goes beyond itself, somehow refers to objects and events from the world beyond the design. Artistic form informs us about things outside itself. These things—as revealed by the artistic form—we shall call the *content* of a work of art. But how does the artistic form do this?

Content

Let us begin to try to answer this question by examining more closely the meanings of the Adams photograph and the Goya painting. Both basically, although oversimply, are about the same abstract idea— human barbarity. In the case of the photograph, we have an example, an instance of this barbarity. Since it is very close to any knowledge-able American's interests, this instance is likely to set off a lengthy chain of thoughts and feelings. These thoughts and feelings, further-more, seem to "lie beyond" the photograph. Suppose a debate devel-oped over the meaning of this photograph. The photograph itself would play an important role primarily as a starting point. From there on the photograph would probably be ignored except for dramatizing points. For example, one person might argue, "Remember that this occurred during the Tet offensive and innocent civilians were being killed by the Vietcong. Look again at that street and think of the consequences if the terrorists had not been eliminated." Another person might argue, "General Loan was one of the highest officials in South Vietnam's government, and he was taking the law into his own hands like a Nazi." What would be very strange in such a debate would be a discussion of every detail or even many of the details of the photo-graph.

In a debate about the meaning of the Goya, on the other hand, every detail and its interrelationships with other details become relevant. The meaning of the painting seems to "lie within" the painting. And yet paradoxically, this meaning, as in the case of the Adams photograph, involves ideas and feelings that "lie beyond" the painting. How can this be? Let us first consider some background information. On May 2, 1808, guerrilla warfare had flared up all over Spain against the occupying forces of the French. By the following day, Napoleon's men were completely back in control in Madrid and the surrounding area. Many of the guerrillas were executed. And, according to tradition, Goya represented the execution of forty-three of these guerrillas on May 3 near the hill of Principe Pio just outside Madrid. This background information is important if we are to understand and appreciate the painting fully. Yet notice how differently this information works in our experience of the painting compared to the way background information works in our experience of the Adams photograph.

With the photograph, the background information is essential because it calls up important questions about the involvement of the United States in Vietnam. It is these questions presumably that make us take such special interest in the photograph. A century from now, the photograph probably will be largely ignored except by historians of the Vietnamese war. If you are dubious about this, consider how quickly most of us pass over photographs of similar scenes from World War I and even World War II. The value of Adams' photograph seems to be closely tied to its historical moment. We pay attention to the photograph mainly because the information it conveys suggests, in turn, important considerations. For example, if General Loan's behavior were representative of the behavior of the Saigon government, should American soldiers have died in support of that government? This kind of consideration, rather than the photograph itself, rapidly becomes the center of our attention. A division develops between the photograph and its meaning. The photograph is *here;* the ideas and feelings it arouses are *over there.* The *here* and the *over there* are not fused in our experience. This happens because the form of the photograph fails to draw us into participation (or at least prolonged participation) with the photograph. There is not much to be gained by continuing to focus on the photograph, and so we turn to what does concern us—its meaning. And the more we do this, the more the photograph fades away. The abstract idea (human barbarity) and the concrete exemplification or specific image of this idea (General Loan executing his captive) are related to each other—the specific image of the photograph calls up the abstract idea. But they are not likely to be fused in our experience. This would be likely only if the photograph had artistic form. Only a powerful form is likely to fuse meaning.

With the Goya, the background information, although very helpful, is not as essential. Test this for yourself. Would your interest in Adams' photograph last very long if you completely lacked background information? In the case of the Goya, the background information helps us understand the where, when, and why of the scene. But even without this information, the painting probably would still grasp and hold the attention of most of us because it would still have significant meaning. We would still have a powerful image of barbarity, and the artistic form would hold us on that image. In the Prado Museum in Madrid, Goya's painting continually draws and holds the attention of innumerable viewers, many of whom know little or nothing about the rebellion of 1808. Adams' photograph is also a powerful image, of course—initially far more powerful probably than the Goya—but the form of the photograph is not strong enough to hold most of us on that image for very long. And so, as we think about the background information, we are led beyond the boundaries of the photograph. The background information of the Goya, on the other hand, comes into our experience in such a way that it merges with our awareness, which stays within the boundaries of the painting. The form of the Goya controls our awareness of the background information so that it is not allowed to escape from the image. With the Goya, the abstract idea (human barbarity) and the concrete image (the firing squad in the process of killing) are tied tightly together because the form of the painting is tight, i.e., artistic. We see the barbarity *in* the lines, colors, masses, shapes, groupings, and lights and shadows of the painting itself. The details of the painting keep referring to other details and to the totality. They keep holding our attention. Thus the ideas and feelings that the details and their organization awaken keep merging with the form. We are prevented from separating the meaning or content of the painting from its form because the form is so fascinating. The form constantly intrudes, however unobtrusively. It will not let us ignore it. We see the firing squad killing, and this evokes the idea of barbarity and the feeling of horror. But the lines, colors, mass, shapes, and shadowings of that firing squad form a pattern that keeps exciting and guiding our eyes. And then that pattern leads us to the pattern formed by the victims. Ideas of fatefulness and feelings of pathos are evoked, but they, too, are fused with the form. The form of the Goya is like a powerful magnet that allows nothing within its range to escape its pull. Strong or artistic form fuses its meaning with itself.

In addition to participation and artistic form, then, we have come upon another basic distinction—content. Unless a work has content—meaning fused with its form—we shall say that the work is not art. Content is the meaning of artistic form. If we are correct (for, of course, our view is by no means universally accepted), artistic form always informs, that is, has meaning or content. And that content, as we experience it when we participate, is always ingrained in the artistic form. We do not perceive an artistic form *and then* a content. We perceive them as inseparable. Of course, we can separate them analytically. But that is also to say that we are not having a participative experience. Moreover, when the form is weak—that is, less than artistic—we experience the form and its meaning separately. We see the form of Adams' photograph, and it evokes thoughts and feelings, indeed, a very powerful meaning. But the form is not strong enough to keep its meaning fused with itself. The photograph lacks content, not because it lacks meaning but because that meaning is not merged with a form. Idea and image break apart.

We have argued that the painting by Goya is a work of art and the photograph by Adams is not. Even if the three basic distinctions we have made so far—artistic form, participation, and content—are useful, we may have misapplied them. Bring out every possible argument against the view that the painting is a work of art and the photograph is not a work of art.

Subject Matter

The content is the meaning of a work of art. The content is embedded in the artistic form. But what is the content giving meaning about? We shall call it "subject matter." The subject matter is what the work of art *is about*. Content is the interpretation—by means of an artistic form—of subject matter. Thus, subject matter is the fourth basic distinction that helps identify a work of art. Since every work of art must have a content, then every work of art must have a subject matter, and this may be any aspect of experience that is an object of some vital human interest. Anything that is related to a human interest is a value. Some values are positive, such as pleasure and health. Other values are negative, such as pain and illness. Human barbarity and executions are very unpleasant. But they are values because they are related to human interests. These values are the subject matter of both Adams' photograph and Goya's painting. They are what both the photograph and the painting *are about*. But the photograph, unlike the painting, has no content. The less-than-artistic form of the photograph simply presents its subject matter. The form does not transform the subject matter, does not enrich the meaning of the subject matter. On the other hand, the artistic form of the painting enriches or interprets its subject matter, says something significant about it. In the photograph the subject matter is directly given. But the subject matter of the painting is not just *there* in the painting. It has been transformed by the form. What is directly given in the painting is the content. You can perceive the content. But you can only imagine the painting's subject matter, for this is not directly given.

The meaning or content of a work of art is what is *revealed* about a subject matter. But in that revelation you must imagine the subject matter. If someone had taken a news photograph of the May third executions, that would be a record of Goya's subject matter. The content of the Goya is its interpretation of human barbarity in those executions. Adams' photograph lacks content because it merely shows us an example of this barbarity. That is not to disparage the photograph, for its purpose was news, not art. A similar kind of photograph—that is, one lacking artistic form—of the May third executions would also lack content. Because both photographs lack artistic form, they directly present their subject matter. Goya's painting has artistic form and content directly presented, whereas its subject matter is only indirectly presented. Now, of course, you may disagree with these conclusions for very good reasons. You may find more transformation of the subject matter in Adams' photograph than in Goya's painting. In any case, such disagreement can help the perception of both parties provided the debate itself is focused. It is hoped that the basic distinctions we are making—subject matter, artistic form, content, and participation—will aid that focusing.

Subject Matter and Artistic Form

Whereas a subject matter is a value that we may perceive before any artistic interpretation, the content is the significantly interpreted subject matter as revealed by the artistic form. Thus, the subject matter is never directly presented in a work of art, for the subject matter has been transformed by the form. Artistic form transforms and, in turn, informs about life. The conscious intentions of the artist may include magical, religious, political, economic, and other purposes; the conscious intentions may not include the purpose of clarifying values. Yet underlying the artist's activity is always the creation of a form that illuminates something from life, some subject matter. Content is the subject matter detached by means of the form from its accidental or insignificant aspects. Artistic form makes the significance of a subject matter more manifest. Artistic form is the means whereby values are threshed from the husks of irrelevancies. A form that *only* entertains or distracts or shocks is less than artistic. Whereas nonartistic form merely presents a subject matter, artistic form makes that subject matter more vivid and clear. On the one hand, artistic form draws from the chaotic state of life—which, as Van Gogh describes it, is like "a sketch that didn't come off,"—a distillation. Adams' photograph is like "a sketch that didn't come off," because it has numerous meaningless details. Goya's form eliminates meaningless detail. On the other hand, because when it is not chaotic life is such a habit-forming drug, artistic form reveals something so vividly the drug fails to work. The work of art creates an illusion that illuminates reality. Thus, such paradoxical declarations as Delacroix's are explained: "Those things which are most real are the illusions I create in my paintings." Or Edward Weston's: The photographer who is an artist reveals "the essence of what lies before the lens with such clear insight that the beholder may find the recreated image more real and comprehensible than the actual object." Aristotle asserts: "Art completes what nature cannot bring to a finish. The artist gives us knowledge of nature's unrealized ends." Hegel: "Art is in truth the primary instructress of peoples." Camus: "If the world were clear, art would not exist." Artistic form is an economy that produces a lucidity that enables us better to understand and, in turn, manage our lives. Hence the informing of a work of art reveals a subject matter with value dimensions that go beyond the artist's idiosyncrasies and perversities. Whether or not Goya had idiosyncrasies and perversities, he did justice to his subject matter: he revealed it. The art of a period is the revelation of the collective soul of its time.

Values in everyday situations are confused and obscured. Art helps us to perceive what we have missed. Anyone who has participated with Cummings' "l(a" will see autumn leaves with heightened sensitivity, and will understand the isolation of loneliness and death a little more poignantly. In clarifying values, art gives us an understanding that supplements the truths of science. Dostoevski teaches us as much about ourselves as Freud. All of us require something that fascinates us for a time, something out of the routine of the practical and the theoretical. But such nonroutine experiences influence our routine experiences, making them more meaningful and thus less routine. Accordingly, if a work of art "works" successfully in us, it is more than a momentary delight, for it deepens our understanding of what matters most. Art adds to the permanent richness of our soul's self-attainment. Art helps us arrange our environment for authentic values. Art makes possible civilization.

Participation, Artistic Form, and Content

Participation is the necessary condition that makes possible our insightful perception of form and content. Unless we participate with the Goya, we will fail to see the power of its artistic form. We will fail to see how the details work together to form a structure. We also will fail to grasp the content fully, for artistic form and content are inseparable. Thus, we will have failed to gain insight into the subject matter. We will have collected just one more instance of human barbarity. The Goya will have basically the same effect upon us as Adams' photograph except that it will be less important to us because it happened long ago. But if, on the contrary, we have participated with the Goya, we probably will never see such things as executions in quite the same way again. The insight that we have gained will tend to refocus our vision so that we will see similar subject matters with a heightened awareness. Look, for example, at the photograph by Ronald L. Haeberle (Figure 2-3), which was published in *Life*, December 5, 1969.

In an interview that accompanied the photograph when it was first published in *The Cleveland Plain Dealer* on November 20, 1969, Haeberle reported that he took this picture in March 1968 while following American troops in an attack upon the South Vietnamese village of My Lai. This incident is much more closely related geographically and historically to Adams' photograph than to Goya's painting.

FIGURE 2-3 Ronald L. Haeberle, *My Lai.* Life magazine, © 1969, Time, Inc.

PERCEPTION KEY PHOTOGRAPHS BY ADAMS AND HAEBERLE AND GOYA'S PAINTING

1. Does Adams' photograph refocus your vision in any important way upon Haeberle's photograph?
2. Does Goya's painting refocus your vision in any important way upon Haeberle's photograph?

3. Why are your answers to these questions fundamentally important in determining whether Adams' photograph and Goya's painting are works of art?

Participation and the Work of Art

The ultimate test for recognizing a work of art is how it works in us, what it does to us. Provided we are able to participate with it, a work of art changes our lives. By its revelation of some subject matter, we now are able to experience similar subject matter with more sensitivity and understanding. Does Mondrian's *Composition in White, Black and Red* (Color Plate 2) heighten your perception of the relationships between sharply edged vertical and horizontal lines, the neatness and "spatial comfortableness" of these kinds of rectangles, and the rich qualities of white, black, and red? Does Cummings' "l(a" heighten your perception of falling leaves and deepen your understanding of loneliness? Do you *see* shovels for the first time, perhaps, after experiencing *Shovel* (Figure 2-1) by Dine? If not, presumably they are not works of art. But this assumes that we have really participated with these works, that we have allowed them to work properly in our experience, so that if content were present it had a chance to come forth into our awareness. Of the four basic distinctions—participation, artistic form, content, and subject matter—the most fundamental is participation. We must not only *understand what it means* to participate but also *be able* to participate. Otherwise, the other basic distinctions, even if they make good theoretical sense, will not be of much practical help in making art more important in our lives. The central importance of participation requires further elaboration.

Participation involves undivided and sustained attention. When attention is sustained, it becomes participative with that which we are attending. Then we no longer *look at* the Goya. We *become* the Goya in the sense that we are not explicitly aware of ourselves standing outside it. Someone watching us would say we are looking at the Goya. But we are so caught up by the power and control of its artistic form that we are unaware of our looking. The subjective and objective sides of experience merge into unity. When we fail to participate, we are spectators. We are aware of ourselves as separate from that which we are attending. In most of our experience of works of art we begin as spectators. Thus, as we settle into our seats and the film begins, we are quite conscious of our place in the theater. But as the film grasps and holds our attention, we lose awareness of such things as our spatial location. Or, as the record begins to play in our living room, our minds and bodies are full of the anxieties of the day, but then, as the music catches us up, our feet may begin tapping, and we "become" the music.

Spectator attention dominates most of our experiences. Spectator attention is more commonsensical, and it works much more efficiently than participative attention in most situations. We would not get very far changing a tire if we only participated with the tire. We would not be able to use the scientific method if we failed to distinguish between ourselves and our data. Practical success on every level requires problem solving. This requires distinguishing the means from the end, and then we must manipulate the means to achieve the end. In so doing, we are aware of ourselves as subjects distinct from the objects involved in our situation. In turn, the habit of spectator attention gets deeply ingrained in all of us because of the demands of survival. That is why, especially after we have left the innocence of childhood, participative attention is so rarely achieved. A child who has not yet had to solve problems, on the other hand, is dominated by participative attention. In this sense, to learn how to experience works of art properly requires a return to the open, receptive attitudes of childhood, for in childhood we were more likely to think *from* things than *at* things. As children, we did not always try to dominate things but, rather, let them reveal themselves to us. Watch young children at play. Sometimes they will just push things around, but often they will let things dominate them. Then, if they are looking at flowers, for example, they will begin to follow the curves and textures with their hands, be entranced with their smell, perhaps even the taste—so absorbed that they seem to listen, as if the flowers could speak.

Mark Twain tells how, as he learned the functions of a steamboat pilot, the Mississippi River became like a book:

> Now when I had mastered the language of this water, and had come to know every trifling feature that bordered the great river as familiarly as I knew the letters of the alphabet, I had made a valuable acquisition. But I had lost something, too. I had lost something which could never be restored to me while I lived. All the grace, the beauty, the poetry, had gone out of the majestic river! . . . All the value any feature of it had for me now was the amount of usefulness it could furnish toward compassing the safe piloting of the steamboat.[1]

In other words, Twain had become so obsessed with using the river that he could no longer participate with it.

Participative experiences of works of art are communions— experiences so full and final that they enrich our entire lives. Such experiences are life-enhancing not just because of the great satisfaction they may give us at the moment but also because they make more or less permanent contributions to our future life. Compare, for example, a photograph of Mont Sainte Victoire (Figure 2-4) and Cézanne's painting (Color Plate 4). It is unlikely that the photograph will be memorable. But if you participate with the painting, you are likely to

---

[1]Mark Twain, "Life on the Mississippi," in *The Family Mark Twain*, Harper, New York and London, 1935, p. 46.

FIGURE 2-4 Mont
Sainte Victoire.
Photograph courtesy of
John Rewald.

see the rhythm and the massiveness of similar mountains with, as
Bernard Berenson put it, a "higher coefficient of meaning."

As participators we do not think of the work of art with reference
to categories applicable to objects—such as what kind of thing it is. We
grasp the work of art directly. When, for example, we participate with
Cézanne's *Mont Sainte Victoire,* we are not making geographical or
geological observations. We are not thinking of the mountain as an
object. For if we did, *Mont Sainte Victoire* would pale into a mere
instance of the appropriate scientific categories. We might judge that
the mountain is a certain type. But in that process the vivid impact of
Cézanne's mountain would dim down as the focus of our attention
shifted beyond in the direction of generality. This is the natural thing
to do with mountains if you are a geologist. It is also the natural thing
to do with this particular photograph of the mountain (Figure 2-4). The
photograph lends itself to the direction of generality because its form
fails to hold us to the photograph in all its specificity. But, on the other
hand, to be only a spectator of the Cézanne is unnatural in the sense
that we block off much of the satisfaction we might have. Also, we
screen ourselves from insights that could make our lives more meaningful. We sell ourselves short.

When we participate, we *think from.* The artistic form initiates
and controls every thought and feeling. When we are spectators, we
think at. We set the object into our framework. We see the Cézanne—
name it, identify its maker, classify its style, recall its background

information—in order, let us say, to do a term paper. We may succeed in getting a passing grade, but this approach will never get us into the Cézanne as a work of art. Of course, such knowledge can be very helpful. But that knowledge is most helpful when it is under the control of the work of art working in our experience. This happens when the artistic form not only suggests that knowledge but also keeps it within the boundaries of the painting. Otherwise the painting will fade away. Its splendid specificity will be sacrificed for some generality. Its content will be missed.

Participators are thrust out of their ordinary, everyday, business-as-usual attitude. They are thrust out of themselves. The content of the work of art makes contact. And then the "concrete suchness" of the work of art penetrates and completely permeates their consciousness. Even if they forget such experiences, which is unlikely, a significant change has taken place in their perceptive organs. New sets of lenses, so to speak, have been more or less permanently built into their vision. After participating with Cézanne's *Mont Sainte Victoire*, participators will automatically see mountains differently.

These are strong claims, and they may not be convincing. In any case, before concluding our search for what a work of art is, let us seek further clarification of our other basic distinctions—artistic form, content, and subject matter. This is worth our trouble. Even if we disagree with the conclusions, clarification helps understanding. And understanding helps appreciation. Anything that can help us appreciate art is exceptionally important, because art is one of the most important things we make. This has a platitudinous ring. But listen to what Alfred North Whitehead, one of the greatest philosophers of the twentieth century, has to say:

> Great art is the arrangement of the environment so as to provide for the soul vivid . . . values. Human beings require something which absorbs them for a time, something out of the routine which they can stare at. But you cannot subdivide life, except in the abstract analysis of thought. Accordingly, the great art is more than a transient refreshment. It is something which adds to the permanent richness of the soul's self-attainment. It justifies itself both by its immediate enjoyment, and also by its discipline of the inmost being. Its discipline is not distinct from enjoyment, but by reason of it. It transforms the soul into the permanent realization of values extending beyond its former self.[2]

Artistic Form: Examples

Let us examine artistic form in a series of examples taken from the work of Roy Lichtenstein, a contemporary American painter, in which

[2]Alfred North Whitehead, *Science and the Modern World*, Macmillan, New York, 1925, pp. 209f.

the subject matter, compared with *May 3, 1808*, is not so obviously important. With such examples, a purely formal analysis should seem less artificial. In the late 1950s and early 1960s, Lichtenstein became interested in comic strips as subject matter. The story goes that his two young boys asked him to paint a Donald Duck "straight," without the encumbrances of art. But much more was involved. Born in 1923, Lichtenstein grew up before television. By the 1930s, the comic strip had become one of the most important of the mass media. Sex, sentimentality, sadism, terror, adventure, and romance found expression in the stories of Tarzan, Flash Gordon, Superman, Steve Roper, Winnie Winkle, Mickey Mouse, Donald Duck, Batman and Robin, etc. Even today, despite the competition of the "soap operas" of television, the comic strip remains an important mass medium.

The purpose of the comic strip for its producers is strictly commercial. And because of the very large market for the comic strip, a premium has always been put on making the processes of production as inexpensive as possible. And so generations of mostly unknown commercial artists, going well back into the nineteenth century, developed ways of cheap, quick color printing. They had to develop a technique that could turn out their cartoons like the products of an assembly line. Moreover, because their market included a large number of children, they developed ways of producing images that were immediately understandable and of striking impact. They evolved a tradition that became a common vocabulary. Both the technique and its product became increasingly standardized. The printed images became increasingly impersonal. Donald Duck, Bugs Bunny, and Batman all seem to come from the same hand, or, rather, the same machine.

Lichtenstein reports that he was attracted to the comic strip by its stark simplicity—the blatant primary colors, the ungainly black lines that encircle the shapes, the "balloons" that isolate the spoken words or the thoughts of the characters. He was struck by the apparent inconsistency between the strong emotions of the stories and the highly impersonal, mechanical style in which they were expressed. Despite the crudity of the comic strip, Lichtenstein saw power in the strong directness of the medium. Somehow something very much about ourselves was mirrored in those cartoons. Lichtenstein set out to clarify what that "something" was. At first people laughed, as was to be expected. He was called "the worst artist in America." Today he is considered one of our best.

The accompanying examples (Figures 2-5 through 2-14) pair the original cartoon with Lichtenstein's transformation.[3] Both the comic strips and the transformations originally were in color, and Lichtenstein's paintings are very much larger than the comic strip. For

[3]These examples were suggested to us by a very interesting article on Lichtenstein's "balloons" by Albert Boime, "Roy Lichtenstein and the Comic Strip," *Art Journal*, vol. 28, no. 2, pp. 155–159, Winter 1968–1969.

FIGURE 2-5   Pair 1, Example *a*.

FIGURE 2-6   Pair 1, Example *b*.

the purposes of analysis, however, our reproductions are presented in black and white, and the sizes more or less equalized. The absence of color and the reduction of size all but destroy the power of Lichtenstein's work, but these changes will help us compare the structures. They will also help us to concentrate upon what is usually the most obvious element of two-dimensional visual structure—line. The five pairs of examples have been scrambled so that either the comic strip or Lichtenstein's painting of it may be on the left or right.

PERCEPTION KEY COMIC STRIPS AND LICHTENSTEIN'S TRANSFORMATIONS

Decide which are the comic strips and which are Lichtenstein's transformations. Defend your decisions with reference to the strength of organization. Presumably Lichtenstein's works will possess much stronger structures than those of the commercial artists. Be as specific and detailed as possible. For example, compare the lines and shapes as they more or less work together in each example. Take plenty of time, for the perception of artistic form is something that must "work" in you. Such perception never comes instantaneously. Compare your judgments with others.

Compare your analysis with ours in the case of Pair 1 (Figures 2-5 and 2-6). Example *a* of Pair 1, we think, has a much stronger structure than *b*. The organization of the parts of *a* is much more tightly unified.

The circles formed by the peephole and its cover in *a* have a graceful rhythmic unity lacking in *b*. Note how in *a* the contour lines, formed by the overlapping of the cover on the right side, have a long sweeping effect. These lines look as if they had been drawn by a human hand. In *b*, the analogous contours as well as the circles to which the contours belong look as if they had been drawn with the aid of a compass. In *a* the circular border of the cover is broken at the right edge and by the balloon above. These devices help soften the hard definiteness not only of this circle but also of the contours it forms with the circle of the peephole. In *a* also, most of the man's face and his entire hand are shadowed. These contrasts help give variety and irregularity to the peephole circle, which blends in smoothly with its surroundings compared to the abrupt insularity of the peephole in *b*. Notice, too, that in *b* a white outline goes almost completely around the cover, whereas in *a* this is avoided. Moreover, the balloon in *a* overlies a significant portion of the cover. In *b* the balloon is isolated and leaves the cover almost alone.

In *a* the line outlining the balloon as it overlies the cover repeats the contours of the overlapping cover and its peephole. Rhythm depends upon repetition, and repetition unifies. But repetition that is absolutely regular is monotonous. Try tapping a pencil with a strong beat followed by a weak beat, and continue to repeat this rhythm as exactly as you can. Against your will and unconsciously you will desire some variations in stress. You will do this because absolute repetition becomes boring. In *a* the repetitions of the contour formed by the peephole and its cover, as well as other repetitions, have variations. The repetitions unify, while the variations excite interest. There are fewer repetitions in *b*. And lacking variations except of the most obvious kind, these repetitions are monotonous. For example, the size of the peephole and cover appear exactly the same. In *a*, on the other hand, sometimes the peephole appears larger and sometimes the cover. This variation very subtly depends on the area on which your eyes focus. And this, in turn, is controlled by the lines and shapes in dynamic interrelationship. In *b* this kind of moving control is missing.

In *a* no part remains isolated. Thus the balloon as it extends over the breadth of the painting helps bind the lower parts together. And at the same time, the shape and contours of the balloon help accent the shape and contours of the other details. Even the shape of the man's mouth is duplicated partially by the shape of the balloon. Conversely, the balloon in *b* is much more isolated from the other details. It just hangs there. Notice, on the other hand, how the tail of the balloon in *a*, just below the exclamation point, repeats the curve of the latch of the cover, and also how the curve of the tail is caught up in the sweep of the curves of the peephole and cover. In *a* the latch of the cover unobtrusively helps to orbit the cover around the peephole. In *b* the latch of the cover is awkwardly large, and this helps to block any sense of dynamic interrelationship between the peephole and its cover.

Whereas the cover seems light and graceful in *a*, and only the top of a finger is needed to turn it back, in *b* a much heavier finger is necessary. Similarly, the lines of face and hand in *a* lightly integrate, whereas in *b* they are heavy and fail to work together very well. Compare, for example, the eye in *a* with the eye in *b*. Finally, there are meaningless details in *b*—the bright knob on the cover, for instance, and the white square with the name of the illustrator. These details are eliminated in *a*. Even the shape of the lettering in *a* belongs to the whole in a way completely lacking in *b*.

Now turn to Pair 2 (Figures 2-7 and 2-8).

PERCEPTION KEY COMIC STRIP AND LICHTENSTEIN'S TRANSFORMATION, PAIR 2.

Limit your analysis to the design functioning of the lettering in the balloons of Pair 2.

1. Does the shape of the lettering in *a* play an important part in the formal organization? Explain your reasons.
2. Does the shape of the lettering in *b* play an important part in the formal organization? Explain your reasons.

Compare your analyses with ours. We think it is only in *b* that the shape of the lettering plays an important part in the formal organization. Conversely, the shape of the lettering is distracting in *a*. In *b* the bulky balloons are eliminated and only two words are kept—"torpedo

FIGURE 2-7   Pair 2, Example *a*.

FIGURE 2-8   Pair 2, Example *b*.

. . . LOS!" The three alphabetic characters of which "LOS" is composed stand out very vividly. The balloon's simple shape helps, a regular shape among so many irregular shapes. Also, "LOS" is larger, darker, and more centrally located than "torpedo." Notice, on the other hand, how no word or lettering stands out very vividly in *a*. Moreover, as Boime points out, the shapes of "LOS" are clues to the structure of the panel.

> The "L" is mirrored in the angle formed by the captain's hand and the vertical contour of his head and in that of the periscope. The "O" is repeated in the tubing of the periscope handle and in smaller details throughout the work. The oblique "S" recurs in the highlight of the captain's hat just left of the balloon, in the contours of the hat itself, in the shadow that falls along the left side of the captain's face, in the lines around his nose and in the curvilinear tubing of the periscope. Thus the dialogue enclosed within the balloon is visually exploited in the interests of compositional structure.

Now consider Pair 3 (Figures 2-9 and 2-10), Pair 4 (Figures 2-11 and 2-12), and Pair 5 (Figures 2-13 and 2-14). Then turn to the perception key on page 46.

PERCEPTION KEY COMIC STRIPS AND LICHTENSTEIN'S TRANSFORMATIONS, PAIRS 3, 4, AND 5

1. Decide once again which are the comic strips and which the transformations.
2. If you have changed any of your decisions or your reasoning, how do you account for these changes?

It should not be surprising to you if you have changed some of your decisions, and it may be that your reasoning has been expanded. Other people's analyses, even when you disagree with them, will usually suggest new ways of perceiving things. In the case of good criticism, this is almost always the case. The correct identifications follow, and they should help you test your perceptive abilities.

Pair 1*a* Lichtenstein, "I Can See the Whole Room . . . and There's Nobody in It!" 1961. Oil on Canvas. Collection, Mr. and Mrs. Burton Tremaine, New York.

Pair 1*b* Panel from William Overgrad's comic strip "Steve Roper."

Pair 2*a* Anonymous comic book panel.

Pair 2*b* Lichtenstein, "Torpedo . . . Los!" 1963. Magna on Canvas. Courtesy of the Leo Castelli Gallery, New York.

Pair 3*a* Anonymous comic book panel.

FIGURE 2-9   Pair 3, Example *a*.

FIGURE 2-10   Pair 3, Example *b*.

FIGURE 2-11   Pair 4, Example *a*.

FIGURE 2-12   Pair 4, Example *b*.

FIGURE 2-14   Pair 5, Example *b*.

FIGURE 2-13   Pair 5, Example *a*.

Pair 3*b*   Lichtenstein, "Image Duplicator." 1963. Magna on Canvas. Courtesy of the Leo Castelli Gallery, New York.
Pair 4*a*   Anonymous comic book panel.
Pair 4*b*   Lichtenstein, "Hopeless." 1963. Magna on Canvas. Courtesy of the Leo Castelli Gallery, New York.
Pair 5*a*   Lichtenstein, "The Engagement Ring." 1961. Courtesy of the Leo Castelli Gallery, New York.
Pair 5*b*   Panel from Martin Branner's comic strip "Winnie Winkle."

If you have been mistaken, do not be discouraged. Learning how to perceive sensitively takes time. Furthermore, it is not possible to decide beyond all doubt, as with the proof that $2 + 2 = 4$, whether Lichtenstein is a creator of artistic form and comic-strip makers are not. We think it is highly probable that this is the case, but absolute certainty here is not possible. And it should be noted that the comic-strip makers generally look upon Lichtenstein's work as "strongly 'decorative' and backward looking."

The examination of these examples makes it fairly evident, we believe, that Lichtenstein is a master at composing forms. But are these paintings works of art? Do these forms inform? Do they have a content? If so, what are their subject matters? What is the subject matter of "Torpedo . . . Los!"? The aggressiveness of submarine commanders? Or, rather, the energy, passion, directness, and mechanicality of comic strips? Or could the subject matter be made up of both these things? Perhaps there is no interpreted subject matter—perhaps the event in the submarine is just an excuse for composing a form. Perhaps this form is best understood and appreciated not as informing but, rather, as simply attractive and pleasing. This kind of form we shall call "decorative form."

Decorative Form or Decoration

Decorative form, unlike artistic form, lacks content. The function of decoration is to be suitable. Wallpaper, for example, is usually chosen because it is pleasing and fitting for an interior wall area. Usually we do not expect wallpaper to have a form that presents a subject matter, as Adams' photograph does. Nor do we expect wallpaper to have a form that interprets a subject matter, as Goya's painting does. If we found wallpaper with artistic form, we would—if we were wise—buy it and frame it as art. The chances of such a discovery, of course, are highly remote. However, if we were that lucky, then the paper would no longer be wallpaper. What we usually expect from wallpaper is a form that neither presents subject matter nor informs about it but, rather, just pleases. If, as sometimes is the case, wallpaper includes subject matter, it is there primarily to add to the pleasure. Then the wallpaper is full of "pretty things," such as idyllic country scenes. We do not expect to find in wallpaper the presentation of powerful images, as in Adams' photograph, that stir up our thoughts and feelings. Maybe, therefore, we should classify Lichtenstein's comic-strip paintings as works of decoration. Admittedly their forms are far stronger than those in things that are usually called "decorative," such as wallpaper and linoleum. Yet are Lichtenstein's forms informing? Do we gain insight from them? Obviously we are into a very complex set of questions. And in the case of Lichtenstein's paintings, these questions are posed in a very difficult way. We need a further analysis of subject matter and content in examples that are less complex. The female nude is such an example and is, perhaps, more interesting.

Subject Matter and Content

The female nude of the *Playboy* type juts out from almost every commercial magazine rack. The subject matter—the female nude—is almost invariably presented without any significant transformation. There is some form, of course, but only enough to display—not interpret—the subject matter. In this respect, this kind of photograph is like Adams' photograph. The nude's position, the lighting, the angle and distance of the shot, etc., have been selected. But this forming or organizing is usually so minimal or uninspired that it fails to inform. Thus these nudes all look pretty much alike. We get clichés of the female body. In other words, we are presented with a subject matter, not a content. Or, if you disagree, what are your arguments?

Compare any photograph of the *Playboy* type—call it Photograph *a*—with Figure 2-15—call it Photograph *b*. Has *b* a stronger form? Are there meaningless details? Do the details interrelate tightly? If so, how is this accomplished? If you agree with us that *b* has a fairly strong

FIGURE 2-15 *Nude under Piano.* 1973. Photograph by Ralph Gibson.

form, would you maintain that this form not only presents but informs? That is, does the form of *b* interpret the female body, reveal it in such a way that you have an increased understanding of and sensitivity to the female body? In other words, does *b* have content? Before deciding, consider the six paintings of the female nude shown in Figures 2-16 through 2-21.

Most of these paintings are very highly valued—some as masterpieces. Why? Surely not because they present the female nude as subject matter. In this respect, *Playboy* does a much better job. These paintings are highly valued as works of art because they are powerful interpretations of their subject matter. *Think from* rather than *at* these paintings. Then notice how different the interpretations are. Any important subject matter has many different facets. That is why shovels and soup cans have limited utility as subject matters. They have very few facets to offer for interpretation. The female nude, on the other hand, is almost limitless. The next artist interprets something about the female nude that had never been interpreted before, because the female nude seems to be inexhaustible as a subject matter.

More precisely, the six paintings all have somewhat different subject matters. All are about the nude. But the painting by Giorgione is about the nude as idealized, as a goddess, as Venus. Now there is a great deal that all of us could say in trying to describe Giorgione's interpretation. But notice how language inevitably fails us. Giorgione has said it in his own language, the language of painting, and any

FIGURE 2-16   Giorgione, *Sleeping Venus*. 1508-1510. Oil on canvas, 43 by 69 inches. Alinari.

FIGURE 2-17   Pierre-August Renoir, *Reclining Nude*. 1902. Oil on canvas, 26½ by 60⅝ inches. Collection, The Museum of Modern Art, New York. Gift of Mr. and Mrs. Paul Rosenberg.

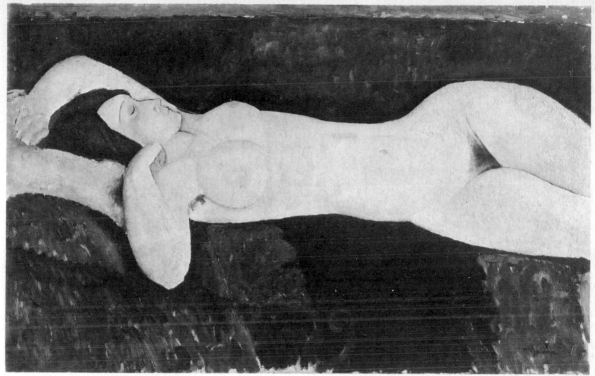

FIGURE 2-18   Amadeo Modigliani, *Reclining Nude* (c. 1919). Oil on canvas, 28½ × 45⅞ inches. Collection, The Museum of Modern Art, New York. Gift of Mr. and Mrs. Paul Rosenberg.

FIGURE 2-19   Pablo Picasso, *Nude on a Black Couch.* 1932. Photograph courtesy of Galerie Louis Leiris. © SPADEM, Paris/VAGA, New York, 1982.

FIGURE 2-20 Tom Wesselmann, *Nude #1*. 1970. Oil on canvas, 25 by 45 inches. Private collection. Photograph by Sidney Janis Gallery, New York.

translation into words falls far short. This is always the case with works of art, including poems and novels. They are their own statement. Their meaning or content is inextricably interwoven in their forms. Thus every time we try to speak about the content of a work of art, we are always at an unbridgeable distance from the fullness of that content. Hence it is usually better to try to describe the subject matter rather than the content. The description of the subject matter can help us perceive the content if we have missed it. In understanding what the form worked on—that is, the subject matter—our perceptive apparatus is better prepared to perceive the "form-content."

The subject matter of Renoir's painting is the nude as earth mother. In the Modigliani, the subject matter is the sensual nude. In the Picasso, it is the nude as abandoned, enfleshed in her sex. In the Wesselmann, it is the nude as exploited. In the Manet, it is the nude as prostitute. In all six paintings the subject matter is the female nude—but qualified. The subject matter is qualified in relation to what the artistic form focuses upon and makes lucid. We believe this qualification is lacking in most *Playboy*-type photographs because usually an artistic form is also lacking.

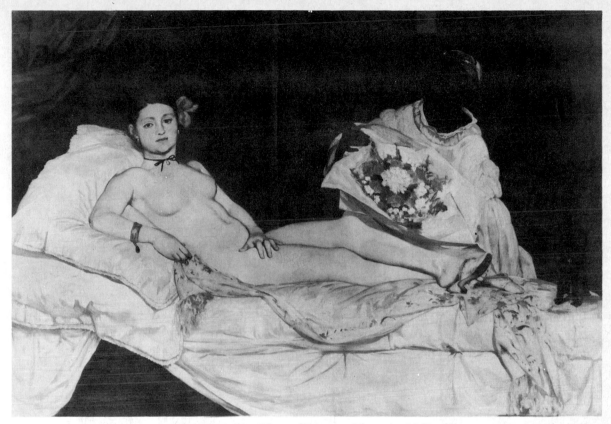

FIGURE 2-21 Edouard Manet, *Olympia*. 1863. Oil on canvas, 51¼ by 74¾ inches. Musée de l'Impressionnisme, Paris.

PERCEPTION KEY NUDE UNDER PIANO

Return to Figure 2-15.

1. Does this photograph have artistic form?
2. If so, how is this accomplished?
3. What is the subject matter of the photograph? Be precise. What is the content of the photograph?
4. Or if you think content is lacking, why?

Summary

A work of art is a form-content. An artistic form is a form-content. An artistic form is more than just an organization of the elements of an artistic medium, such as the lines and colors of painting. The artistic form interprets or clarifies some subject matter. The subject matter, strictly speaking, is not *in* a work of art. Thus, the subject matter is only imaginable, not perceptible. It is only *suggested* by the work of art. The interpretation of the subject matter is the content or meaning of the work of art. Content is enmeshed in the form. The content, unlike the subject matter, is *in* the work of art, fused with the form. We can separate content from form only by analysis. The ultimate justification of any analysis is whether it enriches our participation with that work, whether it helps that work "work" in us. Good analysis or criticism does just that. But conversely, any analysis not based on participation is unlikely to be very helpful. Participation is the way—the only way—of getting into direct contact with the form-content. And so any analysis that is not based upon a participative experience inevitably misses the work of art. Participation and good analysis, although necessarily occurring at different times, always end up hand in hand.

When we get down to specific cases, it is by no means always easy to decide whether something is a work of art. Goya's *May 3, 1808*, it seems to us, is an easy case in the affirmative. But there are hard cases, borderline examples. What about Dine's *Shovel* (Figure 2-1), Lichtenstein's transformations (Figures 2-5 through 2-14), and *Nude under Piano* (Figure 2-15)? The basic distinctions that we have discussed—participation, subject matter, form, and content—provide us with guidelines that help in posing and answering these questions. But how to apply this set of guidelines or other sets of guidelines precisely is not obvious. That job, when done with precision, requires an expertise that only a few highly sensitive and highly trained people—called "critics"—have achieved.

In this chapter, we have elaborated one set of guidelines. Of course, other sets are possible. We have discussed one other set very briefly: that a work of art is significant form. If you can conceive of other sets of guidelines, make them explicit and try them out. The ultimate test is clear: Which set helps you most in appreciating works of art? We think the set we have proposed meets that test better than other proposals. But this is a very large question indeed, and your decision should be delayed. In any event, we will now investigate the principles of criticism. These principles should help show us how to apply our set of guidelines to specific examples. Then we will be properly prepared to examine the uniqueness of the various arts.

Chapter 2 Bibliography

Aldrich, Virgil C. *The Philosophy of Art*. Englewood Cliffs, N.J.: Prentice-Hall, 1963.
Bell, Clive. *Art*. London: Chatto and Windus, 1914.

Collingwood, R. G. *The Principles of Art*. New York: Oxford University Press, 1938.

Dewey, John. *Art as Experience*. New York: Putnam's, 1958.

Ducasse, Curt J. *The Philosophy of Art*. New York: Dover, 1963.

Langer, Susanne K. *Feeling and Form*. New York: Scribner's, 1953.

Maritain, Jacques. *Creative Intuition in Art and Poetry*. Princeton, N.J.: Princeton University Press, 1953.

Merleau-Ponty, Maurice. *The Primacy of Perception*. ed. James M. Edie. Evanston, Ill.: Northwestern University Press, 1964.

Pepper, Stephen C. *The Work of Art*. Bloomington, Ind.: Indiana University Press, 1946.

Rader, Melvin. *A Modern Book of Aesthetics*, 4th ed. New York: Holt, Rinehart & Winston, 1973.

Read, Herbert. *The Meaning of Art*. Baltimore: Penguin Books, 1964.

Reid, Louis Arnaud. *Meaning in the Arts*. London: Allen & Unwin, 1969.

Tolstoy, Leo. *What is Art? and Essays on Art*, trans. Aylmer Maude. New York: Bobbs-Merrill, the Library of Liberal Arts, 1960.

Weiss, Paul. *Nine Basic Arts*. Carbondale: Southern Illinois University Press, 1961.

Weitz, Morris. *Philosophy of the Arts*. Cambridge, Mass.: Harvard University Press, 1950.

BEING A CRITIC
OF THE ARTS

3 The act of criticism is a positive act. When we accept the responsibility of a critic, we aim for the fullest understanding and the fullest participation possible. Being a critic is being at the height of awareness, examining a work of art in detail, establishing its context, and clarifying its achievement. The popular journalistic critic sometimes aims for those qualities, too. But more often the needs of journalism sidetrack the critic into being flashy, negative, and cute. We are not concerned with that negative approach. We are concerned with establishing the methods and means of becoming a good critic and understanding the goals of good criticism. Our purposes are to enjoy our experiences in the arts to the fullest.

You Are Already an Art Critic

Whether we know it or not, we all operate as critics of art much of the time. When we look for a while at a film on television and decide to change the channel to look for something better, we act as critics. This is a particularly broad critical function if someone else is in the room.

The question to ask is not a simple one: On what basis do we change the channel? When we turn a radio dial looking for music we like, we are being critics of music. If we stop to admire a building or a painting, we are being, in a minor way, critics. If we stop to think about it, we become aware that we are critics of art in more ways than we usually realize.

What qualifies us to make the critical judgments we make all the time? What is the training that underlies our constant criticism of such arts as film, music, and architecture? These are embarrassing questions for many people, but they should not be. If we have no special training in any of these fields, we do have—just by virtue of having grown up in a culture saturated with arts of all kinds—considerable background and experience. We probably have listened to music on the radio, watched television, and gone to the movies since before we can remember. The least experienced among us at age twenty can count on fifteen years of seeing architecture, of responding to the industrial design of automobiles and other objects, of seeing public sculpture or any of a host of other works of art and design. Perhaps it is more fair and realistic to say that at age twenty we can count on having had almost twenty years of experience to draw from. This is no inconsiderable background and it makes us all, at almost any age, formidable critics who make critical judgments without hesitation.

But even though all this is true, we realize something further. We have limitations as critics. When we are left to our own devices and grow up with little specific critical training, even in a society rich in art, we find ourselves capable of going only so far. We all know people who have, at age forty, remained the same kinds of critics they were at age twenty. Even if such people were very good critics at age twenty, they must be thought of as emotionally or culturally retarded if they still make the same choices in art twenty years later. This should be obvious if only on the basis that art—not to mention the rest of the society—changes enormously in twenty years. A generation in art in the twentieth century produces the changes a century would have produced in the days of Leonardo. A person who stands still with respect to the arts is a person left behind, a critic whose development stops prematurely, leaving him or her somewhat unable to see what it is other people like about the "new" art.

Each of us is a practicing critic, but if we do nothing to increase our critical skills, they may not grow. When we hear people rebelling against becoming more refined critics because they feel they cannot judge Shakespeare or Mozart or Velasquez, we will see that what they are often rebelling against is the effort it takes to look closely at something and participate with it. As it is, many people stop reading Shakespeare in the middle of a play because they do not feel involved. Similarly, some people turn off Mozart and turn on a popular song. No one can be excused on the "Who am I to judge Mozart?" disclaimer. We are all capable of judging Mozart. Some of us are more capable, of course; and that is the point. By learning some essentials about criticism and how to put them to work more thoughtfully than we do, we will help develop our own capacities as critics.

Participation and the Critic

One of the reasons many of us resist our roles as critics is that we value very highly the participative experience we get from the works of art that excite us. Criticism interferes with that participative delight. For example, most of us lose ourselves in a good film and never think about the film in any objective or "distant" way. It "ruins" the experience to stop and be critical, for the act of criticism is quite different from the act of participative enjoyment. And if we were to choose which act is the more important, then, of course, we would have to stand firm behind enjoyment. Art is, above all, enjoyable. Yet the kinds of enjoyment it affords are sometimes very complex and subtle. Good critics are people who can begin to make the complexities and subtleties more available both to others and to themselves. In other words, taking a moment to reflect upon the participative experience we have had might help any of us deepen our next participation. Thus, the critical act is—at its very best—an act that is very much related to the act of participatory enjoyment. When performed sensitively and knowingly, criticism aids enjoyment. A fine critical sense helps us develop our participatory capacities. The reason is simple: A fine critical sense helps us develop the perceptions essential to understanding what's "going on" in a work of art.

When critics participate with a work of art, they are not doing criticism. When they criticize a work of art, they reflect on their participative experience and the work of art that determined that experience. Unfortunately, there are many people who feel that reflecting on their responses to a work of art is being too analytical, too remote from the act of responding. But we should realize that the act of reflection does not lessen the delights of involvement with a work of art. Those delights have already been achieved. Moreover, reflection can intensify the delight of our next experience with that work if that reflection makes us aware of things we did not notice during our earlier experience.

Seeing a film twice, for instance, is often interesting. At first our personalities may melt away, and we become involved and "lost" in the experience. If the film maker is competent and clever, he or she can cause us to do this quickly and efficiently—the first time. But if the film maker is *only* competent and clever, as opposed to being creative, then the second time we see the film its flaws are likely to be obvious and we are likely to have a less complete participatory experience.

However, when we see a really great film, then the second experience is likely to be more exciting than the first. If we have become good critics and if we have reflected wisely on our first experience, then we will find that the second experience of any great work of art will be more intense and our sense of participation deeper. For one thing, our understanding of the artistic form and content will be considerably more refined in our second experience and in all subsequent experiences.

It is obvious that only those works of art that are successful on most or all levels can possibly be as interesting the second time we experience them as they were the first. This presumes, however, a reliable and full perception of the work. For example, the first experience of most works of art will not be very satisfying—perhaps it will not produce the participative experience at all—if we do not perceive that work fully. Consequently, it is possible that the first experience of a difficult poem, for instance, will be less than enjoyable. If, however, we have gained helpful information from the first experience and thus have made ourselves more capable of perceiving the poem, the second experience will be more satisfying.

When we criticize, one of the first questions we should ask concerns whether or not we actually have had a participative experience. Has the work of art taken us out of ourselves? If it is a good work of art, we should find ourselves "lost" in the delight of experiencing it. However, as we have been suggesting all along, if we are not so carried away by a given work, the reason may not be because it is not successful. It may be because we do not perceive all there is to perceive. We may not "get it" well enough for it to transport us into participation. Consequently, we have to be critical of ourselves some of the time in order to be sure we have laid the basic groundwork essential to participation. When we are sure that we have done as much as we can to prepare ourselves, then we are in a better position to decide whether the deficiency is in the work or in us. In the final analysis, the participative experience can be said to be something that we not only *can* but also *must* have if we are to fully apprehend a work of art.

Kinds of Criticism

Now, with our basic critical purpose clearly in mind—that is, to learn, by reflecting on works of art, how to participate with these works more intensely and enjoyably—let us now analyze the practice of criticism more closely. If, as we have argued in Chapter 2, a work of art is essentially a form-content, then good criticism will sharpen our perception of the form of a work of art and increase our understanding of its content. Take some considerable time now with the following perception key.

Seek out at least five examples of criticism from any available place, including, if you like, Chapters 1 and 2 of this book. Film or book reviews in newspapers or magazines may be used. Analyze these examples with reference to the following questions:

1. Does this criticism focus mainly on the form or the content?
2. Can you find any examples in which the criticism is entirely about the form?
3. Can you find any examples in which the criticism is entirely about the content?
4. Can you find any examples in which the focus is upon neither the form nor the content but on evaluating the work as good or bad or better or worse than some other work?
5. Can you find any examples in which there is not some evaluation?
6. Which kind of criticism do you find most helpful—that bearing on form, content, or evaluation? Why?
7. Do you find any examples in which it is not clear whether the emphasis is upon form, content, or evaluation?

This perception key identifies three basic kinds of criticism: (1) *descriptive*—focusing on form, (2) *interpretive*—focusing on content, and (3) *evaluative*—focusing on the relative merits of a work of art. In the chapters on painting and photography we will also present examples of criticism that are historically oriented. However, historical criticism is, we believe, most usefully classified as a supplemental kind of criticism that enriches the three basic kinds of criticism.

DESCRIPTIVE CRITICISM

Descriptive criticism concentrates on the form of a work of art, describing, sometimes exhaustively, the important characteristics of that form in order to improve our understanding of the entire work. At first glance this kind of criticism may seem unnecessary. After all, the form is all there, completely given—all we have to do is observe. Anybody can do that. But it is not that simple, for the forms of works of art are usually complex and subtle. Even when they are simple, they are usually deceptively simple. Most of us know all too well that we can spend time attending to a work we are very much interested in and yet not perceive all there is to perceive. We miss things, and oftentimes we miss things that are right there for us to observe. For example, did you notice the visual form of E. E. Cummings' "l(a"—the spiraling downward curve (Figure 1-4)—before it was called to your attention? Or did you really see in Goya's painting (Color Plate 3) the way the line of the long dark shadow at the bottom right underlines the line of the firing squad?

Good descriptive critics call our attention to what we otherwise might miss in an artistic form we are concerned about. And even more important, they help us do their work when they are not around. We can, if we carefully attend to descriptive criticism, develop and enhance our own descriptive powers. That is worth thinking about. None of us can afford to have a professional critic with us all the time in order to observe everything that we should. And there are not enough published critical studies of works of art easily available so that we can always consult one if we have questions about something or if we feel that there is something missing in our responsiveness to a work of art. Critics can really help us if we need help, but they are not always available. Consequently, we ourselves must learn to become descriptive critics. No other learning is as likely to improve our participation with a work of art, for such criticism turns us directly to the work itself.

PERCEPTION KEY DESCRIPTIVE CRITICISM AND MODIGLIANI NUDE

---

1. Relying on our discussion of Blume in Chapter 1 and Goya in Chapter 2, descriptively criticize Modigliani's nude (Figure 2-18). Point out every facet of the form that seems important. Discuss the painting in class or with others if possible.
2. After this criticism, return to the painting and participate with it. Do you now have a sharper perception of the painting and, in turn, a more intense feeling of participation?

STRUCTURAL DETAILS

As you worked through Question 1 of this perception key you may have found it difficult to organize your descriptions. After all, we have defined form as the interrelationship of part to part and part to whole in a work of art, and connections like this may seem endless. Two distinctions about form may be of help here—detail and structure.

A connection of one part of form to another part we shall call a relationship of structural details. In poetry, for instance, it would be the relationship of one word to another, one phrase to another, one image to another, or any of these to any other. In the dance, it is the relationship of a given figure's motion at one moment to a motion at another moment, of one dancer's hand as related to another dancer's hand. Structure in music has to do with the relationships of simultane-

FIGURE 3-1   Salve Regina: A Gregorian Chant, "Hail Mary, Mother of Mercy."

FIGURE 3-2   Two bars from Mendelssohn's Violin Concerto.

FIGURE 3-3   Chopin: Three bars from Prelude in C Major.

ously sounded tones or of the relationships of tones sounded one after another. Structural detail has to do with the connections within a limited region in the composition. Even if you do not read music, you can see that there is a considerable difference in the examples of music above (Figures 3-1, 3-2, and 3-3):

PERCEPTION KEY MUSIC AND STRUCTURAL DETAIL

1. Which example has the fewest structural details?
2. Structure usually becomes clearer as the structural details are removed. In which of these examples is the structure most difficult to perceive? In which is it most easy to perceive?
3. Chopin's Prelude is marked "agitato," meaning that the passage is to be played to reveal a state of emotional agitation. Is it possible that emotional agitation is somehow related to the emphasis on textural detail found in this piece of music?
4. If possible, compare the emotional qualities perceptible in these three pieces (when played) and see if there is a relationship between emotional

qualities and the emphasis on structural details. Is it possible that an emphasis on structure produces restfulness in music, while an excess of structural details can produce agitation?

A connection of one part of form to the whole form we shall call a "structural relation." Structure concerns itself with the totality of the work of art and the relationship of any details or regions to that totality. In some works of art the structure is not immediately perceptible. For example, in all forms that take time to unfold because what is perceptible comes to us successively—in literature, music, dance, and film, for example—we are not aware of the totality of structural qualities until the unfolding is over or nearly over. Only then can we begin to grasp the complete structural characteristics. Plot is sometimes the key to the structure of a narrative or a film. The statement, development, and repetition of musical themes or motifs is part of the structural form of a symphony or of a popular song. And in forms such as these we often need some guidance to discover what the structural qualities are. This is basic to all of us in developing an educated sensibility.

The emphasis of structure over structural details—or the reverse—will differ widely from work to work. In the paintings by John F. Peto (Figure 3-4) and Jefferson Davis Chalfont (Figure 3-5) we see two approaches to the problem. We realize that every painting, like every other work of art, will have some structural detail and that structure will emerge from structural detail. When there is less structural detail the structure will emerge more rapidly. An emphasis on structural detail, conversely, will usually obscure structure. Sometimes it will actually obscure structure enough that we will feel the work is not soundly organized, that it is actually deficient in form. In paintings and photographs, often the structural details will be organized into larger, but simpler geometric shapes: circles, rectangles, triangles, polyhedrons, or other recognizable shapes. When this occurs, the work will appear to have strong cohesiveness: its structure is emphasized, and we feel the power of strong, clear organization.

PERCEPTION KEY OFFICE BOARD AND VIOLIN AND BOW

1. In which painting is structural detail more plentiful?
2. Draw the basic geometric shapes used to organize structural details in each painting. For which painting is this job easier?
3. Which painting seems simpler in organization, which more complex?
4. Which painting seems to have random details of everyday life as its subject matter? How does the organization of structure and structural detail relate to the paintings' subject matter?

FIGURE 3-4 John F.
Peto, *Office Board.*
1885. Metropolitan
Museum of Art. Photo
by Jacobus.

We feel that Chalfont's painting stresses structure more than
structural detail because the familiar shape of the violin, overlaid on
the rectangular field, dominates the painting. The structural details are
absorbed in the violin. The structural details in Peto's painting are
letters, pictures, and ribbons holding them to the board. Each structural detail is generally rectangular but they do not cohere in a larger
recognizable shape. Petro seems to organize them in a random manner
to suggest a typical bulletin board of his period on which such items
would build up casually over a period of time. This is the point of
Peto's highly realistic "fool-the-eye" style. Chalfont uses the same
style to achieve a different effect. By simplifying, he reminds us that
music lies dormant in the structure of the violin—a fact we cannot
miss noticing.

FIGURE 3-5 Jefferson Davis Chalfont, *Violin and Bow.* 1889. Metropolitan Museum of Art. Photo by Jacobus.

Interpretive Criticism

Interpretive criticism reveals the content of a work of art. It helps us understand how form transforms subject matter into content. For example, Peto's painting seems to have the randomness of daily life as its subject matter. The disorder of his letters, postcards, tickets, papers, and assorted pamphlets reveals the agitation and dynamics of daily life: it does not boil down to anything simple. It is complex and disordered because each day brings something new, something unexpected. Chalfont's painting is simple, balanced, harmonic. The harmony and orderliness of the structure alludes to those qualities in music. If Peto is revealing that life is so various it has no one structure, then Chalfont reminds us that music has one sure structure revealed by the instantly recognizable form of the violin, whose shape is visually harmonic. These revelations are controlled in part by the relative emphasis on structural details in each work.

The content of any work of art will come clearer when the structure is seen in relationship to the structural details. First, of course, the details must be observed; then, the structure must be perceived. The relationship of the two—the relative importance of each—will help us participate with the work on the level it demands. The following examples (Figures 3-6, 3-7) demonstrate that the same principle holds for architecture as holds for painting. The subject matter of a building—or at least an important component of it—is usually a practical function: the function which the building is to serve. We have no difficulty telling which of these buildings was meant to serve as a bank and which was meant to serve as a church. In the following perception key, consider why it is so easy to tell which building is which, even though neither is typical of its kind of architecture.

PERCEPTION KEY SULLIVAN'S BANK AND LE CORBUSIER'S CHURCH

1. Which of these forms suggests solidity? Which suggests flight and motion? What have these things got to do with practical function?
2. How do the details of each building reinforce the structure?
3. Explain the content of each building.

FORM-CONTENT

The interpretive critic's job is to find out as much about an artistic form as possible in order to explain its meaning. This is a particularly

FIGURE 3-6 Louis Henry Sullivan, Guaranty (Prudential) Building, Buffalo, New York. 1894. Buffalo Historical Society.

FIGURE 3-7 Le Corbusier, Notre Dame-du-Haut, Ronchamps, France, 1950—1955. Ezra Stoller© ESTO.

useful task for the amateur critic—which is to say, for us in particular —since the forms of numerous works of art seem important but are not immediately understandable. When we look at the examples of the bank and the church, we ought to realize that the artistic power of these buildings is expressed by means of the form-content. It is true that without knowing the functions of these buildings we could appreciate them as abstract structures, but knowing about their functions deepens our appreciation. Thus, the lofty arc of Le Corbusier's roof soars heavenward more mightily when we recognize the building as a church. The form takes us up toward heaven, at least in the sense that it moves our eyes upward. For a Christian church such a reference is perfect. The bank, on the other hand, looks like a pile, almost like a pile of square coins or banknotes. Certainly the form "amasses" something, and the sense of this is just what is appropriate for a bank. We will not belabor these examples, since it should be fun for you to do this kind of critical job yourself. Observe how much more you "get out of" these examples of architecture when you consider each form in relation to its meaning—that is, the form as form-content. Furthermore, such analyses should convince you that interpretive criticism operates in a vacuum unless it is based on descriptive criticism. Unless we perceive the form with sensitivity—and this means that we have the basis for good descriptive criticism—we simply cannot understand the content. In turn, any interpretive criticism will be useless.

Consider now Donald Justice's love poem and give some thought to the job an interpretive critic might have in explaining the poem to someone who does not understand or like it. What are the kinds of questions critics might ask about the work as a poem (not, in other words, about themselves or the poet or the woman addressed in the poem)?

LOVE'S MAP

Your face more than others' faces
Maps the half-remembered places
I have come to while I slept—
Continents a dream had kept
Secret from all waking folk
Till to your face I awoke,
And remembered then the shore,
And the dark interior.

[Copyright © 1959 by Donald Justice. Reprinted from *The Summer Anniversaries* by Donald Justice, by permission of Wesleyan University Press. "Love's Map" appeared in *Poetry*.]

This is the kind of poem that one needs to think about for quite a while, for its content is not obvious. And while thinking about it, one could be asking some questions that might help the poem come into sharper focus. In the accompanying perception key, provide some questions of your own. What three questions could you ask that could help put the poem into better perspective, the kind of perspective we think of as "depth" when we talk about a poem as having a "deep" meaning? If you have difficulty doing this, try some questions that deal with the idea of using a map and references to geography in a love poem, or the use of sleep in the poem, or about the poem's rhyme and its effect.

PERCEPTION KEY "LOVE'S MAP"

Questions:

1.

2.

3.

In a way, everyone's serious questions about this poem are relevant, no matter how strange they may seem at first. This is particularly true if a person has the opportunity to talk about his or her questions with others. Questions about this poem can help us gain insight into its content that we could probably get in no other way. Listening to the questions of others should give us some useful ideas about the ways in which works of art are understood by other people, providing us also with ideas about new ways in which we can understand works of art for ourselves. When you see it from this point of view, you realize that an open discussion, far from being vague and irrelevant to the sharpening of our understanding, ought to be one of the most valuable kinds of instruction we can get about the arts.

The relativity of explanations about the content of works of art is important for us to grasp. Even descriptive critics, who try to tell us about what is "really there," will see things in a way that is relative to their own perspective. As N. J. Berrill points out in *Man's Emerging Mind*, "The statement you often hear that 'seeing is believing' is one of the most misleading ones a man has ever made, for you are more likely to see what you believe than believe what you see. To see anything as it really exists is about as hard an exercise of mind and eyes as it is possible to perform. . . ."[1]

[1]N. J. Berrill, *Man's Emerging Mind*, Dodd, Mead: New York, 1955, p. 147.

Two descriptive critics can often "see" quite different things in an artistic form. This is not only to be expected but also desirable; it is one of the reasons great works of art keep us intrigued for centuries. But even though they may see quite different aspects when they look independently at a work of art, when they get together and talk it over, they will usually come to some kind of agreement about the aspects each of them sees. The thing being described, after all, has qualities each of us can perceive and talk about. A work of art possesses objective qualities in the sense that they belong to the work and can be verified by a number of different observers. But they are subjective as well, in the sense that they are observed only by "subjects."

In the case of interpretive criticism, the subjectivity and, in turn, the relativity of explanations are more obvious than in the case of descriptive criticism. The content is "there" in the form, and yet, unlike the form, it is not there in such a directly perceivable way. Thus, if someone were to read "Love's Map" and think that the only "map" in the poem was the face of the beloved woman, that person might well be surprised to learn that there are other references to maps and to kinds of geography—"the interior" usually refers to the unmapped and "dark" places beyond the coasts of continents as yet not totally explored. Then, even if the reader did sense that maps were being used in a very large and meaningful sense, he or she might not be fully aware that the woman in the poem was being loved the way explorers love the country they explore, with all the surprises, terror, uncertainty, and excitement of discovery that famous explorers have written about. The reader might not be fully aware that the act of love can be a way of getting new knowledge, of being in an unfamiliar relationship with someone, and of being in an unfamiliar relationship with oneself. Few people will deny that the concept of the map is present in the poem, but many may disagree that it implies the other ideas we have suggested. For you it may imply something else. But before we can begin to decide what is implied by the poem, we must know what is there that we can agree upon as equally perceivable and conceivable by most readers of the poem. This is descriptive criticism, preliminary to interpretive criticism—to the coming to terms with the content of the poem.

Interpretive critics, more than descriptive critics, must be familiar with the subject matter. Interpretive critics often make the subject matter more explicit for us, at the first stage of their criticism. In doing so, they bring us closer to the work. Perhaps the best way initially to "get at" Picasso's *Guernica* (Figure 1-2) is to discover its subject matter. Is it about a fire in a barn or something else? If we are not clear about this, perception of the painting is obscured. But after that subject matter has been elucidated, good interpretive critics go much further: exploring and discovering meanings about the subject matter as revealed by the artistic form. Now they are concerned with helping us grasp the content directly, in all of its complexities and subtleties. This final stage of interpretive criticism is, undoubtedly, the most demandingly creative of all criticism.

EVALUATIVE CRITICISM

To evaluate a work of art is to judge its artistic merits. At first glance, this seems to suggest that evaluative criticism is prescriptive criticism, which prescribes what is good as if it were a medicine and tells us that this work is superior to that work.

PERCEPTION KEY EVALUATIVE CRITICISM

1. Suppose you are a judge of an exhibition of painting and the six nude paintings discussed in Chapter 2 (Figures 2-16 through 2-21) have been placed into competition. You are to award first, second, and third prizes. What would be your decisions? Why?
2. Suppose, further, that you are asked to judge which is the best work of art from the following selection: Cummings' "l(a," Cézanne's *Mont Sainte Victoire* (Color Plate 4), and Le Corbusier's church (Figure 3-7). What would be your decision. Why?

It may be that this kind of evaluative criticism—sometimes called "judgmental criticism"—makes you a little uncomfortable. If so, we think your reaction is based on good instincts. In the first place, each work of art is such an individual thing that a relative merit ranking of several of them seems arbitrary. This is especially the case when the works are in different media and have different subject matter as in the second question of the perception key. In the second place, it is not very clear how such judging helps us in our basic critical purpose—to learn from our reflections about works of art how to participate with these works more intensely and enjoyably. It is true, of course, that judgmental criticism of some kind is necessary. We have been making such judgments continually in this book—in the selections for illustrations, for example. You are making such judgments when, as you enter a museum of art, you decide to spend your time with this painting rather than that. Obviously, the director of the museum must also make judgmental criticisms, for not everything can be left in. Someone might argue, for example, that his old pair of shoes that have been cemented to a pedestal belong in The Museum of Modern Art. Someone has to decide. If a Velasquez is on sale—and recently one of his paintings was bought by the Metropolitan Art Museum of New York City for over $5 million—someone has to decide its relative worth. Evaluative criticism, then, is always functioning, at least implicitly. Even when we are participating with a work, we are implicitly evaluating its worth. Our participation implies its worth. If it were worthless, we would more or less explicitly judge it so and not even attempt participation.

The problem, then, is how to use evaluative criticism as constructively as possible. How can we use such criticism to help our participation with works of art? Whether Giorgione's painting (Figure 2-16) deserves first prize over Modigliani's (Figure 2-18) seems trivial. Who really cares about that? But if almost all critics agree that Shakespeare's poetry is far superior to Edward Guest's and we have been thinking Guest's poetry is great, we would probably be wise to do some reevaluating. Or if we hear a music critic we respect state that John Cage's music is worth listening to—and up to this time we have dismissed this music as worthless—then we should indeed make an effort to listen. Perhaps the importance of evaluative criticism lies in its commendation of works that we might otherwise dismiss. This may lead us to delightful experiences. Such criticism may also make us more skeptical about our own judgments. If we think that the poetry of Edward Guest and the paintings of Grandma Moses are among the very best, it may be very helpful for us to know that other informed people think otherwise.

Furthermore, when evaluative criticism is done well, it aids descriptive and interpretive criticism. All three kinds of criticism are interdependent. As we have already suggested, it is impossible to describe an artistic form adequately without understanding its content. For example, the line of the shadow in the bottom right of Goya's *May 3, 1808* (Color Plate 3) reinforces the line of the firing squad even if we fail to note what the firing squad is doing. But if we do notice—that is, if we are aware of the form's informing—then the relationship between these lines becomes far stronger. Similarly, any adequate attempt to understand the content necessarily demands attention to the form that is informing. To talk about the executions that Goya portrayed without relating them to such things as those ominous, dreadful lines is to reduce our talk to clichés. Moreover, every effort to describe the form and understand the content implies value judgments that the description and understanding are worth doing, and such value judgments have the power to evoke more adequate descriptions and understandings. One of the authors recalls an example of this. One morning in Florence a historian of architecture and he were conducting a class in the Laurentian Library, designed by Michelangelo. The historian and the author were in disagreement about the architectural merits of the library in general and the stairwell in particular. In order to defend his value judgments, the author began to restate both his descriptions and interpretations. In that process he began to see things he had not seen before. His value judgments not only acted as catalysts to the discussion but also provided precise contexts that centered the issues involved, especially the interpretations. By making explicit our appreciation, evaluation may sharpen our perception and deepen our understanding. Furthermore, truly creative evaluative critics, like creative scientists, ask new questions based on their new way of judging things; in doing so, they help us see anew. They show us how our prejudgments of what is valuable in art may have limited our perception.

Evaluative criticism generally works with three fundamental standards—perfection, insight, and inexhaustibility. When the evaluation centers on the form, it usually values a form highly only if the structural details are tightly organized. If detail fails to cohere with structure, this usually will be condemned as distracting and thus inhibiting participation. An artistic form in which everything works together may be called perfect. A work may have perfect organization, however, and still be evaluated as poor unless it satisfies the standard of insight. If the form fails to inform us about some subject matter—if it just pleases us but doesn't make some significant difference in the way we live our lives—then that form may be called decorative rather than artistic. And decorative form may be valued below artistic form because the participation it evokes, if it evokes any at all, is not as intense, delightful, or as lastingly significant. Finally, works of art may differ greatly in the breadth and depth of their content. The subject matter of Mondrian's *Composition in White, Black and Red* (Color Plate 2)—colors, lines, and space—is not as broad as Cézanne's *Mont Sainte Victoire* (Color Plate 4). And the depth of penetration into the subject matter is far deeper in the Cézanne, we believe, than in the photograph of the mountain (Figure 2-4). The stronger the content—that is, the richer the interpretation of the subject matter—the more intense our participation, for we have more to keep us involved in the work. Such works resist monotony, no matter how often we return to them. Such works apparently are inexhaustible, and evaluative critics usually will rate only those kinds of works as masterpieces.

PERCEPTION KEY EVALUATIVE CRITICISM

1. Evaluate the seven nudes (Figures 2-15 through 2-21) with reference to the perfection of their forms.
2. Evaluate these works with reference to their insight.
3. Evaluate these works with reference to their inexhaustibility.

Notice how unimportant it is how you ultimately rank these works. But notice, also, how these evaluative questions provide precise contexts for your attention. Thus, your evaluations can sharpen your perceptions and broaden and deepen your interpretations.

PERCEPTION KEY EVALUATIVE CRITICISM

1. Evaluate the relative artistic merits of Justice's "Love's Map" and Mondrian's painting (Color Plate 2).

2. Evaluate the relative artistic merits of Mondrian's painting and Rothko's *Earth Greens* (Color Plate 5).

3. What is the point of the above two questions?

Some Examples for Criticism

The following are some examples to study as a critic. You can decide whether or not you have any sense of participation with the works here—but remember that a photograph of a sculpture is not a sculpture, any more than a photograph of a building is a building. No one can hope to have a very intense participative experience except in the presence of the genuine work of art itself. Still, we can sometimes get something of a participative experience even from a photograph.

The following figures are set up in pairs because useful criticisms are more likely to occur when we criticize works of the same artistic medium and at least roughly the same subject matter. (That is why we doubt that Question 1 of the preceding perception key, taken by itself, is of much value.) All criticisms are at least implicitly comparative, although there are some that seem entirely individual. But the important point for us is the fact that when we are beginning to develop our critical sense, we find that comparative judgments are easier and much more valuable than judgments about individual works without reference to any other.

Consider the following perception keys as mere starting points for your criticisms. Go as far beyond them as is useful.

PERCEPTION KEY INTERIORS OF ST. PAUL'S CATHEDRAL, LONDON (FIGURE 3-8), AND ST. ZACCARIAH, VENICE (FIGURE 3-9)

1. Consider the differences between these two church interiors in terms of the attention paid to structural detail. Which is more intricately detailed? Evaluate the effect of the emphasis on structural detail in relation to the function of the space as a church.

2. What are the main structural forms observable in each interior? What is their effect on the space enclosed by these forms? Which space is more dramatic? Which space is more peaceful?

3. Is it possible to evaluate the use of space in these churches without discussing their function as churches? Which space is more suited for public ceremony? Which is more suited for private prayer? How can you tell?

PERCEPTION KEY THREE PORTRAIT BUSTS: EGYPTIAN MUMMY MASK (FIGURE 3-10); GREEK BUST OF ASKLEPIOS (FIGURE 3-11); AFRICAN MASK (FIGURE 3-12)

1. All three of these busts portray the human face. Describe each carefully in terms of its emphasis on structural detail. Which is most dominated by structural detail? Which by structure?

FIGURE 3-8 Interior, Choir of St. Paul's Cathedral, London. Photo by Jacobus.

2. Which of these portraits is most lifelike? Is any, including the funeral mask, reminiscent of death?
3. Which of these portraits seems to express the strongest sense of personality? Why?
4. Which of these portraits expresses power most intensely? What kind of power?
5. Which kind of criticism—descriptive, interpretive, or evaluative—do these portraits seem most to demand?

PERCEPTION KEY STONE 56: STONEHENGE (FIGURE 3-13) AND ARCH OF CONSTANTINE (FIGURE 3-14)

1. Both of these stone pieces were very carefully erected and dressed (finished and smoothed). Which is more emphatically structural in appearance?

FIGURE 3-9   Interior, Chapel, St. Zaccariah, Venice. Photo by Jacobus.

Which emphasizes structural detail?

2. What is the basic structure of the more detailed of these two pieces? Is it difficult to perceive?

3. Stone 56 of Stonehenge was originally one of two stones which held a third stone balanced across their top. What section of the Arch of Constantine is comparable to Stone 56? What is different about it in comparison with Stone 56?

4. Enumerate some of the important structural details of the Arch of Constantine. What might the presence of fluted columns, circular reliefs, and freestanding sculpture have suggested about the richness of Roman society? What does the starkness of Stone 56 suggest about the unknown society that erected it?

5. Which of these pieces reveals more about the basic elemental force of nature? Which reveals more about a civilization's history? Which of these structures is more timeless?

FIGURE 3-10   Plaster Egyptian Mummy Mask, Metropolitan Museum of Art. Photo by Jacobus.

FIGURE 3-11 Marble Greek portrait of Asklepios (the physician), British Museum. Photo by Jacobus.

1. The Church of the Madeleine was constructed under the influence of Napoleon, who was thought to be a champion of the rights of the people. Does the form of the church give expression to the people's rights? Does it give expression to values you associate with churches? What else might the building's function be?

2. What principal details and structural elements are present in the Church of the Madeleine? Compare Figure 3-15 with Figure 6-7, the Parthenon. What are the similarities? Why would a nineteenth-century architect imitate a temple of fifth-century B.C.?

3. Does the Georges Pompidou Center for the Arts look like a museum? Comment on the details and structural forms. Does this building emphasize structure or detail? Compare it with the Church of the Madeleine.

4. The Pompidou Center was built in 1976 and is currently one of the most popular buildings in Paris. It is often called the inside-out building, an example of a modern "high tech" style. Can you make an evaluative comparison between the success of the styles of these two buildings?

Summary

Good critics can help us understand specific works of art while also giving us the means or techniques which will help us become good critics ourselves. By watching the critic perform, we can learn something about what the critical function is and how to adapt it to our purposes. Principally, we can learn a good deal about what kinds of questions to ask about given works of art. Each of the following chapters on the individual arts is designed to do just that—to give some help about what kinds of questions a serious viewer should ask in order to come to a clearer perception and deeper understanding of any specific work. In the arts, unlike many other areas of human concern, the questions are often more important than the answers. The real lover of the arts will often not be the person with all the answers but rather the one who has the best questions. And the reason for this is not that the answers are worthless but that the questions, when properly applied, lead us to a new awareness, a more exalted consciousness of what works of art have to offer us. Then, when we get to the last chapter, we will be better prepared to understand something of how each of the arts is related to the other branches of the humanities.

FIGURE 3-12 Wood African ritual mask, Museum of Ethography, London. Photo by Jacobus.

Chapter 3 Bibliography

Adams, Hazard, ed. *Critical Theory Since Plato*. New York: Harcourt, 1971.
Aschenbrenner, Karl. *The Concepts of Criticism*. Dordrecht, Netherlands: Reidell, 1975.

FIGURE 3-13 Stone 56:
Stonehenge. Photo by
Jacobus.

FIGURE 3-14 Arch of Constantine, Rome. Photo by Jacobus.

FIGURE 3-15 Pierre August Vignon, The Church of the Madeleine, Paris,
1829.

FIGURE 3-16 Richard Rogers and Enzo Piano, The Georges Pompidou Center for the Arts, Paris, 1976. Photo by Jacobus.

Bate, Walter Jackson. *Criticism: The Major Texts.* Enlarged edition. New York: Harcourt, Brace, Jovanovich, Inc., 1970.

Boas, George. *Wingless Pegasus.* Baltimore: John Hopkins, 1950.

Dudley, Louise, Austin Faricy, and James G. Rice. *The Humanities,* 6th edition. New York: McGraw-Hill, 1978.

Frye, Northrop. *Anatomy of Criticism.* Princeton, N.J.: Princeton University Press, 1957.

Greene, Theodore M. *The Arts and the Art of Criticism.* Princeton, N.J.: Princeton University Press, 1940.

Hirsch, E. D. *The Aims of Interpretation.* Chicago: University of Chicago Press, 1976.

Krieger, Murray. *Theory of Criticism.* Baltimore: The Johns Hopkins University Press, 1976.

Margolis, Joseph. *The Language of Art and Art Criticism: Analytic Questions in Aesthetics.* Detroit: Wayne State University Press, 1965.

Olson, Elder. *On Value Judgments in the Arts and Other Essays.* Chicago: University of Chicago Press, 1976.

Osborne, Harold. *Aesthetics and Criticism.* London: Routledge, 1955.

Sontag, Susan. *Against Interpretation and Other Essays.* New York: Farrar, Straus, and Giroux, 1964.

Wellek, René. *Concepts of Criticism.* New Haven: Yale University Press, 1963.

PAINTING

4 Introduction

Painting is the art that has most to do with revealing the visual appearance of objects and events. The eye is the chief sense organ involved in our participation with painting and one of the chief sense organs involved in our dealings with our everyday world. But our ordinary vision of our everyday world is usually very fragmentary. We usually see scenes with their objects and events only to the degree necessary for our practical purposes. The full visual appearance of things is missed. For example, imagine yourself walking along Broadway at Wall Street (Figure 6-5) rather than just looking at the photograph. Is it very likely that you would "see" the patterns formed by the vertical and horizontal lines of that scene? Even in such a simple act as walking safely on a sidewalk, we either ignore or abstract from the qualities of colors, lines, etc. Otherwise we would be late for our appointment or get run down by a car. We hurry on. Usually, when things cannot be ignored, we tend to quantify them. In order to survive, we reduce things to data. In that way we exert our control over things, manage them for our purposes. When we are behind the wheel of a car, our lives depend on our judgment of how far away and how fast-moving that oncoming car really is. We just do not have time to enjoy its splendor of speeding color. Of course, someone

77

else may be driving, and then the qualities of the visually perceptible may be enjoyed for their own sake rather than being mastered by some manner of quantification. Or we may be walking leisurely in the mountains on a safe path, and then the fullness of the scene has a chance to unfold itself.

But this shift to enjoying things as they show themselves rather than passing them by or reducing them to data is not, for most of us, automatic. The habits of practical life tend to harden the lenses of our eyes, so that we become blind both to the qualities of things and the things themselves. Thus, even on that safe path on the mountain, we may miss both the blueness as well as the solidity of that mountain.

Although the habits of practical vision are often necessary for survival, we may make the grand mistake of assuming that we know the thing if we can place a label on it or fit it into a formula. Thus, we learn to notice only the most prominent features of a thing—those features that enable us to place it conveniently into a particular mental slot or category (e.g., mineral, vegetable, animal). Perhaps there is a terrible danger in allowing such a process to dominate our mental activities. Then we regard each two-legged creature with head and arms not as an individual having a particular name and an unusual combination of needs and talents but merely as a *human being*, or—perhaps a bit more specifically—as a Christian, Jewish, American, Chinese, Democratic, Republican, Communist, Socialist, black, white, red, or yellow human, etc. The particular individual becomes lost in these abstract classificational shuffles. Maybe this kind of mental process, if it is not checked by strong qualifications, is the seed bed for racial or religious or political prejudices, hates, and rivalries. In its extreme form, maybe it creates the conditions that permit an Adolph Hitler to practice genocide. Maybe it results in mutually exclusive suspicions and hates between "majority" and "minority" groups whose values permit them to think of themselves first as Catholics or Protestants, second as Christians, and third as members of a universal brotherhood bound together by the common recognition of the fatherhood of God. Maybe this kind of inverted value system permits groups to think of themselves first as Democrats, second as Southerners or Northerners or Westerners or Easterners, third as Americans, and last as citizens of a worldwide society. If there is some truth in these speculations, then sharpening our visual and other perceptual powers to be aware of the qualities of things and the things themselves may have something to do with the moral dimensions of our lives.

Test your visual powers for yourself.

PERCEPTION KEY YOUR VISUAL POWERS

1. What colors are the eyes of members of your family and those of your best friends?

2. Have you ever followed closely the swirl of a falling leaf?
3. Are you aware of the spatial locations of the buildings on the main street of your home town? Are they pleasing or distressing?
4. Are you aware very often of the detailed qualities of things—such as the fluidity of water, the roughness of rocks, or the greenness of grass?
5. Take some green paint and some red paint, a brush, and paper. Or, if these are not readily available, take any materials at hand, such as marbles and chips that are green and red. Now place the green and red side by side in such a way that, as far as possible, you make the greenness of the green shine forth. Maybe this will require a different tone of green or red or a different placement. Or maybe you have to remove the red altogether and substitute another color. Notice how, as you go about this, you must really see the green. This is not like looking at the green of a stop light. Then we see right through the green because it is a signal that directs our safe driving. To hold our sight on the green could be dangerous, and so we give the green no more than a glance and move on. But if we are trying to see the greenness of a green, we must hold on the green itself. We must let the green dominate and control our seeing. The qualities of the green must be allowed to show themselves from themselves for what they are. We must *think from* rather than *think at* the green (see page 36 ff.).
6. Are you aware very often of things as things, their "thingliness"—such as the mountainness of mountains, the marbleness of marble, the glassiness of glass? Do you care about things in this sense?
7. Go into the fields if this is possible and seek a rock that will enhance the appearance of an area of the yard or building or room where you live. Select both the rock and the area so that the rockiness of the rock—its hardness, roughness or smoothness, shape, and especially its solidity—will be perceivable.
8. John Ruskin, the great nineteenth-century critic, noted in his *Modern Painters* "that there is hardly a roadside pond or pool which has not as much landscape *in* it as above it. It is not the brown, muddy, dull thing we suppose it to be; it has a heart like ourselves, and in the bottom of that there are the boughs of the tall trees and the blades of the shaking grass, and all manner of hues, of variable pleasant light out of the sky; nay the ugly gutter that stagnates over the drain bars in the heart of the foul city is not altogether base; down in that, if you will look deep enough, you may see the dark, serious blue of the far-off sky, and the passing of pure clouds. It is at your own will that you see in that despised stream either the refuse of the street or the image of the sky—so it is with almost all other things that we kindly despise." Do you agree with Ruskin? If not, why not?

If you have found yourself tending to answer the questions of this perception key negatively or if you see the assignments about the green and the rock as being difficult and perhaps pointless, you should not be surprised or discouraged. Like the great majority of us, you probably have been educated away from sensitivity to the qualities of things and things as things. We have been taught how to manage and control things by thinking *at* them, as in the scientific method. This does not mean that such education is bad. Without this education the business of the world would come to a halt. But if not supplemented, this training may blind us like some terrible disease of the eye. For help we must go to the artists, especially the painters—those who are most sensitive to the visual appearances of things. With their aid, our vision can be made whole again, as when we were children. Their paintings accomplish this, in the first place, by making things and their qualities much clearer than they are in nature. The artist purges from our sight the films of familiarity. Second, painting, with its "all-at-onceness," more than any other art, gives us the time to allow our vision to focus and participate.

The Clarity of Painting

Examine again the photograph of Mont Sainte Victoire and Cézanne's painting (Figure 2-4 and Color Plate 4). The photograph was taken many years after Cézanne was there, but, aside from a few more buildings and older trees, the scene of the photograph shows us essentially what Cézanne saw. Compare the photograph of the mountain with the painting. At first glance, you might conclude that the photograph is clearer than the painting, for there is a kind of blurry effect about the painting. But look again. Rather, let the painting control your seeing—see from it.

PERCEPTION KEY MONT SAINTE VICTOIRE

1. Why did Cézanne put the two trees in the foreground at the left and right edges? Why are they cut off by the frame? Why are the trees trembling, as if hit by a bolt of lightning?
2. In the photograph, there is an abrupt gap between the foreground and the middle distance. In the painting, this gap is filled in. Why?
3. In the painting the viaduct has been moved over to the left? Why?
4. In the painting the lines of the viaduct appear to move toward the left. Why?
5. Furthermore, the viaduct lines lead to a meeting point with the long road that runs toward the left side of the mountain. The fields and buildings within that triangle all seem drawn toward that apex. Why did Cézanne organize this middle ground more geometrically than the foreground or the mountain? And why is the apex of the triangle the unifying area for that region?
6. Why is the peak of the mountain in the painting given a slightly concave shape?
7. In the painting, the ridge of the mountain above the viaduct is brought into much closer proximity to the peak of the mountain. Why?
8. In the painting, the lines, ridges, and shapes of the mountain are much more tightly organized than in the photograph. How is this accomplished?

The subject matter of Cézanne's painting is surely the mountain. Suppose the title of the painting were *Trees*. This would strike us as strange because when we read a title we usually expect it to tell us what the painting is about, that is, its subject matter. And although the trees in Cézanne's painting are important, they obviously are not as important as the mountain. A title such as *Viaduct* would also be misleading.

The basic content of the painting is, then, the interpretation of the mountain, the insight Cézanne's form gives us about the mountain-ness of the mountain—especially its solid rhythm and massive power. The form accomplishes this in so many ways that a complete description is very difficult. Some of the ways have already been suggested by the questions of the accompanying perception key. Every way helps bring forth the energy of Mont Sainte Victoire, which seems to roll down through the valley and even up into the foreground trees. Everything is dominated by and unified around the mountain. The roll of its ridges are like waves of the sea—but far more durable, as we sense the impenetrable solidity of the masses underneath.

Yet no reproduction, even the best in color, can tell you very much about the subtle relationships of the smaller details of this work. If possible, study this painting in the Phillips Gallery in Washington. Or if this is impossible, study almost any of Cézanne's landscapes after 1885—he did, incidentally, a great many sketches and paintings of Mont Sainte Victoire—in some nearby museum or gallery.

You will notice that the brushstrokes are usually perceptible, angular, and organized in units that function something like pieces in a mosaic. These units move toward each other in receding space, and yet their intersections are rigid, as if their impact froze their movement. Almost all the colors reflect light, like the facets of a crystal, so that a solid color or one-piece effect rarely appears. Generally, you will find within each unit a series of color tones of the same basic tint. The colors, moreover, are laid on in small overlapping patches, often crossed with dark and delicate parallel lines to give shading. These hatchings also model the depth dimension of objects, so we perceive the solidity of their volumes more directly, strangely enough, than we perceive them in nature. Compare again the photograph of Mont Sainte Victoire with the painting. The lines of the painting are not drawn around objects like outlines; rather, the lines emerge from the convergence of color, light, shadow, and volume much as—although this also may seem strange—lines emerge from the objects of nature. And the color tones of the painting, variously modulated, are repeated endlessly throughout the planes of space. For example, the color tones of the mountain are repeated in the viaduct and the fields and buildings of the middle ground and the trees of the foreground. Cézanne's color animates everything, mainly because the color seems to be always moving out of the depth of everything rather than being laid on flat like house paint. The vibrating colors, in turn, rhythmically charge into one another and then settle down, reaching an equilibrium in which everything except the limbs of the foreground trees seems to come to rest.

Cézanne's form distorts reality in order to reveal reality. He makes Mont Sainte Victoire far clearer in his painting than you will ever see it in nature or even in the best of photographs. Once you have participated with this and similar paintings, you will find that you will begin to see mountains like Mont Sainte Victoire with something like Cézanne's vision. A new set of lenses begins to grow in your eyes, and with it a way of seeing such things as mountains with extraordinary clarity and satisfaction.

The "All-at-Onceness" of Painting

In addition to revealing the visually perceptible more clearly, paintings give us time for our vision to focus, hold, and participate. Of course, there are times when we can hold on a scene in nature. We are resting with no pressing worries and with time on our hands, and the sunset is so striking that our attention fixes on its redness. But then darkness descends and the mosquitoes begin to bite. In front of a painting, however, we find that things can "stand still," like the red in Mondrian's *Composition in White, Black and Red* (Color Plate 2). Here the red is peculiarly impervious and reliable, infallibly fixed and settled in its place. It can be surveyed and brought out again and again; it can be visualized with closed eyes and checked with open eyes. There is no hurry, for all of the painting is present and, under normal conditions, it is going to stay present; it is not changing in any significant perceptual sense. The same is true of Cézanne's *Mont Sainte Victoire.*

Painting, more than any other art, presents itself as an entirety. Every part of a painting is all there at once—with a few exceptions, such as gigantic panoramic works—and everything stays put within the frame. The elements of a painting are not presented successively, as with the sound after sound of music or the word after word of literature. This "all-at-onceness" frees our perception from any sense of compulsion. Even our memories are rested. By simply a turn of our eye, the forgotten can be taken in again. Moreover, we can "hold on" any part or region or the totality as long as we like and follow any order of regions at our own pace. No region of a painting strictly presupposes another region temporally. The sequence is subject to no absolute constraint. Whereas there is only one route in listening to music, for example, there is a freedom of routes in seeing paintings.

With *Mont Sainte Victoire* we may focus on the foreground trees, then on the middle ground, and finally on the mountain. The next time around we may reverse the order. "Paths are made," as the painter Paul Klee observed, "for the eye of the beholder which moves along from

COLOR PLATE 1   Peter Blume, *Eternal City* 1937. Oil on composition board, 34 by 47⅞ inches. Collection, The Museum of Modern Art, New York. Mrs. Simon Guggenheim Fund.

COLOR PLATE 2 Piet Mondrian, *Composition in White, Black and Red*. 1936. Oil on canvas, 40½ by 41 inches. Collection, The Museum of Modern Art, New York. Gift of the Advisory Committee.

COLOR PLATE 3 Francisco Goya, *May 3, 1808*. 1814–1815. Canvas, 8 feet 9 inches by 13 feet 4 inches. The Prado, Madrid.

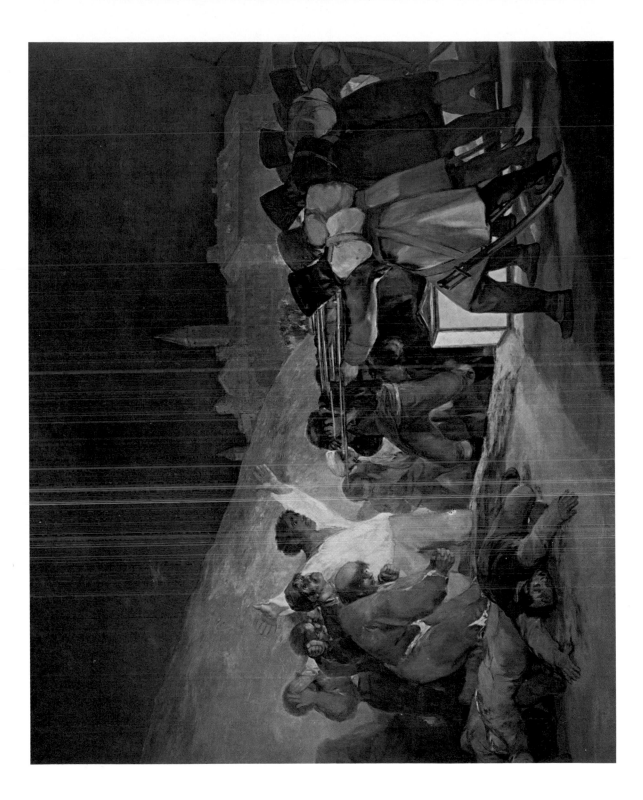

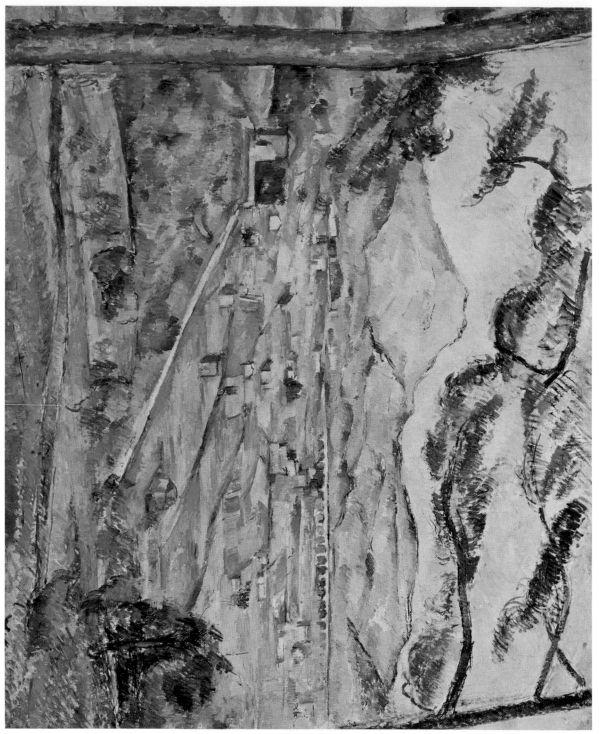

COLOR PLATE 4   Paul Cézanne, *Mont Sainte Victoire*. 1886–1887. Oil on canvas, 23½ by 28½ inches. The Phillips Collection, Washington, D.C.

COLOR PLATE 5 Mark Rothko, *Earth Greens*. 1955. Oil on canvas, 90¼ by 73½ inches. Courtesy of Galerie Beyeler Basel.

COLOR PLATE 6   Henri Matisse, *Pineapple and Anemones*. 1940. Oil on canvas, 29 by 36 inches. Private collection.

COLOR PLATE 7   Parmigianino, *The Madonna with the Long Neck*. ca. 1535. Panel painting, 36⅝ by 53¾ inches. Uffizi, Florence.

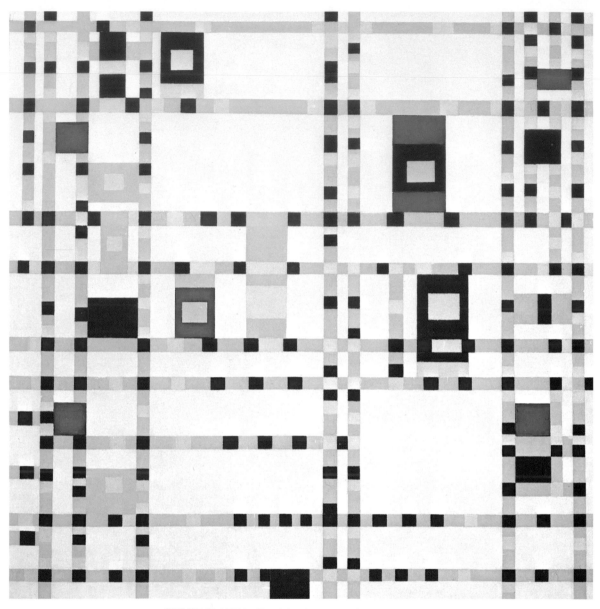

COLOR PLATE 8   Piet Mondrian, *Broadway Boogie Woogie*. 1942–1943. Oil on canvas, 50 by 50 inches. Collection, The Museum of Modern Art, New York. Given anonymously.

patch to patch like an animal grazing." There is a "rapt resting" on any part, an unhurried series of one-after-the-other of "nows," each of which has its own temporal spread. *Mont Sainte Victoire*, like most paintings, has a feudal constitution. Although certain regions—especially the mountain in this case—have hierarchical rights over others, each region maintains its personal rights and particularity, its intrinsic value. Each region has its own center of gravity and thus is a place of rest—of arrest. Each region is a calculated trap for sensuous meditation and consummation. Each region fills our eyes so completely that there is no desire to move to the next region, at least for awhile. Thus we are filled with a sense of the intensified immediate.

Paintings make it possible for us to stop in the present and enjoy at our leisure the sensations provided by the show of the visible. That is the second reason why paintings can help make our vision whole. They not only clarify our world but also free us from worrying about the future and the past, because paintings are a framed context in which everything stands still. There is the "here-now" and nothing but the "here-now." Our vision, for once, has time to let the qualities of things and the things themselves unfold.

Representational and Abstract Painting

The artistic medium of painting is made up of qualities such as colors, lines, and light. These qualities are elements or aspects of the visible, which lend themselves to being organized. They are the "stuff" that the painter forms in order to reveal some subject matter—that is, to transform that subject matter into a content. These qualities we shall call *sensa*.

Sensa

Sensa are the qualities of objects or events that stimulate our sense organs—the causes of sensations, whether visual, tactile, aural, oral, or olfactory. In the case of visual sensations, the sensa are usually a part of such things as white paper, black pencils, or red erasers. But on the painter's palette the white, black, and red are just blobs of differently colored paints ready to be brushed on a canvas. Sensa, in other words, may or may not be associated with specific objects and events. In the case of paper, pencils, and erasers, the sensa appear to us as associated with specific objects. In the case of that student erasing, the sensa are not only associated with specific objects but with a specific event: the act of erasing. In the case of the white, black, and red on the painter's palette, these sensa are disassociated or abstracted from specific objects and events.

Compare Mondrian's *Composition in White, Black and Red* (Color Plate 2), Goya's *May 3, 1808* (Color Plate 3), and Cézanne's *Mont Sainte Victoire* (Color Plate 4).

1. In which painting are the sensa basically associated with only specific objects?
2. In which painting are the sensa associated with both specific objects and events?
3. In which painting are the sensa abstracted from specific objects and events?
4. What is the subject matter, respectively, of each of these paintings?

Representational painting has as its subject matter specific objects and/or events. Thus Cézanne's *Mont Sainte Victoire* basically is about a specific object—that mountain. The painting's form reveals something about that mountain and similar mountains. Thus Goya's *May 3, 1808* basically is about a specific event—that execution. The painting's form reveals something about that execution and similar executions. Representational paintings also reveal something about sensa. *Mont Sainte Victoire* reveals something about colors, lines, and light among other things. And so does Goya's painting. But sensa are not the primary subject matter—not what these paintings are most basically about.

Abstract painting, on the other hand, has sensa or the sensuous as its primary subject matter. Such painting abstracts from specific objects and events and reveals sensa for their own sake. Thus Mondrian's *Composition in White, Black and Red* is basically about the sensa of unvaried white, black, and red in a pattern of rigid lines. Mark Rothko's *Earth Greens* (Color Plate 5) is basically about the sensa of varied reds, greens, and blues in a pattern of soft lines. The sensa *in* both paintings are specific, of course, but they do not refer to any specific object or event *outside* the painting. The basic subject matter of both the Mondrian and the Rothko is sensa or the sensuous. The basic content of both paintings is a clarification of these sensa or the sensuous.

Abstract Painting

Abstract painting might seem to have nothing to do with reality because it contains no reference to things. As we indicated in Chapter 2, some aestheticians even go so far as to proclaim that artistic form is significant not because it informs about our world but because the form is its own significance. And they point to abstract painting along with pure music (as opposed to program music and opera) as prime examples to prove their case. We shall consider this issue in more detail later on in the chapter on music, where the problem is more complex, but with abstract painting we think the "significant form" theory is plainly inadequate. Abstract painting, after all, obviously contains and refers to the sensa of things, and these sensa are with us all the time. There are many times when we are without an awareness of things, for example, when we are waking from a deep sleep. But there is never a time, except when we are totally unconscious, when we are without an awareness of sensa. Of course, because we are necessarily practical beings, we see sensa or qualities most of the time mainly as signs that point to the things of which they presumably are a part. For instance, we see the white shape of the paper only as an indication of a piece of paper we want to use. Our sense of sensa is usually not very vivid. That is one of the reasons why, at first, abstract painting may seem so strange as well as why it is sometimes argued that such painting is totally disconnected from reality.

We see some colored sensa in a certain shape and we conclude: "There is a chair." Alfred North Whitehead remarks:

> But what we have is the mere coloured shape. Perhaps an artist might not have jumped to the notion of a chair. He might have stopped at the mere contemplation of a beautiful colour and a beautiful shape. . . . I am very sceptical as to the high-grade character of the mentality required to get from the coloured shape to the chair. One reason for this scepticism is that my friend the artist, who kept himself to the contemplation of colour, shape and position, was a very highly trained man, and had acquired this facility of ignoring the chair at the cost of great labour.[1]

Ignoring the chair is an abstraction from the chair. But it is not a total abstraction from reality, just an abstraction from the things of reality— its specific objects and events. Thus the Mondrian and the Rothko are not pure forms, as the proponents of significant form claim. They inform about sensa or qualities in various relationships.

PRESENTATIONAL IMMEDIACY

By eliminating reference to everything but sensa from their work, abstract painters liberate us from the habits of referring sensa to specific objects and events. They make it easy for us to focus on the sensa themselves even though we are not artists ourselves. Then the radiant and vivid values of the sensuous are enjoyed for their own sake, satisfying a primal fundamental need. Abstractions can help fulfill this need if we dare, despite our habits of practice and Puritan heritage, to

[1]Alfred North Whitehead, *Symbolism, Its Meaning and Effect*, Macmillan, New York, 1927, pp. 2f.

behold and treasure the images of the sensuous. Then instead of our controlling the sensa, transforming them into data or signs, the sensa control us, transforming us into participators. Moreover, because references to specific objects and events are eliminated, there is a peculiar abstraction from the future and the past. Abstract painting, more than any other art, gives us an intensified sense of "here-now" or *presentational immediacy*. When we perceive representational paintings such as *Mont Sainte Victoire*, we may think about our chances of getting to southern France some time in the future. Or when we perceive *May 3, 1808*, we may think about similar executions. These suggestions bring the future and past into our participation, causing the "here-now" to be somewhat compromised. The "here-now" still dominates because of the "all-at-onceness" of painting. But with abstract painting—because there is no portrayal of specific objects or events that suggest the past or the future—the sense of presentational immediacy is more intense.

Although sensa appear everywhere, in paintings sensa shine forth. This is especially true with abstract paintings, because there is nothing to attend to but sensa. In nature the light usually appears as external to the colors and surface of sensa. The light plays *on* the colors and surface. In paintings the light usually appears immanent *in* the colors and surface, seems to come—in part at least—through them, even in the flat polished colors of a Mondrian. When a light source is represented—the candles in paintings of La Tour, for example, or the sunlight coming through windows in the paintings of Rembrandt or Vermeer—the light seems to be absorbed into the colors and surfaces. There is a depth of luminosity about the sensa of paintings that even nature at its glorious best seldom surpasses. Generally the colors of nature are more brilliant than the colors of painting; but usually in nature sensa are either so glittering that our squints miss their inner luminosity or the sensa are so changing that we lack the time to participate and penetrate. The swift currents of sensa in nature tend to stupefy our sensitiveness. In paintings—except in some Op Art where the sensa of the painting either actually are moved by some device or seem to move because of our movement—glittering change is absent. This is a fixation of the flux. Thus the depth of sensa is unveiled primarily by simply allowing them "to be." This is the respect for sensa that all painters possess. To ignore the allure of the sensa in a painting, and, in turn, in nature, is to miss one of the chief glories life provides. It is especially the abstract painter—the caretaker or shepherd of sensa—who is most likely to call us back to our senses.

Study the Mondrian (Color Plate 2) or the Rothko (Color Plate 5). Then reflect on how you experienced a series of durations, vivid solipsisms of present moments—"spots of time" (Wordsworth)—that are ordered by the relationships between the regions of sensa. Compare your experience with listening to music.

1. The sensa or tones of music come to us successively, and they usually interpenetrate. For example, as we hear the tone C, we also hear the preceding G, and we anticipate the coming E. Do the tones of the music usually interpenetrate more than the sensa of the Mondrian or the Rothko?
2. Is the rhythm of listening to music different from the rhythm in seeing abstractions?

The sensa and regions of abstractions (and the same is largely true of representational paintings) are divided from one another, we think, in a different way from the more fluid progressions of music. Whereas when we listen to music the sensa interpenetrate, when we see an abstraction the sensa are more juxtaposed. Whereas the rhythm of perceiving music is continuous, the rhythm of perceiving abstract painting is discontinuous. Whereas music is perceived as motion, abstract painting is perceived as motionless. We are fascinated by the vibrant novelty and the primeval power of the red of an abstraction for its own sake, cut off from explicit consciousness of past and future. But then, sooner or later, we notice the connection of the red to the blue, and then we are fascinated by the blue. Or then, sooner or later, we are fascinated by the interaction or contrast between the red and blue. Our eye travels over the canvas step by step, free to pause at any step as long as it desires. With music this pausing is impossible. If we "hold on" a tone or passage, the oncoming tones sweep by us and are lost. Music is always in part elsewhere—gone or coming—and we are swept up in the flow of process. The rhythms of hearing music and seeing abstractions are at opposite poles.

Analyze your experiences of Blume's *Eternal City* (Color Plate 1), Matisse's *Pineapple and Anemones* (Color Plate 6), and Rothko's *Earth Greens* (Color Plate 5). Do you find that the Rothko locks you into the "now" more than the Matisse, and the Matisse more than the Blume? If so, why?

The sensa of representational paintings, like those of abstract painting, are not presented successively as in music. Yet because in representational painting the sensa refer to definite objects and events, we inevitably feel process—an awareness of past and future as involved with the present—more than with abstract painting. In the case of a painting that refers primarily to events, such as *May 3, 1808* (Color Plate 3), there is an awareness of the time of the event. But even in a still life where the primary reference is to objects, as in Matisse's

Pineapple and Anemones, the sense of "here-now" is somewhat compromised. Although there may be no definite dating, there is, as in the experience of an eventful painting, a definite placing. Thus our attention is directed from the sensuous surface of the design to the objects designated, such as fruit, flowers, and a table. For participators there will be a fusion of sensa and objects. They will see the fruit and the table *in* the lines, colors, and shapes of the painting. Nevertheless, the awareness of definite objects breaks up the sheer "here-nowness" of the participation. In ordinary, nonparticipative experience, we see, for example, the front side of a table over there. We cannot see the back side simultaneously with the front side. Yet in seeing the front we usually remember, more or less vaguely, the image of the back if we have already seen that table. Or if we have not seen that particular table, we still imagine what its back looks like because we have seen similar tables. Then, too, we are likely to anticipate the possibility of seeing the back simply by moving around the table. Past and future images of the back side synthesize with our present image of the front side. This synthesis introduces an awareness of process, of past and future as immanent in the present experience. The sheer immediacy of the present is fused with past and future; that is to say, there is no longer sheer immediacy. Now when we participate with Matisse's picture and see his table, we know, of course, that we cannot actually see the back side, for this is a painted table rather than an actual table. Yet we carry over from ordinary experience, in most cases completely automatically, the habit of synthesizing images of the absent aspects of an object (like the back side of a table) with the directly given aspect (the front side). Thus, even with a representational painting that is noneventful, such as Matisse's *Pineapple and Anemones*, the sense of "here-now" is not as strong as with abstract paintings.

Just as a still life is likely to stimulate a sense of "here-now" more than a historical painting, so abstractions differ in their ability to stimulate the sense of "here-now." The vast canvas of Pollock's *Autumn Rhythm* (Figure 4-1), full of the chaos of chance, is so forceful, rhythmic, and seemingly spontaneous in the presentation of its sensa that our eye tends to get caught up in the violent rush in a way that inhibits resting on a part. With work such as this—some of the abstractions of Willem de Kooning and Hans Hofmann, for example, and much Op Art with its flashing iridescent colors and shapes— abstract painting comes closest to music in the way it propels perception. Even in our perception of such works, however, there is no more than a sense of the "saddle-back present"—as William James called it—of riding the present with a piece of the past and a piece of the future. There is no long stretch into the past and future as in the perception of most music. And furthermore, the persistent presence of the whole of such abstractions inhibits any feeling of process from becoming compulsive. Malevich's chilly *Supremacist Composition: White on White* (Figure 4-2) illustrates the opposite extreme. The

FIGURE 4 1 Jackson Pollack, *Autumn Rhythm*. 1950. Oil on canvas, 105 by 207 inches. The Metropolitan Museum of Art, Gerald A. Hearn Fund, 1957.

dimensions are so small, the parts and regions so simply and sharply profiled, and the regions so economically interrelated that there tends to be simply one rather than a series of timeless moments. The shades of white sit so quietly and subtly side by side that *Supremacist Composition*, like many of the abstractions of Mondrian, is viewed within such a chaste and unified field of vision that it appears to have no parts or regions. And no matter how long we participate with this painting, it seems as if a single glance has sufficed. The vast majority of abstractions fall between these extremes of restlessness and stillness— for example, Rothko's *Earth Greens* (Color Plate 5)—and at the present time there seems to be no prevailing tendency toward either extreme.

INTENSITY AND RESTFULNESS

Abstract painting presents sensa in their primitive but powerful state of innocence. Furthermore, the persistent presence of abstract painting also helps to arouse our senses from their sleep by attracting our vision so that it holds clearly and distinctly on the bits and pieces and structures of sensa that get lost in theoretical and technical work and get blurred in the crowded confusion of everyday experience. In turn, this intensity of vision renews the spontaneity of our perception and enhances the tone of our physical existence. We clothe our visual sensations in positive feelings, living in these sensations instead of

FIGURE 4-2 Kasimir Malevich, *Supremacist Composition: White on White*. 1918. Oil on canvas, 31¼ by 31¼ inches. Collection, The Museum of Modern Art, New York.

using them as means to ends. And such sensuous activity—sight, for once, minus anxiety and eyestrain—is sheer delight. Abstract painting offers us a complete rest from practical concerns. Abstract painting is, as Matisse in 1908 was beginning to see,

> an art of balance, of purity and serenity devoid of troubling or depressing subject matter, an art which might be for every mental worker, be he businessman or writer, like an appeasing influence, like a mental soother, something like a good armchair in which to rest from physical fatigue.[2]

Or as Hilla Rebay remarks:

> The contemplation of a Non-objective picture offers a complete rest to the mind. It is particularly beneficial to business men, as it carries them away from the tiresome rush of earth, and strengthens their nerves, once they

[2]*La grande revue*, Dec. 25, 1908.

are familiar with this real art. If they lift their eyes to these pictures in a tired moment, their attention will be absorbed in a joyful way, thus resting their minds from earthly troubles and thoughts.[3]

Abstract painting frees us from the grip of the past and future by holding us in relatively isolated durations of "here-nows." The intrinsic values of the sensuous entrance our sight because the "all-at-onceness" of an abstraction and the absence of references to definite objects and events entice us to be one with the sensa. There is a stillness about those areas of red, green, and blue in Rothko's *Earth Greens* (Color Plate 5) that is about as unchanging as anything in this world can be. The only reference of the red, green, and blue are to the reds, greens, and blues of the external world in general. The designations are not to the sensuous as situated in definite objects and events as in representational painting. Thus, specific place and time are irrelevant. Furthermore, even the connections of the regions of sensa to one another within an abstraction have a static character. Thus, the duration of the experience of the red in the Rothko may terminate with the awareness of the red as a stimulus that refers to the green. The duration of the experience of the green, in turn, may terminate with the awareness of green as a stimulus that refers to the blue. The next duration may include the blue and green locked together as crossing vectors in a plane which, in turn, may refer to the red. These reversing and interlocking references of regions further freeze our sense of temporality. Goethe described architecture as frozen music, but abstract painting is a much better example of the metaphor. Abstract painting frees us from explicit awareness of past and future. Once we focus in on the present for its own sake, there results an intensity and exhilaration of experience that is unique.

When we participate with an abstraction, we suspend the habits of ordinary experience. The very framing of an abstraction sets it apart from the tyranny of time and space and the fury of functions. The habit of using sensa as signs of objects and events is abolished. Michel Seuphor claims:

> Every man awaits the revelation. It takes place today through abstract art in particular, in the clearest and simplest language that was ever found. . . . I believe that religious sentiment, in all religions, resides first of all in an immobilization before life, a prolonged attention, a questioning and expectant attitude that suspends all corporeal activity and that is a prelude to an activity of a quite different nature that we call inner life, spiritual life. Now art—and abstract art above all—is the expression of the attentive life, of the free life of the spirit, of this contemplation.[4]

[3]Hilla Rebay, "Value of Non-Objectivity," *Third Enlarged Catalogue of the Solomon R. Guggenheim Collection of Non-Objective Paintings*, Solomon R. Guggenheim Collection, New York, 1938, p. 7.
[4]Michel Seuphor, *The Spiritual Mission of Art*, Galerie Chalette, New York, 1960, p. 26.

Abstract painting holds sensa still without impoverishing them. Thus abstractions rest our restless eyes; abstractions anchor us from transit sickness. If anything is likely to calm our nervous souls, it is an abstraction. Then, as we stand in front of Ad Reinhardt's *Abstract Painting* in The Museum of Modern Art, the guard rails disappear. We forget where we are. Instead of staring from a standpoint at a vast black glob of alien meaninglessness that in saying nothing seems to be conspiring against us, the painting comes to us and we begin to see with insight nine very subtly related squares of luminous blacks. We become what we behold. Our awareness becomes black. And in the inner intimacy of that participative experience is a silence that rings, as in the darkness of night.

TIMELESSNESS

Abstract painters seize sensa with tender care. They take the most transient aspects of reality and make them stand still in their paintings. They purge from our sight the films of familiarity that conceal sensa, let them be as they are, just as the pop artist clears away the covers of mundane objects disguised by repetition. In the structure of an abstraction, sensa take on a powerful and pervasive static quality, timeless within time. The transience of the sensuous gives way to a steadily standing "now" that suggests everlastingness. No other art is as unchangeable—the light changes on the cathedral and the sculpture, music and the dance are always rendered differently, representational painting or literature or drama or the film or photography acquire new connotations more rapidly because they refer to definite objects and events. An abstraction "is." No other thing in art or nature, unless it be the geological patterns in certain rocks, matches its unchangeability. Nothing is as likely to save us from the slavery of functions as abstractions.

PERCEPTION KEY EARTH GREENS

Rothko's *Earth Greens* (Color Plate 5) is, we think, an exceptional example of timelessness. Analyze why this is or is not so. Then compare our analysis which follows.

The underlying blue rectangle of *Earth Greens* is cool and recessive with a pronounced vertical emphasis (91 inches by 74 inches), accented by the way the bands of blue gradually expand upward. However, the green and rusty-red rectangles, smaller but much more prominent because they "stretch over" most of the blue, have a horizontal "lying down" emphasis that quiets the upward thrust. The vertical and the horizontal—the simplest, most universal, and potentially the most tightly "relatable" of all axes, but which in everyday experience usually are cut by diagonals and oblique curves or are strewn about chaotically—are brought together in perfect peace. This fulfilling harmony is enhanced by the way the lines, with one exception, of all these rectangles are soft and slightly irregular, avoiding the stiffness of straight lines that isolate. Only the outside boundary line of the blue rectangle is strictly straight, and this serves to separate the three rectangles from the outside world. Within the firm frontal symmetry of the world of this painting, the green rectangle is the most secure and weighty. It comes the closest to the stability of a square; the upper part occupies the actual center of the picture, which, along with the lower blue border, provides an anchorage; and the location of the rectangle in the lower section of the painting suggests weight because in our world heavy objects seek and possess low places. But even more important, this green, like so many earth colors, is a peculiarly quiet and immobile color. Wassily Kandinsky, one of the earliest abstract painters, finds green generally an "earthly, self-satisfied repose." It is "the most restful color in existence, moves in no direction, has no corresponding appeal, such as joy, sorrow, or passion, demands nothing." Rothko's green, furthermore, has the texture of earth thickening its appearance. Although there are slight variations in hue, brightness, and saturation in the green, their movement is congealed in a stable pattern. The green rectangle does not look as though it wanted to move to a more suitable place.

The rusty-red rectangle, on the other hand, is much less secure and weighty. Whereas the blue rectangle recedes and the green rectangle stays put, the rusty-red rectangle moves toward us, locking the green in depth between itself and the blue. Similarly, whereas the blue is cold and the rusty-red warm, the "temperature" of the green mediates between them. Unlike the blue and green rectangles, the rusty-red seems light and floating, radiating vital energy. Not only is the rusty-red rectangle the smallest but also its winding, swelling shadows and the dynamism of its blurred, obliquely oriented brushstrokes produce an impression of self-contained movement that sustains this lovely shape like a cloud above the green below. This effect is enhanced by the blue, which serves as a kind of firmament for this sensuous world; for blue is the closest to darkness, and this blue, especially the middle band, seems lit up as if by starlight. Yet despite its amorphous inner activity, the rusty-red rectangle keeps its place, also serenely harmonizing with its neighbors. Delicately, a pervasive violet tinge touches everything. And everything seems locked together forever, an image of eternity.

Representational Painting

In the participative experience with representational paintings, the sense of "here-now," so overwhelming in the participative experience with abstractions, is somewhat weakened. Representational paintings situate the sensuous in specific objects and events. These references—unless we arbitrarily ignore them, as the proponents of significant form such as Clive Bell propose—make place and time relevant associations. A representational painting, just like an abstraction, is "all there" and "holds still." But past and future are more relevant than in our experience of abstractions because we are seeing representations of definite objects and events. Inevitably we are aware of place and date, and, in turn, a sense of past and future is a part of that awareness. Our experience is a little more ordinary than it is when we feel the extraordinary isolation from specific objects and events that occurs in the perception of abstractions. Representational paintings always bring in some suggestion of "once upon a time." Hence, we are not held quite so tightly in the immediacy of the present as with abstractions. Moreover, we are kept a little closer to the experience of everyday, because images that refer to specific objects and events usually lack something of the strangeness of images that refer only to sensa. Consequently representational paintings, other things being equal, are not quite so seductive as abstractions in charming us beyond our everyday habits.

Nevertheless, representational paintings entice. Like abstractions, they have a framed "all-at-onceness." A scene or action that in ordinary experience would become lost in another scene or action is isolated. Moreover, the sensa of a representational painting, as of an abstraction, have an inner luminosity that lures our vision, while the form holds everything still for our leisurely contemplation. Hence the references to definite places and times are fused with the sensa. Only abstractions seduce us more securely into durations dominated by the "here-now."

Representational painting furnishes the world of abstractions with definite objects and events. The horizon is sketched out more closely and clearly, and the spaces of the sensuous are filled, more or less, with things. But even when these furnishings (subject matter) are the same, the interpretation (content) of every painting is always different. This point is clarified any time paintings of basically the same subject matter are compared, as, for example, the Madonna holding her Child, a subject matter that fascinated Florentine painters from the twelfth through the sixteenth centuries.

COMPARISONS OF PAINTINGS WITH SIMILAR SUBJECT MATTER

Compare two great Florentine works that helped lead the way into the Italian Renaissance: a *Madonna and Child* (Figure 4-3) by Cimabue, completed around 1290, and a *Madonna Enthroned* (Figure 4-4) by Giotto, completed around 1310.

FIGURE 4-3   Cimabue, *Madonna and Child Enthroned with Angels.* ca. 1285–1290. Panel painting, 151¾ by 78⅞ inches. Uffizi, Florence. Alinari/Editorial Photocolor Archives.

FIGURE 4-4   Giotto, *Madonna Enthroned*. ca. 1310. Panel painting, 128³⁄₁₆ by 80⅜ inches. Uffizi, Florence. Alinari.

Cimabue and Giotto

PERCEPTION KEY CIMABUE AND GIOTTO

These paintings have basically the same subject matter, as their titles indicate. Yet their forms inform about their subject matter very differently. Describe the differences between the forms and contents of these two pictures. Be as specific and detailed as possible. Then compare our attempt at the same analysis. Do not, of course, take our analysis as definitive. There simply is no such thing as a criticism that cannot be improved.

The figures in Cimabue's panel at first sight seem utterly lacking in human liveliness. The fine hands of the Madonna, for example, are extremely stylized. Moreover, the geometricized facial features of the Madonna, very similar to those of the angels, and the stiff, unnaturally regular features of the Child seem almost as unnatural as masks. But Cimabue's *Madonna and Child* begins to grow and glow in liveliness when Cimabue's panel is juxtaposed with contemporary paintings, such as the Magdalen Master's *Madonna Enthroned* (Figure 4-5), ca. 1270, and only in the context of its tradition can a work of art be fully understood and in turn fully appreciated. Thus historical criticism—which attempts to illuminate the tradition of works of art—provides the often indispensable background information for descriptive, interpretive, and evaluative criticism.

Magdalen Master

Everything in this slightly earlier work by the Magdalen Master is subordinated to the portrayal of theoretical, practical, and sociological expressions of the medieval Catholic conception of the sacred. For example, the Child is portrayed as divine (mainly a theoretical expression), as the mediator between us and God (mainly a practical expression), and as a king or prince (mainly a sociological expression). Everything secular in the picture is interpreted as completely dependent on the sacred as its source of existence. Conventional Christian symbols, such as halos, crowns, and the blessing gesture of the Child, dominate everything. Moreover, the sacred comes very close to being represented as totally separate from the secular, for the Madonna and Child are barely incarnated in this world. It is impossible, of course, to interpret the sacred "absolutely," as totally "ab-solved" from our world, for this would negate the possibility of any portrayal of the sacred whatsoever. But the Magdalen Master's panel is typical of the way the artists of the thirteenth and the immediately preceding centuries came as close as possible to representing the sacred absolutely. Thus the Madonna and Child are bilaterally immobile, symmetri-

FIGURE 4-5 Magdalen Master, *Madonna Enthroned*. ca. 1270. Panel painting, 35⅝ by 53¾ inches. Muśee des Arts Decoratifs. Alinari/Editorial Photocolor Archives.

cally and compactly enclosed, and their fantastic sizes relative to the barely visible, bitlike donor at the bottom left of the throne resist references to the sacred as incarnate in this world. The Madonna and Child are interpreted more as emblems rather than as living embodiments of the divine. "Love not the world, neither the things that are in the world. . . . For all that is in the world . . . passeth away" (John 2:15–17). And so the human qualities of the Madonna and Child are barely recognizable. Note, for example, how the fish-shaped, longtailed eyes of the Madonna cannot blink, and how the popping pupils stare out and slightly up in a Sphinxlike glance that seems fixed forever. Her features are written large and seem added to rather than molded with the head. Only in the tender way she holds the Child is there any hint of human sorrow and affection. The spirits of this Madonna and Child belong to a supernatural world; and their bodies are hardly bodies at all but, in the words of St. Thomas Aquinas, "corporeal metaphors of spiritual things." The secular is mainly appearance, a secondary reality. The sacred is the primary reality.

Nevertheless, the secular, even if it is interpreted as appearance, appears very powerfully indeed, for this panel is a very fine work of art. The sensa shine forth, especially in the glimmering gold, the crystal cabochons set in the crowns of the Madonna and Child, and the rhythmic, sharply edged lines. We are lured by the sensa and their designs beyond mere illustrations of doctrine by images. We are caught up in durations of the "here-now." But, unlike our experience of abstractions, these durations include, because of the conventional symbols, doctrinal interpretations of the sacred. And if we participate, we "understand"—even if we disagree—rather than having mere "knowledge of" these doctrines. The expressions of ultimate concern, reverence, and peace in the saints and donor provide a context in which the intent of the Christian conventional symbols are unlikely to be mistaken by sensitive participators, even if they do not know the conventions of the symbols.

Cimabue

When we compare Cimabue's panel with the Magdalen Master's, we can readily see that something of the rigid separation between the sacred and the secular has been relaxed. Cimabue was one of the first to portray, however haltingly, the change in Florentine society toward a more secular orientation. In the twelfth and thirteenth centuries Florence was making great strides in bending nature to human needs for the first time since the Roman Empire. A resurgence in confidence in human powers began to clash with the medieval view that people were nothing without God, that nature was valuable only as a stepping-stone to heaven, that—as St. Peter Damiani in the first half of the eleventh century asserted—"the world is so filthy with vices that any holy mind is befouled by even thinking of it." The emerging view was not yet "man is the measure of all things," but the honor of being human began to be taken seriously, an idea that "was to traverse all later Italian art like the muffled, persistent sound of a subterranean river" (Malraux).

Cimabue had assimilated from the Byzantine tradition its conventions, hierography, technical perfection, and richness of detail. He enriched that inheritance, and in turn helped break ground for the Renaissance, by endowing the old style with more liveliness and mixing the divine into the human, as in this panel, which reveals human emotions in the Madonna. The inert passivity of the Byzantine and the hard dogmatic grimness of the Tuscan style, both so evident in the Magdalen Master's work, are revitalized with a spiritual subtlety and psychic awareness, a warmth and tenderness, that make unforgettable the Madonna's benevolently inclined face, to which one returns with unwearying delight. With this face begins the scaling down of the divine into this world. The anthropocentric view—human beings at the center of things—is beginning to focus. A human face has awakened! And it leans forward to come more closely into spiritual contact with us. Its liveliness fell like a refreshing shower on a parched and long-neglected soil, and from that soil a new world began to rise.

Brown-gold tones play softly across the Madonna's features, merging them organically despite the incisive lines, setting the background for the sweeping eyebrows and large, deep eye sockets that form a stage on which the pathetic eyes play their drama of tragic foreknowledge. These eyes seem to pulsate with the beat of the soul because they are more flexible than the eyes in contemporary paintings—the irises rest comfortably and dreamily within their whites; the delicately curved lids, now shortened, detach themselves gracefully to meet neatly at the inner pockets; and the doubling line of the lower lid is replaced by fragile shadows that flow into the cheeks and nose. Furthermore, although the Greek, or bridgeless, nose is still high and marked by a conspicuous triangle, the sensitive modeling of the nose, its dainty shape, and the tucking in of the pinched tip help blend it into the general perspective of the face. Light shadows fall under the shapely chin to the slender neck and around the cheeks to merge indistinctly with the surrounding veil, whose heavy shadows add to the contemplative atmosphere. But the full lips, depressed at the corners and tightly drawn to the left, add a contrasting touch of intensity, even grimness, to what otherwise would be pure poignancy. The immense, exquisitely decorated throne, with the bristling and curiously vehement prophets below, enhances by its contrasting monumentality the feminine gentleness of the Madonna. Her large size relative to the angels and prophets is minimized by her robe, which, with its close-meshed lines of gold feathering over the cascading folds, is one of the loveliest in western art. In a skillfully worked counterpoint, the angel heads and the rainbow-colored wings form an angular rhythm that tenses toward and then quietly pauses at the Madonna's face. This pause is sustained by the simple dotted edge of the centered halo and by the shape of the pedimental top of the rectangular frame. The facial features of the angels resemble the Madonna's, especially the almond-shaped eyes, separated by the stencillike triangles, and the heavy mouths squared at the corners. Nevertheless, they lack the refined qualities and liveliness that betray so feelingly the soulful sadness of the Madonna. Now in the city of Florence

. . . Mercy has a human heart,
Pity a human face,
And Love, the human form divine,
And Peace, the human dress.

William Blake

But into this peaceful hush that spreads around her sound with anguished apprehension the tragic tones of the Pietà, like the melody of a requiem continued by our imaginations into the pregnant pause.

In Cimabue's panel, unlike the Magdalen Master's, there is no longer the sure suggestion of the sacred as almost completely separate from the secular. The sacred and the secular are only narrowly joined, but the juncture seems much more secure. The sacred is portrayed as clearly immanent in at least some things of our world—the Madonna, Child, and saints having some earthly aspects—but the emphasis, of course, is upon the transcendency of the sacred. There is not the slightest hint of the secular taking precedence over the sacred.

Cimabue and Giotto

According to the legend reported by Ghiberti and embellished by Vasari, Cimabue

> going one day on some business of his own from Florence to Vespignano, found Giotto, while his sheep were browsing, portraying a sheep from nature on a flat and polished slab, with a stone slightly pointed, without having learnt any method of doing this from others, but only from nature; whence Cimabue, standing fast all in a marvel, asked him if he wished to go live with him. The child answered that, his father consenting, he would go willingly. Cimabue then asking this from Bondone, the latter lovingly granted it to him, and was content that he should take the boy with him to Florence; whither having come, in a short time, assisted by nature and taught by Cimabue, the child not only equalled the manner of his master, but became so good an imitator of nature that he banished completely that rude Greek manner and revived the modern and good art of painting, introducing the portraying well from nature of living people.[5]

Giotto's *Madonna Enthroned* and Cimabue's *Madonna and Child*, both originally placed in churches, now hang side by side in the first room of the Uffizi Gallery in Florence. The contrast between the panels is striking. Cimabue's Madonna, who seems to float into our world, is abruptly brought to earth by Giotto; or, as Ruskin puts it, now we have Mama. She sits solidly, bell-shaped, without evasion, in

[5]Giorgio Vasari, *Lives of the Most Eminent Painters*, Gaston Duc Devere (trans.), Macmillan, London, 1912, vol. 1, p. 72.

three-dimensional space subject to gravitational forces, her frank, focused gaze alerted to her surroundings; whereas Cimabue's Madonna, oblivious of space, is steeped in moodiness. The forms of Giotto's Madonna seem to have been abstracted, however radically, from nature, whereas Cimabue seems to have started from Byzantine forms. In subject matter Giotto seems to have begun more from "here," whereas Cimabue seems to have begun more from "hereafter."

The eyes of Giotto's Madonna, surrounded by her high forehead and the immense cheeks, have a fascinating asymmetry that gives her face a mark of idiosyncrasy and adds to its liveliness. The fish-shaped left eye with its half-covered pupil twists to the left, so that it appears to be looking in a different direction than the more realistic right eye. The resulting tension fixes our attention and heightens our feeling of being caught in her level gaze, which gains further intensity by being the focus of the gazes of the saints and angels. Since the open space below the Madonna provides us with a figurative path of access, we are directly engaged with her in a way that Cimabue carefully avoids by, among other devices, putting the throne of his Madonna on a high-arched platform and then placing the little prophets within the arches. The smallness of the sensual mouth of Giotto's Madonna, barely wider than the breadth of her long and snouty nose, accentuates its expressiveness. Also, for the first time, the lips of a Madonna open—however slightly, shyly revealing two teeth—as if she were about to gasp or speak. It does not matter, for the mobility of inner responsiveness is conveyed. Everything else expresses her stoicism, a rocklike kind of endurance—the untooled, centered halo, the steady gaze, the calm, impersonal expression, the cool and silvery skin color with green underpainting that suggests bone structures beneath, the heavy jaw and towerlike neck, the long unbroken verticals and broad sweeping curves of the simply colored robe and tunic, the firm hand that no longer points but holds, and above all her upright monumental massiveness, as solid as if hewn in granite. The saints and angels are compactly arranged in depth and stand on the same ground as the earthly throne. Although the saints express peace and the angels awe, they are natural beings, not imaginary supporters of a heavenly throne as in Cimabue's picture.

The Child shares with his mother the monumentality of Giotto's style—the square, forthright head, the powerful body, the physical density and solidity that make Giotto's figures so statuesque. Giotto's Child, compared with Cimabue's, seems almost coarse, especially in the shaping of the hands and feet, and the incorrect indication of his position from a naturalistic standpoint is physically much more uncomfortable, primarily because such a standpoint is almost irrelevant in Cimabue's picture. The hair and ears are not so stylized as in Cimabue's Child, light and shadow sink more organically into the flesh, the eyes and nose are given the most realistic rendition since Roman times, and the expression is dynamically alert. Yet the lack of irregularity and flexibility in these less conventional features, combined with the effect of maturity in miniature, keep the Child from being a Baby. The content of Giotto's painting is clearly Christian, but not quite so obviously as in the paintings of the Magdalen Master and Cimabue. The portrayal of religious feeling is not quite so strong, and for the first time in Florence there is the suggestion, however muted, of the secular challenging the sacred. If Mama gets much more earthly and independent, then the sacred no longer will be so obviously in control.

Giotto and Parmigianino

Compare now Giotto's painting with *The Madonna with the Long Neck* (Color Plate 7), painted by Francesco Parmigianino in the waning years of the Italian Renaissance, ca. 1535.

PERCEPTION KEY GIOTTO AND PARMIGIANINO

1. *The Madonna with the Long Neck* was never quite finished, and so far as we know, Parmigianino did not provide a title. Later in the sixteenth century, Vasari baptized it *The Virgin and Sleeping Child.* Do you believe Parmigianino would have accepted this naming as appropriate? What about the appropriateness of its present title—*The Madonna with the Long Neck?*
2. How does the content of this picture differ from Giotto's?
3. How does Parmigianino's form accomplish a different interpretation of what apparently is the same subject matter?
4. Jacob Burckhardt, a very knowledgeable and famous critic and historian of the nineteenth century, complained of this work's "unsupportable affection," and, somewhat more tolerantly, of "the bringing of the manners of the great world divertingly into the holy scenes." Generally, until very recent times, this work has been an object of derision. Do you agree with these negative judgments? Explain.

Although natural structures in Parmigianino's painting are suggested, they are not interpreted as natural. The light is neither quite indoors nor outdoors, the perspectives are odd, gravity is defied, the bodies are artificially proportioned and drained of mass and physical power, the protagonists are psychologically detached from one another, and above all the poreless, porcelain facial features allow no hint of liveliness. The head of the Madonna is shaped like a well-wrought urn, while the ears, set out abnormally in order to emphasize their serpentine calligraphy, look like its handles. The nerveless skin is unnaturally cold and pale, glazed like ceramic, and beneath that polished surface the urn seems hollow. Hence the pure geometrical design of the fastidious lines of the eyebrows, eyes, nose, and mouth are assembled on a surface without organic foundation—no pulsating blood coursing through arteries and veins integrates these features, and no muscular structure can move them. And so the gaze down upon the Child—the most lifeless Child of the Renaissance—is too stylized and superficial to be expressive of any psychic, let alone sacramental meaning. Like an Attic amphora, the head of the Madonna rises from its swanlike neck, while the hair decorates the lid with the preciosity of fine goldwork. The features of the angels are similarly constructed, exchangeable like coins. They are made even more masklike by the repetition, a device that almost always increases rigidity.

If the subject matter of *The Madonna with the Long Neck* is a sacred scene, then Burckhardt's denunciation of "unsupportable affection" is certainly justified. If, however, the Christian symbols are no more than a support or an excuse for an interpretation of line, color, and volume, then Burckhardt's denunciation is irrelevant. To meet this painting halfway—and surely this is the responsibility of every serious perceiver—the religious symbols can be dismissed, and then the subject matter can be experienced as secular. The design of this delicate work, this splendor of form shining on the proportionate parts of matter, ought to bring one to a better understanding and appreciation of the rhythmic qualities of line, the sinuous sensuousness of spiraling shapes, the fluidity of bulkless volumes, and the cooling, calming powers of certain surfaces and colors. But this heretical design, despite its lifting flow, will never waft you to a Christian heaven on the wings of faith.

The Madonna with the Long Neck is such a magnificently secular work of art that the excommunication of the Christian symbols is rather easily accomplished, at least in our day. That is why the present title seems more appropriate to most of us than Vasari's title. Abstract painting has opened our eyes to the intrinsic values of sensa, and a strong case can be made that *The Madonna with the Long Neck* is a kind of abstract painting. An even more appropriate title today might be *Sinuous Spiraling Shapes*.

Bronzino

PERCEPTION KEY CHRIST IN LIMBO

In 1552, a few years after Parmigianino's work, Angelo Bronzino completed *Christ in Limbo* (Figure 4-6). This work also possesses Christian symbols.

1. Is the content of this work religious, as in the works of the Magdalen Master, Cimabue, and Giotto?
2. Is this work a kind of abstract painting, as is the case, perhaps, of *The Madonna with the Long Neck?*

FIGURE 4-6 Bronzino, *Christ in Limbo.* 1552. Panel painting, 174⅜ by 114½ inches. Museum of Santa Croce, Florence, Alinari/Editorial Photocolor Archives.

The quality of Bronzino's painting is so much poorer, we think, that the use of Christian symbols is a parody rather than an excuse. Christ advances with an affected dancing step, his curled hair and perfumed face almost indistinguishable from the man in profile immediately to the right and the man whose figure is cut by the frame. The aphrodisiac figure of the woman posing between these two men would better grace a poster of a Pigalle nightclub. All the bodies are overmuscular but unexercised and listless, a cold, contorted, claustrophobic display of striptease sensuality. Despite the inclusion of Christian symbols, it is difficult to discover a work of art that is so clearly nonreligious. And whereas in Parmigianino's painting the sensa shine forth and are revealed, in Bronzino's painting the sensa—unlike the brilliance of sensa in almost all his portraits—are as dull as in a typical advertising poster.

A work such as *The Madonna with the Long Neck* makes plain that the subject matter of a painting is not always easily ascertained, and in answering such questions historical information can be of great help. Nevertheless, historical information is not necessarily decisive. Thus, there can be little doubt that in Parmigianino's time its subject matter was understood as Christian—the work, for example, was commissioned for a church by the clergy. Yet today the subject matter is likely to be understood, and properly so we believe, as the sensuous. The decisive test is what we perceive as the content.

Determining the Subject Matter

Consider a contemporary example by Arshile Gorky (Figure 4-7).

PERCEPTION KEY A PAINTING BY ARSHILE GORKY

---

1. Is this painting abstract or representational? Take plenty of time before you decide, but disregard the title.
2. The title is *Waterfall*. Do you see a waterfall when you ignore the title? Do you see a waterfall when you take the title into consideration?
3. If you do, in fact, see a waterfall when taking notice of the title, does this make the painting representational?

The last question of the perception key is tricky. We suggest the following principle as a basis for answering such questions. If a work only "shows" (presents) but does not interpret (reveal) the objects and events that the title indicates, this is not enough to make it representational. These objects and events must be interpreted if the work is to be usefully classified as representational. *The Madonna with the Long Neck* shows a Madonna and Child, but they are not interpreted as a Madonna and Child. Thus to call this work representational is misleading, because the Madonna and Child are not part of the content. Our view is that the waterfall in Gorky's painting is interpreted, that our perception of the bounce and rhythm of colors of waterfalls is intensified by Gorky's work. If this judgment is correct, then the work is representational. On the other hand, your view may be that recognition of a waterfall in the painting only helps intensify your perception of sensa—the bounce and rhythm of colors. If this judgment is correct, then the work is abstract.

FIGURE 4-7 Arshile Gorky, *Waterfall*, ca. 1943. Oil on canvas, 60½ by 44½ inches. The Tate Gallery, London.

PERCEPTION KEY MOUNTAIN, TABLE, ANCHORS, NAVEL

1. What is the subject matter of this work?
2. Does Arp succeed in revealing a mountain, a table, anchors, and a navel (the navel is invisible in the reproduction) so that you have a heightened awareness of similar objects?

Study Jean Arp's *Mountain, Table, Anchors, Navel* (Figure 4-8).

FIGURE 4-8   Jean Arp, *Mountain, Table, Anchors, Navel.* 1925. Oil on cardboard with cutouts, 29⅝ by 23½ inches. Collection, The Museum of Modern Art, New York.

If your answer to Question 2 in the perception key is negative, then you should deny that the objects listed in the title are the subject matter of this painting.

It is true, of course, that the references of the title are supported by the painting, for we can see a mountain, etc., in the painting once we have noted the title. But these references are misleading, if taken as anything more than identification tags, because the recognition of the objects designated is of little importance in our perception. *Colors and Positions*—for they seem to us to be the subject matter of Arp's painting—perhaps would be a much more appropriate title.

Sometimes, as we have seen with Gorky's *Waterfall,* it is extremely difficult to distinguish between abstract and representational painting. Whether the recognition of definite objects and events in a painting intensifies perception may differ with the differences in temperament and background of the recipients. Nevertheless, the distinction between abstract and representational painting is very useful because it points up this important fact: whereas in abstract painting definite objects and events are not a part of the content, in representational paintings they are. And by being clear about this, we can better focus upon what is most important in any particular painting.

Recent Painting

Painting, whether abstract or representational, sets forth the visually perceptible in such a way that it works in our experience with heightened intensity. Every style of painting finds facets of the visually perceptible that had previously been missed. For example, the painting of the last hundred years has given us Impressionism, a style that reveals the play of sunlight on color, as in the work of Renoir (Figure 2-17); Post-Impressionism, using the surface techniques of Impressionism but drawing out the solidity of things, as in Cézanne (Color Plate 4); Expressionism, scenes portraying strong emotion, as in Munch; Cubism, showing the permanent properties of things and their three-dimensional qualities splayed out in closed space—without perspective or cast light—through geometrical crystallization, as in Picasso; Dada, poking fun at the absurdity of everything including painting, as in Duchamp; Surrealism, the expression of the subconscious, as in Dali; Futurism, the portrayal of sensa and things in motion, as in Severini; Suprematism or Constructivism, the portrayal of sensa in sharp geometrical patterns, as in Mondrian and Malevich (Color Plate 2 and Figure 4-2); Abstract Expressionism, the portrayal of sensa in movement with—as in Expressionism—the expression of powerful emotion or energy, as in Pollock (Figure 4-1); Pop Art, the revelation of mass-produced products, as in Dine and Lichtenstein (Figures 2-1 and 2-5); Op Art, the glittering show of sensa in motion or in different aspects as the participator changes his perspective, as in Larry Poons; etc. And today and tomorrow new dimensions are and will be portrayed. Never in the history of painting has there been such rapid change and vitality. Never in history has there been so much help available for those of us who, in varying degrees, are blind to the fullness of the visually perceptible. If we take advantage of this help, the rewards are priceless:

For don't you mark, we're made so that we love
First when we see them painted, things we have passed
Perhaps a hundred times nor cared to see.

Robert Browning, "Fra Lippo Lippi"

Summary

Painting is the art that has most to do with revealing the visual sensa and the visual appearance of objects and events. Painting shows the visually perceptible more clearly. Because a painting is usually presented to us as an entirety, with an all-at-onceness, it gives us time for our vision to focus, hold, and participate. This makes possible a vision that is both extraordinarily intense and restful. Sensa are the qualities of objects or events that stimulate our sense organs. Sensa can be disassociated or abstracted from the specific objects or events in which they are usually joined. Sensa are the primary subject matter of abstract painting. Specific objects and events are the primary subject matter of representational painting.

Chapter 4 Bibliography

Abell, Walter. *Representation and Form*. New York: Scribner, 1936.

Arnheim, Rudolf. *Art and Visual Perception*. Berkeley: University of California Press, 1954.

Bell, Clive. *Art*. London: Chatto & Windus, 1914.

Blanshard, Frances B. *Retreat from Likeness in the Theory of Painting*. New York: Arno, 1949.

Canaday, John. *Keys to Art*. New York: Tudor, 1963.

———. *Mainstreams of Modern Art*. New York: Holt, Rinehart and Winston, 1959.

Elsen, Albert E. *Purposes of Art*; 3rd ed. New York: Holt, Rinehart and Winston, 1972.

Fry, Roger. *Vision and Design*. New York: New American Library, 1974.

———. *Transformations*. London: Chatto and Windus, 1920.

Gombrich, E. H. *The Story of Art*. New York: Phaidon, 1962.

———. *Art and Illusion*, 2nd ed. London: Phaidon, 1962.

Hauser, Arnold. *The Social History of Art*. 4 vols. New York: Vantage Books, 1960.

Janson, H. W. *History of Art*. Englewood Cliffs, N.J.: Prentice-Hall, 1963.

Kuh, Katherine. *Art Has Many Faces*. New York: Harper, 1951.

Pandofsky, Erwin. *Meaning in the Visual Arts*. Garden City, New York: Doubleday Anchor, 1955.

Read, Herbert. *The Philosophy of Modern Art*. New York: Meridian, 1955.

Steinberg, Leo. *Other Criteria: Confrontations with Twentieth-Century Art*. New York: Oxford University Press, 1972.

Wölfflin, Heinrich. *Principles of Art History*, trans. W. D. Hottinger. New York: Dover, 1950.

Zucker, Paul. *Styles in Painting*. New York: Viking, 1950.

SCULPTURE

5 Sculpture and Touch

Painting and sculpture, along with architecture, are sometimes but not very usefully classified as visual arts. Such classification suggests that the eye is the chief sense organ involved in our participation with sculpture, as it is with painting. Yet observe participants at an exhibition of both paintings and sculptures. Usually at least a few will touch some of the sculptures—despite the "Do Not Touch" signs—whereas the paintings are usually left alone. Some kinds of sculpture invite us to explore and caress them with our hands, and even, if they are not too large or heavy, to pick them up. Marcel Duchamp noticed this and experimented with a kind of sculpture not to be seen but only to be touched. Within a box with an opening at the top large enough to allow passage of the hand, he placed forms with varying shapes and textures. And Brancusi created a *Sculpture for the Blind*.

PERCEPTION KEY EXPERIMENT WITH TOUCH

Using scissors or some similar tool, cut out four approximately 6-inch cardboard squares. Shape them with curves or angles into abstract patterns (structures that do not represent definite objects), and put one into a bag. Ask a

111

friend to feel that sample in the bag without looking at the sample. Then ask him or her to (1) draw with pencil on paper the pattern felt. Then ask your friend to (2) model the pattern in putty. Continue the same procedure with the other three samples. Have your friend make four samples for you, and follow the same procedures yourself. Analyze both your results. Were the drawings or the modelings more closely imitative of the samples? What is the significance, if any, of this experiment?

Sculpture and Density

Somehow, it seems, sculpture engages our senses differently than does painting. And somehow this seems to have something to do with the fact that sculpture occupies space as a three-dimensional mass, whereas painting is essentially a two-dimensional surface that can only represent ("re-present") three-dimensionality. Of course, painting can *suggest* density—for example, *Mont Saint Victoire* (Color Plate 4)—but sculpture *is* dense. Henry Moore, one of the best of contemporary sculptors, states that the sculptor "gets the solid shape, as it were, inside his head—he thinks of it, whatever its size, as if he were holding it completely enclosed in the hollow of his hand. He mentally visualizes a complex form *from all round itself;* he knows while he looks at one side what the other side is like; he identifies himself with its center of gravity, its mass, its weight; he realizes its volume, as the space that the shape displaces in the air."[1] Apparently we can only fully apprehend sculpture by senses that are alive not only to visual and tactile (touchable) surfaces but also to the weight and volume lying behind those surfaces.

Sensory Interconnections

It is surely an oversimplification to distinguish the various arts on the basis of any one sensation or sense organ; for example, to claim that painting is experienced solely by sight and sculpture solely by touch. Our nervous systems are far more complicated than that. Generally no clear separation is made in experience between the faculties of sight and touch. The sensa of touch, for instance, are normally joined with other sensa—visual, aural, oral, and olfactory. Even if only one kind of sensum initiates a perception, a chain reaction triggers off other sensations, either by sensory motor connections or by memory associations. We are constantly grasping and handling things as well as seeing, hearing, tasting, and smelling them. And so when we see a

[1] Henry Moore, "Notes on Sculpture," in David Sylvester (ed.), *Sculpture and Drawings 1921–48*, 4th rev. ed., George Wittenborn, Inc., New York, 1957, pp. xxxiii f.

thing, we have a pretty good idea of what its surface would feel like, how it would sound if struck, how it would taste, and how it would smell if we approach. And if we grasp or handle a thing in the dark, we have some idea of what its shape looks like.

We see someone sitting on a bench. But do we? Only if our vision includes information gathered from other sources. "Sitting on" is not the same as "situated above." "Sitting on" is possible because of gravity, and we do not see gravity but, rather, sense it in our bodies. When we stand, we feel gravity bearing down. And we feel the ground as support against that force. Memories of such feelings are touched off when we see someone "situated above" the bench. And so we say "sitting on." As we approach a stone wall, we see various shapes. And these shapes recall certain information. We know something about how the surface of those stones would feel and that it would hurt if we walked into them. We do not know about the surface, volume, and mass of these stones by sight alone but by sight associated with manual experience. Both painting and sculpture involve especially sight and touch. But touch is much more involved in our participation with sculpture. If we can clarify such differences as these, our understanding of sculpture will be deeper and, in turn, our participation more rewarding.

Sculpture and Painting Compared

Compare Rothko's *Earth Greens* (Color Plate 5) with Arp's *Growth* (Frontispiece).

PERCEPTION KEY EARTH GREENS AND GROWTH

1. Would you like to touch either of these works?
2. Would you expect either the Rothko or the Arp to feel hot or cold to your touch?
3. Which work seems to require the more careful placement of lighting?
4. Is space perceived differently in and around these two works? How?
5. Which of the two works appears to be the more unchangeable in your perception?
6. Which of the two works is more abstract?

Both works are abstract, we suggest, for neither has as its primary subject matter specific objects or events (see Chapter 4, page 83 ff.). Arp's sculpture has something to do with growth, of course, as confirmed by the title. But is it human, animal, or vegetable growth? Male or female? Clear-cut answers do not seem possible. Specificity of reference, just as in the Rothko, is missing. And yet, if you agree that the subject matter of the Rothko is sensa, would you say the same for the Arp? To affirm this may bother you, for Arp's marble is dense material. This substantiality of the marble is very much a part of its appearing as sculpture. Conversely, *Earth Greens* as a painting—that is, as a work of art rather than as a physical canvas of such and such a weight—does not appear as a material thing. The weight of the canvas is irrelevant to our participation with *Earth Greens* as a work of art. Indeed, if that weight becomes relevant, we are no longer participating with the painting. That weight becomes relevant if we are hanging *Earth Greens* on a wall, of course, but that is a procedure antecedent to our participation with it as a painting.

Rothko has abstracted sensa, especially colors, from objects or things, whereas Arp has brought out the substantiality of a thing—the marbleness of the marble. Rothko has left behind things such as earth and grass and sky. Conversely, Arp has kept his marble as a thing relevant to his sculpture. This kind of difference, incidentally, is perhaps the underlying reason why the term "abstract painting" is used more frequently than the term "abstract sculpture." There is an awkwardness about describing something as material as most sculpture as abstract. Picasso once remarked: "There is no abstract art. You must always start with something. There is no danger then anyway because the idea of the object will have left an indelible mark." This may be an overstatement with respect to painting, but this point rings true with sculpture. Still, the distinction between abstract and representational sculpture is worth making, just as with painting, for being clear about the subject matter of a work of art is the sine qua non of all sensitive participation. It is the key to understanding the content, for the content is the subject matter interpreted by means of the form. Abstract sculpture, like abstract painting, abstracts from specific objects and events. On the other hand, abstract sculpture generally does not, unlike abstract painting, abstract from the materiality of things. Arp brings out, rather than abstracts from, his marble.

Most sculpture, whether abstract or representational, returns us to the voluminosity (bulk), density (mass), and tactile quality of things. Thus, sculpture has touch or tactile appeal. Even if we do not actually "handle" a work of sculpture, we can imagine how it would feel with reference to its surface, volume, and weight. Sculpture brings us back into touch with things by allowing the thickness of things to permeate its surface. Most sculptures make us feel them as resistant, as substantial. Hence the primary subject matter of most abstract sculpture is the density of sensa. Sculpture is more than skin deep. Abstract painting can only *represent* the density of sensa, whereas sculpture, whether abstract or representational, *presents* that density. Abstract painters generally emphasize the surfaces of sensa, as in *Earth Greens*. Their interest is in the vast ranges of color qualities and the play of light to bring out the nuances. Abstract sculptors, on the other hand, generally restrict themselves to a minimal range of color qualities and emphasize light not only to play on these qualities but also to bring out the inherence of these qualities in things. Whereas abstract painters are shepherds of surface sensa, abstract sculptors are shepherds of depth sensa.

Sculpture has many species, and even within the species of abstract sculpture any general statement, such as the one that concludes the previous paragraph, should be understood as subject to qualification and exception. Any art is too creative, too expansive, to lend itself to significant unexceptional generalizations. And in our time, the art of sculpture is one of the most adventurous. It is even difficult sometimes to know how to distinguish sculpture from painting at one extreme and architecture at the other, and this difficulty began long before our time.

Sunken-Relief Sculpture

Compare, for example, Figure 5-1, a detail of an Egyptian work in limestone from about 2100 B.C., with a work of Pollock (Figure 4-1). We usually think of sculpture, with its emphasis on density, as projecting out into space. Yet sometimes some of the lines and patches of paint in Pollock's works, which are generally described as paintings, are laid on so thickly that they stand out as much as a half inch or so from the flat surface of the canvas. In the Egyptian work there is no projection whatsoever. Rather, the carving cuts grooves of various depths into the surface plane of the stone to outline each object, a technique called "sunken relief." The firmness, clarity, and brilliance of these linear grooves in the Egyptian work is brought out by the way their sharp outside edges catch the light. Did this technique in this instance produce sculpture rather than painting? Only if it brings out in some significant sense the voluminosity or density or surface feel of its materials: only then will the tactile appeal be significant as well as the visual. This work, we think, has significant tactile appeal. The density of the limestone is especially evident. In other words, we are suggesting that this work is more than a linear drawing—it is a *limestone* linear drawing. Pollock's work, on the other hand, lacks significant tactile appeal despite the projection of its heavy thick oils. It is conceivable that this work could have been made in some other medium—aluminum paint or paint with more white lead, for example —and still be essentially the same work. It is inconceivable that the Egyptian relief could have been carved out of different material and still be essentially the same work. The surface as seen is what counts in Pollock's painting—the materials that make that surface possible are basically irrelevant in perceiving the work as painting (although for a restorer of the painting, the materials would be very relevant indeed). In the Egyptian relief, the surface as seen shows forth, unlike the

FIGURE 5-1   King Akhenaten and Queen Nefertiti, Egyptian sunken relief from El-Amarra. XVIII dynasty. Photograph, The Metropolitan Museum of Art.

Pollock, the depth of the material. Thus the materials that make the surface possible are basically relevant in perceiving the work as sculpture, and, in turn, the surface is perceived more tactually than the surface of the Pollock. And yet, the differences between Pollock's painting and this Egyptian work are hardly clear-cut. You may disagree with good reasons.

PERCEPTION KEY CEMETERY SCULPTURE, HEULER, AND NICHOLSON

1. Visit a cemetery. Make a rough estimate of the sculpture that is low relief—that is, sculpture that projects only slightly from its background plane—as in Figure 5-11. Then estimate roughly the percentage of relief that is sunken, as in Figure 5-1. In all probability, you will find a high percentage of sunken relief. If so, what is the explanation? Does the presence or absence of first-rate sculptors doing cemetery sculpture have any relevance to the question?
2. Pick out a couple of examples of the worst sculpture in the cemetery and a couple of examples of the best. Can you find in the cemetery any sculpture that approaches the artistic quality of Heuler's war memorial (Figure 5-2)? Then analyze the presuppositions or assumptions that were the basis for your judgments.
3. The title of Ben Nicholson's *Painted Relief* (Figure 5-3)—made of painted synthetic board mounted on plywood—is ambiguous. Would you classify this work as painting or sculpture? Or do you think it would be more useful to classify this kind of work as a hybrid between painting and sculpture?

FIGURE 5-2 Heuler, War Memorial in Würzburg. Photograph by R. Kellner.

FIGURE 5-3 Ben Nicholson, *Painted Relief.* 1939. Synthetic board mounted on plywood, painted; 32⅞ by 45 inches. Collection, The Museum of Modern Art, New York. Gift of H. S. Ede and the artist.

Surface-Relief Sculpture

Study Ghiberti's bronze doors of the Baptistry of Florence (Figure 5-4), completed in 1452, and called by Michelangelo "The Gates of Paradise." How different are the panels of these doors from representational paintings? There are some clearly noticeable projections out into space, but almost every device available to the Florentine painter of the fifteenth century for creating the *illusion* rather than the actuality of spatial depth—foreshortening, landscape vistas, perspective effects, etc.—is used. When used with sculptural materials, these pictorial methods produce what is called "surface relief." The surface planes of Ghiberti's panels are part of the composition, and there is no clear perceptual distinction between the relief that comes out into space and the surface planes. Behind the surface planes the backgrounds are nonplanar; thus, no limits to the backgrounds are perceptible, suggesting an infinity of space. The perspective of such things as the lines of trees, the retreating undulations of the ground, the receding arches, the overlapping and diminishing sizes of people, the increase in delicacy of modeling as the size of objects decreases, and even a progression from clear to hazy atmosphere all suggest an unlimited background space in which the various biblical actions take place. In other words, there are no background starting points that function as the bases for the planar organizations. Rather, the surface planes of the panels function as the basic organizing planes: hence the expression "surface relief." Does Ghiberti's "surface relief" produce sculpture? We think so (although some critics think otherwise), because the tactile qualities of the

FIGURE 5-4 Lorenzo Ghiberti, doors of the Baptistry of Florence. 1425–1452. Bronze, 16½ feet high. Alinari.

bronze significantly stimulate our tactile senses. Some desire, admittedly not very strong, to touch as well as look at these doors is aroused.

Sculpture and Architecture Compared

Architecture is the art of separating inner from outer space in such a way that the inner space can be used for practical purposes. There is much more to architecture than that, of course, as we shall discuss in the next chapter. But how can sculpture be distinguished from architecture? Despite the architectural monumentality of Goeritz's *Five Towers of the Satellite City* (Figure 5-5), this is clearly sculpture because there is no inner space. But what about the Sphinx and the Pyramid at Memphis (Figure 5-6)? Like *The Five Towers of the Satellite City*, both the Sphinx and the Pyramid are among the densest and most substantial of all works. They attract us visually and tactilely. Since there is no space within the Sphinx, it is sculpture. But within the Pyramid, space was provided for the burial of the dead. There is a separation of inner from outer space for the functional use of the inner space. Yet the use of this inner space is so limited that the living often have a very difficult time finding it. The inner space is functional *only* in a very restricted sense—for the dead only. Is then this Pyramid sculpture or architecture? We shall delay our answer until the next chapter. The difficulty of the question, however, points up an important factor that we should keep in mind. The distinctions between the arts that we have and will be making are necessary in order to talk about them intelligibly, but the arts resist neat pigeonholing and any attempt at that would be futile.

Compare Arp's *Growth* (Frontispiece), Chryssa's *Times Square Sky* (Figure 5-7), Calder's *Ghost* (Figure 5-8), and Calder's *Three Arches* (Figure 5-9).

PERCEPTION KEY ARP, CHRYSSA, AND CALDER

1. Which of these four works is most obviously sculpture? Why?
2. In some of Pollock's paintings (Figure 4-1), as we have already indicated, the paint stands out from the canvas surface somewhat the way the aluminum and neon tubing in Chryssa's work stand out from the flat surface of the steel. These Pollocks are usually classified as paintings, the Chryssas as sculpture. Do you agree? Why or why not?
3. Both *Ghost* and *Three Arches* are usually classified as sculpture. Do you agree? Why or why not?
4. How is space perceived differently around the Calders compared with the space around the Chryssa and the space around the Arp? As you reflect about this, consider how your body is involved with these works.
5. Which of the four works are abstract and which representational?

Low-Relief Sculpture

Relief sculpture projects from a background plane such as a wall or column. Low-relief sculpture projects relatively slightly from its background plane, and so its depth dimension is diminished or condensed. Medium and high-relief sculpture project further from their backgrounds, and so their depth dimensions are expanded. Sculpture in the round is freed from any background plane, and so its depth dimension is completely unrestricted. *Times Square Sky* is, we

FIGURE 5-5   Mathias Goeritz, *The Five Towers of the Satellite City.* 1957.
Painted concrete pylons, 121 to 187 feet high, near Mexico City. Photograph
from *Matrix of Man*, 1968, by Sibyl Moholy-Nagy, Praeger Publishers.
Courtesy of Hattula Moholy-Nagy Hug.

FIGURE 5-6 Great Sphinx and Pyramid at Memphis, Egypt. IV dynasty, ca. 2850 B.C. Rock-cut limestone and masonry; base of Pyramid, about 13 acres; Sphinx, 66 feet high, 172 feet wide.

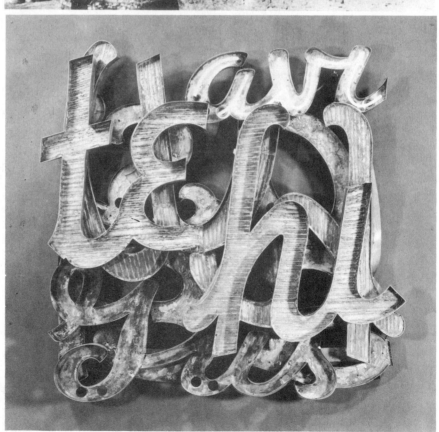

FIGURE 5-7 Chryssa, *Times Square Sky*. 1962. Neon, aluminum, steel; 60 by 60 by 9½ inches. Collection, Walker Art Center, Minneapolis. Gift of the T. B. Walker Foundation.

FIGURE 5-8 Alexander
Calder, *Ghost*. 1964.
Mobile of sheet metal
and metal rods, 288 by
414 inches. Philadelphia
Museum of Art.
Purchased with the New
Members' Fund.

FIGURE 5-9 Alexander
Calder, *Three Arches*.
1963. Painted metal
stabile, 9 feet high, 9 feet
4½ inches wide, 12 feet
long.
Munson-Williams-Proctor
Institute, Utica, New
York.

think, most usefully classified as sculpture of the low-relief species. The materiality of the steel, neon tubing, and especially the aluminum is brought out very powerfully by their juxtaposition. Unfortunately, this is difficult to perceive from a photograph. Because of its three-dimensionality, sculpture generally suffers even more than painting from being seen only in a photograph. But if you cannot get to the Walker Art Center in Minneapolis, you can see works in a style similar to Chryssa's at almost any museum, gallery, or exhibition of contemporary sculpture. Note how in such works the sculptors—unlike painters—allow the substantiality of the materials that make up their work to come forth. Sculptors usually are possessed with care for the materiality of things. In *Times Square Sky* Chryssa is especially sensitive to aluminum, the neon light helping to bring out the special sheen of that metal, which flashes forth in smooth and rough textures through subtle shadows.

Yet *Times Square Sky*, as the title suggests, is representational. The subject matter is about a quite specific place, and the content of *Times Square Sky*—by means of its form—is an interpretation of that specific subject matter. Times Square is closed in almost entirely by manufactured products, such as aluminum and steel, animated especially at night by a chaos of flashing neon signs. Letters and words—often as free of syntax as in the sculpture—clutter that noisy space and noxious air with an overwhelming senselessness. The feel of that fascinating square is Chryssa's subject matter, just as it is in Mondrian's *Broadway Boogie Woogie* (Color Plate 8). Both works reveal something of the rhythm, bounce, color, and chaos of Times Square, but *Times Square Sky* interprets more of its physical character. Whereas Mondrian abstracts from the physicality of Broadway, Chryssa gives us a heightened sense of the way Broadway feels as our bodies are bombarded by the street and its crowds. Those attacks—tactile, visual, aural, and olfactory—can have a metallic, mechanical, impersonal, and threatening character, and something of those menacing qualities is revealed in *Times Square Sky*. The physicality of that effect is, we suggest, what distinguishes this work as sculpture rather than painting. And yet the line here cannot be too sharply drawn. For if the neon tubing and aluminum were flattened down on the steel somewhat or if Pollock had laid on his paints an inch or so thicker, would these works then be sculpture or painting?

PERCEPTION KEY THE CITY OF THE CIRCLE AND THE SQUARE AND TIMES SQUARE SKY

Compare Paolozzi's *City of the Circle and the Square* (Figure 5-10), entirely in aluminum, with *Times Square Sky*.

1. Do Paolozzi's shapes reveal anything about our urban world? Be specific.
2. Are these shapes as revelatory as Chryssa's of a large contemporary city? Or of Times Square?

FIGURE 5-10 Eduardo Paolozzi, *The City of the Circle and the Square*. 1963. The Tate Gallery, London.

FIGURE 5-11 *Running Animals.* Impression from a seal cylinder, Sumerian, Jamdet Nasr period. Walters Art Gallery, Baltimore.

3. In Paolozzi's sculpture, unlike Chryssa's, much of the aluminum is masked by paint. Is this not a kind of "untruth" to his materials? If so, is this artistically justifiable.

Relief sculpture—with a few exceptions such as those previously discussed—allows its materials to stand out from a background plane, as in *Times Square Sky.* Thus relief sculpture in at least one way reveals its materials simply by showing us—directly—their surface and something of their depth. By moving to a side of *Times Square Sky,* we can see that the steel, neon tubing, and aluminum are of such and such thickness. However, this three-dimensionality in relief sculpture, this movement out into space, is not allowed to lose its ties to its background plane. Hence relief sculpture, like painting, is usually best viewed from a basically frontal position. You cannot walk around a relief sculpture and see its back side as sculpture any more than you can walk around a painting and see its back side as painting. That is why both relief sculptures and paintings are usually best placed on walls or in niches.

Low-relief sculpture comes closest to painting when the movement out from the background plane is very slight, as in that very ancient and lovely Sumerian seal called *Running Animals* (Figure 5-11). Even here, however, we are aware of the smoothness of the material as it takes on the configurations of graceful animal movement. And this awakens our sense of touch. Even if we were blind, we could get some feeling of this work's fluidity and what this work is about by passing our hands over its surface. Even the temperature of the stone would be a significant element in our perception. But would passing our hands over *Earth Greens* (Color Plate 5) enhance our perception of that work as a painting? Would our sensing its temperature? Or what about a canvas of Pollock's (Figure 4-1)? Our hands would feel the rhythmic textures of the Pollock, no doubt, but would the feel of the oil paints as oil be of any significance? Would we be aware of the concentration of white lead? And even if we were, would that awareness be significant in our experience of the canvas and its contents as a work of art? Would it make sense to talk about the oiliness of its oil paint? Would touching alone give us any significant understanding of what the work is about?

Charles Biederman's *Structurist Relief, Red Wing #6* (Figure 5-12), like *Times Square Sky,* is in considerably higher relief than *Running Animals.*

PERCEPTION KEY STRUCTURIST RELIEF, RED WING #6

Biederman's sculpture is made of sheet aluminum, machine-tooled and sprayed with several coats of paint in order to build up bright, lustrous surfaces. The placement of the squares and rectangles with their right-angled

FIGURE 5-12   Charles Biederman, *Structurist Relief, Red Wing #6.* 1957–1963. Painted aluminum, 38⁷⁄₁₆ by 26¼ by 8⅝ inches. Collection, Walter Art Center, Minneapolis. Gift of the artist through the Ford Foundation Purchase Program.

lines is reminiscent of Mondrian's style (Color Plates 2 and 8). And, in fact, Biederman was strongly influenced by Mondrian. Unlike *Times Square Sky*, the metallic character of the aluminum of *Structurist Relief, Red Wing #6* is covered over rather than brought out. Despite the close relationship in style to Mondrian's paintings, would you be satisfied describing Biederman's work as a painting? Explain.

Structurist Relief, Red Wing #6 differs from most sculpture in several respects. In the first place, Biederman—unlike Chryssa, for example—covers up his material, the aluminum. Second, he uses a wider color range than most sculptors and even painters such as Mondrian. Yet we think *Structurist Relief, Red Wing #6* is an example of sculpture. The squares and rectangles, unlike Mondrian's, possess some density. Moreover, they move strongly with clean simplicity out into space, and their smooth surfaces lure our hands. In contrast to our participation with *Broadway Boogie Woogie* (Color Plate 8), our tactile sense is strongly aroused. If we were blindfolded and felt this work, we would be able to make some sense of it. Furthermore, these sharply edged planes with their high-luster skins reflect the play of light out into and through space in a way that suggests the luminosity of crystals. And perhaps this is the key to the content of this abstract sculpture—the interpretation of the molecular and crystal structures of nature. And perhaps, also, there is the suggestion of how the kinetics of modern technology are derivative from these natural structures, for in the absolute precision of this work there is something very machinelike. Biederman covers up his aluminum, but in such a way that he uncovers something of the matter of nature and its relationship to the machine. This is a highly debatable interpretation, of course. As you debate, reconsider your answer to Question 3 of the perception key on pages 124–125.

High-Relief Sculpture

FIGURE 5-13 Dancing Asparas. XII to XIII century. Rajasthan, India. Relief, sandstone, 28 inches high. The Metropolitan Museum of Art. Gift of Mrs. John D. Rockefeller, Jr., 1942.

The voluptuous Hindu *Nymph* (Figure 5-13), from a temple of the thirteenth century after Christ at Rajasthan in India, is an example of high-relief sculpture. Bursting with energy, the nymph almost escapes from her pillar. On the other hand, the small admiring handmaiden is in relatively low relief, closely integrated with the pillar. Partly because the nymph is almost completely in the round, we sense her bulk and mass with exceptional force. Rather than starting with the appearance of a naked woman, the sculptor must have started with the appearance of his stone and allowed that stone to suggest a naked woman capable of providing an eternity of sexual delight. He allowed woman to come forth as that kind of sandstone would say it, and rarely has such stone revealed such erotic qualities. Sensuality and sexuality

FIGURE 5-14
Michelangelo Buonarroti,
Pietà. ca. 1550–1555.
Marble, 7 feet 8 inches
high; in Florence
Cathedral. The Bettmann
Archive, inc.

are completely embodied in a shape that attracts our need to touch. Indeed, it may even be, at least for older westerners with Puritan roots, that the erotic excitation reduces us to dwarfs like the handmaiden. In any case, there is a great deal of humor in this remarkable work.

Sculpture in the Round

Michelangelo's *Pietà* (Figure 5-14) of the Cathedral of Florence, one of his last sculptures, ca. 1550–1555, was unfinished. According to Vasari and Condivi, Michelangelo originally wanted to be buried at the foot of this sculpture, which was to be placed in Santa Maria Maggiore in Rome. Hence he portrayed his own features in the head of Joseph of Arimathea, the figure hovering above, and apparently was making good progress. But then a series of accidents occurred, some involuntary and some probably voluntary. In carving the left leg of Christ, a vein in the marble broke, and the leg was completely destroyed. There are also breaks above the left elbow of Christ, in his chest on the left, and on the fingers of the hand of the Virgin. The story goes that, in despair, Michelangelo did some of this damage himself. In any case, he gave it up as a monument for his tomb and sold it in 1561, deciding that he preferred burial in Florence.

PERCEPTION KEY PIETÀ

1. Of the four figures of this statue—Joseph, Christ, the Virgin to the right, and Mary Magdalene to the left—one seems to be not only somewhat stylistically out of harmony with the other three but of lesser artistic quality. Historians and critics generally agree that this figure was not done or at least not completed by Michelangelo but rather by a second-rate sculptor, presumably Tiberio Calcagni. Which figure is this? What are your reasons for choosing it?
2. Michelangelo, perhaps more than any other sculptor, was obsessed with marble. He spent months at a time searching the hills of Carrara near Pisa for those marble blocks from which he, like a midwife, could help sculptural shapes emerge. Something of his love for marble, perhaps, is revealed in this *Pietà*. Do you perceive this? And if so, how do you think it was achieved?
3. Is this sculpture in the round? The figures are freed from a base as background, and one can walk around the work. But is this *Pietà* in the round in the same way as Arp's *Growth* (Figure 5-15)?

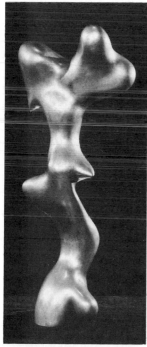

FIGURE 5-15 Jean Arp, *Growth*. 1938. Philadelphia Museum of Art. Photograph by A. J. Wyatt, staff photographer.

The answer to the first question is the Magdalene. Her figure and pose, relative to the others, are artificial and stiff. Her robe—compare it with the Virgin's—fails to integrate with the body beneath. For no accountable reason she is both very aloof and much smaller, and the rhythms of her figure fail to harmonize with the others. Finally, the marbleness of the marble fails to come out with the Magdalene.

In the other figures—and this is the key to the second question—Michelangelo barely allows his shapes, except for the polished surfaces of the body of Christ, to emerge from the marble block. The features of the Virgin's face, for example, are very roughly sketched. It is as if she were still partially a prisoner in her stone. The Virgin is a marble Virgin; the Magdalene is a Magdalene and marble. Or, to put it another way, Michelangelo saw the Virgin in the marble and helped her image out without allowing it to betray its origin. Calcagni, or whoever did the Magdalene, saw the image of Magdalene and then fitted the marble to the image. Thus the claim that the face of the Virgin was unfinished is mistaken. It is hard to conceive, for us at least, how more chiseling or any polishing could have avoided weakening the expression of tender sorrow. The face of the Magdalene is more finished in a realistic sense, of course, but the forms of art reveal rather than reproduce reality. In the case of the body of Christ—compared with the rest of the statue except the Magdalene—the much more "finished" chiseling and the high polish was appropriate because it helped reveal the bodily suffering that preceded death.

Since there is no background plane from which the figures emerge, the *Pietà* is usually described as sculpture in the round. Yet when compared with Arp's *Growth*, it is obvious that the *Pietà* is not so clearly in the round. There is no "pull" around to the rough-hewn back side, except our need to escape from the intensity of the awesome compassion. And when we do walk behind the *Pietà*, we find the back side unintegrated with the sides and front and of little intrinsic interest. Michelangelo intended this essentially three-sided pyramid, as with practically all of his sculptures, to be placed in a niche so that it could be seen principally from the front. In this sense, the *Pietà* is a transition piece between high-relief sculpture, such as the *Nymph* (Figure 5-13), and unqualified sculpture in the round, such as *Growth*.

Sensory Space

The space around a sculpture is sensory rather than empty. Despite its invisibility, sensory space—like the wind—is felt. Sculptures such as *Growth* are like magnets from which radiating vectors flow. As we focus on such sculptures, we find ourselves being drawn in and around by these invisible but perceptible radiating forces. With relief sculptures, except for very high relief such as the *Nymph* (Figure 5-13), our bodies tend to get stabilized in one favored position. The framework of front and sides meeting at sharp angles, as in *Running Animals* (Figure 5-11) and *Times Square Sky* (Figure 5-7), limits our movements to 180 degrees at most. Although we are likely to move around within this limited range for awhile, our movements gradually slow down, like finally getting settled in a comfortable chair. We are not Cyclops with just one eye, and so we see something of the three-dimensionality of things even when restricted to one position. But even low-relief sculpture encourages some movement of the body, because we sense that a different perspective, however slight, may bring out something we have not directly perceived, especially something more of the three-dimensionality of the materials. With paintings, since there is no significant three-dimensionality of materials, this tendency is much more restricted, and that is one of the reasons why paintings come at us with such "all-at-onceness." With paintings there is usually one principal position from which to participate, and it does not take long to find it. In short, the space in front of a painting is relatively free of forces; low-relief sculpture projects some force; high-relief more; and, finally, the space in front of a sculpture in the round is full of forces because the frontal space is usually dynamically integral with the spaces of the sides and back.

PERCEPTION KEY GROWTH—TWO VERSIONS

1. Compare the two versions of *Growth* (Frontispiece and Figure 5-15). Do the planes and masses stretch out and pull back more strongly from the marble or the bronze? As you reflect about this, compare the way light acts on the two statues. On which one does the light reflect and contrast more sharply and rapidly? As a consequence, does the sensory character of the respective spaces surrounding the two statues differ? In what ways?
2. Suppose the marble *Growth* were backed into a corner in such a way that it would be difficult to walk around it. Would you feel that somehow the natural forces of the statue had been disturbed?
3. Imagine the bronze *Growth* in the same position. Would you feel that the space of the bronze was being violated more or less than the space of the marble? Why? In thinking about this, recall your answers to the first question.
4. If you agree that somehow our bodies are more actively involved with sculpture—especially sculpture in the round—than with paintings, how is this to be explained? Is it simply because with most sculpture we have to move our bodies around in order to see the whole sculpture as a succession of two-dimensional images? Or is there more to it than this? Reflect on the following statement by Naum Gabo, one of the most innovative sculptors of the twentieth century: "To think about sculpture as a succession of two-dimensional images would mean to think about something else, but not sculpture."[2] Consider also the fact that the subject matter of most sculpture—roughly estimated as close to 90 percent—is the human body. Even if this estimate is too high (and if restricted to contemporary sculpture, it surely is), nevertheless it remains generally true that sculptors usually find the human body a far more interesting subject matter than most painters. How is this to be explained?

Most of us believe that perceiving painting and sculpture are very similar acts.

PERCEPTION KEY PERCEIVING PAINTING AND SCULPTURE

Go to a museum and participate with a painting that is especially interesting to you. Then describe as accurately as possible *how* you perceived that painting. Describe every significant detail of your perception. Do the same

[2]Quoted by Herbert Read and Leslie Martin in *Gabo: Constructions, Sculpture, Drawings, Engravings*, Harvard University Press, Cambridge, Mass., 1957, p. 156.

FIGURE 5-16 Rebrandt van Rijn, *Portrait of Nicolaes Ruts.* 1631. Copyright the Frick Collection, New York.

with a sculpture that is especially interesting to you. Compare the differences, if any, between the two perceptions. Finally, compare what you have done with the following analysis.

As I walk into a room in the Philadelphia Museum of Art, my attention is drawn to an early Rembrandt portrait[3] on a wall and the bronze version of Arp's *Growth* (Figure 5-15) near the center of the room. I find the space in front of the Rembrandt vacuous. The space around the Arp is dense. Deciding to concentrate first on the Rembrandt, I seek and find an optimal or privileged position, eliminating the glare on the surface of the painting and allowing the painting to be seen most clearly within one basic view, all elements being simultaneously perceivable. From that position awareness of real space (the space between the painting and me) and its irrelevancies disappears, and I focus upon the imaginary space of the painting. I stand before the painting, and my body comes to rest (if a chair were available I would surely sit down), and only slight turns of my eyes and head are necessary to participate with the painting. One aspect suffices. Although I find myself shifting my stance occasionally in order to observe a color or shading or line or shape from a slightly different angle, still I relate and subordinate these observations to the privileged position. In memory, I seem to be able to see the Rembrandt from only the privileged position. That position produces the image of the essential relationships against which all other images are counterpointed. Moreover, perspective centers every region of space within the portrait, and, as R. L. Gregory points out, "paintings are generally more compelling in depth when viewed with . . . the head held still."[4] The painting as perceived from that fixed-focus position makes itself felt as a norm. The Rembrandt is like a face with one set expression.

Turning to the Arp, I find a more warm and friendly presence. I find myself reaching toward the statue rather than keeping my distance (if a chair were available I would not use it). Whereas my perceptual relationship to the Rembrandt required my getting to and settling in the privileged position, similar to finding the best seat in the theater, my perceptual relationship to the Arp is much more mobile and flexible. I want to touch and caress the shining bronze, despite the "Do Not Touch" signs and the guards. The smooth rounded shapes with their swelling volumes move gently out into space, turn my body around the figure and control the rhythm of my walking. My perception of the Arp seems to take much more time than my perception of the Rembrandt. This is a "seeming," for in fact I probably spent as much time perceiving the Rembrandt. But the dominance of the view

[3]This Rembrandt is no longer in the Philadelphia Museum. However, the Rembrandt reproduced here—*Portrait of Nicolaes Ruts* (Figure 5-16)—is very similar.
[4]R. L. Gregory, *Eye and Brain*, McGraw-Hill, New York, 1966, p. 169.

of the Rembrandt from the privileged position made it seem as if only the time spent in that view really counted, as if a single, timeless glance had sufficed. The power of that moment was so overwhelming that it made me forget "the spots of time" spent in other views.

Conversely, the Arp seems not only three-dimensional but four-dimensional, because it brings in the element of time so discernibly—a cumulative drama. Not only does each aspect make equal demands upon my contemplation, but, at the same time, each aspect is incomplete, enticing me on to the next for fulfillment. As I move, volumes and masses change, and on their surfaces points become lines, lines become curves, and curves become shapes. As each new aspect unrolls, there is a shearing of textures, especially at the lateral borders. The bronze flows. The leading border uncovers a new aspect and the textures of the old aspect change. The light flames. The trailing border wipes out the old aspect. The curving surface continuously reveals the emergence of volumes and masses in front, behind, and in depth. What is hidden behind the surfaces is still perceived, for the textures indicate a mass behind them. As I move, what I have perceived and what I will perceive stand in defined positions with what I am presently perceiving. My moving body links the aspects. A continuous metamorphosis evolves, as I remember the aspects that were and anticipate the aspects to come, the leaping and plunging lights glancing off the surface helping blend the changing volumes, shapes, and masses. The remembered and anticipatory images resonate in the present perception. My perception of the Arp is alive with motion. The sounds in the museum room are caught, more or less, in the rhythm of that motion. As I return to my starting point, I find it richer, as home seems after a journey. With the Rembrandt, on the other hand, there seemed to be no motion and thus no journey. And also no sound. In the inner intimacy of the moment there was, instead, a silence that rang. "Give her a silence, that the soul may softly turn home into the flooding and fullness in which she lived" (Rilke).

Any photograph of the Arp is necessarily unsatisfactory, for it must isolate a single aspect, whereas a photograph of the Rembrandt taken from the privileged position may be satisfactory. The static camera cannot capture the three-dimensional world, especially when, as with the Arp, the sculpture is not set up in a pictorial manner, for example, in front of a flat wall at right angles to the perceiver. Unlike my participation with the Rembrandt, there is no privileged position for participating with the Arp. I have no single memory image of the sculpture but a series of images, none of which is necessarily dominant, the shades of the various images passing into one another. Moreover the drawing of my body around the sculpture, following the concavities and convexities, had an "in-and-out" quality, like breathing. Sometimes I wanted to touch the surfaces, and sometimes I drew back. When I moved in, the textures, shapes, and volumes appeared larger and the reflected lights diffused. When I moved back, the textures, shapes, and volumes appeared smaller and the reflected lights sharpened. In close, the mass of *Growth* seemed heavier. On the other hand, I had no desire to touch the Rembrandt or even to get closer than the privileged position. The Rembrandt discourages embrace. Nor could I have grasped the painted man by the nose. If I had walked closer, at a certain point the portrait would have ceased to be a portrait and become blurred blotches. Nor could I have walked into the depth of the painted space, for its surface would have resisted like a wall. Nor were there any holes in that surface that would have enabled me to reach into that painted space and touch the chair in front or the man behind. Even if I had put my nose on the surface, the painted depth, being imaginary, would have remained beyond my physical reach. And, furthermore, as Rembrandt remonstrated: "Don't poke your nose into my pictures, the smell of paint will poison you." The imaginary space of the portrait and the real space of the museum room were like parallel lines that never meet. Thus touching the Rembrandt was no help in my perception of that painting. Touching the Arp, on the other hand, helped my perception of that sculpture by informing me about its surface. Grasping the Arp—impossible with the Rembrandt—informed me about its shape, size, weight, and its ridigity-plasticity. With the Rembrandt my hands were usually clasped behind my back, whereas with the Arp my hands were usually moving, even when I was not touching or grasping the sculpture. Unlike my perception of the Rembrandt, continual bodily adjustments were necessary in my perception of the Arp. Consequently, in the perception of the Rembrandt there was little co-perception of my body, whereas with the perception of the Arp there was considerable co-perception of my body.

The space between the Rembrandt and myself ideally is transparent, a clear and motionless atmosphere. I felt entirely alone with the painting when this was the case. Sensory awareness of the space between—such as glare coming off the surface of the painting, smoke coming from a neighboring spectator, sounds, or smells—distracted me from the painting. The space between was necessary, of course, but ideally only as an unfelt access. With the Arp the space between was furrowed with forces: the shadows, for example, intruded into that space, stretching, shrinking, warping and twisting, while the burning lights bounced off the bronze and seemed to warm the atmosphere. The smoke of the neighboring spectator and the sounds and smells of the museum room were not nearly so distracting as with the Rembrandt, to some extent being absorbed into the space between the Arp and me as if they belonged there.

The Rembrandt had a light of its own, generated within the frame, simultaneously illuminating and dissolving the man and the chair within a rich engulfing darkness. My activity of seeing was emphasized by being made difficult by the flickering inadequacy of the light rendered in chiaroscuro. This light appeared to be entirely distinct from the light of the museum room. The man and the chair of the painting seemed to struggle with the painting's light, oblique and falling in shafts, in order to capture its moving nature and make it static, and they seemed to have nothing to do with the light of the museum room. Conversely, *Growth* had no light of its own, and the material body, like the flower to the sun, seemed to reach out for the light of the room. As it reached that light, the bronze dramatically enhanced it by reflection, even seeming to make the light move. With the Rembrandt, awareness of real space and light and people were disturbances. I wanted to feel entirely alone with the portrait, conscious only of its imaginary world. With the Arp awareness of real space and light were not disturbances but welcome necessities, and even the awareness of other people in the room was not necessarily distracting.

The swelling shapes of *Growth* interact with real space. If *Growth* were crowded into a corner, its vitality would be weakened, for *Growth* needs a complete surrounding space, which it can penetrate with its forces. (Unfortunately, *Growth* has recently been exiled high against a wall in the Philadelphia Museum of Art, apparently to save space.) Unlike the Rembrandt, *Growth* breathes into the atmosphere. Its concavities inhale; its convexities exhale. Its surrounding space is a perceptible part of the statue. As Henry Moore points out, sculpture needs

> more care in its placing than paintings do. With a picture, the frame keeps you at a distance and the picture goes on living in its own world. But if a sculpture is placed against the light, if you come into a room for instance and see it against the window, you just see a silhouette with a glare around it. It can't mean anything. If a thing is three-dimensional and meant to have a sense of complete existence, it won't do to back it up against a wall like a child that's been put in the corner.[5]

Like a magnet, Arp's bronze sends out vectors that fill its environment with directed paths. If an object had entered that field, I would have felt that it would have been drawn at once into some orbit. And, indeed, I was pulled and drawn around the bronze and controlled by its rhythm. A sense of gravity united the sculpture and myself in a common space. *Growth* articulates the emptiness around it, making what otherwise would be a void both visible and tactile. The surrounding space has a curious curvature, a moving volume filled with currents. To perceive this vortex along with the material body is to perceive the totality of this sculpture. The space between myself and the Arp was not a mere adjunct, as in the case of the Rembrandt, but integral. Whereas the forces of the Rembrandt—determined by the relationships of lines, colors, shapes, lights, and textures—stay within the frame, the forces of the Arp—determined by the relationships of the parts of the material body of the sculpture—thrust out into the surrounding space and seem

[5]Quoted by John Russell in *Henry Moore*, G. P. Putnam's Sons, New York, 1968, p. 156.

to push or pull into my perceptions. The frame of the Rembrandt helps contain its forces within an imaginative space, helping to bracket them, as it were, between quotation marks. Claims such as Dewitt Parker's—"By placing the statue on a pedestal, we indicate its isolation from the space of the room, as by putting a frame around a picture we isolate it, too, from everything else in the world"[6]—fail to recognize the impact of a sculpture into its surrounding space. It is true that large pedestals may make the material bodies of their sculptures inaccessible to touch, and pedestals usually separate their sculptures from the earth. But to the degree that a pedestal needlessly obscures our perception of the impact of the material body of a sculpture into its surrounding space, the sculpture is weakened. With the Arp, in contrast, the pedestal, like a stem of a plant leading to its flower, is continuous with and prepares for the spiraling form above. The pedestal helps that form push out spiraling lines of force into its environment. Moreover, the pedestal adds to the sense of the pull of gravity that I share with the sculpture, reinforcing the weight of forces in the surrounding atmosphere. The pedestal works as an entering rather than as a distancing device. Whereas the Arp possesses its environment (with or without a pedestal), the Rembrandt dispossesses itself of its environment (with or without a frame).

Sculpture and the Human Body

Sculptures generally are more or less a center—the place of most importance which organizes the places around it—of actual three-dimensional space: "more" in the case of sculpture in the round, "less" in the case of low relief. That is why sculpture in the round is more typically sculpture than the other species. Other things being equal, sculpture in the round, because of its three-dimensional centeredness, brings out the voluminosity and density of things more certainly than any other kind of sculpture. First of all, we can see and touch all sides. But more important, our sense of density has something to do with our awareness of our bodies as three-dimensional centers thrusting out into our surrounding environment. Gaston Bachelard remarks that "immensity is within ourselves. It is attached to a sort of expansion of being which life curbs and caution arrests, but which starts again when we are alone. As soon as we become motionless, we are elsewhere; we are dreaming in a world that is immense. Indeed, immensity is the movement of a motionless man."[7] Lachaise's *Floating Figure* (Figure 5-17), with its ballooning buoyancy emerging with lonely but powerful internal animation from a graceful ellipse, not only expresses this

---

[6]Dewitt Parker, *The Analysis of Art*, Yale University Press, New Haven, 1926, p. 36.
[7]From *The Poetics of Space* by Gaston Bachelard. Translation © 1964 by The Orion Press, Inc. Reprinted by permission of Grossman Publishers.

FIGURE 5-17 Gaston Lachaise, *Floating Figure*, 1927. Bronze (cast in 1935), 51¾ by 96 inches. Collection, The Museum of Modern Art, New York. Given anonymously in memory of the artist.

feeling but also something of the instinctual longing we have to become one with the world about us. Sculpture in the round, even when it does not portray the human body, often gives us something of an objective image of our internal bodily awareness as related to its surrounding space. Furthermore, when the human body is portrayed in the round, we may have the most vivid material counterpoint of our internal feelings and mental images of our bodily existence.

1. Take a pencil and paper. Close your eyes. Now draw the shape of a human being but leave off the arms.
2. Take some clay or putty elastic enough to mold easily. Close your eyes. Now model your material into the shape of a human being, again leaving off the arms.
3. Analyze your two efforts. Which was easier to do? Which produced the better result? What do you mean by "better"? Was your drawing process guided by any other factor than your memory images of the human body? What about your modeling process? Did any significant factors other than your memory images come into play? Was the feel of the clay or putty important in your shaping? Did the awareness of your internal bodily sensations contribute to the shaping? Did you exaggerate any of the functional parts of the body where movement originates, such as the neck muscles, shoulder bones, knees, or ankles? Could these exaggerations, if they occurred, have been a consequence of your inner bodily sensations?

In Greek mythology, the young Narcissus fell in love with his image as reflected in a clear spring. Unfortunately, being unable to endow that image with corporeality, he pined away and died. In this as in most myths, there is an element of profound truth. The Narcissus myth expresses the insatiable desire most of us have to arrive at a satisfactory image of our bodily selves. Mirror images help, of course, but they are always seen as far behind the mirror as we are in front. We cannot rub against or even touch our image, for what is "in" the mirror is not there at all. The image has no being of its own, entirely dependent upon what it reflects. A mirror image, like the image of a painting, has no tangibility. And as with a painting, the mirror image can only present the surface of our bodies; the mass is represented by cues of perspective. Such images with their unreal quality are not very satisfactory material counterpoints of our mental images of ourselves. The nonreflected sight of ourselves helps, but we can see only a part of ourselves. Touch of ourselves and other people helps, but usually such perceptions are blurred with irrelevancies, such as concealing clothes. Sculpture can strip away the irrelevancies. It can bring out density directly and powerfully—that "strange thickness" so basic to our awareness of our bodies—presenting clarifying images of both the exterior and interior of our bodies.

TACTILITY: INWARD AND OUTWARD SENSATIONS

Tactile or touch sensations are both inward and outward. We feel our internal bodily sensations—such as muscular tension and relaxation, strength and lassitude, pleasure and pain, and desire—as three-dimensional forces filling out our bodily space and, in turn, being met by external forces or bodies. We feel gravity, for example, as a force limiting our bodily forces. Through our inward sensations we perceive ourselves constantly. Only in deep sleep do these sensations cease. Our outward sensations—that is, sensations of the outside of our bodies, as when we scratch our skin—are usually less constant. Moreover, usually our outward sensations are directed toward external things rather than our bodies. Our visual sensations of ourselves are even more sporadic than our external tactile sensations of ourselves. We can still perceive ourselves inwardly even if we are blind and paralyzed. Once we can no longer feel ourselves inwardly, we no longer are. Even the so-called totally paralyzed person feels something in his head.

Our first experiences are tactile rather than visual. Babies feel their hunger and thirst inwardly. And they touch their mother's breast before they see it. Most psychologists are convinced that young children are severely handicapped in their development if they are shut off from fondling. However that may be, all of us have learned something about the limits of our bodies the harder way—as toddlers trying to stand up and banging into things. Our bumps and bruises have told us more about our bodies than mirrors. Our body image is built primarily from our contacts with other bodies, our visual sensations of ourselves being supplemental. The boundaries of our bodies are based upon the obstruction of those objects that "object" to being incorporated. Our inward sensations thrust outward to meet and be bounded by our outward sensations of other bodies. Without outward sensations, we would be unaware of things beyond us. Without inward sensations, our outward sensations would have no center.

Sculpture in the Round and the Human Body

No object is more important to us than our body, and it is always "with" us. Yet when something is continually present to us, we find great difficulty in focusing our attention upon it. Thus we are usually only vaguely aware of air except when it is deficient in some way. Similarly, we usually are only vaguely aware of our bodies except when we are in pain. Nevertheless, our bodies are part of our most intimate selves—we are our bodies—and, since most of us are narcissists to some degree, we have a deep-down driving need to find a satisfactory material counterpoint for the mental images of our bodies. If that is the case, we are lovers of sculpture in the round. All sculpture always evokes our outward sensations and sometimes our inward sensations. Sculpture in the round often evokes our inward sensations, for such sculpture often is anthropomorphic in some respect. And sculpture in the round that has as its subject matter the human body—as in the *Aphrodite* (Figure 5-18), Michelangelo's *David* (Figure 5-19), or Rodin's *Danaïde* (Figure 5-20)—not only often evokes our inward sensations but also interprets them. Rodin, one of the greatest sculptors of the human body, wrote that "instead of imagining the different parts of the

FIGURE 5-18 *Aphrodite* (Venus Anadyomene). ca. first century B.C. Marble, slightly under life size. Found at Cyrene. Museo Nazionale delle Terme, Rome.

FIGURE 5-19 Michelangelo Buonarroti, *David*. 1501–1504. Marble, 13 feet high. Accademia, Florence.

body as surfaces more or less flat, I represented them as projections of interior volumes. I forced myself to express in each swelling of the torso or of the limbs the efflorescence of a muscle or a bone which lay beneath the skin. And so the truth of my figures, instead of being merely superficial, seems to blossom from within to the outside, like life itself."[8] Such sculpture presents an objective correlative—an image that is objective in the sense that it is "out there" and yet correlates or is similar to a subjective awareness—that clarifies our internal bodily sensations as well as our outward appearance.

These are large claims and highly speculative. You may disagree, of course, but we hope they will stimulate your thinking.

[8]Auguste Rodin, *Art*, Romilly Fedden (trans.), Small, Boston, 1912, p. 65.

FIGURE 5-20 Auguste Rodin, *Danaïde*. 1885. Marble, 35 by 73 by 57 centimeters. Musée Rodin, Paris. © SPADEM, Paris/VAGA, New York, 1982.

PERCEPTION KEY APHRODITE AND GIORGIONE'S VENUS

The marble *Aphrodite* (Figure 5-18), slightly under life size, found at Cyrene, is a Roman copy of a Greek original of the first century B.C. It is extraordinary both for the delicacy of its carving, for most Roman copies of Greek works crudely deaden their liveliness, and the translucency of its marble, which seems to reflect light from below its surface. Compare this work with Giorgione's *Venus* (Figure 2-16).

1. Which of the two would you rather touch?
2. Which of the two evokes more inward sensations?
3. In both these works, graceful lassitude and sexuality have something to do with their subject matter. Yet they are interpreted, we think, quite differently. What do you think?
4. If the head and arms of the *Venus* were represented as broken off, would this injure the work as much as the *Aphrodite?* Some critics claim that the *Aphrodite* is not very seriously injured as an artistic object by the destruction of her head and arms. Yet how can this be? As you reflect about this, ask yourself why we excluded the arms in the drawing and modeling exercises of the previous perception key. Suppose the *Aphrodite* were to come off her pedestal and walk. Would you not find this monstrous? Yet many people treasure her as one of the most beautiful of all females. How is this to be explained? As you consider this question, review the discussion on inward sensations as a possible clue.

When we participate with sculpture such as the *Aphrodite*, we find something of our bodily selves confronting us. If we demanded all of our bodily selves, we would be both disappointed and stupid. Art is always a transformation of reality, never a duplication. Thus the absence of head and arms in the *Aphrodite* does not shock us as it would if we were confronting a real woman. Nor does their absence ruin our perception of the beauty of this statue. Even before the damage, the work was only a partial image of a female. Now the *Aphrodite* is even more partial. But even so, she is in that partiality exceptionally substantial. The *Aphrodite* is more substantial than a real woman because the female shape, texture, grace, sensuality, sexuality, and beauty are interpreted by a form and thus clarified. And with all those feminine qualities, density is present in a more vivid way than in reality. Even the most perfect real woman—at least from a male chauvinist viewpoint—is always moving away, or covering up, or talking too much, or in bad light, or sick, or getting old. The sculptor can make her stand still, strip her, shut her up, give her good light, and keep her in good health and young. The painter also can do this, of course, except that, unlike the sculptor, he has to sacrifice the density.

Giorgione's *Venus* is perhaps even lovelier than the *Aphrodite*. Yet the body of *Venus* is only represented; the body of *Aphrodite* is presented. And this difference makes our participations with the two works quite different. We are bound to be drawn close to *Aphrodite* and to circle her. And if the guards are not looking—she is watched over in Rome's Museo Nazionale delle Terme by some of Italy's most zealous puritans—to touch and caress her. Such does not seem to be the case with the *Venus*. Paintings, even one so erotically attractive as this, tend to keep their distance. For one thing, if we get too close, we lose our best view. Although this also happens with sculpture, the visual loss is often compensated by the tactile gain. Second, there is no thrust forward into the space in front of the picture plane. Hence there are no channeling forces—except the need to find the position of best sight— to draw us in. And so the picture plane remains a dividing plane that we have no desire to penetrate.

PERCEPTION KEY HUMAN BODY AS SCULPTURAL SUBJECT MATTER

Considerations such as we have been discussing may account, perhaps, for some of the less conscious motivations that lead sculptors to the human body as subject matter. Are there other motivations? In thinking about this, imagine yourself a sculptor. Are there any three-dimensional shapes more subtle or complex than that of the human body?

The human body is supremely beautiful. To begin with, there is its sensuous charm. There may be other things in the world as sensuously attractive—for example, the full glory of autumnal leaves—but the human body also possesses a sexuality that greatly enhances its sensuousness. Moreover, in the human body, mind is incarnate. Feeling, thought, purposefulness—what in sum is loosely called "spirit"—have taken shape. Thus, the absent head of the *Aphrodite* (Figure 5-18) is not really so absent after all. There is a dignity of spirit that permeates her body. It is abhorrent to conceive of her as having an idiotic or wrathful head. Better no head at all. It is the manifestation of Aphrodite's composed spirit in the shaping of her body that, in the final analysis, explains why we are not repulsed by the sight of the absent head and arms.

Compare Michelangelo's *David* (Figure 5-19) and *Pietà* (Figure 5-14) with the *Aphrodite*.

PERCEPTION KEY DAVID, APHRODITE, AND THE PIETA.

1. Suppose the head of the *David* were broken off and, like the head of *Aphrodite*, you had never seen it. Is it conceivable that a head something like that of the Christ of the *Pietà* could be satisfactorily substituted?
2. Both the *Aphrodite* and the *David* are in marble, although of very different kinds. Which statue is more evocative of your outward sensations? Your inward sensations? Henry Moore claims that "sculpture is more affected by actual size considerations than painting. A painting is isolated by a frame from its surroundings (unless it serves just a decorative purpose) and so retains more easily its own imaginary scale." He makes the further claim that the actual physical size of sculpture has an emotional meaning. "We relate everything to our own size, and our emotional response to size is controlled by the factor that men on the average are between five and six feet high."[9] Does the fact that the *David* is much larger in size than the *Aphrodite* make any significant difference with respect to your tactile sensations?
3. Both statues respect the relative proportions of the human body. Yet one of the statues has one part of its anatomy greatly out of proportion to the other parts. Identify this part and explain why this is the case.

FIGURE 5-21   *Venus of Willendorf.* ca. 15,000 to 10,000 B.C. Stone, 4⅜ inches high. Naturhistorisches Museum, Vienna.

Both the *Aphrodite* and the *David* are exceptional examples of idealized sculpture—that is, figures more beautiful than those found in nature. Compare the *Aphrodite* with one of the earliest known sculptures, also in the round—the compact *Venus of Willendorf* (Figure 5-21) from the Paleolithic period, in limestone and just over 4 inches in height. Apparently there was no attempt to idealize this *Venus* even granting the technical limitations of the sculptor.

---

[9]Moore, "Notes on Sculpture," p. xxxiv.

1. Can you suggest a more appropriate title than the *Venus of Willendorf?* In reflecting about this, identify the subject matter. Perhaps the fact that the sculpture is small enough to be encompassed by your hands is a clue.
2. Does it follow, because of the lack of idealization, that the *Venus* is of lesser artistic quality than the *Aphrodite?* Explain.
3. Which of the two works arouses your outward sensations more? Inward sensations? Why? Be specific.
4. Is the limestone of the *Venus* an appropriate material for the forming of this figure? Consider how the figure would appear if carved in a marble like that of the *Aphrodite.* Would its artistic quality have been enhanced? Suppose the material had been relatively light, like rubber. Would this change our perception of the figure greatly?
5. Is the head of the *Venus*, with its very abstract treatment, suitable to the body?
6. The structure of the *Venus* is composed of parts that suggest geometrical shapes. Analyze these parts in relation to the whole. Do the same with the *Aphrodite.* Which of the two works has the more complex part-to-whole composition?

Return once again to the marble and bronze version of Arp's *Growth* (Frontispiece and Figure 5-15).

1. The Arp statues certainly do not look like any human beings in a realistic sense. If someone resembling these statues came walking down the street, we would be horrified. Yet is there nothing revealingly human about these figures?
2. Compare these figures with the waxworks of Colonel Glenn and John F. Kennedy (Figure 5-22) in Madame Tussaud's collection. Are the waxworks more revealingly human?
3. Is one of the versions of *Growth* more feminine than the other? If so how is this to be explained?

Sculptural Orientation

Relief sculpture tends to be horizontally oriented because generally it is placed on or against a wall or in a niche,[10] that background serving as the basic "plane of departure" for the relief. Thus its basic three-dimensionality extends from a background plane toward a frontal plane. Sculpture in the round, on the other hand, tends to be vertically oriented because generally it is placed on the earth (inclusive of floors

[10]Recumbent tomb figures placed on the floors of churches and chapels, as commonly done in the medieval period, are a notable exception.

FIGURE 5-22 Colonel Glenn and John F. Kennedy in wax. Madame Tussaud's Wax Museum, London. British Tourist Authority, New York.

FIGURE 5-23 Constantin Brancusi, *Bird in Space.* 1925. Polished bronze, marble and oak base; 50¼ inches high. Philadelphia Museum of Art, The Louise and Walter Arensberg Collection. Photograph by A. J. Wyatt, staff photographer.

and bases). Thus its basic three-dimensionality extends upward. There are three main possibilities for the relation of sculpture in the round to the earth: the sculpture is either rooted in the earth, resting on it, or rising above it.

PERCEPTION KEY SCULPTURES IN THE ROUND

The *Aphrodite* (Figure 5-18), *David* (Figure 5-19), *Danaïde* (Figure 5-20), Brancusi's *Bird in Space* (Figure 5-23), Lachaise's *Floating Figure* (Figure 5-17), and Moore's *Reclining Figure* (Figure 5-24) are all sculptures in the round.
1. Which ones are rooted in the earth? Which rest on it? Which rise above it?
2. Return to Calder's *Ghost* (Figure 5-8) and *Three Arches* (Figure 5-9) and your answers to Questions 3 and 4 of the perception key on page 120. *Ghost* is based neither on a wall nor on a floor but hung from the ceiling so that you can walk under it. Most of its materials move with the air currents and have little significant density. *Three Arches* is based on the earth, but its materials also have little density and you can walk under it. Once again, are these sculptures?

Space Sculpture

The history of sculpture shows something of an evolution from low to high relief to sculpture in the round. But this is an exceedingly rough generalization. For example, the *Venus of Willendorf* (Figure 5-21) is

FIGURE 5-24 Henry Moore, *Reclining Figure.* 1945–1946. Elmwood, 90 inches. By permission of the artist.

one of the earliest known sculptures, and she is very much in the round. What can be claimed with little qualification, however, is that work such as *Ghost* and *Three Arches* has emerged in the last half-century. So new is this species that it has yet to be baptized with a universally accepted name. We shall call it "space sculpture." What distinguishes space sculpture from the earlier kinds is its emphasis upon spatial relationships and, consequently, its tendency to deemphasize the density and materiality of its materials. As a further consequence, the appeal of space sculpture is more visual and less tactile than that of earlier sculpture. Nevertheless, the tactile appeal remains to some degree. Work that lacks significant tactile appeal completely, it seems to us, is not usefully described as sculpture. More precisely, space sculpture differs from sculpture in relief and in the round in technique, in density, and in its relationships with space. If we can be clear about these differences, we should have a better appreciation of the various species of sculpture.

Techniques of Sculpture

Sculpture in relief and in the round generally is made either by modeling or carving. Space sculpture, on the other hand, generally is made by assembling preformed pieces of material.

The modeler starts with some plastic or malleable material such as clay, wax, or plaster and "builds" the sculpture. If the design is complex or involves long or thin extensions, the modeler probably will have to use an internal wooden or metal support (armature) that functions something like a skeleton. Whereas *Floating Figure* (Figure 5-17) and *Bird in Space* (Figure 5-23) required armatures, the *Venus of Willendorf* (Figure 5-21) did not. In either case, the modeler builds from the inside outward to the surface finish, which then may be scratched, polished, painted, etc. But when nonplastic materials such as bronze are used, the technical procedures are much more complicated. Bronze cannot be built up like clay. Nor can bronze be carved like stone, although it can be lined, scratched, etc. And so the sculptor in bronze or any material that is cast must use further processes. We can present here only a grossly oversimplified account. For those who want to pursue the techniques of sculpture further—and this can be very helpful in sharpening our perceptual faculties—a large number of excellent technical handbooks are available.[11]

The sculptor in bronze begins with clay or some similar material and builds up a model to a more or less high degree of finish. This is a solid or *positive* shape. Then the sculptor usually makes a plaster mold—a hollow or *negative* shape—from the solid model. This negative shape is usually divisible into sections, so that the inside can easily be worked on to make changes or remove any defects that may have developed. Then, because plaster or similar material is much better than clay for the casting process, the sculptor makes a positive or solid plaster cast from his negative plaster mold and perfects its surface. This plaster cast is then given to a specialized foundry, unless the sculptor does this work for himself or herself, and a negative mold is again made of such materials as plaster, rubber, or gelatin. Inside this mold—again usually divisible into sections to allow for work in the interior—a coating of liquid wax is brushed on, normally at least ⅛ inch in thickness but varying with the size of the sculpture. After the wax dries, a mixture of materials, such as sand and plaster, is poured into the hollow space within the mold. Thus the wax is completely surrounded.

Intense heat is now applied, causing the wax to melt out through channels drilled through the outside mold and the molds on both sides of the wax are baked hard. Then the bronze is poured into the space the wax has vacated. After the bronze hardens, the surrounding molds are removed. Finally, the sculptor may file, chase, polish, or add patinas (by means of chemicals) to the surface. One of the most interesting and dramatic descriptions of casting, incidentally, can be found in the *Autobiography* of Benvenuto Cellini, the swashbuckling Renaissance sculptor. His *Perseus*, probably his finest sculpture, was almost still-born in the casting process.

The carver uses nonmalleable material, such as marble, that cannot be built up, and so the carver must start with a lump of material

[11]For example, William Zorach, *Zorach Explains Sculpture*, American Artists Group, New York, 1947. Learning the techniques of handling various artistic media is one of the best ways of improving our perception and understanding of the arts. We do not have the space to go into these techniques, but good technical handbooks in all the arts abound.

and work inward from the outside by removing surplus material until arriving at the surface finish. Thus for his *David* (Figure 5-19), Michelangelo was given a huge marble block that Agostino di Duccio had failed to finally shape into either a David or, more likely, a prophet for one of the buttresses of the Cathedral of Florence. Agostino's carving had reduced the original block considerably, putting severe restrictions upon what Michelangelo could do. This kind of restriction is foreign to the modeler, for there is no frame such as the limits of a marble block to prevent the expansion of the sculpture into space. And when a model is cast in materials of great tensile strength, such as bronze, this spatial freedom becomes relatively unlimited.

It should be noted that many carvers, including Michelangelo, sometimes modeled before they carved. A sketch model often can help carvers find their way around in such materials as marble. It is not easy to visualize before the fact the whereabouts of complicated shapes in large blocks of material. And once a mistake is made in nonplastic materials, it is not so easily remedied as with plastic materials.

The shapes of the *David* had to be ordered from the outside inward, the smaller shapes being contained within the larger shapes. Whereas the modeler works up the most simplified and primary shapes that *underlie* all the secondary shapes and details, the carver roughs out the simplified and primary shapes *within* which all the secondary shapes and details are contained. For example, Michelangelo roughed out the head of the *David* as a solid sphere, working down in the front from the outermost planes of the forehead and nose to the outline of the eyes and then to the details of the eyes, etc. Hence the primary shape of the head, the solid sphere, is not only preserved to some extent but also points to its original containment within the largest containing shape, the block itself. Consequently, we can sense in the *David* something of the block from which Michelangelo started. This original shape is suggested by the limits of the projecting parts and the high points of the surfaces. We are aware of the thinness of the *David* as a consequence of the block Michelangelo inherited. There remains the huge imprint of that vertical block that had been sliced into. This accounts in part for the feeling we may have with some carved works of their being contained within a private space, introverted and to some extent separate. Modeled sculpture generally is more extroverted.

PERCEPTION KEY GROWTH—TWO VERSIONS

1. Compare again the marble and bronze versions of *Growth* (Frontispiece and Figure 5-15). If the bronze were made first, then the modeling technique was basic to both versions. If the marble were made first—assuming that no sketch model played a dominant role—then the carving technique was basic to both versions. Which technique do you think was basic?

2. Which statue is the more private and introverted?
3. Do you believe that your answer to Question 2 has something to do with your knowledge of the technical processes of how these statues were made? But if so, is this legitimate, since you were, presumably, judging the sculpture produced and not the producing process?

Ghost (Figure 5-8) and *Three Arches* (Figure 5-9) obviously were neither modeled nor carved. Their wires and sheets of metal have little mass to be shaped and no interior to be structured. Although the materials of these works exist in three-dimensional space, as does everything else in this world, they are not themselves significantly three-dimensional. Calder preformed these pieces and then assembled them, attached, furthermore, at clearly discernible joints and intersections. These pieces relate across and frame space; in the case of *Ghost*, there is even movement through space. The appeal of these works, therefore, is more visual than that of earlier sculpture. Calder's materials fill space only slightly, and so their tactile appeal, while still present, is considerably reduced.

The assemblage technique does not rule out the presentation of density—Paolozzi's *The City of the Circle and the Square* (Figure 5-10), for example, was assembled and yet is quite dense—but assemblage lends itself to the lightening of materials. This, in turn, lends itself to the creating of spatial relationships that become at least as interesting as the materials. Moore's *Reclining Figure* (Figure 5-24) is hollowed out with holes that open up space within the figure. Brancusi's *Bird in Space* (Figure 5-23) rises above the earth and opens up the space outside the figure. But in both these examples, the density of the materials, the wood and the bronze, respectively, dominates space. With *Ghost* and *Three Arches*, however, space is opened up both within and without, sliced up in such a way that the spatial relationships become more interesting than or at least as interesting as the materials.

Calder's *Bougainvillea* (Figure 5-25), made of wire and sheet metal, is an especially lovely example of spatial relationships. It is as if we were standing under a large vine, as the title suggests. The sinuous wires expand in all directions with the fibrous strength of wood branches, and the graceful disks, like blossoms, ride the breezes. Here our visual perception of spatial relationships is clearly more important than the tactile qualities of wire and metal. We have little desire to touch these pieces. Yet in their flowing movement to and from each other, they help bring out the tactile qualities of the open air. To cage *Bougainvillea* in a museum or any inside place would be as deadening to its natural forces as to back either version of Arp's *Growth* (Frontispiece and Figure 5-15) into a corner. *Bougainvillea*, much more than *Ghost*, belongs to the wind and sky.

Bougainvillea and *Ghost* are rather aptly described as "space

FIGURE 5-25 Alexander Calder, *Bougainvillea.* 1947. Mobile of wire and sheet metal, 76 inches high. Collection of Mr. and Mrs. Burton Tremaine, Meriden, Connecticut. Photograph by Herbert Matter.

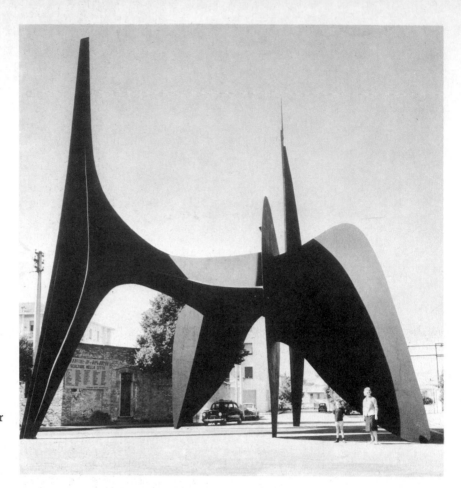

FIGURE 5-26 Alexander Calder, *The Gates of Spoleto*. 1962. Steel. Photograph by Edvard Trier.

drawings." Their primarily visual appeal, like very low-relief sculpture (Figure 5-11), has close affinities to painting. On the other hand, Calder's *Gates of Spoleto* (Figure 5-26) and, to a lesser extent, his *Three Arches* are examples of space sculpture with close affinities to architecture. As with many of the materials of architecture, Calder's ·materials sometimes are not only preformed and assembled but also massive. This makes it easily possible for inner space to be separated from outer space for practical purposes. If, for example, Calder had extended the upper steel sheets of *The Gates of Spoleto* horizontally, this work could serve as a functional shelter.

Tactility, Mass, and Space

Space sculpture never loses completely its ties to the materiality of its materials. Otherwise tactile qualities would be largely missing also, and then it would be doubtful if such work could usefully be classified as sculpture. The materials of *Ghost* and *Bougainvillea* carry with them the feel of the air. The sheets of steel of *Three Arches* and *The Gates of Spoleto*, despite their thinness, appear heavy. Naum Gabo, one of the fathers of space sculpture along with his brother Antoine Pevsner, often uses translucent materials, as in *Spiral Theme* (Figure 5-27). Although the planes of plastic divide space with multidirectional movement, no visual barriers develop. Each plane varies in translucency as our angle of vision varies, and in seeing through each, we see them all—allowing for freely flowing transitions between the space without and the space within. In turn, the tactile attraction of the plastic, especially its smooth surface and rapid fluidity, is enhanced. As Gabo has written: "Volume still remains one of the fundamental attributes of sculpture, and we still use it in our sculptures. . . . We are not at all intending to dematerialize a sculptural work. . . . On the contrary, adding Space perception to the perception of Masses, emphasizing it and forming it, we enrich the expression of Mass, making it more essential through the contact between them whereby Mass retains its solidity and Space its extension."[12]

PERCEPTION KEY RECLINING FIGURE, PELAGOS, BRUSSELS CONSTRUCTION, AND SPACE SCULPTURE

1. Compare Moore's *Reclining Figure* (Figure 5-23), Hepworth's *Pelagos* (Figure 5-28), Rivera's *Brussels Construction* (Figure 5-29), and Kricke's

[12]Quoted by Herbert Read and Leslie Martin in *Gabo: Constructions, Sculpture, Drawings, Engravings*, Harvard University Press, Cambridge, Mass., 1957, p. 168.

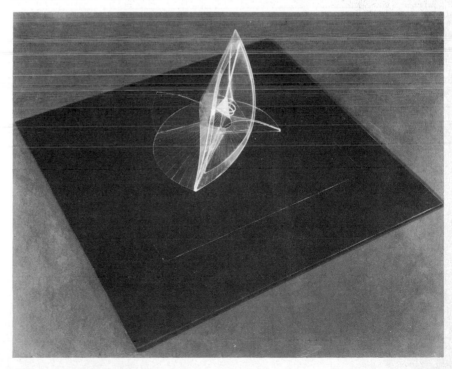

FIGURE 5-27 Naum Gabo, *Spiral Theme*. 1941. Construction in plastic, 5½ by 13¼ by 9⅜ inches, on base 24 inches square. Collection, The Museum of Modern Art, New York. Advisory Committee Fund.

FIGURE 5-28   Barbara Hepworth, *Pelagos*. 1946. Wood with color and strings, 16 inches in diameter. The Tate Gallery, London.

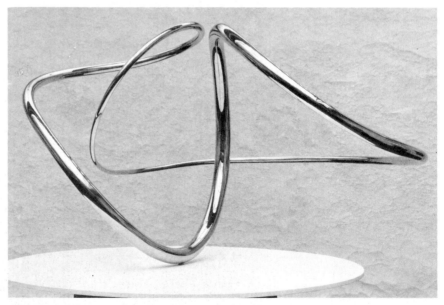

FIGURE 5-29   Jose de Rivera, *Brussels Construction*. 1958. Stainless steel. The Art Institute of Chicago. Gift of Mr. and Mrs. R. Howard Goldsmith.

FIGURE 5-30 Norbert Kricke, *Space Sculpture.* 1958. Stainless steel. Photograph by Edvard Trier.

Space Sculpture (Figure 5-30). Is there in these four works, as Gabo claims for his, an equal emphasis on mass and space? If not, in which one does mass dominate space? Vice versa?

2. Moore has written that "The first hole made through a piece of stone [or most three-dimensional materials] is a revelation. The hole connects one side to the other, making it immediately more three-dimensional. A hole can itself have as much shape-meaning as a solid mass."[13] Is Moore's claim applicable to all four of these works?

3. Compare another *Reclining Figure* (Figure 5-31) by Moore with an earlier one (Figure 5-32). Both are in Hornton stone, although of different colors. Do the holes in Figure 5-31 help bring out the stoniness of the stone? Or in this respect is Figure 5-32 more revealing?

4. Compare Moore's sculptures in Figures 5-24 and 5-31 with those in Figure 5-32. Do you sense in the figures with holes any suggestion of the rhythm of breathing? What role do the holes play with reference to the content of the first two works? Do the holes increase or decrease the liveliness of the figures, for example? What is Moore saying differently about women in the first two works compared with the third?

5. How many holes are there in *Pelagos*? What is the function of the strings? Why did Hepworth color the inside white?

6. *Brussels Construction* is mounted on a flat disk turned by a low-revolution motor. Is it useful to refer to holes in this sculpture? The three-

[13]"Notes on Sculpture," op. cit., p. xxxiv.

FIGURE 5-31 Henry Moore, *Reclining Figure.* 1938. Green Hornton stone, 54 inches long. By permission of the artist.

FIGURE 5-32 Henry Moore, *Reclining Figure.* 1929. Brown Hornton stone, 32 inches long. By permission of the artist.

dimensional curve of *Brussels Construction* proceeds in a long, smooth, continuous flow. Does this have anything to do with the changing diameter of the chromium-plated stainless steel? Suppose the material absorbed rather than reflected light. Would this change the structure significantly? Do you think this sculpture should be displayed under diffused light, or in dim illumination with one or more spotlights? Is there any reference to human life in the simplicity and elegant vitality of this work? Or is the subject matter just about stainless steel and space? Or is the subject matter about something else? Do you agree that this work is an example of space sculpture? And what about *Pelagos?* Note that there is no assemblage of pieces in the case of *Brussels Construction*, whereas, because of the addition of strings, there is some assemblage in *Pelagos.* Would you classify Moore's works in Figures 5-24 and 5-31 as space sculptures?

7. Kricke's *Space Sculpture* is an assemblage of welded metal strips. Does this work require, as does *Bougainvillea* (Figure 5-25), the open air? Could it be appropriately placed in Times Square? Suppose it were to be placed either at the entrance of Kennedy Airport or on a Hudson River pier. Which would provide the more suitable space? Can you think of a specific place where this work could be best displayed? Is this work an example of space sculpture? Is the title an index to the subject matter or nothing more than an identification tag? Can you think of a more appropriate title?

It seems to us that *Pelagos* and the works by Moore in Figures 5-24 and 5-31 are not space sculptures because, although they open up space within, the density of their materials dominates space. *Brussels*

Construction, on the other hand, is space sculpture because the spatial relationships are at least as interesting as the stainless steel. The fact that *Pelagos* was assembled in part and *Brussels Construction* was not is not conclusive. Assemblage is the technique generally used in space sculpture, but what we are perceiving and should be judging is the product, not the producing process. Of course, the producing process affects what is produced, and that is why it can be helpful to know about the producing process. That is why we went into some detail about the differences between modeling, carving, and assemblage. But the basis of a sound judgment about a work of art is that work as it is given to us in perception. Any kind of background information is relevant *provided* it aids that perception. But if we permit the producing process rather than the work of art itself to be the basis of our judgment—in the jargon of the critics this is called the "intentional fallacy"—we are led away from, rather than into, the work. This destroys the usefulness of criticism.

PERCEPTION KEY THE INTENTIONAL FALLACY

We have argued that we should not permit the producing process to be the basis of our critical judgments about what is produced—i.e., the work of art. But consider counterarguments. For example, suppose as you participate with *Brussels Construction* you imagine the alternatives Rivera had open to him. He could have used aluminum instead of stainless steel, made the work larger or smaller, or made the curves more or less complex, etc. Do not such conjectures enrich our participative experience? And if so, why shouldn't our understanding of the producing process have priority over the product in our critical judgments? These questions are subtle and difficult. Discuss them with others, for in being clear about these questions, you will, in turn, be clearer about many of the basic issues of criticism.

Contemporary Sculpture

Developments in sculpture are emerging and changing so quickly that no attempt can be made here even to begin to classify them. These developments fall into the species of low, medium, and high relief, sculpture in the round, space sculpture, earth sculpture, and some hybrids of these. But beyond that not-very-helpful generalization, the innovations of contemporary sculptors escape pigeonholing.

TRUTH TO MATERIALS

There is, however, at least one tendency, more of a reaffirmation than an innovation, that is fairly pervasive—respect for the materials used in the sculpture. In the flamboyancy of much of late Baroque, in the early-nineteenth-century Neoclassicism of many of the followers of Canova such as Thorwaldsen, and in some of the Romanticism of the later nineteenth century, respect for materials was ignored. In the twentieth century the realistic waxworks (Figure 5-22) of Madame Tussaud arc the ultimate conclusion of this ignorance. Karl Knappe refers to

> the crisis through which art [sculpture] is passing [is] one that concerns . . . the artistic media. An image cannot be created without regard for the laws of nature, and each kind of material has natural laws of its own. Every block of stone, every piece of wood is subject to its own rules. Every medium has, so to speak, its own tempo; the tempo of a pencil or a piece of charcoal is quite different from the tempo of a woodcut. The habit of mind which creates, for instance, a pen drawing cannot simply be applied mechanically to the making of a woodcut; to do this would be to deny the validity of the spiritual as well as the technical tempo.[14]

In contemporary sculpture, perhaps in part as a reaction, respect for materials has come back with a vengeance. It has even been given a name—"truth to materials."

PERCEPTION KEY TRUTH TO MATERIALS

1. Review the examples of twentieth-century sculpture we have discussed. Assuming that these examples are fairly representative, do you find a pervasive tendency to truth to materials? Do you find exceptions, and, if so, how might these be explained?
2. Henry Moore has stated that "Every material has its own individual qualities. It is only when the sculptor works direct, when there is an active relationship with his material, that the material can take its part in the shaping of an idea. Stone, for example, is hard and concentrated and should not be falsified to look like soft flesh—it should not be forced beyond its constructive build to a point of weakness. It should keep its hard tense stoniness."[15] Figures 5-31 and 5-32 by Moore are both in stone. Do they illustrate Moore's point? If so, point out as specifically as possible how this is done.
3. Can you imagine how human figures could be made in wax, as in Figure 5-22, and yet truth to wax as a material be maintained? If you think wax is a weak or even impossible material for the sculpture of human figures, try to see a wax work by Medardo Rosso (1858–1928). Some of his wax sculptures are in the Hirshhorn Museum in Washington, D. C. We are not including an illustration of them because the special quality of wax is completely lost in a photograph.

---

[14]Karl Knappe, quoted in Kurt Herberts, *The Complete Book of Artists' Techniques*, Thames and Hudson, 1958, p. 16. Published in the United States by Frederick A. Praeger.
[15]Quoted by Herbert Read, *Henry Moore, Sculptor*, A. Zwemmer, London, 1934, p. 29.

FIGURE 5-33 *Mother and Child*. From the Ivory Coast: Senufo. Wood, 26¾ by 7 inches. Private collection, Amsterdam.

In Moore's *Reclining Figure* (Figure 5-24), notice how the grains of wood flow over the shoulders and arms and down the body, and how these grains lead into the concavities and climax at the convexities, for example, the upper knee. The silhouette and contour lines were carved to conform to those grains, which, in turn, bring out the woodiness of the wood. This truth to materials can be found in the best of every sculptural tradition, even Canova's, but it is found almost everywhere in so-called primitive sculpture. Go to any such exhibition (North American Indian art is rather widely accessible) and you will invariably find this care for materials. African sculpture—the *Mother and Child* (Figure 5-33), for example, from the Ivory Coast—is especially notable in this respect. Societies in which technology has not been developed very far live much closer to nature than we do, and so their feeling for natural things usually is reverent.

As technology has gained more and more ascendancy, reverence toward natural things has receded. In highly industrialized societies, people tend to revere artificial things, and the pollution of our environment is one result. Another result is the flooding of the commercial market with imitations of primitive sculpture, which are easily identified because of the lack of truth to the materials (test this for yourself). Even the contemporary sculptors, as distinguished from the "hackers," have lost some of their innocence toward things simply because they live in a technological age. Most of them, however, are far more innocent than the rest of us. Many sculptors still possess something of the primitive way of feeling things, and so they find in primitive sculpture inspiration, even if to reach it requires repentance. Despite its abstract subject matter, Marta Pan's *Balance en deux* (Figure 5-34), with its reverence to walnut wood, has a close spiritual affinity to the *Mother and Child* (Figure 5-33).

Truth to material sculpture—such as Hepworth's (Figure 5-28), Moore's (Figures 5-24, 5-31, and 5-32) and Pan's (Figure 5-34)—is an implicit protest against technological ascendancy.

PROTEST AGAINST TECHNOLOGY

PERCEPTION KEY TROVA, SEGAL, GIACOMMETTI, AND TRŠAR

Is protest expressed against our technologically dominated culture in Trova's *Study; Falling Man (Wheelman)* (Figure 5-35)? Segal's *Bus Driver* (Figure 5-36)? Giacometti's *City Square* (Figure 5-37)? Tršar's *Demonstrators II* (Figure 5-38)? If so, is this protest implicit or explicit? If explicit, how is this accomplished in each of these four works?

Explicit protest is part of the subject matter of all these works, we think, although perhaps only in *Wheelman* is that protest unequivo-

FIGURE 5-34 Marta Pan, *Balance en Deux*. 1957. Collection of the artist.

cally directed at technology. Flaccid, faceless, and sexless, this anonymous robot has "grown" spoked wheels instead of arms. Attached below the hips these mechanisms produce a sense of eerie instability, a feeling that this antiseptically cleansed automaton with the slack, protruding abdomen may tip over from the slightest push. In this inhuman mechanical purity, no free will is left to resist. Human value, as articulated in Aldous Huxley's *Brave New World*, has been reduced to humanpower, functions performed in the world of goods and services. Since another individual can also perform these functions, the given person has no special worth. His or her value is a unit that can easily be replaced by another.

The Bus Driver is an example of "environmental sculpture." Grimly set behind a wheel and coin box taken from an old bus, the driver is a plaster cast made in sections over a living well-greased model. Despite the "real" environment and model, the stark white figure with its rough and generalized features is both real and strangely unreal. In the air around him, we sense the hubbub of the streets, the smell of fumes, the ceaseless comings and goings of unknown customers. Yet despite all these suggestions of a crowded, nervous atmosphere, there is a heartrending loneliness about this driver. Worn down day after day by the same grind, Segal's man, like Trova's, has been flattened into an *x*—a quantity.

In Giacometti's emaciated figures, the huge, solidly implanted feet suggest nostalgia for the earth; the soaring upward of the elongated bodies suggests aspiration for the heavens. The surrounding environment has eaten away at the flesh, leaving lumpy, irregular surfaces with dark hollows that bore into the bone. Each figure is without contact with anyone, as despairingly isolated as *The Bus Driver*. They stand in or walk through an utterly alienated space, but, unlike *Wheelman*, they seem to know it. And whereas the habitat of *Wheelman* is the clean, air-conditioned factory or office of *Brave New World*, Giacometti's people, even when in neat galleries, always seem to be in the grubby streets of our decaying cities. The cancer of the city has left only the armatures of bodies stained with nicotine and scarred with sickness. There is no center in this city square nor any exit, nor can we imagine any communication among these citizens. Their very grouping in the square gives them, paradoxically, an even greater feeling of isolation. Even the naked female, the only figure at a standstill, is ignored by the males. Each Giacometti figure separates a

FIGURE 5-35 Ernest Trova, *Study: Falling Man (Wheelman)*. 1965. Silicon bronze, one of six casts, 60 by 48 by 20^{13}⁄₁₆ inches. Collection, Walker Art Center, Minneapolis. Gift of the T. B. Walker Foundation.

FIGURE 5-36   George Segal, *The Bus Driver*. 1962. Figure of plaster over cheesecloth with bus parts, including coin box, steering wheel, driver's seat, railing, dashboard, etc. Figure, 53½ by 26⅞ by 45 inches; wood platform, 5⅛ inches by 6 feet 3 inches; overall height, 6 feet 3 inches. Collection, The Museum of Modern Art, New York. Philip Johnson Fund.

spot of space from the common place. The disease and utter distress of these vulnerable creatures demands our respectful distance, as if they were lepers to whom help must come, if at all, from some public agency.

The Demonstrators II is a powerful visual and tactile image of the potential violence embedded in mass demonstrations. More specifically, although the work was completed in 1957, it is an exceptional prophecy of the 1960s in the United States. To take just one example,

FIGURE 5-37   Alberto Giacometti, *City Square (La Place).* 1948. Bronze, 8½ by 25⅜ by 17¼ inches. Collection, The Museum of Modern Art, purchase.

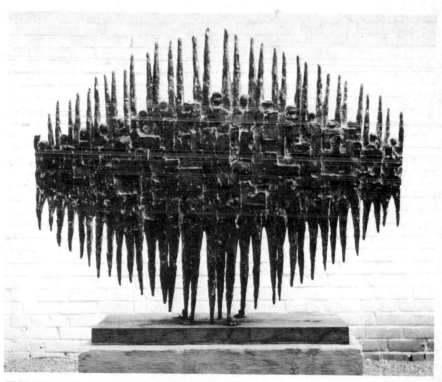

FIGURE 5-38   Drago Tršar, *The Demonstrators II.* 1957. Bronze, 53⅞ by 66⅞ inches. Photograph by Edvard Trier.

The Demonstrators II evokes images of the Kent State massacre: the anonymous mass of gas-masked guardsmen and their rifles, and the upraised arms of those in defiance packed together in a design that expresses blind, fanatical rigidity. No smiles lighten this rough dark mass. Light flashes like lightning. Irrationality reigns, as in a machine which has gotten beyond human control.

PERCEPTION KEY THE DEMONSTRATORS II AND KENT STATE

1. Do you believe it would be appropriate to place *The Demonstrators II* on the Kent State campus as a memorial?
2. Is it possible or likely that works of art can play a healing function in such highly explosive situations? Or can works of art make such a situation worse? Discuss with others.

To blame technology entirely for the dehumanization of man interpreted in these sculptures is a gross oversimplification, of course. But this kind of work does bring out something of the horror of technology when it is misused. Look around—there are people who have become scheduled by-products of the power plants. Technology can drive us into the dubious safety zones of isolation, as in Figure 5-37, or the herd, as in Figure 5-38. Works such as these vividly illuminate what we are all up against.

Accommodation with Technology

Not all contemporary sculptors are concerned in their work with the misuses of technology. Many see in technology blessings for human-kind. It is true that sculpture can be accomplished with the most primitive tools (that, incidentally, is one of the basic reasons why sculpture in primitive cultures apparently not only precedes painting but also usually dominates both qualitatively and quantitatively). Nevertheless, sculpture in our day, far more than painting, can take advantage of some of the most sophisticated advances of technology, surpassed in this respect only by architecture. Many sculptors today interpret the positive rather than the negative aspects of technology. This respect for technology is expressed by (1) truth to its materials or (2) care for its products or (3) showing forth its methodology.

David Smith's *Cubi X* (Figure 5-39), like Chryssa's *Times Square Sky* (Figure 5-7), illustrates truth to technological materials. But unlike Chryssa, Smith usually accomplishes this by wedding these materials to nature. The stainless steel cylinders of the *Cubi* support a juggling act of hollow rectangular and square cubes that barely touch one another as they cantilever out into space. Delicate buffing modulates

FIGURE 5-39 David Smith, *Cubi X.* 1963. Stainless steel; 10 feet 1⅜ inches × 6 feet 6¾ inches × 24 inches, including steel base 2⅞ × 25 × 23 inches. Collection, The Museum of Modern Art, New York. Robert G. Lord Fund.

the bright planes of steel giving the illusion of several atmospheric depths and reflecting light like rippling water. Occasionally, when the light is just right, the effect is like the cascading streams of fountains, recalling the Arabic inscription on the *Fountain of the Lions* in the Alhambra, Granada: "Liquid and solid things are so closely related that none who sees them is able to distinguish which is motionless and which is flowing." Usually, however, the steel reflects with more constancy the colorings of its environment. Smith writes, "I like outdoor sculpture and the most practical thing for outdoor sculpture is stainless steel, and I make them and I polish them in such a way that on a dull day, they take on the dull blue, or the color of the sky in the late afternoon sun, the glow, golden like the rays, the colors of nature. And in a particular sense, I have used atmosphere in a reflective way on the surfaces. They are colored by the sky and the surroundings, the green or blue of water. Some are down by the water and some are by the mountains. They reflect the colors. They are designed for outdoors."[16] But Smith's steel is not just a mirror, for in the reflections the fluid surfaces and tensile strength of the steel emerge in a structure that, as Smith puts it, "can face the sun and hold its own." There is a care for this manufactured material comparable to Pan's care for natural material (Figure 5-34).

Kurt Schwitters' *Merz Konstruktion* (Figure 5-40) is—except for the old wood—an assemblage of worn-out, discarded, and despised manufactured materials such as cardboard, wire mesh, paper, and nails. The waste of our world is brought to our attention. With sensitive ordering with respect to shape, texture, color, and density, these rejects are rehabilitated. We see and feel them, perhaps for the first time, as things in themselves, a little like returning to an old abandoned house we once lived in but ignored except for practical purposes. We made and used these things, Schwitters is informing us, and we should recognize that, despite their lowly status, they have a dignity, over and above their utility, that demands our respect.

John Chamberlain's *Velvet White* (Figure 5-41) is an example of "junk sculpture." Whereas Schwitters delicately assembled small industrial debris, Chamberlain roughly assembled large sheets of twisted, torn metal from junkyards. Most of these macabre shapes carry with them the gashes of violence—accident and death. A walk through a junkyard can be a terrifying experience. And Chamberlain preserves and makes even more vivid this fury and horror in the discipline of his composition. It is as if the torn metal were screaming. But there is something more—the metallic character of these industrial materials is allowed to shine forth, powerfully and even monumentally, for its own sake.

Pop sculpture respects the products of technology as well as its materials. Duchamp's *Bottle Rack* (Figure 5-42) of 1914 was probably not so intended. Duchamp at that time was poking fun at overblown artistic pretensions. One of his more hilarious inventions, for example, was a urinal placed on a pedestal and signed R. Mutt, the name of the manufacturer. Nevertheless, *Bottle Rack* and works like it became prototypes for the Pop sculptor of the 1950s and 1960s. By separating an industrial product from its utilitarian context and isolating it for our contemplation, the sculptor gives us opportunity to appreciate its intrinsic values. *Bottle Rack* is a "ready-made," for Duchamp had nothing to do with its making. But Duchamp was apparently the first to recognize the artistic qualities of what was then a very familiar object. The contrast of the diminishing rings with their spikey "branches" makes an interesting spatial pattern, especially if, as in Man Ray's photograph, light is played rhythmically on the rough surfaces of galvanized iron. Duchamp saw this possibility, for rarely are

[16]David Smith in Cleve Gray (ed.), *David Smith*, Holt, Rinehart and Winston, New York, 1968, p. 123.

FIGURE 5-40   Kurt Schwitters, *Merz Konstruktion.* 1921. Painted wood, wire, and paper; 14½ by 8½ inches. Philadelphia Museum of Art. The A. E. Gallatin Collection. Photograph by A. J. Wyatt, staff photographer.

FIGURE 5-41 John Chamberlain, *Velvet White*. 1962. Metal, 81½ inches high, 61 inches wide, 54½ inches deep. Collection of Whitney Museum of American Art, New York. Gift of the Albert A. List family.

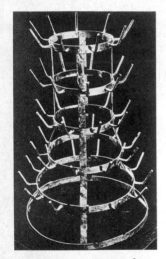

FIGURE 5-42 Marcel Duchamp. *Bottle Rack*. 1914. Galvanized iron, 23¼ inches high. Photograph of lost original by Man Ray.

bottle racks—or any other industrial products, for that matter—so effectively displayed.

Most Pop sculpture in recent years does not incorporate "ready-mades." By using material different from the original, attention often can be drawn more strongly to the product itself. For example, Oldenburg's *Giant Soft Fan* (Figure 5-43) is made in the functionally impossible materials of vinyl, wood, and foam rubber. Someone might be tempted to use *Bottle Rack* for practical purposes, but *Giant Soft Fan* completely frustrates such temptation. The scale and character of the fans of the marketplace, the ones we usually see only dimly, are completely changed. This 10-foot shining giant opens our eyes to the existence of all those everyday fans. As Oldenburg comments: "I want people to get accustomed to recognize the power of objects. . . . I alter to unfold the object and to add to it other object qualities."[17] This kind of sculpture is concerned not so much with the materials of our consumer world but with its products.

MACHINE SCULPTURE

Some avant garde sculptors are interested not so much in the materials and products of technology but rather in revealing the machine and its powers: their works are known as "machine sculpture." As in Calder's *Ghost* (Figure 5-8) and *Bougainvillea* (Figure 5-25), machine sculpture usually is "kinetic" or moving sculpture; but the motion of machine sculpture, unlike these works of Calder, is primarily a result of mechanical rather than natural forces. Sculptors in this tradition, going back to the ideas and work of László Moholy-Nagy after World War I, welcome the machine and its sculptural possibilities. Rivera hides his machine under *Brussels Construction* (Figure 5-29), but many machine sculptors expose their machines. They are interested not only in the power of the machine but also in the mechanisms that make that power possible. George Rickey, the literary prophet of machine sculpture, writes that "A machine is not a projection of anything. The crank-shaft exists in its own right; it *is* the image. . . . The concreteness of machines is heartening."[18]

PERCEPTION KEY TWO LINES—TEMPORAL I AND HOMAGE TO NEW YORK

1. Although depending upon air currents for its motion, Rickey's *Two Lines—Temporal I* (Figure 5-44) is basically a machine—two 35-foot stainless steel "needles" balanced on knife-edge fulcrums. Is this work just

[17]Quoted by Robert Goldwater in *What is Modern Sculpture?* The Museum of Modern Art, New York, n.d., p. 113.
[18]George Rickey, *Art and Artist*, University of California Press, Berkeley and Los Angeles, 1956, p. 172.

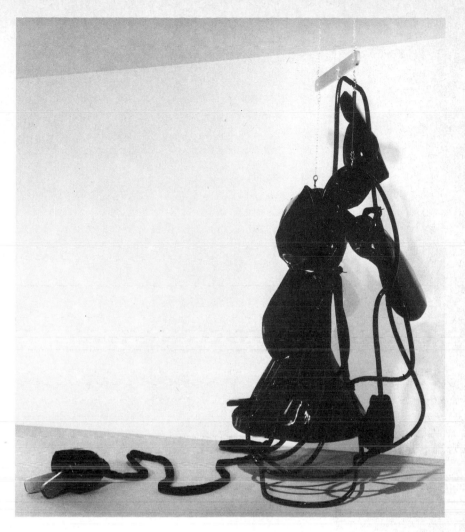

FIGURE 5-43 Claes Oldenburg, *Giant Soft Fan.* 1966–1967. Construction of vinyl with wood, foam rubber, metal, and plastic tubing; 10 feet by 58⅞ inches by 61⅞ inches, variables, plus cord and plug, 24 feet 3¼ inches. The Museum of Modern Art, New York. The Sidney and Harriet Janis Collection.

an image of itself as a machine? Or does it suggest other images? Does its subject matter include more than just machinery? As you reflect about this, can you imagine perhaps more appropriate places than the garden of The Museum of Modern Art for this work?

2. Is Jean Tinguely's *Homage to New York* (Figure 5-45) an image of itself as a machine? Does its subject matter include more than just machinery?

A good case can be made, we believe, for placing *Two Lines—Temporal I* in a grove of tall trees. Despite its mechanical character, this work belongs, like Calder's *Bougainvillea* (Figure 5-25) and Smith's *Cubi X* (Figure 5-39), in nature. Otherwise the lyrical poetry of its gentle swaying is reduced to a metronome. But even in its location

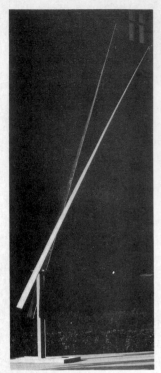

FIGURE 5-44 George Rickey, *Two Lines—Temporal I.* 1964–1967. Two stainless steel mobile blades on a painted steel base, 35 feet 4⅝ inches high. Collection, The Museum of Modern Art, New York. Mrs. Simon Guggenheim Fund.

FIGURE 5-45 Jean Tinguely, *Homage to New York.* 1960. Exhibited at the Museum of Modern Art, New York. Photograph by David Gahr.

in New York, it is much more than just an image of itself. *Two Lines—Temporal I* suggests something of the skeletal structure and vertical stretch of New York's buildings as well as something of the sway of the skyscrapers as we see them against the sky.

Tinguely is dedicated to humanizing the machine. His *Homage to New York,* exhibited at The Museum of Modern Art (New York) in

1960, is a better example than *Two Lines—Temporal I* of the image of the machine in its own right. The mechanical parts, collected from junk heaps and dismembered from their original machines, apparently stood out sharply, and yet they were linked together by their spatial locations, shapes, and textures, and sometimes by nervelike wires. Only the old player piano was intact. As the piano played, it was accompanied by howls and other weird sounds in irregular patterns that seemed to be issuing from the wheels, gears, and rods, as if they were painfully communicating with each other in some form of mechanical speech. Some of the machinery that runs New York City was exposed as vulnerable, pathetic, and comic, but Tinguely humanized this machinery as he exposed it. Even death was suggested, for *Homage to New York* was self-destructing: the piano was electronically wired for burning and, in turn, the whole structure collapsed.

Rather than exposing the machine, sculptors such as Len Lye are more interested in manifesting the powers of the machine. Works of this type are usually highly expensive and, up to the present time, rarely exhibited. Unfortunately, it is also very difficult to appreciate their effectiveness except by direct participation. One hopes, however, that more of this kind of sculpture will be made available. Lye's *The Loop* (Figure 5-46) was first exhibited in Buffalo in 1965, and he provided the following description in the exhibition catalogue:

> *The Loop*, a twenty-two foot strip of polished steel, is formed into a band, which rests on its back on a magnetized bed. The action starts when the charged magnets pull the loop of steel downwards, and then release it suddenly. As it struggles to resume its natural shape, the steel band bounds upwards and lurches from end to end with simultaneous leaping and rocking motions, orbiting powerful reflections at the viewer and emitting fanciful musical tones which pulsate in rhythm with *The Loop*. Occasionally, as the boundless Loop reaches its greatest height, it strikes a suspended ball, causing it to emit a different yet harmonious musical note, and so it dances to a weird quavering composition of its own making.[19]

FIGURE 5-46 Len Lye, *The Loop*. 1963. Stainless steel, 60 by 6 inches. The Art Institute of Chicago.

In work such as *The Loop*, the machine is programmed independently of the environment. In "cyborg [cybernetic organism] sculpture," the machine, by means of feedback, is integrated with its environment, often including the participant. Thus the sixteen pivoting polychromed plates of Nicolas Schöffer's aluminum and steel frame *CYSP I* (Figure 5-47)—a name composed of the first letters of "cybernetics" and "spatio-dynamics"—are operated by small motors located under their axes. Built into the structure are photoelectric cells and microphones sensitive to a wide range of variations in the fields of color, light, and sound. These changes feed into an electronic brain (housed in the base of the sculpture) which, in turn, activates four sets of motor-powered wheels. Depending on the stimuli, the sculpture

[19]*Len Lye's Bounding Steel Sculptures*, Howard Wise Gallery, New York, 1965.

FIGURE 5-47 Nicolas Schöffer, *CYSP I.* 1956. Aluminum and steel. Courtesy of Nicolas Schöffer.

will move more or less rapidly about the floor, turning more or less sharp angles. Blue, for example, excites rapid movement and makes the plates turn quickly. Darkness and silence are also exciting, whereas intense light and noise are calming. Complex stimuli produce, as in human beings, unpredictable behavior. Moreover, the participant takes part in making the sculpture "come alive." In such work, technical methodology is extended not only to the sculpture but also to ourselves.

PERCEPTION KEY CYSP I

Does it strike you as surprising that with *CYSP I* darkness and silence are activating stimuli, whereas intense light and sound are nonactivating? Can you explain why Schöffer did this?

Harold Lehr has created machine sculptures with an ecological function. Looking like buoys or markers (Figure 5-48), they are placed in waters such as the East River of New York City, where they were first exhibited in 1971. Inside the sculptures are pumps and filters, powered by the sun and wind, which constantly clean the surrounding water. Lehr sees his sculptures as

a visual connection between two primordial forms of nature—water and air. The sculpture's interaction takes many forms. It is seen on two levels. One when tides, winds, waves and currents affect movement and they skim across the water as a group or divide and scatter randomly. Weather, light, and the water's surface also affect this visual appearance. Secondly, interaction is visible over a period of time. It involves the sculpture's response to the animating variety of nature. As it responds to the wind and ocean, it moves and changes. Some of this energy is converted into electricity, which is stored and used to purify water. As a result, positive change is created. Cleaner water is a better environment. Sea life is attracted to the man-made structures, and the area is improved.[20]

PERCEPTION KEY MACHINE SCULPTURE

Can you conceive of any other kind of machine sculpture that would have an ecological function? Try your hand at some designs.

Machine sculptures are being developed in many forms. For example, there are water-driven sculptures, works suspended in midair by magnets or by jets of air or water, synthetic membranes stretched like sails by mechanical forces, color and motion produced by polarized light, and mechanically powered environmental sculpture (although such power is absent in *The Bus Driver*, Figure 5-36). Many of these developments are more experimental than artistic—the engineer often dominates the artist. But the story is just beginning, and it will be fascinating to watch its unfolding. At the very least, machine sculpture has had considerable stimulating effect upon the more conventional species of sculpture. No machinery, for instance, is involved in Marta Pan's *Floating Sculpture* (Figure 5-49). The structure was based on carved wood and then cast in polyester. But like much of the work of Rickey (Figure 5-44) and Schöffer (Figure 5-47), Pan calls on the environment—in this case the movement of water and wind—for assistance. And, of course, the right kind of landscape is all-important for the full realization of this graceful structure.

EARTH SCULPTURE

Finally, another avant garde sculpture—"earth sculpture"—even goes so far as to make the earth itself the medium, the site, and the subject matter. The proper spatial selection becomes absolutely essential, for

FIGURE 5-48 Harold Lehr, Ecological sculptures. 1971. Courtesy of Harold Lehr.

[20]*The New York Times*, January 23, 1972. © by The New York Times Company. Reprinted by permission.

FIGURE 5-49 Marta Pan, *Floating Sculpture.* 1967. Polyester, 180 centimeters high. Rijksmuseum Kröller-Moller, Otterlood (G.). Copyright Holland.

the earth usually must be taken where it is found. Forms are traced in plains, meadows, sand, snow, etc., in order to help make us stop and perceive and enjoy the "form site"—the earth transformed to be more meaningful. Usually nature rapidly breaks up the form and returns the site to its less ordered state. Accordingly, many earth sculptors have a special need for the photographer to preserve their art.

PERCEPTION KEY EARTH SCULPTURE

Study Michael Heizer's *Circumflex* (Figure 5-50), a 120-foot-long design "carved" out of the bed of a dry lake in Nevada.

1. Does the fact that probably the circumflex will be silted up in time disqualify this work as art? As you reflect about this, does the fact that the work has been elegantly photographed become relevant? Discuss with others.
2. Does the circumflex help bring out and make you notice the "earthiness" of the earth? The line of the mountain in the distance? The relation of the plain to the mountain?
3. Does the circumflex appear too large, too small, or just right in relation to the landscape?
4. Why do you think Heizer used such a long, free-flowing line juxtaposed against an almost geometrical oval?
5. Suppose works like this were found abundantly throughout the United States. Would you find this objectionable?

Sculpture and Architecture

All sculpture requires a proper spatial placement. Thus architecture, the most spatial of all the arts, has always been closely associated with sculpture. Indeed, architect and sculptor were usually the same person until after the Renaissance. And it has only been in our time that sculpture has gained complete independence. With works in the open air such as Calder's *Bougainvillea* (Figure 5-25), Smith's *Cubi X* (Figure 5-39), Pan's *Floating Sculpture* (Figure 5-49), and Heizer's *Circumflex* (Figure 5-50), sculpture has proved that it can be autonomous. The partnership of sculpture and architecture remains very close, nevertheless, for both must often share the same space. And despite the orientation of much contemporary sculpture to open air landscape,

FIGURE 5-50 Michael Heizer, *Circumflex*. 1968. Massacre Creek Dry Lake, 120 feet long.

that landscape often necessarily and sometimes happily includes buildings. The sculpture of Rome's famous Trevi Fountain, for example, is much more effective against its building than it would be in an entirely open space. Rickey's *Two Lines—Temporal I* (Figure 5-44) is a rather exceptional example because it can work well with or without architecture. Sculpture can be effectively related to city squares as centers of traffic, as so often with fountains; to the approaches to large cities, as with *The Five Towers of the Satellite City* (Figure 5-5) outside Mexico City; to factories, as with Pevsner's *Bird Soaring*,[21] in front of the General Motors Company Technical Center in Detroit; to schools and churches and airports, etc. Every building, if it has architectural value, seems to lend itself to appropriate sculpture. Gabo's *Rotterdam Construction* (Figures 5-51 and 5-52) in front of De Bijenkorf, a store in Rotterdam designed by Marcel Breuer, is a monumentally successful solution to what might seem to have been an impossible commission. The open vertical construction, rooted like a tree but branching out more like the cranes and bridges of Rotterdam, brings out with striking clarity the compact horizontal mass of the building. Rarely have sculpture and architecture achieved such powerful synthesis. But we are leaping ahead. Such a judgment is surely dogmatic without a better understanding of architecture.

Summary

Sculpture is perceived differently from painting, engaging more acutely our sense of touch and the motion of our body. Whereas painting is more about the visual appearance of things, sculpture is more about things as three-dimensional masses. Whereas painting only *represents* voluminosity and density, sculpture *presents*. Sculpture in the round, especially, brings out the three-dimensionality of objects. No object is more important to us than our body, and its "strange thickness" is always "with" us. When the human body is the subject matter, sculpture more than any other art reveals a material counterpoint for our mental images of our body. Traditional sculpture is made either by modeling or carving. Many contemporary sculptures, however, are made by assembling preformed pieces of material. New sculptural techniques and materials have opened up developments in avant-garde sculpture that defy classification. Nonetheless, contemporary sculptors, generally, have emphasized "truth to materials," respect for the media that is organized by their forms. They have also had to come to grips with modern technology, either protesting its misuses or interpreting its positive aspects.

[21]It is noteworthy that this work was placed by Eero Saarinen, an architect. He made an enlarged bronze cast from Pevsner's *Column of Victory* (1946) and erected it with a new name in 1956 in a site that enhances both the sculpture and the architecture.

FIGURE 5-51 Naum Gabo, *Rotterdam Construction.* 1954–1957. Steel, bronze wire, free stone substructure; 85 feet high. Copyright, Tom Kroeze, Rotterdam.

Chapter 5 Bibliography

Adriani, Bruno. *Problems of the Sculptor.* New York: Nierendorf Gallery, 1943.

Anderson, Wayne. *American Sculpture in Process: 1930/1970.* Boston: New York Graphic Society, 1975.

Burnham, Jack. *Beyond Modern Sculpture.* New York: George Braziller, 1967.

Elsen, Albert E. *Origins of Modern Sculpture.* New York: George Braziller, 1974.

FIGURE 5-52 Naum Gabo, *Rotterdam Construction*. 1954–1957. Netherlands National Tourist Office, New York.

Giedion-Welker, Carola. *Contemporary Sculpture: An Evolution in Volume and Space.* New York: George Wittenborn, 1960.

Hammacher, A. M. *The Evolution of Modern Sculpture.* New York: Abrams, n.d.

James, Phillip, ed. *Henry Moore on Sculpture.* London: Macdonald, 1966.

Kelly, James J. *The Sculptural Idea.* 2d ed. Minneapolis: Burgess, 1974.

Krauss, Rosalind E. *Passages in Modern Sculpture.* New York: Viking, 1977.

Licht, Fred. *Sculpture: 19th & 20th Centuries.* Greenwich, Conn.: New York Graphic Society, 1967.

Martin, F. David. *Sculpture and Enlivened Space: Aesthetics and History.* Lexington, Ky.: University Press of Kentucky, 1981.

Read, Herbert. *The Art of Sculpture.* 2d ed. Princeton, N. J.: Princeton University Press, 1961.

Rodin, Auguste. *Art* (any edition).

Trier, Eduard. *Form and Space.* New York: Frederick A. Praeger, 1962.

Wittkower, Rudolf. *Sculpture: Processes and Principles.* New York: Harper and Row, 1977.

ARCHITECTURE

Buildings constantly assault us. Our only temporary escape is to the rarely accessible wilderness. We can close the novel, shut off the music, refuse to go to a play or dance, sleep through a movie, shut our eyes to a painting or a sculpture. But we cannot escape from buildings for very long, even in the wilderness. Fortunately, however, sometimes buildings possess artistic quality—that is, they are architecture—drawing us to them rather than pushing us away or making us ignore them. They make our living space more livable.

Space in General

Space is a relation of things, not a thing itself. Space in its full reality is the power we feel in the positioned interrelationships of things. Space is not reducible to a mere collection of given things. Nor is space an envelope containing the sum of such given things, although since Newton—and despite Einstein—space is usually so conceived. Space is not a thing, and yet, because of the positioned interrelationships of things, space "spaces"; it manifests itself somewhat like a thing. Space shows a vitality that can be felt. Usually we pass by this power, however, because we tend to notice explicitly the position of things only when we use them. We abstract from the full reality of space and see space only as a means. We *know* space, for we perceive and understand things in their positioned interrelationships; but because of the anaesthesia of practicality, we fail to *feel* space, the power of these interrelationships.

PERCEPTION KEY SPACE AS THE POSITIONED INTERRELATIONSHIPS OF THINGS

1. How often in the last few days have you felt space as the positioned interrelationships of things? For example, did the furniture of some room bother you because it cramped your movement? Did the ceiling of some room give you a feeling of claustrophobia because it was too low in relation to the width and length of the room? Did the space around and between some buildings make you feel comfortable or uncomfortable?
2. Is there any space that seems to give your community a center, something like the hub of a wheel? Do the positioned interrelationships of buildings in your nearest shopping center invite you gracefully into the center? Are there any spaces in your community that draw you to them? That stand out? That you are blind to? That are repulsive? Are there any buildings in your community that seem to draw the sky and earth together harmoniously?

Centered Space

Painters do not command real three-dimensional space: they only feign it. Sculptors can mold out into space, but generally they do not enfold an enclosed or inner space for our movement. The "holes" in the sculpture of Henry Moore (Figures 5-24 and 5-31), for example, are to be walked around, not into, whereas our passage through its inner spaces is one of the conditions under which the solids and voids of a work of architecture have their effect. In a sense, architecture is a great hollowed-out sculpture that we perceive by moving about both outside and inside. Space is the material of the architect, the primeval cutter,[1] who carves apart an inner space from an outer space in such a way that both spaces become more fully perceptible and, in turn, more intrinsically valuable. Invisible air is rendered perceivable. Inside the building, space is filled with emergent forces. Outside, space becomes organized and focused. The enfolded inner space is anchored to the earth. The convergent outer space is oriented around the inner space. Sunlight, rain, snow, mist, and night fall gracefully upon the cover protecting the inner space as if drawn by a channeled and purposeful gravity, as if these events of the outside belonged to the inside as much as the earth from which the building rises.

Inner and outer space come together to the earth to form a

[1]This meaning is suggested by the Greek *architectón*.

centered and illuminated context or clearing. Centered space is the positioned interrelationships of things organized *around* some paramount thing as the place to which the other things seem to converge. Sometimes this center is a natural thing, such as a great mountain, river, canyon, or forest. Sometimes the center is a natural site enhanced by a work of architecture. Listen to Martin Heidegger, the great German thinker, describing a bridge:

> The bridge swings over the stream "with ease and power." It does not just connect banks that are already there. The banks emerge as banks only as the bridge crosses the stream. The bridge designedly causes them to lie across from each other. One side is set off against the other by the bridge. Nor do the banks stretch along the stream as indifferent border stripes of the dry land. With the banks, the bridge brings to the stream the one and the other expanse of the landscape lying behind them. It brings stream and bank and land into each other's neighborhood. The bridge *gathers* the earth as landscape around the stream. Thus, it guides and attends the stream through the meadows. Resting upright in the stream's bed, the bridge piers bear the swing of the arches that leave the stream's waters to their own course. The waters may wander on quiet and gay, the sky's floods from storm or thaw may shoot past the piers in torrential waves—the bridge is ready for the sky's weather and its fickle nature. Even where the bridge covers the stream, it holds its flow up to the sky by taking it for a moment under the vaulted gateway and then setting it free once more.
>
> The bridge lets the stream run its course and at the same time grants their way to mortals so that they may come and go from shore to shore. Bridges lead in many ways. The city bridge leads from the precincts of the castle to the cathedral square; the river bridge near the country town brings wagons and horse teams to the surrounding villages. The old stone bridge's humble brook crossing gives to the harvest wagon its passage from the fields into the village and carries the lumber cart from the field path to the road. The highway bridge is tied into the network of long-distance traffic, paced as calculated for maximum yield. Always and ever differently the bridge escorts the lingering and hastening ways of men to and fro, so that they may get to other banks and in the end, as mortals, to the other side.[2]

If we are near such bridges we tend to be drawn into their clearing, for—unless practical urgencies have completely desensitized our senses either momentarily or habitually—centered space has an overpowering dynamism that captures both our attention and our bodies. Centered space propels us out of the ordinary modes of experience in which space is used as a means. Centered space is centripetal, insisting upon drawing us in. There is an inrush that is difficult to escape, that overwhelms and makes us acquiescent. We perceive space not as a receptacle containing things but rather as a context energized by the positioned interrelationships of things. Centered space has a pulling power that, even in our most harassed moments, we can hardly help

[2]Martin Heidegger, *Poetry, Language, Thought*, trans. Albert Hofstadter, Copyright © 1971 by Martin Heidegger. By permission of Harper & Row, Publishers, Inc. pp. 152f.

FIGURE 6-1   Piazza
before St. Peter's. Alinari.

feeling. In such places as the Piazza before St. Peter's (Figure 6-1), we walk slowly and speak softly. We find ourselves in the presence of a power that seems beyond our control. We feel the sublimity of space, but, at the same time, the centeredness beckons and welcomes us.

No special training is required to feel the sublimity of space, its overwhelming power. Space is breathing space, a clearing, and yet space exerts its power by pushing in on us. Gravitational force is the most obvious manifestation of this power, for gravity works continuously on every aspect of our lives. Without some sensitivity to space we could not survive. But because of life's exigencies, we learn to push things around in space. Insofar as this pushing succeeds easily and efficiently (and in a technological age such success becomes increasingly possible), space tends to become no more than a framework—a vacuous place—within which we manipulate the positions of things. We become insensitive to the intrinsic values of the positioned interrelationships of things. We become explicitly conscious of space only when things in their interrelationships frustrate us, and then only as an area within which we have to work. Space becomes a part of a problem. In this aggressiveness we enslave space to the point that we pass by the power of space. Then it takes either the embracing thrust of the great spaces of nature (and these spaces, such as in and around the Grand Canyon, are always centered to some significant extent) or the centered spaces of architecture to return us to an explicit awareness of the power and the embrace of the positioned interrelationships of things.

Space and Architecture

Architecture—as opposed to mere engineering—is the creative conservation of space. Architects perceive the centers of space in nature, and build to preserve these centers and make them more vital. Architects are confronted by centered spaces that desire to be made, through them, into works. These spaces of nature are not offspring of architects alone but appearances that step up to them, so to speak, and demand protection. If an architect succeeds in carrying through these appeals, the power of the natural space streams forth through that person and the work arises. Architects are the shepherds of space. In turn, the paths around their shelters lead us away from our ordinary preoccupations demanding the use of space. We come to rest. Instead of our using up space, space takes possession of us with a ten-fingered grasp. We have a place to dwell.

CHARTRES

On a hot summer day some years ago, following the path of Henry Adams, one of the authors was attempting to drive from Mont Saint Michel to Chartres in time to catch the setting sun through the western rose window of Chartres Cathedral. The following is an account of this experience:

> In my rushing anxiety—I had to be in Paris the following day and I had never been to Chartres before—I became oblivious of space except as providing landmarks for my time-clocked progress. Thus I have no significant memories of the towns and countrysides I hurried through. Late that afternoon the two spires of Chartres (Figures 6-2 and 6-3), like two strangely woven strands of rope let down from the heavens, gradually came into focus. The blue dome of the sky also became visible for the first time, centering as I approached more and more firmly around the axis of those spires. "In lovely blueness blooms the steeple with metal roof" (Hölderlin). The surrounding fields and then the town, coming out now in all their specificity, grew into tighter unity with the church and sky. Later, I recalled a passage from Aeschylus: "The pure sky desires to penetrate the earth, and the earth is filled with love so that she longs for blissful unity with the sky. The rain falling from the sky impregnates the earth, so that she gives birth to plants and grain for beasts and men." No one rushed in or out or around the church. The space around seemed alive and dense with slow currents all ultimately being pulled to and through the central portal.[3] Inside, the space (Figure 6-4), although spacious far

[3]Chartres, like most Gothic churches, is shaped roughly like a recumbent Latin cross:

The front (Figure 6-3)—with its large circular window shaped like a rose and the three vertical windows or lancets beneath—faces west. The apse or eastern end of the building contains the high altar. The nave (Figure 6-4) is the central and largest aisle leading from the central portal to the high altar. But before the altar is reached, the transept cuts across the nave. The crossing is the meeting point of the nave and the transept. Both the north and south facades of the transept of Chartres contain, like the western facade, glorious rose windows.

FIGURE 6-2 Chartres Cathedral. Courtesy Cliché HOUVET.

beyond the scale of practical human needs, seemed strangely compressed, full of forces thrusting and counterthrusting in dynamic interrelations. Slowly, in the cool silence inlaid with stone, I was drawn down the long nave, following the stately rhythms of the columns. But my eyes also followed the vast vertical stretches far up into the shifting shadows of the vaultings. It was as if I were being borne aloft. Yet I continued down the narrowing tunnel of the nave, but more and more slowly as the pull of the space above held back the pull of the space below. At the crossing of the transept, the flaming colors, especially the reds, of the northern and southern roses transfixed my slowing pace, and then I turned back at last to the western rose and the three lancets beneath—a delirium of color, dominantly blue, was pouring through. Earthbound on the crossing, the blaze of the Without was merging with the Within. Radiant space took complete possession of my senses. In the protective grace of this sheltering space, even the outer space which I had dismissed in the traffic of my driving seemed to converge around the center of this crossing. Instead of being *alongside* things—the church, the town, the fields, the sky, the sun—I was *with* them, at one with them. This housing of holiness made me feel at home in this strange land.

FIGURE 6-3 Chartres Cathedral, the west front. 1194–1260. Copyright A. F. Kersting.

Living Space

Living space is the feeling of the positioning of things in the environment, liberty of movement, and the appeal of paths as directives. Taking possession of space is our first gesture as infants, and sensitivity to the position of other things is a prerequisite of life. Space infiltrates through all our senses, and our sensations of everything

FIGURE 6-4 Chartres
Cathedral, interior.
Courtesy Editions
HOUVET Cliché
FRANCESCHI.

influence our perception of space. A breeze broadens the spaciousness of a room that opens on a garden. A sound tells us something about the surfaces and shape of that room. A cozy temperature brings the furniture and walls into more intimate relationships. The smell of books gives that space a personality. Each of our senses helps record the positioning of things, expressed in such terms as "up–down," "left–right," and "near–far." These recordings require a reference system with a center. With abstract space, as when we estimate distances visually, the center is the zero point located between the eyes. With living space, since all the senses are involved, the whole body is a center. Furthermore, when we relate to a place of special value, such as the home, a "configurational center" is formed, a place that is a gathering point around which a field of interests is structured. If we oversimplify, we can say that for peasants their farms, those places to which they most naturally belong, constitute their configurational center—with Romans it was Rome, with medieval people the church and castle, with Babbitt the office, with Sartre the café, and with De Gaulle the nation. But for most people at almost any time, although probably more so in contemporary times, there are more than a couple of centers. Often these are more or less confused and changing. In living space, nevertheless, places, principal directions, and distances arrange themselves around configurational centers.

The configurational center is our personal space, to some extent private and protected. Outside the configurational center, space is more public and dangerous. The security of the home gradually lessens as we step out through the door into the yard, into the immediate neighborhood, and then into more remote places. As we move onto the typical super highway in the northeastern United States, for example, the concrete cuts abusively into the earth and through the landscape as straight as possible, with speed the only aim. The arteries of commerce pump efficiency, and there is no time for piety to space. Everyone passes hurriedly, aloof from both other people and centered spaces. There is no place for pedestrians or vistas or peace. Even the roadside rests, if any, for the fatigued driver are drowned in the whine of tires. The necessities such as gas stations, restaurants, and motels are usually repetitious vulgarities that excite us to move on. Everyone from the hitchhiker to the other motorist is a threat. Only a police car or a severe accident is likely to slow us down. The machine takes over, and when we have reached our destination *on time*, the machine mentality is likely to maintain its grip. Space is sacrificed to time.

Such desecration of space may even lead us to forget our configurational center that gives orientation and meaning to other spaces. Then orientation with reference to intrinsic values is lacking. We become displaced persons, refugees from ourselves. Then living space, private as well as public, becomes merely used space. And then used space tends to become geometrical space, for the efficient use of used space requires precise placements. Space becomes a static schematic vacuum. The geometricians measure out coordinate systems whereby everything is related quantitatively. The centers now are entirely impersonal, for the basic characteristic of geometrical space is its homogeneity. No center and no direction in this democracy of places has more value than another. When we want to move through space most efficiently, geometrical space provides the map. To the degree that efficiency of movement dominates our concerns, living space becomes abstract space. Like the lumber barons of California ripping out the redwoods, we see straight through space. We still see things and the "between" of things, but only as means. Space itself—the power and hospitality of the positioned interrelationships of things—is ignored. Space becomes a wasteland.

PERCEPTIONAL KEY NON-ARCHITECTURAL BUILDINGS

1. Select a house that strikes you as the ugliest or one of the ugliest in your community. Now analyze why you make this judgment.
2. Do the same for an apartment house, a school building, an office building, a gas station, a supermarket, a city street, a bridge.

FIGURE 6-5   Richard Upjohn, Trinity Church. 1839–1846. Broadway at Wall Street, New York City. Photograph by Eric Hass.

A building that is not architecture, even if it encloses a convenient void, encourages us to ignore it. Normally we will be blind to such a building and its space as long as it serves its practical purposes. If the roof leaks or a wall breaks down, however, then we will see the building, but only as a damaged instrument. A building that is a work of architecture—by being a place around which other things appear to converge—brings us back to living space by centering space. Such a building raises to clarity preceding impressions of the scene that were obscure and confused. The potentialities of power in the positioned interrelationships of things are captured and channeled. Our feeling for space is reawakened. We become aware of the power and embrace of space.

PERCEPTION KEY CHARTRES AND TRINITY CHURCH

Compare the facade and spires of Chartres Cathedral (Figure 6-3) with the facade and spire of Trinity Church (Figure 6-5) in New York City.

1. The spire of Trinity Church is higher than the spires of Chartres. Is this surprising? Why?
2. Do you believe that a church ought to dominate strongly the space that surrounds it? Would you expect a building that houses a dental clinic, for example, to dominate its surrounding space as strongly as a church does? Does Trinity Church dominate its surrounding space as strongly as does Chartres?

3. Which church seems best able to perform its function as a place of worship?
4. Which church seems to reveal religious values more profoundly?

When it was built in the nineteenth century, the spire of Trinity Church must have brought the sky of Manhattan into intimate relationship with the earth, somewhat the way Chartres still does for its region. But now the thrust of the spire of Trinity is impotent, because the outer space it once centered is swamped by skyscrapers. Now the office buildings of Wall Street dominate that space. Commercial values look down upon religious values. If the church were a dental clinic, this would not seem odd. Or maybe this does not seem odd to you—but imagine how Richard Upjohn, the architect, would feel at the sight of his church if by some miracle he were to return to Wall Street.

The Architect

The architect's professional life is perhaps more difficult than that of any other artist. Architecture is a peculiarly public art because buildings generally have a social function, and many buildings require public funds. More than other artists, the architects must consider the public. If they do not, very few of their plans are likely to materialize. Thus architects must be psychologists, sociologists, economists, business people, politicians, and courtiers. They must also be engineers, for they must be able to construct structurally stable buildings. And even then they need luck. Upjohn could hardly have foreseen the fate of his church. And even as famous an architect as Frank Lloyd Wright could not prevent the destruction, for economic reasons, of one of his masterpieces—the Imperial Hotel in Tokyo.

Architects have to take into account four basic and closely interrelated necessities: technical or structural requirements, functioning or use, spatial relationships, and content. To succeed, their structures must adjust themselves to these necessities. As for what time will do to their creations, they can only prepare with foresight and hope. Wright's hotel withstood all the earthquakes, but ultimately every building is peculiarly susceptible to the whims of future taste.

Technical Requirements of Architecture

The structural requirements of a building are the most obvious of architects' necessities. Their buildings must stand (and withstand). Architects must know the materials and their potentialities, how to put the materials together, and how the materials will work on a particular site. Stilt construction, for instance, will not withstand earthquakes—and so architects are also engineers. But they are something more as well—artists. In solving their technical problems, they must also make their forms revelatory. Their buildings must illuminate something significant that we would otherwise fail to perceive.

Consider, for example, the relationship between the engineering requirements and artistic qualities of the Parthenon, 447–432 B.C. (Figures 6-6 and 6-7). The engineering was superb, but unfortunately the building was almost destroyed in 1687, when it was being used as an ammunition dump by the Turks and was hit by a shell from a Venetian gun. Basically the technique used was post-and-lintel (or beam) construction. Set on a base or stylobate, columns (verticals) support the architrave (horizontals) which, in turn, composes, along with the frieze, the entablature that supports the pediment and roof.

PERCEPTION KEY PARTHENON AND CHARTRES

Study the schematic drawing of the Doric order (Figure 6-8), the order followed in the Parthenon, and Figures 6-6 and 6-7.

1. Why were the narrow vertical grooves or flutes carved into the marble columns of the Parthenon?
2. Why do the columns bulge or swell slightly? (This curvature is called "entasis.")
3. Why are the columns wider at the base than at the top?
4. Why is there a capital between the top of the shaft and the architrave (the

FIGURE 6-6 The Athenian Acropolis, with the Parthenon. 447–432 B.C. Photograph by Greek National Tourist Office, New York.

FIGURE 6-7 The Parthenon. 447–432 B.C. Photograph by Greek National Tourist Office, New York.

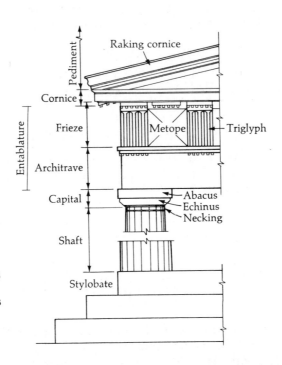

FIGURE 6-8 Elements of the Doric order. Adapted from John Ives Sewell, *A History of Western Art*, rev. ed., Holt, Rinehart and Winston, New York, 1961.

Pediment

Raking cornice

Cornice

Frieze

Metope

Triglyph

Entablature

Architrave

Capital

Abacus
Echinus
Necking

Shaft

Stylobate

Upper diameter

Entasis (shaded)

Entasis begins

About $\frac{1}{3}$ height

Lower diameter

Entasis of a column (slightly exaggerated)

plain lintels that span the voids from column to column and compose the lowest member of the entablature)?

5. The capital is made up of three parts: the circular grooves at the bottom (called the necking); the bulging cushionlike molding (called the echinus); and the square block (called the abacus). Why the division of the capital into these three parts?

6. The columns at the corners are a couple of inches thicker than the other columns. Why?

7. The corner and adjacent columns are slightly closer together than the other columns. Why?

8. All the columns slant slightly inward. Why?

9. Subtle refinements such as those mentioned above abound throughout the Parthenon. Few if any of them are necessary from a technical standpoint, nor were these irregularities accidental. They are found repeatedly in other Greek temples of the time. Presumably, then, they are a result of a need to make the form of the temple mean something, to be a form-content. Presumably then the Parthenon can still reveal something of the values of the ancient Greeks. What? Compare those values with the values revealed by Chartres. For example, which building seems to reveal a society that places more trust in God? And what kind of God? And in what way are those subtle refinements we have cited above relevant to these questions?

Functional Requirements of Architecture

Architects must make their buildings not only stand but also usually stand them in such a way that they reveal their function or use. One contemporary school of architects even goes so far as to claim that form must follow function. If the form succeeds in this, that is all the form should do. In any case, a form that disguises the function of a building seems to irritate almost everyone.

PERCEPTION KEY FUNCTION AND ARCHITECTURE

1. If the interior of Trinity Church (Figure 6-5) were remodeled into a dental clinic, would you feel dissatisfied with the relationship between the new interior and the old exterior?

2. Study Figure 6-9. What is the function of this building?

3. Are you surprised to learn that this is a high school?

4. Is this building architecture?

5. Would you like to have such a building as a high school in your community? Does this involve you in the question of what architecture is?

6. In your opinion, what must a building be to be a work of architecture?

If form follows function in the sense that the form "stands for" the function of its building, then conventional forms or structures are often sufficient. No one is likely to mistake Trinity Church for an

FIGURE 6-9 High school in Edinburgh.

office building. We have seen the conventional structures of too many churches and office buildings to be mistaken about this. Nor are we likely to mistake the surrounding office buildings for churches. We recognize the functions of these buildings because they are in the conventional shapes that such buildings so often possess.

PERCEPTION KEY FORM, FUNCTION, CONTENT, AND SPACE

Study Figures 6-10 and 6-11.

1. What is the basic function of each of these buildings?
2. Notice that neither building has the commonplace conventional shapes that are seen in Figure 6-5. Then how do you know what the functions are? How have the respective forms revealed the functions of their buildings? And does it seem more appropriate to use the term "reveal" for Figures 6-10 and 6-11, suggesting that these buildings have content, that their forms are revelatory, whereas the forms in Figure 6-5 are not? In other words, that in Figure 6-5 the forms are basically clichés and less than artistic because they fail to interpret the functions of their buildings? Would you agree that the buildings in Figure 6-5 are less than architecture, whereas the buildings in Figures 6-10 and 6-11 *are* architecture? And that they are architecture because the form of the building in Figure 6-11 is revelatory of the subject matter—of the tension, anguish, striving, and ultimate concern of religious faith; whereas in Figure 6-10 the form of the building is revelatory of the stripped-down, uniform efficiency of an American business corporation? Consider every possible relevant argument.
3. In Figures 6-10 and 6-11, do the buildings center and organize their surrounding spaces? If so, how is this accomplished?

Study one of Frank Lloyd Wright's last and most famous works, the Solomon R. Guggenheim Museum in New York City (Figures 6-12

FIGURE 6-10 Union Carbide Building, New York City. Photograph by Public Relations Department, Union Carbide Company.

and 6-13), constructed in 1957–1959 but designed in 1943. Wright wrote:

> Here for the first time architecture appears plastic, one floor flowing into another (more like sculpture) instead of the usual superimposition of stratified layers cutting and butting into each other by way of post-and-beam construction. The whole building, cast in concrete, is more like an egg shell—in form a great simplicity—rather than like a crisscross

FIGURE 6-11 Le Corbusier, Notre Dame-du-Haut, Ronchamps, France 1950–1955. Ezra Stoller © ESTO.

structure. The light concrete flesh is rendered strong enough everywhere to do its work by embedded filaments of steel either separate or in mesh. The structural calculations are thus those of cantilever and continuity rather than the post and beam. The net result of such construction is a greater repose, the atmosphere of the quiet unbroken wave: no meeting of the eye with abrupt changes of form.[4]

PERCEPTION KEY GUGGENHEIM MUSEUM

1. Does the exterior of this building harmonize with the interior?
2. Does the form reveal the building as an art museum?
3. Elevators take us to the top of the building, and then we participate with the exhibited works of art by walking down the spiraling ramp. This enables us to see each work from many perspectives. Does this seem to you to be an interesting, efficient, and comfortable way of exhibiting works of art?
4. The front of the museum faces Fifth Avenue. The surrounding buildings are tall rectangular solids evenly lined up along the sidewalks. Did Wright succeed in bringing his museum into a harmonius spatial relationship with these other buildings? Or was his purpose perhaps to make his museum stand out in sharp contrast, like a plant form among inorganic shapes? But if so, does the museum fit successfully into the spatial context—"the power and embrace of the positioned interrelationships of things"?
5. Originally the museum was to have been situated in Central Park. Do you think that a park site would have been better than its present site?

[4]Reprinted from *The Solomon R. Guggenheim Museum*, copyright 1960, by permission of the publishers, The Solomon R. Guggenheim Foundation and Horizon Press, New York, pp. 16f.

FIGURE 6-12 Frank Lloyd Wright, The Solomon R. Guggenheim Museum, New York City. 1957–1959. Photograph, The Solomon R. Guggenheim Museum.

FIGURE 6-13 Frank Lloyd Wright, The Solomon R. Guggenheim Museum, interior. Courtesy of the Solomon R. Guggenheim Museum.

Spatial Requirements of Architecture

Wright solved his technical problems (cantilevering,[5] etc.) and his functional problems (efficient and commodious exhibition of works of art) with considerable success. Moreover, the building functions well as a museum and reveals itself as a museum. But, if you can, check the site for yourself and see if you are satisfied with the spatial relationships between the museum and the surrounding buildings. It seems to us that Wright was not completely successful in this respect, and this, in turn, detracts from some of the "rightness" of the building. In any case, the technical, functional, and spatial necessities are obviously interdependent. If a building is going to be artistically meaningful—that is to say, if it is to be architecture—it must satisfy all of those necessities to some degree at least or its form will fail to be a form-content. A building that is technically awry with poor lighting or awkward passageways or cramped rooms will detract us from its form, and so usually will a form that fails to reveal the function of its building, or a form that fails to fit into its spatial context. We will go about our business and ignore those kinds of forms as much as possible.

Revelatory Requirements of Architecture

The function or use of a building is an essential part of the subject matter of that building, what the architect interprets or gives insight into by means of his form. The function of the Union Carbide Building (Figure 6-10) is to house offices. The form of that building reveals that function. But does this function exhaust the subject matter of this building? Is only function revealed? Would we, perhaps, be closer to the truth by claiming that involved with this office function are values closely associated with, but nevertheless distinguishable from, this function? That somehow other values, beside functional ones, are interpreted in architecture? That values from the architect's society somehow impose themselves and the architect must be sensitive to them? We think that even if architects criticize or react against the values of their time, they must take account of them. Otherwise architects' buildings would stand for little more than clichés or their personal idiosyncrasies.

We are claiming that the essential values of contemporary society are a part of all artists' subject matter, part of what they must interpret in their work, and this—because of the public character of architecture —is especially so with architects. The way architects (and artists

[5]A *cantilever* is a projecting beam or structure anchored at only one end to a pier and extending over a space to be bridged. Manuals that describe the technical problems of architecture and explain possible solutions are readily available. They can deepen our appreciation of architecture.

generally) are influenced by the values of their society has been given many explanations. According to the art historian Walter Abell, the state of mind of a society influences architects directly. The historical and social circumstances generate psychosocial tensions and latent imagery in the minds of the members of a culture. Architects, among the most sensitive members of a society, release this tension by condensing this imagery in their art. The psyche of the artist, explained by Abell by means of psychoanalytic theory and social psychology, creates the basic forms of art; but this psyche is controlled by the state of mind of the artist's society, which, in turn, is controlled by the historical and social circumstances of which it is a part.

> Art is a symbolical projection of collective psychic tensions. . . . Within the organism of a culture, the artist functions as a kind of preconsciousness, providing a zone of infiltration through which the obscure stirrings of collective intuition can emerge into collective consciousness. The artist is the personal transformer within whose sensitivity a collective psychic charge, latent in society, condenses into a cultural image. He is in short the dreamer . . . of the collective dream.[6]

Whereas Abell stresses the unconscious tensions of the social state of mind that influence the architect's creative process, Erwin Panofsky, another art historian, stresses the artist's mental habits, conscious as well as unconscious, that act as principles to guide the architect. For example:

> We can observe [between about 1130 and 1270] . . . a connection between Gothic art and Scholasticism which is more concrete than a mere "parallelism" and yet more general than those individual (and very important) "influences" which are inevitably exerted on painters, sculptors, or architects by erudite advisors. In contrast to a mere parallelism, the connection which I have in mind is a genuine cause-and-effect relation; but in contrast to an individual influence, this cause-and-effect relation comes about by diffusion rather than by direct impact. It comes about by the spreading of what may be called, for want of a better term, a mental habit—reducing this overworked cliché to its precise Scholastic sense as a "principle that regulates the act." Such mental habits are at work in all and every civilization.[7]

Whatever the explanation of the architect's relationship to society —and Abell's and Panofsky's are two of the best[8]—the forms of architecture reflect and intepret some of the fundamental values of the

[6]Walter Abell, *The Collective Dream in Art*, Harvard University Press, Cambridge, Mass., 1957, p. 328.
[7]Erwin Panofsky, *Gothic Architecture and Scholasticism*, 2nd Wimmer Lecture, 1948. St. Vincent College. Archabbey Press, Latrobe, Pa., 1951, pp. 20f. New American Library, New York, 1957, Meridian Books, p. 44.
[8]For an evaluation of these and other explanations, see F. David Martin, "The Sociological Imperative of Stylistic Development," *Bucknell Review*, vol. XI, no. 4, pp. 54–80, December, 1963.

society of the architect. Yet even as these forms are settling, society changes. Thus, while keeping the past immanent in the present, architecture takes on more and more the aura of the past, especially if the originating values are no longer viable or easily understandable. The Tomb of the Pulcella (young girl) in Tarquinia was built about the same time as the Parthenon, but because we have much more rapport with Greek than with Etruscan values, the tomb seems far older.

Anything that now exists but has a past may refer to, or function as, a sign of the past, but the forms of architecture interpret the past. The structures of architecture not only preserve the past more carefully than most things, for most architects build buildings to last, but also these structures enlighten that past. They inform about the values of the artists' society. Architects did the forming, of course, but from beginning to end that forming, insofar as it succeeded artistically, brought forth something of their society's values. Thus architectural structures are weighted with the past—a past, furthermore, that is more public than private. The past is preserved in the structures as part of the content of architecture.

Every stone of the Parthenon, in the way it was cut and fitted, reveals something about the values of the Age of Pericles—for example, the emphasis upon moderation and harmony, the importance of mathematical measurement and yet its subordination to human aesthetic needs, the respect for the "thingliness" of things, the eminence of humans and their rationality, the immanence rather than the transcendence of the sacred.

Chartres is an exceptional example of the preservation of the past. The structure reveals three principal value areas of that medieval region: the special importance of Mary, to whom the cathedral is dedicated; the cathedral school, one of the most important centers of learning in Europe in the twelfth and thirteenth centuries; and the value preferences of the main patrons—the royal family, the lesser nobility, and the local guilds. The windows of the 175 surviving panels and the sculpture, including over two thousand carved figures, were a Bible in glass and stone for the illiterate, but they were also a visual encyclopedia for the literate. From these structures the iconographer—the decipherer of the meaning of icons or symbols—can trace almost every fundamental value of the society that created Chartres Cathedral: the conception of human history from Adam and Eve to the Last Judgment; the story of Christ from his ancestors to his Ascension; church history; ancient lore and contemporary history; the latest scientific knowledge; the curriculum of the cathedral school as divided into the trivium and the quadrivium; the hierarchy of the nobility and the guilds; the code of chivalry and manners; and the hopes and fears of the time. Furthermore, the participator also becomes aware of a society that believed God to be transcendent but the Virgin to be both transcendent and immanent, not just a heavenly queen but also a mother. Chartres is Mary's home. For, as Henry Adams insisted: "You had better stop here, once for all, unless you are willing to feel that Chartres was made what it was, not by the artist, but by the Virgin." Even if we disagree with Adams, we understand, at least to some extent, Mary's special position within the context of awe aroused by God as "wholly other." The architecture of Chartres does many things, but, above all, its structures preserve that awe. Something of the society of the Chartres that was comes into our present awareness with overwhelming impact. And then we can understand something about the feelings of such medieval men as Abbot Haimon of Normandy who, after visiting Chartres, wrote to his brother monks in Tutbury, England:

> Who has ever heard tell, in times past, that powerful princes of the world, that men brought up in honor and wealth, that nobles, men and women, have bent their proud and haughty necks to the harness of carts, and that, like beasts of burden, they have dragged to the abode of Christ these waggons, loaded with wines, grains, oil, stone, wood, and all that is necessary for the wants of life, or for the construction of the church . . .? When they have reached the church, they arrange the waggons about it like a spiritual camp, and during the whole night they celebrate the watch by hymns and canticles. On each waggon they light tapers and lamps; they place there the infirm and sick, and bring them the precious relics of the Saints for their relief.

PERCEPTION KEY VALUES AND ARCHITECTURE

1. Describe other values in addition to the functional that are interpreted by the form of the Union Carbide Building (Figure 6-10).
2. Do the same for Upjohn's Trinity Church (Figure 6-5) and Le Corbusier's Notre Dame du Haut (Figure 6-11). Is it easier to describe the values related to Le Corbusier's church? If so, how is this explained?
3. Compare the Palazzo Vendramin-Calergi in Venice, completed in 1534 (Figure 6-14), with the building at 23 Havnegade in Copenhagen, completed in 1865 (Figure 6-15). Which one seems to you better architecturally? Explain. Ask yourself the same question about Chartres and the Trinity Church, but try to imagine the latter before it was submerged by skyscrapers.

To participate with a work of architecture fully, we must have as complete an understanding as possible of its subject matter—the function of the building and the relevant values of the society which subsidized the building. The more we know about the region of Chartres in medieval times, the more we will appreciate its cathedral. The more we understand our own time, the more we will appreciate the Union Carbide Building. Similarly, the more we understand about the engineering problems involved in a work of architecture, including especially the potentialities of its materials, the better our apprecia-

FIGURE 6-14 Palazzo
Vendramin-Calergi,
Venice. 1534. Photograph
by P. Lombardo,
Anderson, Rome.

tion. And, of course, the more we know about the stylistic history of
architectural elements and structures and their possibilities, the
deeper will be our appreciation. That tradition is a long and complex
one, but you can learn its essentials in any good book on the history of
architecture.

FIGURE 6-15 23
Havnegade, Copenhagen.
Completed 1865.
Architect, F. Meldahl.

Let us return again to architecture and space, for what most clearly distinguishes architecture from painting and sculpture is the way it works in space. Works of architecture separate an inside space from an outside space. They make that inside space available for human functions.[9] And in interpreting their subject matter (functions and their society's values), architects make space "space." They bring out the power and embrace of the positioned interrelationships of things. Architecture in this respect can be divided into three main types—the earth-rooted, the sky-oriented, and the earth-resting.

Earth-Rooted Architecture

The earth is the securing agency that grounds the place of our existence, our center. In most primitive cultures it is believed that people are born from the earth. And in many languages people are the "Earth-born." In countless myths, Mother Earth is the bearer of humans from birth to death. Of all things the expansive earth, with its mineral resources and vegetative fecundity, most suggests or is symbolic of security. Moreover, since the solidity of the earth encloses its depth in darkness, the earth is also suggestive of mystery.

No other thing exposes its surface more pervasively and yet hides its depth dimension more completely. The earth is always closure in the midst of disclosure. If we dig below the surface, there is always a further depth in darkness that continues to escape our penetration. Thus the Earth Mother has a mysterious, nocturnal, even funerary aspect—she is also often a goddess of death. But, as the theologian Mircea Eliade points out, "even in respect of these negative aspects, one thing that must never be lost sight of, is that when the Earth becomes a goddess of Death, it is simply because she is felt to be the universal womb, the inexhaustible source of all creation."[10] Nothing in nature is more suggestive or symbolic of security and mystery than the earth. Earth-rooted architecture accentuates this natural symbolism more than any other art.

SITE

Architecture that is earth-rooted discloses the earth by drawing our attention to the building's site, or to its submission to gravity, or to its raw materials, or to its centrality in outer and inner space. Sites whose surrounding environment can be seen from great distances are especially favorable for helping a building bring out the earth. The site of

[9]Since the inside space of the Memphis Pyramid (Figure 5-6) is useful only for the dead, the pyramid is not clearly classifiable as either architecture or sculpture.
[10]Mircea Eliade, *Myths, Dreams and Mysteries*, Philip Mairet (trans.), Harper, New York, 1961, p. 188.

the Parthenon (Figures 6-6 and 6-7), for example, is superior in this respect to the site of Chartres (Figures 6-2 and 6-3), because the Acropolis is a natural center that stands out prominently within a widespread concave space. Thus the Parthenon is able to emphasize by continuity both the sheer heavy stoniness of the cliffs of the Acropolis and the gleaming whites of Athens. By contrast, it sets off the deep blue of the Mediterranean sky and sea and the grayish greens of the encompassing mountains that open out toward the weaving blue of the sea like the bent rims of a colossal flower. All these elements of the earth would be present without the Parthenon, of course, but the Parthenon, whose columns from a distance push up like stamens, centers these elements more tightly so that their interrelationships add to the vividness of each. Together they form the ground from which the Parthenon slowly and majestically rises.

GRAVITY

The Parthenon is also exceptional in the way it manifests a gentle surrender to gravity. The horizontal rectangularity of the entablature follows evenly along the plain of the Acropolis with the steady beat of its supporting columns and quiets their upward thrust. Gravity is accepted and accentuated in this serene stability—the hold of the earth is secure.

The site of Mont Saint Michel (Figure 6-16) can also be seen from great distances, especially from the sea, and the church, straining far up from the great rock cliffs, organizes a vast scene of sea, sand, shallow hills, and sky. But the spiny, lonely verticality of the church overwhelms the pull of the earth. We are lured to the sky, to the world of light, whereas the Parthenon draws us back into the womb of the earth. Mont Saint Michel discloses the earth, for both the earth and a world to be opened up require centering and thus each other, but the defiance of gravity weakens the securing sense of place. Mont Saint Michel rapidly moves us around its walls, when the tides permit, with a dizzying effect, whereas the Parthenon moves us around slowly and securely so that our orientation is never in doubt. The significance of the earth is felt much more deeply at the Parthenon than at Mont Saint Michel.

The complex of skyscrapers that composes Rockefeller Center (Figure 6-17) in New York City is an exceptional example of an architecture that allows for only a minimal submission to gravity. The surrounding buildings, unless we are high up in one nearby, block out the lower sections of the Center. If we are able to see the lower sections by getting in close, we are blocked from a clear and comprehensive view of the upper sections. The relationships between the lower and upper sections are, therefore, somewhat disintegrated, and there is a sense of these tapering towers, especially the R. C. A. Building, not only scraping but being suspended from the sky. The Union Carbide

FIGURE 6-16 Mont Saint Michel. Photograph from French Government Tourist Office, New York.

Building (Figure 6-10), not far away, carries this feeling even further by the placement of the shaftlike box on stilts. This apparently weightless building mitigates but does not annihilate our feeling of the earth, for despite its arrowlike soaring, we are aware of its base. Even at night, when the sides of this structure become dark curtains pierced by hundreds of square lights, we feel these lights, as opposed to the light of the stars, as somehow grounded. Architecture in setting up a world always sets forth the earth, and vice versa.

RAW MATERIALS

When the medium of architecture is made up totally or in large part of unfinished materials furnished by nature, especially when they are from the site, these materials stand forth and also help reveal the earthiness of the earth. In this respect stone, wood, and clay in a raw or relatively raw state are much more effective than steel, concrete, and glass. If the Parthenon had been made in concrete rather than in native Pentelic marble—the quarries can still be seen in the background—the building would not grow out of the soil so organically and some of the feeling of the earth would be dissipated. On the other hand, if the paint that originally covered much of the Parthenon had remained, the effect would be considerably less earthy than at present. Wright's Kaufman house (Figure 6-18) is an excellent example of the combined use of manufactured and raw materials that helps set forth the earth. The

FIGURE 6-17
Rockefeller Center, New
York City. 1931–1940.
Courtesy of Rockefeller
Center, Inc. Photograph
by Wendell MacRae.

concrete and glass bring out by contrast the textures of stone and wood taken from the site, while the lacelike flow of the falling water is made even more graceful by its reflection in the smooth clear flow of concrete and glass. Like a wide-spreading plant, drawing the sunlight and rain to its good earth, this home seems to breathe within its homeland.

CENTRALITY

Finally, a building that is strongly centered, both in its outer and inner space, helps disclose the earth. Perhaps no building is more centered in

FIGURE 6-18 Frank Lloyd Wright, Kaufman house *(Falling Water)*, Bear Run, Pennsylvania. 1937–1939. Photograph by Bill Hedrich, Hedrich-Blessing, Chicago.

its site than the Parthenon, but the weak centering of its inner space slackens somewhat the significance of the earth. Unlike Chartres, there is no strong pull into the Parthenon, and when we get inside, the inner space, as we reconstruct it, is divided in such a way that no certain center can be felt. There is no place to come to an unequivocal standstill as at Chartres. Even Versailles (Figure 6-19), despite its seemingly never-ending partitions of inner space, brings us eventually to somewhat of a center in the bed of the bedroom of Louis XIV. Yet this centering is made possible primarily by the view from the room that focuses both the pivotal position of the room in the building and the placement of the room on a straight-line axis to Paris in the far distance. Conversely, the inner space of Chartres, most of which from the crossing can be taken in with a sweep of the eye, achieves centrality without this kind of dependence upon outside orientation. Buildings such as the Parthenon and Versailles, which divide the inner space with solid partitions, invariably are weaker in inner centrality than buildings without such divisions. The endless boxes within boxes of the Union Carbide Building (Figure 6-10) negate any possibility of significant inner centering, adding to the unearthiness of this cage of steel.

Buildings whose inner space not only draws us to a privileged position—that position which gives us the best perception—but whose inner space or most of it can also be seen from that privileged position evoke a feeling of powerful inner centeredness. This feeling is further

FIGURE 6-19 Palace of Versailles. 1661–1687. Photograph from French Government Tourist Office, New York.

enhanced when the expanses of inner space are more or less equidistant from the privileged position. Greek-cross buildings,[11] such as Giuliano da Sangallo's Santa Maria delle Carceri (Figures 6-20 and 6-21) in Prato, are likely to center us in inner space more strongly than Latin-cross buildings, such as Chartres (Figure 6-4). If Bramante's and Michelangelo's Greek-cross plan for St. Peter's had been carried out, the centrality of the inner space would have been greatly enhanced. It does not follow, however, that all centrally planned buildings that open up all or almost all of the inner space will be strongly centered internally. San Vitale (Figures 6-22 and 6-23) in Ravenna, for example, is basically an octagon, but the enfolded interior spaces are not clearly outlined and differentiated as in Santa Maria delle Carceri. There is a floating and welling of space working out and up through the arcaded niches into the outer layers of the ambulatory and gallery that fade into semidarkness. The dazzling colors of the varied marble slabs and the mosaics lining the piers and walls, unlike the somber static grays and whites of Sangallo's inner church, add to our sense of spatial uncertainty. We can easily discover the center of San Vitale if we so desire, but there is no directed movement to it because the indeterminacy of the surrounding spaces makes the feeling of the center insecure and insignificant. The unanchored restlessness of the interior of San Vitale belies its solid weighty exterior.

FIGURE 6-20 Giuliano da Sangallo, Santa Maria delle Carceri, Prato, Italy. 1485. Alinari.

[11]The arms of a Greek cross, unlike those of a Latin cross, are equal in length. Thus, the ground dimensions of a building in the shape of a Greek cross can be encompassed, more or less, within a circle.

FIGURE 6-21 Santa Maria delle Carceri, interior. Alinari.

FIGURE 6-22 San Vitale, Ravenna, Italy. 526–547. Alinari.

Buildings in the round, other things being equal, are the most internally centered of all. In the Pantheon (Figure 6-24), almost all the inner space can be seen with a turn of the head, and the grand and clear symmetry of the enclosing shell draws us to the center of the circle, the privileged position, beneath the "eye" of the dome opening to a bit

FIGURE 6-23 San Vitale, interior. Alinari.

FIGURE 6-24 Giovanni Paolo Panini, *Interior of the Pantheon, Rome.* 1691–1692. Canvas, 50½ by 39 inches. National Gallery of Art, Washington, D. C. Samuel H. Kress Collection. The Pantheon itself dates from the second century after Christ.

of the sky. Few buildings root us more firmly in the earth. The massive dome with its stony bluntness seems to be drawn down by the funneled and dimly spreading light falling through the "eye." This is a dome of destiny pressing tightly down. We are driven earthward in this crushing ambience. Even on the outside the Pantheon seems to be forcing down. In the circular interior of Wright's Guggenheim Museum (Figure 6-13) not all of the inner space can be seen from the privileged position, but the smoothly curving ramp that comes down like a whirlpool makes us feel the earth beneath as our only support. The chapel of M.I.T. by Saarinen, also circular, accents the earth somewhat differently. No natural light is allowed to come inside directly; but natural light falls upon pools of water that lie below the floor and around the perimeter of the drum, the light flickering up the undulating interior walls. Thus in a strange way it appears as if the light, like the water, were coming up from the earth. This helps draw the drum down into the ground. In buildings such as these, especially in their centers, we are made to feel the presence of the earth with exceptional force. Whereas in buildings such as Mont Saint Michel and Chartres, mass seems to be overcome, the weight lightened, and the downward motion thwarted, in buildings such as the Pantheon, the Guggenheim Museum, and the chapel of M.I.T., mass comes out heavily and down.

The importance of a center, usually within a circle, as a privileged and even sacred position in relation to the earth, is common among the spatial arrangements of ancient cultures, for example, the Stonehenge on the Salisbury Plain of England. And the first city of Rome, according to Plutarch,[12] was laid out by the Etruscans around a circular trench or *mundus*, over which was placed a great capstone. Around the *mundus*, the Etruscans outlined a large circle for the walls which would enclose the city. Following a carefully prescribed ritual, a deep furrow was plowed along the circle and the plow was lifted from the ground wherever a gate was to appear. This circular plan was subdivided by two main cross streets: the *cardo*, running north and south in imitation of the axis of the earth, and the *decumanus*, running east and west, dividing the city into four equal parts. These streets crossed at the site of the *mundus*, believed to be the entrance to the underworld, and the capstone was removed three times each year to allow the spirits passage between the world of the living and the world of the dead. Although such beliefs and customs have long been dead in Western civilization, we still can feel the power of the earth in circular city plans and buildings.

Sky-Oriented Architecture

Architecture that is sky-oriented suggests or is symbolic of a world as the generating agency that enables us to project our possibilities and realize some of them. A horizon, always a necessary part of a world, is symbolic of the limitations placed upon our possibilities and realizations. The light and heat of the sun are more symbolic than anything else in nature of generative power. Dante declared, "there is no visible thing in the world more worthy to serve as symbol of God than the Sun; which illuminates with visible life itself first and then all the celestial and mundane bodies." The energy of the moving sun bright-

---

[12]John Dryden (trans.) *Plutarch's Lives*, Random House, Modern Library, New York, 1932, p. 31.

ens the sky which, in turn, opens up for us a spacious context or world within which we attempt to realize our possibilities. In total darkness we may be able to orient ourselves to the earth, but in order to move with direction, as do the blind, we must imagine space as open in some way, as a world enlightened with light even if our imaginations must provide that light. Total darkness, at least until we can envision a world, is terrifying. That is why, as the Preacher of Ecclesiastes proclaims, "the light is sweet, and a pleasant thing it is for the eyes to behold the sun." "The light of the living" is a common Hebrew phrase, and in Greek "to behold light" is synonymous with "to live." The light of the sky reveals space—the positioned interrelationships of things. The dome of the sky, with its limits provided by the horizon, embraces a world within which we find ourselves. But a world is above all the context for activity. A world stirs our imaginations to possibilities. A world, with its suggestion of expectation, turns our faces to the future, just as the smile of the sun lures our eyes. Architecture organizes a world, usually far more tightly than nature, by centering that world on the earth by means of a building. By accentuating the natural symbolism of sunlight, sky, and horizon, sky-oriented architecture opens up a world that is symbolic of our projections into the future.

Such architecture discloses a world by drawing our attention to the sky bounded by a horizon. It accomplishes this by means of making a building appear high and centered within the sky, or defying gravity, or tightly integrating the light of outer with inner space. Negatively, architecture that accents a world deemphasizes the features that accent the earth. Thus the manufactured materials, such as the steel and glass, of the Union Carbide Building (Figure 6-10) help separate this building from the earth. Positively, the most effective means at the disposal of architects for accenting a world is turning their structures toward the sky in such a way that the horizon of the sky forms a spacious context. Architecture is an art of bounding as well as opening.

AXIS MUNDI

Even before buildings become architecture, primitive people often express this need for a world by centering themselves in relation to the sky by means of an *axis mundi*. Eliade presents many instances, for example, among the nomadic Australians, whose economy is still at the stage of gathering food and hunting small game:

> According to the traditions of an Arunta tribe, the Achipla, in mythical times the divine being Numbakula cosmicized their future territory, created their Ancestor, and established their institutions. From the trunk of a gum tree Numbakula fashioned the sacred pole *(kauwa-auwa)* and, after anointing it with blood, climbed it and disappeared into the sky. This pole (the *axis mundi*) represents a cosmic axis, for it is around the sacred pole that territory becomes habitable, hence is transformed into a

world. The sacred pole consequently plays an important role ritually. During their wanderings the Achipla always carry it with them and choose the direction they are to take by the direction toward which it bends. This allows them, while being continually on the move, to be always in "their world" and, at the same time, in communication with the sky into which Numbakula vanished. For the pole to be broken denotes catastrophe; it is like "the end of the world," reversion to chaos. Spencer and Gillen report that once, when the pole was broken, "the entire clan were in consternation; they wandered about aimlessly for a time, and finally lay down on the ground together and waited for death to overtake them."[13]

When buildings accent a world, their turning to the sky usually suggests a kind of *axis mundi*. The perpendicularity and centering of the Acropolis (Figure 6-6), for example, make it a kind of natural *axis mundi* that would open up the sky to some extent even if the Parthenon had never been built. But the flat plains around Chartres (Figure 6-2) would rarely turn us to the sky without the spires of the cathedral. At one time the spire of Trinity Church (Figure 6-5), beautifully proportioned despite its lack of originality, must have organized the sky. Buildings that stretch up far above the land and nearby structures, such as Mont Saint Michel (Figure 6-16), Durham Cathedral, Chartres (Figures 6-2 and 6-3), and Rockefeller Center (Figure 6-17), not only direct our eye to the sky but also act as a center that orders the sunlight in such a way that a world with a horizon comes into view. The sky both opens up and takes on limits. Such buildings reach up like an *axis mundi*, and the sky reaches down to meet them in mutual embrace. And we are blessed with an orienting center, our motion being given direction and limits.

DEFIANCE OF GRAVITY

The more a building appears to defy gravity, the more it is likely to disclose the sky, for this defiance draws our eyes upward. The thrust against gravity is not simply a question of how high the building goes. Most of the skyscrapers of New York City, like the Woolworth Building (Figure 6-25) and unlike the Union Carbide Building (Figure 6-10), seem to stop finally not because they have reached a more or less perfect union with the sky but because the space used up had exhausted them. They hang lifelessly despite their great height. They seem to have just enough strength to stand upright but no power to transcend the rudimentary laws of statics. Gravity wins out after all. The up and the down frustrate each other, and their conflict dims the world that might have been. Chartres is not nearly so tall as the Woolworth Building, and yet it appears far taller. The stony logic of the

[13]Mircea Eliade, *The Sacred and the Profane*, Williard R. Trask (trans.), Harcourt Brace Jovanovich, Inc., 1959, pp. 32f.

FIGURE 6-25 Cass Gilbert, Woolworth Building, New York City. 1913. Photograph from Ely-Cruikshank Company, Inc.

press of the flying buttresses of Chartres and the arched roof, towers, and spires that carry on their upward thrust seem to overcome the binding of the earth, just as the stone birds on the walls seem about to break their bonds and fly out into the world. The reach up is full of vital force and finally comes to rest comfortably and securely in the bosom of the heavens. Mont Saint Michel and Durham Cathedral are even more impressive in this respect, mainly because of the advantages of their sites. But perhaps Brunelleschi's dome of the Cathedral of Florence (Figure 6-26) is the most powerful structure ever built in

FIGURE 6-26 Filippo Brunelleschi, dome of the Cathedral of Florence. 1420–1436. Italian Government Travel Office.

seeming to defy gravity and achieving height in relation to its site. The eight outside ribs spring up to the cupola with tremendous energy, in part because they repeat the spring of the mountains that encircle Florence. The dome, visible from almost everywhere in and around Florence, appears to be precisely centered in the Arno Valley, precisely as high as it should be in order to organize its sky. The world of Florence begins and ends at the still point of this dome of aspiration. On the other hand, Michelangelo's dome of St. Peter's (Figure 6-1), although grander in proportions and over 50 feet higher, fails to organize the sky of Rome as firmly, mainly because the hills of Rome do not lend themselves to centralized organization.

INTEGRATION OF LIGHT

When the light of outer space suffuses the light of inner space, especially when the light from the outside seems to dominate or draw the light from the inside, a world is accented. Inside Chartres the light is so majestic that we cannot fail to imagine the light outside that is generating this transfiguration inside. For a medieval man like Abbot Suger the effect was mystical, separating the earth from Heaven:

> When the house of God, many colored as the radiance of precious jewels, called me from the cares of the world, then holy meditation led my mind to thoughts of piety, exalting my soul from the material to the immaterial, and I seemed to find myself, as it were, in some strange part of the

universe which was neither wholly of the baseness of the earth, nor wholly of the serenity of heaven, but by the grace of God I seemed lifted in a mystic manner from this lower toward the upper sphere.

On the other hand, for a contemporary person the stained glass is likely to be felt more as integrating rather than separating us from a world. We sense the unity of inner with outer space by means of the light, the effect that Saarinen avoids in the chapel at M.I.T. The upper chapel of Sainte-Chapelle in Paris, built by order of St. Louis, is an extraordinary example of how even a small building can accent a world by means of its stained glass. The inner space is so full of moving color energized by the sun, the power of which changes with the hours and the seasons, that we imagine a great world outside even though we cannot see it directly and even though the structure of the building has little centralizing effect upon the sky. Unlike Sainte-Chapelle, Hagia Sophia in Istanbul (Figure 6-27) has no stained glass, and its glass areas are completely dominated by the walls and dome. Yet the subtle placement of the little windows, especially around the perimeter of the dome, seems to draw the light of the inner space up and out. Unlike the Pantheon (Figure 6-24), the great masses of Hagia Sophia seem to rise. The dome floats gently, despite its diameter of 107 feet, and the great

FIGURE 6-27 Hagia Sophia, Istanbul, Turkey, interior. 532–537; restored 558, 975. From Turkish Tourism and Information Office, New York.

enfolded space beneath is absorbed into the even greater open space outside. We imagine a world.

Sky-oriented architecture reveals the generative activity of a world. The energy of the sun is the ultimate source of all life. The light of the sun enables us to see the physical environment and guides our steps accordingly. "Arise, shine, for thy light is come" (Isaiah 60:1). The sky with its horizon provides a spacious context for our progress. The world of nature vaguely suggests the potentialities of the future. Architecture, however, tightly centers a world on the earth by means of its structures. This unification gives us orientation and security.

PERCEPTION KEY SKY-ORIENTED ARCHITECTURE AND HUMAN SCALE

Sky-oriented architecture tends to disregard the human scale, as in the case of Rockefeller Center (Figure 6-17) and so much of New York City. Lawrence Durrell in his *Sicilian Carousel* observes with reference to secular buildings: "The minute your architecture dwarfs people, shows disrespect for the purely human scale, you start to stunt their minds and chill their spirits." Do you agree? If so, do you think that sky-oriented architecture should be used mainly for religious buildings?

Earth-Resting Architecture

Most architecture accents neither earth nor sky but rests on the earth, using the earth like a platform with the sky as background. Earth-resting buildings may either dominate the earth, as in the case of the Palazzo Farnese (Figures 6-28 and 6-29) in Rome, or relate harmoniously to the earth, as in the case of Mies van der Rohe's residence of Dr. Edith Farnsworth (Figure 6-30) in Plano, Illinois. Generally, earth-resting buildings are not very tall, have flat roofs, and avoid strong vertical extensions such as spires and chimneys. Thus—unlike sky-oriented architecture—the earth-resting type does not strongly organize the sky around itself, as with Chartres (Figure 6-2) or the Cathedral of Florence (Figure 6-26). The sky is involved with earth-resting architecture, of course, but more as a setting.

With earth-resting architecture—unlike earth-rooted architecture —the earth does not appear as an organic part of the building, as in Wright's Kaufman house (Figure 6-18), or as an integral part, as in Saarinen's chapel at M.I.T. Rather, the earth appears as a stage. Earth-resting buildings, moreover, are usually cubes that avoid canti-levering structures, as in the Kaufman house, as well as curving lines, as in the chapel at M.I.T. Earth-rooted architecture seems to "hug to" the earth, as with the M.I.T. chapel and the Pantheon (Figure 6-24), or to grow out of the earth, as with the Kaufman house. Earth-resting architecture, on the other hand, seems to "sit on" the earth. Thus, because it does not relate to its environment quite as strongly as earth-rooted and sky-oriented architecture, this kind of architecture usually tends to draw to itself more isolated attention with reference to its shape, articulation of the elements of its walls, lighting, etc.

Earth-resting architecture is usually more appropriate than earth-rooted architecture when the site is severely bounded by other buildings. Perhaps this is a basic deficiency of Wright's Guggenheim Museum (Figure 6-12). In any case, it is obvious that if buildings were constructed close to the Kaufman house—especially earth-resting or sky-oriented types—they would destroy much of the glory of Wright's creation.

PERCEPTION KEY PALAZZO FARNESE

Study the Palazzo Farnese (Figures 6-28 and 6-29) by Antonio da Sangallo and Michelangelo.

1. The façade of this building is 185 feet by 96½ feet. Is there any particular significance to the large size and proportion of these dimensions? Suppose, for example, that the construction had stopped with the second floor. Would the relationship between width and height be as "right" as it now appears?
2. Does the relationship between the sizes of the three floors have a "rightness"? If so, how is this to be explained?
3. The window pediments of the first floor are all alike. On the second floor, however, there is an a/b rhythm. The windows at the ends of the façade are topped by triangles, and as we move toward the center of the façade, semicircular pediments interrupt the triangular pediments. Why this rhythm? Why not have the same rhythm on the first and third floors? Why do semicircular rather than triangular pediments lead to the central window, with its large family insignia and porch?
4. The cornice—the horizontal molding projecting along the top of the building—is very large, and the corners of the façade are accented by roughly cut stones. Why?
5. Sangallo designed the first two floors and Michelangelo designed the third. The differences between their two styles are more evident in the courtyard (Figure 6-29). What are these differences? For example, which architect stresses restlessness? How? Why? Did Michelangelo successfully unite his third floor with Sangallo's?
6. In answering the above questions are you inevitably led to consider the function of this building? If you were told that this building was a church, for example, would you be both surprised and distressed? Would your answers be different?
7. What function and what values are revealed in this building? In other words, what is the subject matter that the form informs about? And how does the form achieve its content?

The residence of Dr. Edith Farnsworth (Figure 6-30), designed by Mies van der Rohe, exemplifies his paradoxical doctrine that "less is

FIGURE 6-28 Antonio da Sangallo and Michelangelo Buonarroti, Palazzo Farnese, Rome, 1534. Alinari.

FIGURE 6-29 Palazzo Farnese, courtyard. Alinari.

FIGURE 6-30 Ludwig Mies van der Rohe, Farnsworth residence, Plano, Illinois. 1950. Photograph from Hedrich-Blessing, Chicago.

more." On the Palazzo Farnese much ornament—for example, all the elements around the windows—could be removed and the building would still stand. But with Mies' work, it seems as if nothing is there that is not necessary for the technical solutions of making the building stand.

PERCEPTION KEY FARNSWORTH RESIDENCE AND THE PALAZZO FARNESE

1. The simplicity of Mies' house may be misleading. Analyze the placement of the elements and their proportions, and see if you can discover why this work is considered to be a small masterpiece by one of the greatest of modern architects. For instance, why are the posts not out at the corners? Why do the posts meet a projecting line of the roof rather than coming up under the roof?
2. How are light and outer space related differently here than in the Palazzo Farnese?
3. Why is absolute symmetry absent here, whereas in the Palazzo Farnese it is closely approached?
4. What is the content of this home? And how does the form achieve it?
5. Mies' houses have sometimes been criticized as buildings made to be looked at rather than lived in. In the case of the Farnsworth residence, do you agree?
6. Try your hand at designing your ideal home. What form will reveal *your* home?

The Palazzo Farnese reveals the authority and power of a palace. It commands the earth and everything around it. Michelangelo's third floor, compared with Sangallo's floors, is even awesome, as if the power can no longer be contained. Only the third floor in this mighty, sharply outlined, indestructible cube expresses movement. Conversely, Mies' quiet house rests on the earth and is a home. Its dignity is private rather than public, expressive of an efficiency that has learned much from the machine but has also learned how to humanize the machine. Light and air interpenetrate through the glass and post-and-lintel construction. This wedding of nature and the manufactured is all the more impressive for its economy of means.

Study the Wiley House (Figure 6-31) by Philip Johnson, very much in the style of Mies. The functions of this house are explicitly separated—the ground floor contains the "private functions," and the open social functions are reserved for the modular glass pavilion above. Nothing seems to be there that does not work as a practical function.

PERCEPTION KEY WILEY HOUSE

1. Do you think the ground floor and the pavilion relate to one another in a satisfactory way?
2. Are light and air integrated with the structure of the building as gracefully as in Mies' building? Explain.
3. Some critics have remarked of Wiley House that "less is a bore." Comment.

FIGURE 6-31 Philip Johnson, Wiley house, New Canaan, Connecticut. 1953. Photograph from Ezra Stoller © ESTO.

The problem of when to use earth-rooted or earth-resting or sky-oriented buildings is usually easily solved: The function of the building generally is the key. Churches and large office buildings, especially in crowded sites, lend themselves to sky orientation. Homes in rural areas lend themselves to earth orientation. Homes in crowded urban areas present special problems. Earth-rooted buildings, such as the Kaufman house (Figure 6-18), normally require relatively large open areas. Thus, most urban dwellings are earth-resting. But as our populations have become increasingly dense, sky-oriented apartment buildings have become a common sight. In Reston, Virginia, for example, clusters of one-family houses of the earth-resting type are strewn over 7,400 acres of landscape. In the village plaza, however, one apartment tower rises (Figure 6-32), apparently to provide both more living space and a vertical accent that, like Chartres, would center the surrounding buildings.

PERCEPTION KEY RESTON AND LAFAYETTE PARK

1. Does the Reston tower apartment spatially unify the one-family units around it?

FIGURE 6-32
Apartment complex in Reston, Virginia. 1965. Conklin and Rossant, architects. Photograph from *Matrix of Man*, 1968, by Sibyl Moholy-Nagy, Praeger Publishers. Courtesy of Hattula Moholy-Nagy Hug.

FIGURE 6-33   Ludwig Mies van der Rohe, Lafayette Park, Detroit, Michigan. 1955–1963. Photograph from Hedrich-Blessing, Chicago.

2. Compare the one-story townhouses and the twenty-two-story high-rise apartment building (Figure 6-33) by Mies in Lafayette Park, Detroit. Does Mies succeed in integrating more harmoniously the earth-resting townhouses with the sky-oriented apartment building? If so, how?

We think Mies' solution is more successful than the one in Reston. The windows of Mies' townhouses are broad horizontal rectangles that flow rhythmically along the earth, with just enough vertical lines to prepare for the sky orientation of the apartment building. The vertical lines of the apartment building dominate the horizontals because the height of the building somewhat exceeds its breadth. Nevertheless, the thickest lines are horizontals, and a delicate balance is achieved. Just as the horizontals slightly dominate the townhouses, the verticals slightly dominate the apartment building. The two sets of buildings require each other, and the power of their positioned relationships—their space—is brought out vividly and harmoniously.

In Reston, on the other hand, the vertical and horizontal lines of the one-family houses and the apartment tower fail to relate quite so effectively. The verticals of the tower, perhaps in part because of the isolation of the tower, lack the restraint that would bring them into complete harmony with the family units. The latter, partly because we see them in relation to the tower, seem to be truncated towers, cut off

FIGURE 6-34 National Gallery of Art, Washington, D. C., mall entrance. 1941. Photograph from the National Gallery of Art.

before reaching their proper height. Both the family units and the tower fail to fit nicely into the landscape, nor does the tower organize the surrounding buildings in a way that unifies them. Yet it is obvious that unity was intended, and this failure is disturbing.

Consider another earth-resting building, one of the most expensive ever built in this country—the National Gallery of Art (Figure 6-34) in Washington, D.C.

PERCEPTION KEY THE NATIONAL GALLERY OF ART

1. Would you know the function of this building just by observing it from the outside?
2. Do you find its entrance inviting? Compare St. Peter's (Figure 6-1).
3. Does its form inform you about anything?

Combining the portico of the Temple of Diana and the dome of the Pantheon with vast wings that stretch out to a total length of 785 feet, this monstrous building, despite the very expensive materials and the great engineering skill that went into its making, reveals little except the imitative conservatism of its designers and the wealth and conservatism of its patrons. In the 1930s, when the National Gallery was planned, mainly by John Russell Pope, the United States had risen from its worst depression and was beginning to face, as potentially the most powerful nation in the world, the crisis of the coming Second World War. At the dedication of the gallery in March 1941, President Roosevelt concluded his address:

Seventy-eight years ago, in the third year of the war between the States, men and women gathered here in the capitol of a divided nation, here in Washington, to see the bronze goddess of liberty set upon its top.

It had been an expensive, a laborious business, diverting money and labor from the prosecution of the war and certain critics . . . found much to criticize. . . . But the President of the United States, whose name was Lincoln, when he heard those criticisms, answered: "If people see the Capitol going on it is a sign that we intend this Union shall go on."

We may borrow the words for our own. We, too, intend the Union to go on. We intend it shall go on, carrying with it the great tradition of the human spirit which created it.

The dedication of this gallery to a living past and to a greater and more richly living future is the measure of the earnestness of our intention that the freedom of the human spirit shall go on too.

Brave words by a brave president. But what living past does the architecture of this building disclose? And in what way does this building bring forth the freedom of the human spirit that shall go on? The gallery reveals rather the taste—derived from Jefferson's belief that the beautiful in architecture had been forever established in Roman masterpieces—that has bound the architecture of Washington to pale imitations of what had once been a living art. Nothing of the thrusting optimism of the United States, its ceaseless and ingenious ferment, its power and pragmatism comes out. Even the superb technology of our country is masked. The engineering excellence of the steel structure is covered up, as if there were something shameful about the steel that helped make the United States prosperous. Even the immense dome gets lost in the mass of marble, and so the building spreads out without centering the outer space. Instead, the gallery somewhat awkwardly imposes its bulk into the graceful open ensemble of the Mall as planned by L'Enfant. Even the function of the building is hidden. The exterior tells us nothing about the use or even the structuring of the inner space. The building could have been constructed for just about any purpose that requires great inner dimensions. Even a "draw" by the inner into the outer space is lacking, surely an adjunct that a museum of art should provide. Indeed, the forty granite steps of mighty spread which mount up from the Mall to the main entrance, like the terror-inspiring stairways to the Mayan sacrificial platforms, either weaken visitors or drive them away. The architecture, if it can be called that, goes unnoticed. Neither the earth nor the sky comes into focus. Unimaginatively conceived, the National Gallery of Art was stillborn.

City Planning

No use of space has become more critical in our time than in the city. In conclusion, therefore, the issues we have been discussing about

FIGURE 6-35 Paul Rudolph, Municipal Garage, New Haven, Connecticut. 1961. Photograph by Ezra Stoller Associates © ESTO.

space and architecture take on special relevance with respect to city planning. For example in New Haven, Connecticut, the home of Yale University, the largest and most grandiloquent building is the Municipal Garage (Figure 6-35). In an article in *Show*, December 1963, Wolf von Eckhardt describes this building as "the most imposing shrine yet built to the automobile." With reference to the shopping center to be built next to it, Eckhardt declares that "its only virtue is that it will largely hide Mr. Rudolph's monstrous prehistoric garage." The nearby city hall, the three old churches on the lovely green, Yale University, and all other buildings of the central city tend to be dominated by this enormous storage facility.

PERCEPTION KEY NEW HAVEN MUNICIPAL GARAGE

1. Does it strike you that something is wrong about a garage having such dominance? What would you think of a house whose most predominant feature was its garage or its septic tank? Past cultures have built monuments to God and man. Does it worry you that our culture is building monuments to the automobile?
2. On the other hand, if you drive—as usually you must—into almost any city today, you find parking a tormenting, hazardous enterprise that is liable to reduce you to a nervous wreck. Then is not the New Haven garage, spacious and convenient, an excellent solution? Or, if not, what do you propose? Discuss with others.

Suppose spacious parking lots were located around the fringes of the city, rapid public transportation were readily available from those lots into the city, and in the city only public and emergency transportation—most of it underground—were permitted. In place of poisonous fumes, screeching noises, and jammed streets, fresh air, fountains and sculpture, talk and music, and wide open spaces to walk and enjoy would be possible. Buildings could be participated with. All the diversified character of a city—its theaters, opera, concert halls, museums, shops, stores, offices, restaurants, markets, parks, lakes, squares, outdoor cafes—would take on some spatial unity again. If for no other reason, we could get to those various places without nervous prostration and the risk of life and limb. The city would be taken away from the automobile and given back to us.

One of the solutions proposed for the city is to decentralize. One area would be set aside for offices, another for factories, another for stores, another for residences, another for recreation, etc. Another solution is to move residences to the suburbs. But now suburbia is becoming as tyrannized by the automobile as the big city. Another solution is to develop outlying villages with a rural atmosphere, such as Reston (Fig. 6 32).

PERCEPTION KEY CITY PLANNING

1. Do you think the city ought to be saved? What advantages does only the city have? What still gives glamour to such cities as Florence, Rome, Paris, and London?

2. Suppose you agree that New York City is worth saving. Suppose further that you are a city planner for New York City, and assume that funds are available to implement your plans. What would you propose? For example, would you destroy all the old buildings? Joseph Hudnut has written, "There is in buildings that have withstood the siege of centuries a magic which is irrespective of form and technical excellence. . . . the wreckage of distant worlds are radioactive with a long-gathered energy."[14] Do you agree? Would you be satisfied with high-rise apartments such as those on a bluff above the Bronx River (Figure 6-36)? Or what do you think of the cluster of apartment buildings of Stuyvesant Town (Figure 6-37) in Manhattan? What would you do with the Manhattan area in Figure 6-38? Would you separate areas by function? The Wall Street area, for example, contains the financial interests. Is this a good idea? Would you allow factories within the city limits? Or do you think factories are cancers within the city? How would you handle transportation to and within the city? For instance, would you allow expressways to slice through the city, as in Detroit and Los Angeles? If you outlawed the private car from the city, what would you do with the streets? Could the streets become a unifier of the city?

3. Suppose one side of an old residential street is salvageable, as with these row houses (Figure 6-39) in Brooklyn Heights, and the other side is to be

[14]Joseph Hudnut, *Architecture and the Spirit of Man*, Harvard University Press, Cambridge, Mass., 1949, pp. 15f.

FIGURE 6-36 High-rise apartments above the Bronx River, New York. Photograph from *Matrix of Man*, 1968, by Sibyl Moholy-Nagy, Praeger Publishers. Courtesy of Hattula Moholy-Nagy Hug.

FIGURE 6-37 Stuyvesant Town, New York. Photograph from *Matrix of Man*, 1968, Sibyl Moholy-Nagy, Praeger Publishers. Courtesy of Hattula Moholy-Nagy Hug.

FIGURE 6-38 A section of Manhattan, New York. Photograph from *Matrix of Man*, 1968, by Sibyl Moholy-Nagy, Praeger Publishers. Courtesy of Hattula Moholy-Nagy Hug.

put to nonresidential use. Would you necessarily design your new buildings in the same style as the old? As you reflect about this, study Dieter Osterleen's Historical Museum (Figure 6-40) in Hanover, Germany, built in 1964, in its relation to the old half-timbered houses across the street.

If we have been near the truth, then architects are the shepherds of space. And to be sensitive to their buildings is to help, in our more humble way, to preserve their preservation. Architects make space a gracious place. Such places, like a home, give us a center from which we can orient ourselves to other places. And then we can be at home in the homeland.

Summary

Architecture is the creative conservation of space—the power of the positioned interrelationships of things. The spatial centers of nature organize things around them, and architecture enhances these centers. Architects carve apart an inner space from an outer space in such a way that both spaces become more fully perceptible and the inner space is made useful. A work of architecture is a configurational center, a place

FIGURE 6-39 Row houses, Brooklyn Heights, New York. Photograph from *Matrix of Man*, 1968, by Sibyl Moholy-Nagy, Praeger Publishers. Courtesy of Hattula Moholy-Nagy Hug.

FIGURE 6-40 Osterleen Historical Museum, Hanover, Germany. 1964. Photograph by Hans Wagner, Hanover.

of special value, a place to dwell. Architects must account for four basic and closely interrelated necessities: technical or structural requirements, functioning or use, spatial relationships, and content. To succeed, their forms must adjust to these necessities. Because of the public character of architecture, moreover, the common or shared values of contemporary society usually are in a very direct way a part of architects' subject matter. Finally, architecture can be classified into three main types. Earth-rooted architecture brings out with special force the earth and its symbolisms. Such architecture appears organically related to the earth, the site and its materials, and gravity. Sky-oriented architecture brings out with special force the sky and its symbolisms. Such architecture discloses a world by drawing our attention to the sky bounded by a horizon. It accomplishes this by means of making a building high and centered within the sky, or defying gravity, or tightly integrating the light of outer with inner space. Negatively, this kind of architecture deemphasizes the features that accent the earth. Earth-resting architecture accents neither earth nor sky but rests on the earth, using the earth as a platform with the sky as background. These distinctions should help us solve one of our most pressing problems—city planning. Is it possible to make the city a place to dwell?

Chapter 6 Bibliography

Arnheim, Rudolf. *The Dynamics of Architectural Form.* Berkeley: University of California Press, 1977.

Burchard, John. *The Architecture of America.* Boston: Little, Brown, 1966.

Coles, William A. and Reed Jr., Henry Hope. *Architecture in America: A Battle of Styles.* New York: Appleton-Century-Crofts, 1961.

Coppleston, Trewin, ed. *World Architecture.* London: The Hamlyn Publishing Group, 1973.

Davern, Jeanne M., ed. *Places for People.* New York: McGraw-Hill, 1976.

Fletcher, Banister. *A History of Architecture on the Comparative Method.* 17th ed. New York: Scribner's, 1963.

Giedion, Sigfried. *Space, Time and Architecture.* Cambridge, Mass.: Harvard University Press, 1941.

Gloag, John. *The Architectural Interpretation of History.* New York: St. Martin's, 1977.

Greene, Herb. *Mind and Image.* Lexington, Ky.: University Press of Kentucky, 1976.

Gropius, Walter. *The New Architecture and the Bauhaus.* London: Faber & Faber, 1965.

———. *The Scope of Total Architecture.* New York: Harper and Row, 1955.

Heyer, Paul. *Architects on Architecture.* New York: Walker, 1966.

Jacobs, Jane. *The Death and Life of Great American Cities.* New York: Random House, 1961.

Jordan, R. Furneaux. *A Concise History of Western Architecture.* New York: Harcourt Brace, 1969.

Le Corbusier. *Towards a New Architecture.* New York: Payson and Clark, 1927.

Mumford, Lewis. *The City in History.* New York: Harcourt Brace and World, 1961.

———. *The Roots of Contemporary American Architecture.* New York: Grovc, 1951.

Nervi, Pier Luigi. *Aesthetics and Technology in Building.* Cambridge, Mass.: Harvard University, 1965.

Oliver, Paul, ed. *Shelter and Society.* New York: Praeger, 1969.

Pevsner, Nikolaus. *An Outline of European Architecture.* Baltimore: Penguin, 1961.

Rudofsky, Bernard. *Architecture without Architects.* Garden City, N.Y.: Doubleday, 1964.

Scott, Geoffrey. *The Architecture of Humanism.* London: Norton, 1974.

Scruton, Roger. *The Aesthetics of Architecture.* Princeton, N.J.: Princeton University Press, 1979.

Soleri, Paolo. *The City in the Image of Man.* Cambridge, Mass.: M.I.T., 1973.

Wittkower, Rudolf. *Architecture Principles in the Age of Humanism.* New York: Columbia University Press, 1965.

Wright, Frank Lloyd. *Modern Architecture.* Princeton, N.J.: Princeton University Press, 1931.

———. *The Living City.* New York: Horizon, 1958.

———. *The Natural House.* New York: Horizon, 1954.

———. *A Testament.* New York: Horizon, 1957.

LITERATURE

7 Introduction

Spoken language is the basic medium of literature. Therefore, in this chapter we will stress the fact that literature was designed to be active—literally to be spoken or to be witnessed in an active context. Since we are the inheritors of the printing press and since we no longer read aloud to ourselves, we lose sight of literature's connection with living sound. Once everyone read everything out loud, but since the time of St. Augustine in the fifth century, there has been steady progress toward reading silently. It may be good for developing reading speed, but it is bad for appreciating the subleties and the excitement of literature.

Geoffrey Chaucer wrote down his *Canterbury Tales* for convenience, more than a century before the invention of the printing press. But he read his tales out loud to an audience of courtly listeners who were much more attuned to hearing a good story than to reading it. Today, people interested in literature are usually described as readers, which underscores the dependence we have developed on the printed word for our literary experience. However, since words "sound" even when read silently and the "sound" is an essential part of the "sense" or meaning of the words, we will reemphasize the tradition. The medium of literature is spoken language. If possible, you should hear all the literature in this chapter in recitation. If this is not possible, let the sound of the words ring in your inner ear. Do not attempt speed reading literature. Let your eye follow the pace of the words as controlled by the way your mouth, tongue, and vocal chords form the words, even silently. Do not let sight overwhelm sound.

Interestingly enough, E. E. Cummings' poem, which we discussed on pages 12–14, might seem to be an exception. Based upon the arrangement of the *littera* (Latin for "letters"), the most basic elements of literature, the visual structure may seem more important than the sound structure. If Cummings' poem were to be recited aloud, it would take at least two people to recite it, since one word, "loneliness," has to be sustained while the other words, "a leaf falls," are spoken.

PERCEPTION KEY RECITING CUMMINGS' "1(a"

1. With a group of readers, try to stage a recitation of Cummings' "1(a" on page 13. Several groups could try different approaches using individuals to be responsible for specific letters or syllables or a given word.
2. Comment at length on the recitations and evaluate them. Can this poem be effectively recited?

Treating literature as spoken language points up its relationship to other serial arts such as music, dance, and film. Literature happens in time. In order to perceive it, we must be aware of what is happening now, remember what happened before, and anticipate what is to come. This is not so obvious to us in a short lyric poem or in Cummings' "1(a" because we are in the presence of something akin to a painting: It seems to be all there in front of us at once. But this is far from the truth. To prove this, simply read a short poem, either aloud or silently. One letter follows another; one word another; one sentence another; one line or one stanza another. There is no way for us to perceive the "all-at-onceness" of a literary work as we sometimes perceive a painting, although Cummings' poem comes close.

There is a sense in which a work of literature is a construction of separable elements like architecture. The structural details of a scene, a character or event, or a symbol pattern can be conceived as the bricks in the wall of a literary structure. If one of them is weakly conceived, it can weaken the entire structure. Likewise, if one of those details is imperfectly perceived, our understanding of the function of that detail—and, in turn, of the total structure—will be imperfect. The theme of a literary work is comparable to the architectural decision about the kind of space being enclosed: is it that of a house, church, shopping center, ballroom? The characters, the setting, the sound of the language, the uses of the decisions regarding the materials, size, shape, and landscaping of architecture. Here, perhaps, the analogy ends. But its usefulness will be seen as we proceed in our discussions about the details and structure of literature. It is not just useful but essential to think of literature as works composed of elements that can be discussed individually in order to gain a more thorough perception of them. And it is equally important to realize that the discussion of these individual elements conduces to a fuller understanding of the whole structure.

Our structural emphasis in the following pages will be on the nature of the narrative, both the organic narrative, in which all or most of the individual structural details have a direct bearing on all other details, and the episodic narrative, in which the interdependence of the details is not so tightly organized. Once we have explored some of the basic structures of literature, we will examine some of the more important textural elements. Here our attention will be focused on linguistic details. If the medium of literature is language, we must be sensitive to the fact that literature explores the sounds and meanings of language. In everyday language situations, what we say is often what we mean. But in a work of literature things are rarely that simple. Language has denotation and connotation: a literal and obvious level and a more subtle and suggestive level. When we are being denotative, we say the rose is sick and mean nothing more than that. But if we are using language connotatively, we might mean any of several things by such a statement. When the poet William Blake says the rose is sick, he is describing a symbolic rose, something very different from a literal rose.

The literary symbol, which stretches language's capacity for meaning, is only one kind of use of literary language. Similes, metaphors, images (which make a more direct appeal to our sensory experience), and certain uses of language that have become conventionally acceptable, such as the sounds of the language of the psalms in the King James Bible, will concern us when we analyze the textural elements in literature. All these qualities are found in poetry, fiction, drama, and even the essay.

Our emphasis on narrative and lyric structures in the following pages is not meant to imply that other structures—expository, argumentative, and other essayistic writings—are not worth close examination from a literary point of view. Nor is it meant to imply that the narrative and lyric structures are superior to others or totally independent of them. Some essays have narrative or story structure; some focus on a relatively isolated emotional situation, which is the hallmark of lyric. The urge to tell a story and to explore an emotional situation seems basic to most literature. Moreover, some lyrics are narrative in that they tell a story that centers on an emotional situation. Likewise, some narratives can be regarded as lyric in some ways. It is important, therefore, to understand that we are not arguing for excluding the narrative from the lyric or vice versa. We are separating, for the purpose of examination, structural approaches to the use of language which can intersect and which can help us to understand all forms of literature.

Literary Structures

We begin with the narrative—a basic structural principle that is often used to hold together the details of character, setting, theme, language, and action.

THE NARRATIVE AND THE NARRATOR

The narrative implies a story told by a teller who controls the order of events and the emphasis the events will receive. It also implies an audience to whom the story is told. Some kinds of narrative have very little action. They reveal character through a careful examination of the details of response of the characters to their experiences. Sometimes the teller of the narrative is himself or herself a character; sometimes he or she pretends an awareness of the audience to whom he or she speaks. Our understanding of the narrative will be controlled by the choice the writer makes in creating a narrative, imagining an audience, and deciding which events will give us an understanding of the characters and their situation. By way of becoming acquainted with these concepts, consider the following narrative poem, which is presented in its entirety:

PIANO

Softly, in the dusk, a woman is singing to me;
Taking me back down the vista of years, till I see
A child sitting under the piano, in the boom of the tingling strings
And pressing the small, poised feet of a mother who smiles as she sings.

In spite of myself, the insidious mastery of song
Betrays me back, till the heart of me weeps to belong
To the old Sunday evenings at home, with winter outside
And hymns in the cozy parlor, the tinkling piano our guide.

So now it is vain for the singer to burst into clamor
With the great black piano appassionato. The glamor
Of childish days is upon me, my manhood is cast
Down in the flood of remembrance, I weep like a child for the past.

From *The Complete Poems of D. H. Lawrence*, edited by Vivian de Sola Pinto and F. Warren Roberts. Copyright © 1964, 1971 by Angelo Ravagli and C. M. Weekley, Executors of the Estate of Frieda Lawrence Ravagli. All rights reserved. Reprinted by permission of the Viking Press, Inc.

PERCEPTION KEY "PIANO"

1. What is narrated here—a story of events or a story of character? How do you decide?
2. What do we know about the narrator?
3. Is the narrator aware of the audience to whom the narrative is addressed? If so, what words or lines show concern for the audience?

Lawrence's poem concentrates on the narrator, but it also concentrates on the specific situation that has given rise to the narrative itself. It is what makes possible the double focus of the man as man and as child, with all the ambiguities that the narrator's memory evokes. Many narratives avoid such ambiguities in order to present a more directly focused view. Consider the beginning of the short story, *"My Oedipus Complex,"* by Frank O'Connor:

> Father was in the army all through the war—the first war, I mean—so, up to the age of five, I never saw much of him, and what I saw did not worry me. Sometimes I woke and there was a big figure in khaki peering down at me in the candlelight. Sometimes in the early morning I heard the slamming of the front door and the clatter of nailed boots down the cobbles of the lane. These were Father's entrances and exits. Like Santa Claus he came and went mysteriously.
>
> In fact, I rather liked his visits, though it was an uncomfortable squeeze between Mother and him when I got into the big bed in the early morning. He smoked, which gave him a pleasant musty smell, and shaved, an operation of astounding interest. Each time he left a trail of souvenirs—model tanks and Gurkha knives with handles made of bullet cases, and German helmets and cap badges and button-sticks, and all sorts of military equipment—carefully stowed away in a long box on top of the wardrobe, in case they ever came in handy. There was a bit of the magpie about Father; he expected everything to come in handy. When his back was turned, Mother let me get a chair and rummage through his treasures. She didn't seem to think so highly of them as he did.[1]

PERCEPTION KEY "MY OEDIPUS COMPLEX"

1. What does the narrator reveal about himself in this passage? What can you consider as hard information? What conclusions can be drawn from the information the narrator gives us?
2. Taking the title into consideration (an Oedipus complex is a sexual "orientation" toward the parent of the opposite sex), what do the events narrated in these paragraphs suggest? Can you imagine how the story will unfold?

[1]Reprinted from *The Stories of Frank O'Connor* by Frank O'Connor, by permission of Alfred A. Knopf, Inc. Copyright 1950, 1952 by Frank O'Connor.

One interesting feature of both these examples is that in order to be consistent we must treat the narrator as a character in the literary work. Thus, we understand the "I" of "Piano" as a character in the poem just as much as we understand the mother. But the problem with that is curious. Since each of us conceives of him or herself as "I," we also accept the "I" of a narrative with the same kind of lack of examination we apply to accepting ourselves. Lawrence or O'Connor is the "I," and that is all there is to it for some readers. Yet, there is no compelling reason for us to think this; it is merely a matter of psychological habit and convenience, leading, it may be, to misinterpretations that weaken the power of the poem.

The following poem is a powerful example of the way in which a writer uses the first person but clearly creates a character apart from her. It is told by someone in an iron lung:

PARALYTIC

It happens. Will it go on?—
My mind a rock,
No fingers to grip, no tongue,
My god the iron lung

That loves me, pumps
My two
Dust bags in and out,
Will not

Let me relapse
While the day outside glares by like ticker tape
The night brings violets,
Tapestries of eyes,

Lights,
The soft anonymous
Talkers: "You all right?"
The starched, inaccessible breast.

Dead egg, I lie
Whole
On a whole world I cannot touch,
At the white, tight

Drum of my sleeping couch
Photographs visit me—
My wife, dead and flat, in 1920 furs,
Mouth full of pearls,

Two girls
As flat as she, who whisper "We're your daughters."
The still waters
Wrap my lips,

Eyes, nose and ears,
A clear
Cellophane I cannot crack.
On my bare back

I smile, a buddha, all
Wants, desire
Falling from me like rings
Hugging their lights.

The claw
Of the magnolia,
Drunk on its own scents,
Asks nothing of life.

"Paralytic" from *Ariel* by Sylvia Plath (published by Faber &
Faber, London). Copyright © 1965 by Ted Hughes. By
permission of Harper & Row, Publishers, Inc.

Once we know this poem is by a woman who did not live in an
iron lung, we begin to accept the person speaking as a character in the
narrative rather than as a projection of a poet-narrator addressing us.
Yet, without this outside information, the poem could never have
revealed this "reality." Consequently, it has become a convention in
literature to treat all narrators as part of the narrative, just as we would
treat all words used in the piece as part of the narrative.

PERCEPTION KEY "PARALYTIC"

1. Analyze the narrative. What are the problems of telling a story from the
   point of view of a person who is paralyzed?
2. What is the role of the magnolia claw—a living but not a moving
   instrument, as with people's hands—in the poem?
3. Explore some of the implications of the fact that the narrator of the poem
   is an imaginary character invented by the poet. Is this information crucial
   to a full understanding of the poem?
4. Sylvia Plath committed suicide not long after writing this poem. Does that
   information add intensity to your experience of the poem?

THE EPISODIC NARRATIVE

The term "episodic" implies significant disconnectedness in the parts
of the structure. The episodic narrative is one of the oldest forms of
literature—Homer's *Odyssey* is an example. We are aware of the
overall structure of the story centering on the adventures of Odysseus,
but each adventure is almost a complete structure in itself. We develop
a clear sense of the character of Odysseus as we follow him in his

adventures, but this does not always happen in episodic literature. Often the adventures are completely disconnected from one another, and the thread that is intended to connect everything—the character of the protagonist—is not strong enough to keep things together. Sometimes the character may even seem to be a different person from one episode to the next. This is often the case in oral literature, compositions that were "written" by tellers or singers of stories rather than by persons who wrote their narratives. In the former cases, the singers gathered adventures from many sources and joined them in one long narrative. The chances of disconnectedness, then, are naturally quite strong.

But disconnectedness is sometimes not undesirable. It is risked in the episodic narrative in order to gain several things: compression, speed of pacing, plenty of action, and variety that sustains attention. Some of the most important famous episodic narratives are novels: Fielding's *Tom Jones*, Cervantes' *Don Quixote*, Defoe's *Moll Flanders*. These are older works, but Graham Greene's *Power and the Glory* and J. P. Donleavy's *Ginger Man* both give evidence that the mode is viable in contemporary literature.

PERCEPTION KEY THE EPISODIC NARRATIVE

1. Consider any episodic narratives you have read or heard. What are their strong points? Why do people continue to like episodic narratives? Why are they the chief narrative structure used for mystery or adventure novels like the James Bond adventures?
2. Aristotle considered episodic structure as second-rate. Why would he do so? Is there any inherent weakness in the episodic structure that would cause it to be looked down upon?

Novels and epics are not the only literary modes to use episodic structures, nor are all episodic structures long works. One very popular episodic structure is the ballad. It usually tells a story about a specific hero or heroine, and it has a peculiar quality of not respecting strict chronology or strict consistency of events. Since it was originally sung in the streets and along the byways of Europe, the ballad tends to be a casual genre. Heroes die in stanza four only to show up again hale and hearty in stanza eight. Such poems are usually the work of several wandering singers; each wishes to contribute something without undoing the work of predecessors.

Langston Hughes' "Ballad of the Landlord" reads somewhat like a sequence of events reported in a newspaper. The time frame seems to shift forward and backward, and a variety of events are recounted without worrying about how they are tied together. Because we are familiar with the sequence of such events, we can easily **understand** the relative importance of each.

BALLAD OF THE LANDLORD

Landlord, Landlord,
My roof has sprung a leak.
Don't you 'member I told you about it
Way last week?

Landlord, Landlord,
These steps is broken down.
When you come up yourself
It's a wonder you don't fall down.

Ten bucks you say I owe you?
Ten bucks you say is due?
Well, that's Ten bucks more'n I'll pay you
Till you fix this house up new.

What? You gonna get eviction orders?
You gonna cut off my heat?
You gonna take my furniture and
Throw it on the street?

Um-huh! You talking high and mighty.
Talk on—till you get through.
You ain't gonna be able to say a word
If I land my fist on you.

Police! Police!
Come and get this man!
He's trying to ruin the government
And overturn the land!
Copper's whistle!
Patrol bell!
Arrest.

Precinct Station.
Iron cell
Headlines in press:

MAN THREATENS LANDLORD

TENANT HELD NO BAIL

JUDGE GIVES NEGRO 90 DAYS IN COUNTY JAIL

Reprinted by permission of Harold Ober Associates, Inc.
Copyright 1951. From *Montage of a Dream Deferred*, by
Langston Hughes.

1. What are the main episodes in the ballad? Are any of them out of usual time order? Are there any unusual techniques that emphasize the breaking off of action or events?
2. Why is this poem not titled "Ballad of the Negro Tenant"?
3. Who is the main character in the ballad? What do we really know about him? And how?
4. Hughes was a black writer, a member of the "Harlem Renaissance" of the 1920s and 1930s. Does this make a difference in the way we read the poem?

THE QUEST NARRATIVE

Any reader of mystery stories—such as those by Arthur Conan Doyle, which feature Sherlock Holmes, or the Miss Marple mysteries by Agatha Christie—will realize that one of the chief ingredients of many and perhaps most narratives is the quest. By quest is meant more— even in mystery stories—than just a quest for a murderer or a searching for clues and objects. Often, particularly in modern fiction, the quest is by the main character, or *protagonist*, for self. Since it is clear that most humans feel uncertain about their own nature—where they have come from, who they are, where they are going—it is natural that writers from all cultures should invent fictions that string adventures and character development and changes on the thread of the quest for self-identity. This quest is so attractive to our imaginations that we find it sustains our attention almost all the time. And while our attention is arrested by the narrative, the author can broaden and deepen the meaning of the question until it engages our conceptions of ourselves. When it becomes literature—that is, takes on an artistic quality—the quest almost always becomes a search for self-identity. And such a search in quest literature usually reveals in some ways the identity of both the protagonist and the reader.

One of the most important recent novels that employs this structure is Ralph Ellison's *Invisible Man*. The quest is so deeply rooted in the novel that the protagonist has no name. We know a great deal about him, though, because he narrates the story and tells us much about himself. He is black, southern, and, as a young college student, ambitious. His heroes are George Washington Carver and Booker T. Washington. He craves the dignity and the opportunity he associates with their lives. But things go wrong. He is dismissed unjustly from his college in the South and must, like Odysseus, leave his home to seek his fortune. He imagines himself destined for better things and eagerly pursues his fate, finding a place to live and work up North, beginning to find his identity as a black man. He discovers the sophisticated urban society of New York City, the political subtleties of communism, the pains of black nationalism, and the realities of his relationship to white people, to whom he is an invisible man. Yet he does not hate the whites, and in his own image of himself he remains an invisible man. The novel ends with the hero in an underground place he has found and which he has lighted, by tapping the electric company's lines, with almost two thousand electric light bulbs. Still, he cannot consider himself—despite this colossal illumination—visible. He ends his quest without finding out who he is beyond this fundamental fact: he is invisible.

The quest narrative is native to American culture. Mark Twain's *Huckleberry Finn* is one of the most important examples of the structure in American literature. But whereas *Invisible Man* is an organic quest narrative, because the details of the novel are closely interwoven, *Huckleberry Finn* is an episodic quest narrative. Huck's travels along the great Mississippi River qualify as episodic in the same sense that *Don Quixote*, to which this novel is closely related, is episodic. Huck is questing for freedom for Jim, but also for freedom from his own father. Like Don Quixote, Huck comes back from his quest rich in the knowledge of who he is. In this sense one might say Don Quixote's quest is for the truth about who he is and was, since he is an old man when he begins. But Huck Finn is a child, so his quest must be for knowledge of who he is and can be.

PERCEPTION KEY THE QUEST NARRATIVE

Read a quest narrative. Some suggestions, in addition to those given above are: Herman Melville, *Moby Dick*; T. S. Eliot, *The Waste Land*; William Faulkner, *Absalom, Absalom!*; Ernest Hemingway, *The Old Man and the Sea*; J. D. Salinger, *The Catcher in the Rye*; Graham Greene, *The Third Man*; Franz Kafka, *The Castle*; and Albert Camus, *The Stranger*. You may get other suggestions from friends or teachers. What is the quest and what is actually found? How different are the various quests and their outcomes? How does the quest help the protagonist get to know himself better? How does the quest structure help you get to know the character better? Does the quest help you understand yourself better?

Long poems, those we sometimes refer to as epic poems, seem natural for the quest motif, but they are not the only poems that use the structure. Lewis Carroll's famous nonsense poem "Jabberwocky" is fairly short, but it is the story of a boy's knightlike adventures in pursuit of the Jabberwock, whom he finds and slays. We can read the poem with understanding because it is held together by the orderliness of the quest, an order we already understand from our experiences with other literature. If there were not that kind of order in the poem, Carroll would not be able to ignore the usual logic of language, as he does throughout the poem:

JABBERWOCKY

'Twas brillig, and the slithy toves
    Did gyre and gimble in the wabe:
All mimsy were the borogoves,
        And the mome raths outgrabe.

"Beware the Jabberwock, my son!
    The jaws that bite, the claws that catch!
Beware the Jubjub bird, and shun
        The frumious Bandersnatch!"

He took his vorpal sword in hand:
    Long time the manxome foe he sought—
So rested he by the Tumtum tree,
        And stood awhile in thought.

And, as in uffish thought he stood,
    The Jabberwock, with eyes of flame,
Came whiffling through the tulgey wood,
        And burbled as it came!

One, two! One, two! And through and through
    The vorpal blade went snicker-snack!
He left it dead, and with its head
        He went galumphing back.

"And, hast thou slain the Jabberwock?
    Come to my arms, my beamish boy!
O frabjous day! Callooh! Callay!"
        He chortled in his joy.

'Twas brillig, and the slithy toves
    Did gyre and gimble in the wabe:
All mimsy were the borogoves,
        And the mome raths outgrabe.

PERCEPTION KEY "JABBERWOCKY"

1. If we assume that this poem is a condensed quest narrative, what seem to be the main elements of the quest?
2. What does the boy gain in terms of self-knowledge in this poem?
3. Does it matter that the Jabberwock actually finds the boy rather than the boy finding the Jabberwock?
4. When Alice, in *Alice in Wonderland*, comes across this poem it is printed backwards and must be placed before a mirror to be understood. Does this have any bearing on its value as a quest narrative?

THE LYRIC

The lyric is a structure, virtually always a poem, that is used primarily to reveal a relatively limited but deep feeling. The lyric is almost always associated with the feeling of a given poet, although we have already seen that it is not difficult for poets to create narrators distinct from themselves. In any case, someone in the lyric poem is speaking to us, and usually it is the poet's or author's emotional situation that is explored in the lyric modes.

If we participate, we find ourselves caught up in the emotional situation of the lyric. It is usually revealed to us through a recounting of the circumstances the poet is reflecting on. T. S. Eliot has spoken of an objective correlative: an object that correlates with the poet's feeling. Eliot has said that poets must find the situation, event, or person that correlates with their emotion so that they can interpret the emotion and readers can comprehend it. Perhaps this is too narrow a view of the poet's creative process, for it seems quite possible for poets to understand and interpret emotions without necessarily undergoing them. Otherwise, it would seem that Shakespeare, for example, and even Eliot would have blown up like overcompressed boilers if they had had to experience directly all the feelings they interpreted in their poems. But in any case, it seems clear that the lyric has feeling—emotion, passion, or mood—as basic in its subject matter.

The word "lyric" implies a personal statement by an involved writer who feels deeply. In one limited sense, lyrics are poems to be sung to music. Most lyrics before the seventeenth century were set to music. Thus, most Medieval and Renaissance lyrics were written to be sung with musical accompaniment, usually performed on a lute or other portable string instrument. And the writers who composed the words were usually the composers of the music—at least until the seventeenth century, when specialization began to separate those functions. Some of the examples that follow are meant to be sung to music; most of them could be sung if you wanted to find a tune that would suit them.

John Keats (1795–1821), an English poet of the romantic period, died of tuberculosis. His sonnet, written in 1818, has a basis in biographical fact:

When I have fears that I may cease to be
Before my pen has glean'd my teeming brain,
Before high-piled books, in charact'ry,
Hold like rich garners the full-ripen'd grain;
When I behold, upon the night's starr'd face,
Huge cloudy symbols of a high romance,
And think that I may never live to trace
Their shadows, with the magic hand of chance;
And when I feel, fair creature of an hour!
That I shall never look upon thee more,
Never have relish in the faery power
Of unreflecting love! then on the shore
Of the wide world I stand alone, and think
Till love and fame to nothingness do sink.

1. First establish what, for you, is the emotional situation in this lyric. Then, by asking others who have read the poem, find out how much of a range of understanding there is. Do most readers achieve approximately the same interpretation of the poem?
2. This poem has no setting, yet it establishes an atmosphere of uncertainty and, possibly, of terror. How does Keats create this atmosphere?

Keats is interpreting a terrible personal feeling. He realizes he may die before he can write his best poems. In fact, the epitaph Keats chose for his headstone just before he died is: "Here lies one whose name was writ on water." He felt his poems would not be read by posterity. He was wrong. Moreover, his work is so brilliant that we cannot help wondering what else he might have done. Had Chaucer, Shakespeare, Milton, or Joyce died at twenty-six, we might not know their names at all. All their most important work was yet to come.

It is not difficult to understand how Keats must have felt when he had fears that he might die before he had written what he wanted. But it is also important for us to understand that the lyric mode makes it difficult for him to communicate his feelings to us. He has no story to tell and very little in the way of a setting to create an atmosphere that might give us a clue about his feelings. His interest in character is limited, even though he is himself the narrator of the poem. What, then, are his resources?

One is the fact that since we all will die, we can sympathize with the thought of death cutting a life work short. The tone Keats establishes in the poem—one of direct speech, honestly said, not overdone or melodramatic—is one of the most important resources he has. It gives the poem an immediacy: one human being telling something straight from the heart to another. Keats modulates the tone slightly, slowing things down enough at the end of the poem for us to sense and share the contemplative mood.

An entirely different mood established by quite different means characterizes the next poem. It was written in the second half of the nineteenth century by a poet who was also a Jesuit priest. It is very personal but also, like the psalms of the Bible, something of a prayer or hymm of praise.

PIED BEAUTY

Glory be to God for dappled things—
    For skies of couple-colour as a brinded cow;
      or rose-moles all in stipple upon trout that swim;

Fresh-firecoal chestnut-falls; finches' wings;
    Landscape plotted and pieced—fold, fallow, and plough;
      And all trades, their gear and tackle and trim.

All things counter, original, spare, strange;
    Whatever is fickle, freckled (who knows how?)
      With swift, slow; sweet, sour; adazzle, dim;
He fathers-forth whose beauty is past change:
Praise him.[2]

Gerard Manley Hopkins

PERCEPTION KEY "PIED BEAUTY"

1. Hopkins reveals joy in this poem. How? Are there elements inconsistent with joyousness?
2. How many senses does Hopkins make reference to in the poem? Is the awareness of the sensory important in our experience of the poem?
3. See what range of responses you can discover in those who read this poem. Query people who have read the poem under the same circumstances you have, then query people who come to it "cold." How different is their understanding of the poem?
4. God is referred to as him rather than Him in the last line. Is this simply a printer's convention?

The range of the lyric is enormous. We have been talking about it as centering on a single powerful emotion, avoiding the narrative mode. But this is not quite accurate, for the lyric is often able to "narrate" the poet's range of interest in a subject matter; it is a structure that gives him free rein to explore a subject matter of almost any kind. One may wish to see in any such exploration the feelingful response of the poet, but such considerations ought not to delimit the lyric in any way.

The usefulness of the lyric for bringing out the significance of things as felt meditatively is so great that perhaps this is its most important purpose. It is a mode that, in its meditativeness, can explore any number of aspects of a subject matter. Without necessarily having a story to tell, the poet need not rush off into something that is not central to the meditation itself. One famous meditative poem is Walt Whitman's "A Noiseless Patient Spider," a poem that is perhaps as much a tribute to the patience of Walt Whitman as it is to the spider.

[2]*Pied:* spotted, like "dappled" and "couple-colour." *Brinded:* spots or streaks on a buff-colored background. *Chestnut-falls:* the skin of the hot chestnut, stripped off. *Plotted and pieced:* fields of different shaped rectangles. *Fold, fallow, and plough:* fields used for different purposes, and that look different to the eye.

But it goes beyond such tributes, because out of Whitman's contemplation of the spider comes insight into the human soul.

A NOISELESS PATIENT SPIDER

A noiseless patient spider,
I mark'd where on a little promontory it stood isolated,
Mark'd how to explore the vacant vast surrounding,
It launch'd forth filament, filament, filament, out of itself,
Ever unreeling them, ever tirelessly speeding them.

And you O my soul where you stand,
Surrounded, detached, in measureless oceans of space,
Ceaselessly musing, venturing, throwing, seeking the spheres to
    connect them,
Till the bridge you will need be form'd, till the ductile
    anchor hold,
Till the gossamer thread you fling catch somewhere, O my soul.

PERCEPTION KEY "A NOISELESS PATIENT SPIDER"

1. Whitman sees a connection between the spider and the human soul. What, exactly, is that connection? How reasonable does it seem to you?
2. Explore the meaning of this poem with other readers. Is there a consensus about the connection Whitman makes between the spider and the soul?

Three lyrics follows. They are very different in nature, although each one focuses on strong feelings. Symbols, metaphors, and images interpret those feelings for the attentive reader. Blake's "Tyger" seems to be about many things, especially the nature of evil and the nature of nature itself. The tiger is a powerful symbol in the poem, but it is not easy to say precisely what it symbolizes. It is a poem that, of the three, has most frequently been set to music. Matthew Arnold's "Dover Beach" has been set to music as well. It focuses on the isolation of two people who contemplate the uncertainties and terror of the future. For the modern reader, this is a particularly timely poem, since the "armies of the night"—to use Norman Mailer's paraphrase of Arnold—seem to have been more highly visible in the last fifty years than in the more distant past. Rolfe Humphries' lyric is less theological, less cosmically historical than the other two and it seems not to have been set to music. It concentrates on one man's reactions to a spectacle that becomes symbolic and meaningful to him: baseball at the old Polo Grounds. He finds a symbol that permits him to take a measure of himself and develop a useful perspective for contemplating his own nature. In this selection consider the rich varieties of the lyric.

THE TYGER

Tyger! Tyger! burning bright
In the forests of the night,
What immortal hand or eye
Could frame thy fearful symmetry?

In what distant deeps or skies
Burnt the fire of thine eyes?
On what wings dare he aspire?
What the hand dare seize the fire?

And what shoulder, and what art,
Could twist the sinews of thy heart?
And when thy heart began to beat,
What dread hand? and what dread feet?

What the hammer? what the chain?
In what furnace was thy brain?
What the anvil? what dread grasp
Dare its deadly terrors clasp?

When the stars threw down their spears,
And water'd heaven with their tears,
Did he smile his work to see?
Did he who made the Lamb make thee?

Tyger! Tyger! burning bright
In the forests of the night,
What immortal hand or eye
Dare frame thy fearful symmetry?

William Blake

DOVER BEACH

The sea is calm to-night.
The tide is full, the moon lies fair
Upon the straits;—on the French coast, the light
Gleams and is gone; the cliffs of England stand,
Glimmering and vast, out in the tranquil bay.
Come to the window, sweet is the night air!
Only, from the long line of spray
Where the sea meets the moon-blanch'd land,
Listen, you hear the grating roar
Of pebbles which the waves draw back, and fling,
At their return, up the high strand,
Begin, and cease, and then again begin,
With tremulous cadence slow, and bring
The eternal note of sadness in.

Sophocles long ago
Heard it on the Ægæan, and it brought
Into his mind the turbid ebb and flow
Of human misery; we
Find also in the sound a thought,
Hearing it by this distant northern sea.

The Sea of Faith
Was once, too, at the full, and round earth's shore
Lay like the folds of a bright girdle furl'd.
But now I only hear
Its melancholy, long, withdrawing roar,
Retreating, to the breath
Of the night-wind, down the vast edges drear
And naked shingles of the world.

Ah, love, let us be true
To one another! for the world, which seems
To lie before us like a land of dreams,
So various, so beautiful, so new,
Hath really neither joy, nor love, nor light,
Nor certitude, nor peace, nor help for pain;
And we are here as on a darkling plain
Swept with confused alarms of struggle and flight,
Where ignorant armies clash by night.

Matthew Arnold

POLO GROUNDS

Time is of the essence. This is a highly skilled
And beautiful mystery. Three or four seconds only
From the time that Riggs connects till he reaches first,
And in those seconds Jurges goes to his right,
Comes up with the ball, tosses to Witek at second
For the force on Reese, Witek to Mize at first,
In time for the out—a double play.

(Red Barber crescendo. Crowd noises, obbligato;
Scattered staccatos from the peanut boys,
Loud in the lull, as the teams are changing sides) . . .
Hubbell takes the sign, nods, pumps, delivers—
A foul into the stands. Dunn takes a new ball out,
Hands it to Danning, who throws it down to Werber;
Werber takes off his glove, rubs the ball briefly,
Tosses it over to Hub, who goes to the rosin bag,
Takes the sign from Danning, pumps, delivers—
Low, outside, ball three. Danning goes to the mound,
Says something to Hub. Dunn brushes off the plate,
Adams starts throwing in the Giant bull pen,
Hub takes the sign from Danning, pumps, delivers,
Camilli gets hold of it, a *long* fly to the outfield,

Ott goes back, back, back, against the wall, gets under it,
Pounds his glove, and takes it for the out.
That's all for the Dodgers. . . .

Time is of the essence. The rhythms break,
More varied and subtle than any kind of dance;
Movement speeds up or lags. The ball goes out
In sharp and angular drives, or long, slow arcs,
Comes in again controlled and under aim;
The players wheel or spurt, race, stoop, slide, halt,
Shift imperceptibly to new positions,
Watching the signs, according to the batter,
The score, the inning. Time is of the essence.
Time is of the essence. Remember Terry?
Remember Stonewall Jackson, Lindstrom, Frisch,
When they were good? Remember Long George Kelly?
Remember John McGraw and Benny Kauff?
Remember Bridwell, Tenney, Merkle, Youngs,
Chief Myers, Big Jeff Tesreau, Shufflin' Phil?
Remember Matthewson, and Ames, and Donlin,
Buck Ewing, Rusie, Smiling Mickey Welch?
Remember a left-handed catcher named Jack Humphries,
Who sometimes played the outfield, in '83?

Time is of the essence. The shadow moves
From the plate to the box, from the box to second base,
From second to the outfield, to the bleachers.

Time is of the essence. The crowd and players
Are the same age always, but the man in the crowd
Is older every season. Come on, play ball!

Rolfe Humphries

From *Collected Poems of Rolfe Humphries*. Copyright © 1965 by
Indiana University Press. Reprinted by permission.

PERCEPTION KEY VARIETIES OF LYRIC

1. Begin by establishing a taxonomy of the lyric. This means drawing up a list
   of the qualities you feel the lyric possesses. Try to decide which qualities
   are most important and which are least important for the lyric.
2. Select a favorite song lyric. What does it have in common with the lyrics of
   Blake, Arnold, and Humphries? What different elements or qualities does
   it seem to have? Are these important to lyrics in general?
3. If possible, listen to Ralph Vaughan-Williams' musical setting of Blake's
   "Tyger." Does it help clarify the poem to hear music with it? Are any of
   your ideas about the poem altered by hearing it sung? If you cannot find
   this particular setting, experiment with some song lyrics you find more
   convenient. What is the relative importance of the words to the music?
4. Is it possible to talk about lyric structure? On the basis of your experience,

can you contrast narrative expectations with lyric expectations in literature? Does the focus on feeling—emotion, passion, or mood—help in
establishing the concept of lyric structure?

5. Try your hand at writing a lyric poem. Decide before or as you write what
   you are trying to achieve, then keep refining your lines in order to help
   achieve what you want. After you have written your lyric, give it to
   someone to read and find out what he or she thinks you have achieved.

Literary Details

So far we have been speaking of literature in terms of its structures,
those principles of organization that give it an overall order and shape.
But within every structure are details or individual elements that need
close examination in many cases before structural principles can be
fully understood.

Literature uses language in ways that are somewhat different from
everyday uses. This is not to say literature is artificial and unrelated to
the language we speak but, rather, that we sometimes do not see the
fullest implications of our speech and rarely take full advantage of the
opportunities language affords us to say what we mean. Literature uses
language to reveal meanings that are usually absent from our daily
speech.

Our emphasis here in treating matters of detail will be upon
several special kinds of language usages; the image, the metaphor and
simile, the symbol. There are other, often more subtle, usages of
language also worthy of our attention, but those named are so central
to literature of all genres that they will stand as introduction enough
for our purposes. To these particular usages of language we will add one
further: diction. The term is ambiguous and so must be defined here. It
is the choice of words for a given situation. The diction of a piece of
literature will sometimes tend to make that piece seem "inevitable,"
as if there were no other way of saying the same thing. Oddly enough,
sometimes the most artificial and stilted diction will produce results
that will be perfect for the situation at hand. Other times, however, the
most conversational diction will produce better results. Each situation
must be examined independently, since no rules will serve for all.

THE IMAGE

Imagery involves any use of language that asks us to imagine what is
being described. It may appeal to our sense of sight, sound, taste, odor,
or touch—or any combination of these. The richness of the image
partly depends on our capacity to reconstruct fully the image in our
imagination. And much of this depends upon the care and creativity
with which the writer has presented the images for our consideration.
One of the most striking resources of any kind of literature is the

capacity of language to help us reconstruct in our minds the "reality" of perceptions that the author wishes to reveal. This resource is as important in prose as in poetry. Consider, for example, the following passage from Joseph Conrad's "Youth":

> The boats, fast astern, lay in a deep shadow, and all around I could see the circle of the sea lighted by the fire. A gigantic flame arose forward straight and clear. It flared fierce, with noises like the whirr of wings, with rumbles as of thunder. There were cracks, detonations, and from the cone of flame the sparks flew upwards, as man is born to trouble, to leaky ships, and to ships that burn.

PERCEPTION KEY YOUTH

1. Which of our senses is most powerfully appealed to in this passage?
2. How would this passage differ from the average, "nonliterary" description of a burning boat? If possible, read a description of a burning boat (perhaps one written by yourself or one of your friends) that does not specifically try to involve the reader in the occurrence itself. What are the differences between it and Conrad's passage? Examine and compare the images in each.
3. What are the ways in which Conrad uses imagery to help us participate with the experience he describes?

In *Youth* this scene is fleeting, only an instant in the total structure of the book. But the entire book is composed of such details, ensuring the reader's participation.

For some writers, such as poet Ezra Pound, the image is almost all there is. Pound and several other writers of the early twentieth century grouped together and became known as Imagist poets. One classic example of this school is Pound's famous poem:

IN A STATION OF THE METRO

The apparition of these faces in the crowd.
Petals on a wet, black bough.

Ezra Pound, *Personae*, Copyright 1926 by Ezra Pound. Reprinted by permission of New Directions Publishing Corporation.

The Metro is the Paris subway. The poem really does not make direct comment about the character of these faces—they are not good, not bad, not threatening, not loving. We really do not know much more about them in these respects than if we had been there ourselves to see them as Pound did. The poem asks us to "image" the scene; we must reconstruct it in our imagination. And in doing so we participate with the appearance of these faces: They are like petals on a wet black bough. This device is a metaphor (see the next section on this subject), and in this case, its function is to clarify our imagining of the scene.

Pound was influenced in this poem and others by the achievement of Chinese and Japanese poets. Their use of image stimulated him to consider the possibilities in a language and in a culture that had not fully explored their techniques. The following poem is by the Chinese poet Tu Mu.

THE RETIRED OFFICIAL YÜAN'S HIGH PAVILION

The West River's watershed sounds beyond the sky.
Shadows of pines in front of the studio sweep the clouds flat.
Who shall coax me to blow the long flute
Leaning together on the spring wind with the moonbeams for our toys?

From *Poems of the Late T'ang*, A. C. Graham (trans.), Penguin Books Ltd. (Penguin Classics 1965. © A. C. Graham, 1965.)

PERCEPTION KEY "THE RETIRED OFFICIAL YÜAN'S HIGH PAVILION"

---

1. What are the most significant images in this poem?
2. How completely do you find yourself actively imagining scenes in response to the poem?
3. Do these images take you beyond yourselves into meanings that are not immediately apparent? If so, how?
4. We think these images do go far beyond perception into concepts or ideas. In discussion with others, try to make explicit the concepts of the poem as evoked by the percepts.

THE METAPHOR

Metaphor helps writers intensify language. Metaphor is a class of linguistic comparisons designed to change our conception of the things being compared. Poets or writers will usually let us know which of the two things compared is the main object of their attention. They will usually expect that the comparison will have a greater effect on that object than on the thing they use to make the comparison. For example:

Art is long, and Time is fleeting,
    And our hearts, though stout and brave,
Still, like muffled drums, are beating
    Funeral marches to the grave.

Henry Wadsworth Longfellow, from "A Psalm of Life"

The expression of sentiment in this poem is ancient, dating back to the Roman maxim: *"Ars longa, vita breva est,"* which translates: "Art is long, life is short." Longfellow adds to it a metaphor that he found in Henry King's seventeenth-century poem, "The Exequy": the comparison of the pulse rate with a drum measuring the distance to the grave. The pulse rate and the drumbeat are not the only comparisons here. There is the obvious comparison with art and life, two very different things—perhaps even more different than the heart and the drum, which themselves do not seem at first glance to have much in common. Such a surprising comparison is often one of the most important features of the metaphor. It takes a poet to show us fresh relationships between things.

PERCEPTION KEY METAPHOR

What is the result of Longfellow's comparing the heartbeat with the beat of funeral drums? Does the comparison reveal any unexpected and significant truths about hearts, drums, funerals, or life itself? Is the metaphor particularly economical in its ability to impart meaning to the stanza? How is metaphor different from the ordinary speech of our everyday life?

The standard definition for the metaphor is that it is a comparison made without any explicit words to tell us a comparison is being made. The simile is the kind of comparison that has explicit words: "like," "as," "than," "as if," and a few others. We have no trouble recognizing the simile, although we get so used to seeing similes in literature that we accept them usually with no special degree of awareness.

Some people make a fuss over the difference between a metaphor and a simile. We will not do so because basically both are forms of comparison for effect, and both are part of a general class of language uses called tropes (linguistic changes for effect). Our discussion, then, will use the general term "metaphor" and use the more special term "simile" only when necessary. On the other hand, the term "symbol," which is also metaphoric, will be treated separately, since its effect is usually much more specialized than either the nonsymbolic metaphor or simile.

Metaphoric language is not limited, of course, to the poetry and prose of Western culture. Non-Western writing finds the metaphor as congenial to its various languages as Western writing does. The use of metaphor seems to pervade all cultures. Daily conversation—usually none too literary in character—is full of metaphoric language used to emphasize our points and to give color and feeling to our speech (check this for yourself). The Chinese poet Li Ho shows us that the resources of metaphor and simile function for all of us:

THE GRAVE OF LITTLE SU

I ride a coach with lacquered sides,
My love rides a dark piebald horse.
Where shall we bind our hearts as one?
On West Mound, beneath the pines and cypresses.

(Ballad ascribed to the singing girl Little Su, ca. A.D. 500).

Dew on the secret orchid
No thing to bind the heart to.
Misted flowers I cannot bear to cut.
Grass like a cushion,
The pine like a parasol:
The wind is a skirt,
The waters are tinkling pendants.
A coach with lacquered sides
Waits for someone in the evening.
Cold blue candle-flames
Strain to shine bright.
Beneath West Mound
The wind puffs the rain.

From *Poems of the Late T'ang*, A. C. Graham (trans.), Penguin Books Ltd. (Penguin Classic 1965).© A. C. Graham, 1965.

Clearly, Little Su was important to the narrator. But the portrayal of his feeling for her is oblique—which is, perhaps, the reason for the use of so many metaphors in such a short poem. Instead of striking bluntly and immediately, the metaphoric language delicately resounds with nuances, so that we are aware of its cumulative impact only after the moment of reading.

PERCEPTION KEY "THE GRAVE OF LITTLE SU"

1. Enumerate the uses of metaphor in the poem. Compare what you find with the findings of other readers. Do you find disagreement on how many uses of metaphor there are? If so, what does that mean?

2. Along with two or three other readers, select for yourself the most impressive use of metaphor. The likelihood is that you and others will choose different examples. Explain to one another the reasons for the effectiveness of the metaphor you have chosen.

We accept metaphor in poetry, but we do not always realize how extensive the device is in other kinds of literature. Prose fiction, essays, drama or literature meant for the stage, and almost every form of writing we knows uses the metaphoric mode to some extent or another. Poetry in general tends to have a higher metaphoric density than other forms of writing, partly because poetry is somewhat distilled and condensed to begin with. Rarely, however, is the density of metaphor quite as thick as in "The Grave of Little Su."

Since literature depends so heavily on metaphor, it is essential that we reflect on its use. One kind of metaphor tends to evoke an image and involves us mainly on a perceptual level—because we perceive in our imagination something of what we would perceive were we there. This kind we shall call a "perceptual metaphor." Another kind of metaphor tends to evoke ideas, give us information that is mainly conceptual. This kind of metaphor we shall call a "conceptual metaphor." To tell us the pine is like a parasol is basically perceptual: Were we there, we would see that the cone shape of the pine resembles that of a parasol. But to tell us the wind is a skirt is to go far beyond perception and simple "likeness." The metaphor lures us to reflect upon the suggestion that the wind resembles a skirt, and we begin to think about the ways in which this might be true. Then, once we have understood the ways in which this is true, we are lured further—this is an enticing metaphor—to explore the implications of this truth. If the wind is like a skirt, what then is the significance of this in the poem? In what ways does this conceptual metaphor help us to understand the poet's insights at the grave of Little Su? In what ways does the perceptual metaphor of the pine/parasol help us?

The answer to how the wind is a skirt is by no means simple. Its complexity is one of the most precious qualities of this poem. It is also one of the most precious possibilities of the conceptual metaphor, for then one can go beyond the relatively simple perceptual comparison into the more suggestive and significant act of understanding. We might suggest, for instance, that if the wind is like a skirt, it clothes a girl: Little Su. But Little Su is dead, so perhaps it clothes her spirit. The comparison is between the wind and the spirit. Both things are impossible to see, but their effects can be felt by writers and—when the idea is communicated by their readers.

The same kind of complexity is present in Tu Mu's poem, "The Retired Official Yüan's High Pavilion." The last line suggests that the moonbeams are toys. The metaphor is quiet, restrained, but as direct as the wind/skirt metaphor. Moreover, the last line suggests that the wind is something that can be leaned against. It would be worth turning back to that poem to see just how these metaphors expand the mysterious quality of the poem.

THE SYMBOL

The symbol is a further use of metaphor. Being a metaphor, it is a comparison between two things, but unlike most perceptual and conceptual metaphors, only one of the things compared is clearly stated. The symbol is clearly stated, but what it is compared with (sometimes a very broad range of meaning) is only hinted at, more or less. For instance, the white whale in Herman Melville's novel, *Moby Dick*, is a symbol both in the novel and in the mind of Captain Ahab, the novel's main character. Ahab sees the whale as a symbol of all the malevolence and evil in a world committed to evil. But we may not necessarily share Ahab's views. We may believe that the whale is simply a beast and not a symbol at all. Or, we may believe that the whale is a symbol for nature, which is constantly being threatened by human misunderstanding. Such a symbol can mean more than one thing. It is the peculiar quality of most symbols that they do not sit still; even their basic meanings keep changing or expanding. Symbols are usually vague, always ambiguous. It is said that many symbols are a product of the subconscious, which is always treating things symbolically and always searching for implicit meanings. If this is so, it accounts for the persistence of symbols in even the oldest literature.

Perhaps the most important thing to remember about the symbol is that it implies rather than explicitly states meaning. We sense that we are dealing with a symbol in those situations in which we feel there is more to what is said than meets the eye. Most writers are quite open about their symbols; they let us know that they are using symbols and that it is up to us to understand the meaning of their symbols in our own terms and in our own way. William Blake's poetry is filled with symbols. He saw God's handiwork everywhere, but he also saw forces of destruction everywhere. Thus, his poetry discovers implied meaning in almost every situation and thing, not just in those situations and things that are usually accepted as meaningful. The following poem is an example of his technique. At first the poem may seem needlessly confusing, because we do not know how to interpret the symbols. But the meanings of the symbols begin to come clear to some extent with some examination:

THE SICK ROSE

O rose, thou art sick!
    The invisible worm,
That flies in the night,
    In the howling storm,

Has found out thy bed
    Of crimson joy;
And his dark secret love
    Does thy life destroy.

William Blake

1. The rose and the worm stand as opposites in this poem, and as opposites they are symbolically antagonistic. In discussion with other readers, explore possible meanings for the rose and the worm. What might they be symbols for? Begin with examining all that roses mean to most readers; then reflect on our reactions to worms.
2. The bed of crimson joy and the dark secret love are also symbols. What are their meanings? Consider them closely in relation to the rose and the worm.

Blake enjoyed working with such symbols because he saw a richness of implication in them that linked him to God. As a symbolist, he thus shared in a way the creative act with God and helped others understand the world in terms of symbolic meaningfulness. For most other writers, the symbol is used more modestly as a means of expanding meaning, of including larger ranges of suggestion than a nonsymbolic statement can encompass. The symbol has been compared with a stone dropped into the still waters of a lake: The stone itself is very small, but the effects radiate from its center of action to all the edges of the lake. The symbol is dropped into our imagination, and it, too, radiates with meanings. But the curious thing about the symbol is that its meanings tend to be permanently expansive: who knows where the meaningfulness of Blake's rose ends?

Prose fiction has made extensive use of the symbol. In Melville's *Moby Dick,* the white whale is a symbol, but so, too, is Ahab, and so is the entire journey they undertake. The quest for Moby Dick is itself a symbolic quest. The albatross in Samuel Coleridge's *The Ancient Mariner* is a symbol, and so is the Ancient Mariner's stopping one of the wedding guests to make him hear the entire narrative. In these cases the symbols are operating both structurally, in terms of the entire narrative, and detailedly, in terms of only a part of it. There is nothing incoherent about this; it shows, rather, the enormous resources of the symbol.

In Dostoevky's *Crime and Punishment,* there is a symbolic dream that the murderer-to-be, Raskolnikov, has shortly before he is to kill the old woman, Alёna. In the dream Raskolnikov is a child again, walking through city streets with his father:

Suddenly there was a great explosion of laughter that drowned everything else: the old mare had rebelled against the hail of blows and was lashing out feebly with her hoofs. Even the old man could not help laughing. Indeed, it was ludicrous that such a decrepit old mare could still have a kick left in her.

Two men in the crowd got whips, ran to the horse, one on each side, and began to lash at her ribs.

"Hit her on the nose and across the eyes, beat her across the eyes!" yelled Mikolka.

"Let's have a song, lads!" someone called from the wagon, and the others joined in. Somebody struck up a coarse song, a tambourine rattled, somebody else whistled the chorus. The fat young woman went on cracking nuts and giggling.

. . . The boy ran towards the horse, then round in front, and saw them lashing her across the eyes, and actually striking her very eyeballs. He was weeping. His heart seemed to rise into his throat, and tears rained from his eyes. One of the whips stung his face, but he did not feel it; he was wringing his hands and crying aloud. He ran to a grey-haired, grey-bearded old man, who was shaking his head in reproof. A peasant-woman took him by the hand and tried to lead him away, but he tore himself loose and ran back to the mare. She was almost at her last gasp, but she began kicking again.

"The devil fly away with you!" shrieked Mikolka in a fury.

He flung away his whip, stooped down and dragged up from the floor of the cart a long thick wooden shaft, grasped one end with both hands, and swung it with an effort over the wretched animal.

Cries arose: "He'll crush her!" "He'll kill her!"

"She's my property," yelled Mikolka, and with a mighty swing let the shaft fall. There was a heavy thud.[3]

The symbolic value of this passage becomes clearer in the context of the entire novel. Raskolnikov is planning a brutal murder of an aged shopkeeper. Only a couple of pages later, Raskolnikov reflects on his dream:

"God!" he exclaimed, "is it possible, is it possible, that I really shall take an axe and strike her on the head, smash open her skull . . . that my feet will slip in warm, sticky blood, and that I shall break the lock, and steal, and tremble, and hide, all covered in blood . . . with the axe . . . ? God, is it possible?"[4]

PERCEPTION KEY *CRIME AND PUNISHMENT*

1. What is the old mare symbolic of in Raskolnikov's dream? What is the entire situation symbolic of?
2. Sample opinion from others and explore the effectiveness of having the beating of the horse revealed in a dream. Is this weaker or stronger for the symbolic value than if the scene had actually taken place on the streets in front of Raskolnikov? Why?
3. How much does this symbolic action reveal about Raskolnikov? Does he seem—considering what he is actually about to do—different as a boy than as an adult? How would you characterize his sensitivities and his compassion?

[3]From Dostoevsky's *Crime and Punishment*, translated by J. L. Coulson, published by Oxford University Press, 1953. Reprinted by permission of the publisher.
[4]Ibid.

The problem most readers have with symbols centers either on the question of recognition—is this a symbol?—or on the question of what the symbol stands for. Usually an author will use something symbolically in situations that are pretty clearly identified. Blake does not tell us that his rose and worm are symbolic, but we readily realize that the poem says very little worth listening to if we do not begin to go beyond its literal meaning. The fact that worms kill roses is more important to gardeners than it is to readers of poetry. But that there is a secret evil that travels mysteriously to kill beautiful things is not so important to gardeners as to readers of poetry.

Some readers tend to see everything as symbolic. This is as serious a problem as being unable to identify a symbol at all. The best rule of thumb is based on experience. Symbols are very much alike from one kind of literature to another. Once you begin to recognize symbols—the several presented here are various enough to offer a good beginning—other symbols and symbolic situations will be clearer and more unmistakable. But the symbol should be compelling. The situation should be clearly symbolic before we begin to explore what the symbols mean. Not all black objects are symbolic of death; not all predators are symbolic of evil. Moreover, all symbols should be understood in the context in which they appear. Their context in the literature is what usually reveals their meaning, as we can see from the dream of Raskolnikov.

In those instances, as often in Blake's poems, in which there is no evident context to guide us, we should interpret the symbols with extreme care and tentativeness. Symbolic objects usually have a fairly well-understood range of meaning that authors such as Blake depend upon. For instance, the rose is often thought of in connection with beauty, romance, love. The worm is often thought of in connection with death, the grave, and if we include the serpent in the Garden of Eden (Blake, of course, had read Milton's *Paradise Lost*), the worm also suggests evil, sin, and perversion. Most of us know these things. Thus, the act of interpreting the symbol is usually an act of bringing this knowledge to the forefront of our minds so we can use it in our interpretations.

DICTION

"Diction" is a term that describes the language used in a piece of literature, the "choice of words." Because the entire act of writing involves the choice of words, the term "diction" is usually reserved for literary acts (they can be speech as well as the written word) that use words chosen especially carefully for their impact. In Robert Herrick's poem below, we see an interesting example of the poet calculating the effect of specific words in their context. Basically, the words in "Upon Julia's Clothes" are single-syllable words, such as "Then," "my," "goes." But the few polysyllables—"vibration" with three syllables and the most unusual four-syllable word, "liquefaction"—lend an air of intensity and special meaning to themselves simply by means of contrast. There may also be an unusual sense in which those words "act out" or imitate what they describe.

UPON JULIA'S CLOTHES

Whenas in silks my Julia goes,
Then, then, methinks, how sweetly flows
That liquefaction of her clothes.

Next, when I cast mine eyes, and see
That brave vibration, each way free,
O, how that glittering taketh me!

PERCEPTION KEY "UPON JULIA'S CLOTHES"

1. The implications of the polysyllabic words in this poem may be quite different for different people. Have the poem read aloud, give people a minute to think about it, then ask for suggestions about what the polysyllables *do* for the reader. Is there a sense in which their complexity invites more participation with the poem's expression of feeling about Julia?
2. Read the poem to some listeners who are not likely to know it beforehand. Do they notice such words as "liquefaction" and "vibration"? When they talk about the poem, do they observe the use of words? Compare their observations with those who read the poem in this book.

But this example is isolated. A more interesting example is that of language used in a more even fashion, a fashion that produces a sense of inevitability, that what has been expressed is in the most perfect form the expression could possibly have. We have this sense probably most profoundly in the psalms of the King James version of the Bible. The inevitability is partly a product of conditioning. Most of us have heard the psalms in the King James version many times, and thus all other versions sound "wrong" to our ears. But the fact is that the King James version was only one of a good number of English translations. Because of the accuracy of its translation and the "rightfulness" of its diction, the King James version, completed in 1611, was recognized even in its own time as a literary triumph.

Compare the following versions of the familiar Psalm 23:

My shepherd is the living Lord; nothing, therefore, I need.
In pastures fair, with waters calm, he set me for to feed.
He did convert and glad my soul, and brought my mind in frame
To walk in paths of righteousness for his most holy name.
Yea, though I walk in the vale of death, yet will I fear none ill;
Thy rod, thy staff doth comfort me, and thou art with me still.
And in the presence of my foes, my table thou has spread;
Thou shalt, O Lord, fill full my cup and eke anoint my head.
Through all my life thy favor is so frankly showed to me
That in thy house forevermore my dwelling place shall be.

Sternhold and Hopkins, 1567

The Lord is my shepherd, I shall not want.
He maketh me to lie down in green pastures: he leadeth me beside
   the still waters.
He restoreth my soul: he leadeth me in the paths of righteousness
   for his name's sake.
Yea, though I walk through the valley of the shadow of death,
I will fear no evil: for thou art with me; thy rod and thy staff they
   comfort me.
Thou preparest a table before me in the presence of mine enemies:
   thou anointest my head with oil; my cup runneth over.
Surely goodness and mercy shall follow me all the days of my life;
   and I will dwell in the house of the Lord forever.

King James Version, 1611

PERCEPTION KEY PSALM 23

1. Compare the Sternhold-Hopkins version with the King James version. What word choices are particularly strong or weak in either version? Does the lack of rhyme in the King James version weaken or strengthen the diction? Explain.
2. As an experiment, read the Sternhold-Hopkins version to a friend and ask him what the name of the piece of poetry is. Does it come as a surprise when he realizes which psalm it is?
3. With a group of other readers of this psalm, try your hand at revision. "Translate" it into contemporary English. Compare the best translation in your group with the King James version. How does the diction in each contribute to the effectiveness of the translation?

The careful use of diction can sometimes conceal a writer's immediate intention, making it difficult for us to ignore the words until they have, indeed, made their point. One classic example of this is Jonathan Swift's essay, *A Modest Proposal*, in which he most decorously suggests that the solution to the povertry-stricken Irish farmer's desperation was the sale of his infant children—for the purpose of serving them up as plump, tender roasts for Christmas dinners in England. The diction is so subtly ironic that it is with some difficulty that many readers finally realize Swift is writing satire. By the time one reaches the following passage in the essay, one hardly knows quite how to take it:

> I have been assured by a very knowing American of my acquaintance in London, that a young healthy child well nursed is at a year old a most delicious, nourishing, and wholesome food, whether stewed, roasted, baked, or boiled; and I make no doubt that it will equally serve in a fricasee or a ragout.

This matter-of-fact tone, with such careful choice of words and an apparently totally innocent approach, has fooled more than one reader into accepting the whole idea.

There are many kinds of diction available to the writer, from the casual and conversational to the archaic and the formal. Every piece of writing considers the problem of diction afresh, and every piece of writing solves the problem in its own way for its own purposes. Sometimes a literary work will suggest a prophetic quality through its diction; sometimes it will suggest a holy quality by borrowing biblical diction; sometimes a work can be frightening, arrogant, humble, or vindictive—all through the diction. There are times, too, when the choice of words seems so exact and right that any tampering destroys the value of the work for us almost entirely. No writer can tell you exactly how he or she achieves this "inevitability," but it seems to depend in part upon experimenting with word sounds and rhythms. It is an act of finding the best combination of those elements that a choice of words will affect.

PERCEPTION KEY DICTION

1. Compare the following sets of lines:
   a. "Belching black disagreeable breath,
      They count the ways to love. . . ."
   b. "Belching black cacophonous breath,
      They count the ways to love. . . ."
      Which version seems better to you? Why?
2. In the following examples, all nineteenth-century works, the problems of diction are different from those discussed above. Describe for a friend exactly what seems to be achieved by the diction of these examples. Compare your findings with others.
3. Does there seem to be a significant difference between the prose and the poetry in terms of their ability to exploit the resources of diction?

But there can hardly be a doubt that we are descended from barbarians. The astonishment which I felt on first seeing a party of Fuegians [savages living on Tierra del Fuego in South America] on a wild and broken shore will never be forgotten by me, for the reflection at once rushed into my mind—such were our ancestors. These men were absolutely naked and bedaubed with paint, their long hair was tangled, their mouths frothed with excitement, and their expression was wild, startled, and distrustful. They possessed hardly any arts, and like wild animals lived on what they could catch; they had no government and were merciless to everyone not of their own small tribe. He who has seen a savage in his native land will not feel much shame, if forced to acknowledge that the blood of some more humble creature flows in his veins. For my own part I would as soon be descended from that heroic little monkey, who braved his dreaded enemy in order to save the life of his keeper; or from that old baboon, who, descending from the mountains, carried away in triumph his young comrade from a crowd of astonished dogs—as from a savage who delights to torture his enemies, offers up wives like slaves, knows no decency, and is haunted by the grossest superstitions.[5]

TO HELEN

Helen, thy beauty is to me
    Like those Nicean barks of yore,
That gently, o'er a perfumed sea,
    The weary, way-worn wanderer bore
To his own native shore.

On desperate seas long wont to roam,
    Thy hyacinth hair, thy classic face,
Thy Naiad airs have brought me home
    To the glory that was Greece
And the grandeur that was Rome.

Lo! in yon brilliant window-niche
    How statue-like I see thee stand!
    The agate lamp within thy hand,
Ah! Psyche, from the regions which
    Are Holy Land!

                    Edgar Allen Poe

OZYMANDIAS

I met a traveler from an antique land
Who said: Two vast and trunkless legs of stone
Stand in the desert . . . Near them, on the sand,
Half sunk, a shattered visage lies, whose frown,
And wrinkled lip, and sneer of cold command,
Tell that its sculptor well those passions read
Which yet survive, stamped on these lifeless things,

[5]From Charles Darwin, *The Descent of Man.*

The hand that mocked them, and the heart that fed:
And on the pedestal these words appear:
"My name is Ozymandias, king of kings:
Look on my works, ye Mighty, and despair!"
Nothing beside remains. Round the decay
Of that colossal wreck, boundless and bare,
The lone and level sands stretch far away.

Percy Bysshe Shelley

Summary

Our emphasis throughout this chapter has been on literature as spoken language. Because we stress the spoken qualities of language, whether in poems or prose, we want to give proper credit to the active character of literature. It is not passive; it does not sit on the page; it is engaged actively in the lives of those who give it a chance. Reading the literary samples in this chapter aloud will help clarify that point.

Moreover, we have been especially interested in two aspects of literature: its structure and its structural details. Structure involves the larger issues of literature—how a piece of literature is put together, what its overall strategies are—and structural details, the smaller issues. Clearly, any artifact is composed of structural details that are gathered into larger structures. It is the same in literature, and one of the prerequisites of coming to an understanding of how writers can reveal to us the visions they have of their subject matter is the awareness of how details create structure. The use of metaphor, symbol, diction, and many more details will determine the specifics of a given work of literature.

Structural strategies, such as the choice between a lyric or a narrative approach, will determine how details are used. There are many kinds of structures beside the narrative and the lyric, although these two offer convenient polarities that help define the nature of literary structure. It would be useful for any student of literature to see how many kinds of structures there may be to supplement these two. And it would be useful to see what kinds of revelations can be achieved by different structural approaches. We have made some suggestions as starters: pointing out the capacity of the lyric for revealing feeling, and the capacity of the narrative for revealing mythic and psychological truths that underlie everyday experience. Your own further study should point you toward more such revelations and deeper participation with literature.

Chapter 7 Bibliography

Auerbach, Erich. *Mimesis.* Princeton, N.J.: Princeton University Press, 1953.
Boas, George A. *A Primer for Critics.* Baltimore, Md.: Johns Hopkins University Press, 1937.

Bodkin, Maud. *Archetypal Patterns in Poetry.* New York: Oxford University Press, 1934.

Brooks, Cleanth. *The Well-Wrought Urn.* London: Reynal and Hitchcock, 1947.

Burke, Kenneth. *The Philosophy of Literary Form.* Baton Rouge: Louisiana University Press, 1941.

Eliot, T. S. *Selected Essays: New Edition.* New York: Harcourt Brace & World, 1960.

Fish, Stanley. *Is There a Text in This Class?* Cambridge: Harvard University Press, 1980.

Forster, E. M. *Aspects of the Novel.* New York: Harcourt Brace & World, 1947.

Frye, Northrop. *Anatomy of Criticism.* Princeton, N.J.: Princeton University Press, 1957.

Hayman, Stanley Edgar. *The Armed Vision.* New York: Knopf, 1948.

Hirsch, E. D. *The Aims of Interpretation.* Chicago: University of Chicago Press, 1978.

James, Henry. *The Art of the Novel.* New York: Scribner's, 1934.

Leavis, F. R. *The Great Tradition.* London: Chatto and Windus, 1934.

Stoll, E. E. *From Shakespeare to Joyce.* New York: Doubleday, 1944.

Wellek, Rene, and Warren, Austin. *Theory of Literature.* New York: Harcourt Brace & World, 1949.

Wimsatt, William K. and Brooks, Cleanth. *Literary Criticism: A Short History.* New York: Knopf, 1957.

DRAMA

The word "drama" comes from a Greek word meaning "act." A drama is an action; and according to a long tradition, it is an imitation of an action. Drama is an action onstage that interprets another action—which we may loosely call "life"—offstage. From the Greeks to the present, dramatic theory and criticism have been concerned with the relationship between dramatic action and the action it imitates, although some contemporary drama has aimed at being action without imitating anything. The question of whether this is possible will be deferred until we discuss experimental contemporary theater. Before that, however, we will consider some of the long-standing ideas relating to the concept that underlies much of Western theories of dramatic literature: the concept of *mimesis*. The word is related to mime, mimic, and pantomime, all having a special meaning relative to imitating life.

Aristotle developed a theory of art as imitation of nature—nature being life in general, not just the outdoors. In his analysis of Sophocles' *Oedipus Rex*, he claimed that tragedy is the imitation of human action. From other comments he made, we can safely assume he meant to include comedy and other forms of drama. Some ways in which this concept can be applied to dramatic arts are fairly obvious. For instance, certain kinds of drama imitate an action by allusion. The recent musical dramas *Godspell*, *Jesus Christ Superstar,*, and *Your Arms too Short to Box with God* all allude to the story of Christ. They do not, however, aim at representing the gospel with accuracy. Because they imitate an action by allusion, they can admit purposeful distortion. Another way of imitating an action is by retelling, which requires accuracy. Historical plays, such as Shakespeare's *Henry V*, strive for enough accuracy to seem a reasonable interpretation of what happened. Plays on the assassinations of Lincoln, John F. Kennedy, and Malcolm X all depend on historical accuracy to some extent. Such retellings seem particularly popular on television, spawning numerous one-person dramas such as Hal Holbrook's imitation of Mark Twain, Julie Harris's imitation of Emily Dickinson (Figure 8-1), and James Whitmore's imitations of Will Rogers and Harry Truman. There are many more than these, and there will probably be many more to come.

PERCEPTION KEY VARIETIES OF IMITATION

1. What recent imitations of famous persons or historical events have you witnessed? What is their appeal? Is the accuracy of the portrayals an important source of your pleasure in witnessing these imitations?
2. Two kinds of imitation have been noted: allusion, which depends upon

FIGURE 8-1 Julie Harris as Emily Dickinson in *The Belle of Amherst.* Produced for the Public Broadcast Service by KCET/Los Angeles.

alluding to a well-known action, and retelling, which depends upon recreating a well-known action with careful attention to the accuracy of the imitation. What other kinds of imitation can you recall from your experience with drama? Ask people what they think drama best imitates. Ask also what people may think it means for drama to imitate life.

Realism

Because drama is there in front of us in three-dimensional space and because the actors are people like us, often conducting life as we ourselves live it, we have developed a popular critical standard: realism. Many kinds of drama are labeled fantasy simply because they have an important element that is not realistic. *Harvey*, a comedy in which a mythical rabbit, or pookah, is imagined onstage, and Gore Vidal's *Visitor from a Small Planet*, about interstellar travel, are only two of countless such plays—most of which seem to use almost overly realistic sets and situations to surround the nugget of fantasy at their core. The critical standard of realism is often applied even to these plays because people seem to say, "All right, given this nugget of fantasy, is everything as real as it would be if that nugget of fantasy were real, too?"

Realism is not an adequate basis for critical discussion of drama even though the question of *mimesis* may be central to most dramatic concerns. This is primarily because the term "realism" has taken on much more explicit limits of meaning than *mimesis* has. For a play to be realistic, its plot must have a high degree of probability; its characters must act with a high degree of plausibility and be recognizable by an audience as people they might know; the sets should be accurate representations of real places; the dialogue and the delivery should be as natural as possible. When these conditions are met, we consider the play realistic. But we all realize that if absolute realism were achieved onstage, we would abominate it. If characters really went to sleep onstage instead of pretending to, if they really got drunk and forced us to wait for them to sober up instead of pretending to, if they really murdered their victims instead of pretending to, then we would have much more realism onstage. But we would have much less drama. It is a paradox, but it has proved an easy one to live with. Too much realism is undesirable. From what we can tell of the history of realistic drama (the bulk of what we are likely to see), art should be realistic only to the extent that it allows a meaningful interpretation of life. Otherwise the work would lack content: the revelation of some subject matter.

PERCEPTION KEY THE LIMITS OF REALISM

1. Is absolute realism possible in a drama? In any work of art?
2. Since no one can really lay down the "law" on how much realism is too

much in drama, one useful project is that of determining by experience what an audience's limits seem to be. Set up a series of brief interviews, asking people how realistic they think a drama should be. Do their answers help you clarify the limits of realism that seem acceptable to audiences?

The history of drama is filled with amusing anecdotes about the extent to which a drama has been realistic enough to cause an audience to mistake drama for real life. For instance, in Royall Tyler's play *The Contrast* (1787), one of the earliest American plays, it was not uncommon for members of frontier audiences to rush onstage to try to stop the villain from his villainy. Anyone who has seen or read *The Contrast* will wonder how naive an audience would have to be to take for real what to our ears and eyes sounds peculiarly stilted and artificial. For eighteenth-century America, however, it was a very realistic play. Even some contemporary New York theatergoers have made the same mistake. Arthur Miller's *Death of a Salesman* (1949) played to some early audiences that included salesmen at New York conventions. Stories have circulated that several salesmen rose in anguish to help the hero, Willy Loman, by offering good business advice to help him from losing his "territory." These are breakdowns of a "distance" that we should maintain with all art, and they help explain why realism has limits. The distance we maintain between ourselves and art, between our awareness of the difference between life and *mimesis*, is sometimes described as "psychical distance" or "aesthetic distance." Maintaining that distance in our experience of drama implies the possibility of truly participating with the drama, since it implies the loss of self that participation demands. When spectators leap onstage to right the wrongs of drama, they show that there has been no loss of self. Indeed, because they see themselves as capable of changing the action, they are projecting their own ego rather than participating with the dramatic action unfolding before them.

Archetype

Realistic drama often relies upon the constant details of life as we know it or of life as it was once lived. Occasionally it dulls us with its sheer amount of detail and its sheer delight in accuracy, as if these were ends in themselves. Other kinds of drama avoid realism, while Archetypal drama aims at symbolic or mythic interpretations of experience. Archetypal drama often combines realism with its mythic interpretations, but the power of this kind of drama depends on the use of structural patterns that seem to have their origin in our psyche as determined by culture and nature. For instance, the individual's search for personal identity, since it is a pattern apparently repeated in all ages, can serve as a primary archetypal structure for drama. This particular archetype is the driving force in *King Lear*, and it is present in *Oedipus Rex, Hamlet,* and many more plays—notably, but by no means exclusively, tragedies. As we shall see, comedy also has appropriate archetypes. The biological pattern of birth (a return to the soil from whence we came) can be seen as part of the archetypal structure of *Romeo and Juliet,* as our later discussion will demonstrate.

Archetypal patterns proliferate in dramas of all ages. The power of the archetype derives, in part, from our conscious or unconscious recognition of a pattern as one that has been repeated by the human race throughout history. The psychologist Carl Jung, whose work spurred critical awareness of archetypal patterns in all literature, believes that the archetype's greatest power lies in its capacity to reveal through art the "imprinting" of racial experience. Maud Bodkin, a critic who developed Jung's views, explains them this way: "The special emotional significance possessed by certain poems [as well as drama]—a significance going beyond any definite meaning conveyed—[Jung] attributes to the stirring in the reader's mind, within or beneath his conscious response, of unconscious forces which he terms 'primordial images', or archetypes. These archetypes he describes as 'psychic residua of numberless experiences of the same type', experiences which have happened not to the individual but to his ancestors, and of which the results are inherited in the structure of the brain."[1]

The quest narrative mentioned in Chapter 7 is an example of an archetypal structure, one that recurs in drama frequently. For instance, Hamlet is seeking the truth about his father's death. Even Vladimir and Estragon, in Samuel Beckett's *Waiting for Godot,* are searching, in a modern way, for Godot himself—whoever Godot may be. Sophocles' *Oedipus Rex* tells about a man who kills his father, marries his mother, suffers a plague on his lands, and is ultimately blinded and ostracized. Freud thought the play so archetypal that he saw in it a profound human psychological pattern, which he called the Oedipus complex: the desire of a child to "get rid of" the same-sex parent and to have a sexual union with the parent of the opposite sex. Not all archetypal patterns are this thrilling, but most reveal something about basic human needs and experiences. Drama seems to be one of the most powerful means of expression for such archetypes.

We cannot delineate all the archetypes there are to be found in drama. But some suggestions should help establish the more important patterns. Some of the common archetypes are those of an older man, usually a king, who is betrayed by a younger man, his trusted lieutenant, in regard to a woman. This is the theme of Richard Wagner's *Tristan and Isolde.* The loss of innocence, a variation on the Garden of Eden theme, is another favorite, although we may associate it more with Milton's *Paradise Lost* than with plays, such as Ibsen's *Ghosts* or his *The Wild Duck,* to which they are related. The archetypal quest for oneself is so common in all literature that it is even

[1]Maud Bodkin, *Archetypal Patterns in Poetry,* Oxford University Press, New York, 1934, p. 1.

sometimes parodied, as in Oscar Wilde's *The Importance of Being Earnest*. The very successful popular play by Anthony Shaffer, *Sleuth*, is an instance of an adaptation of the pattern, including the use of disguise to get at the truth, another common variation on the theme.

The four seasons have been suggested as models for the development of archetypes because the seasons are intertwined with patterns of growth and decay. The origins of drama, which are obscure beyond recall, may have been linked with rituals associated with the birth and death of a king, the planting of seed, the reaping of crops, and the entire complex issue of fertility. In *Anatomy of Criticism*, Northrop Frye associates comedy with spring, romance with summer, tragedy with autumn, irony and satire with winter. His associations may not be completely accurate, but they suggest that some archetypal drama may be rooted in human relationships to the rhythms of nature. Such origins may account for part of the power that archetypal drama has on our imagination, for the influences that derive from such origins are pervasive in all of us. These influences may also help explain why tragedy usually involves the death of a hero—although sometimes, as in the case of Oedipus, death is withheld—and why comedy frequently ends with one or more marriages, as in Shakespeare's *As You Like It*, *Much Ado About Nothing*, and *A Midsummer Night's Dream*. Rhythmic patterns of the seasons have permeated archetypal drama. Such drama seems to thrive on seasonal patterns and on the capacity to excite in us a recognition of events that on the surface may not seem important, but that underneath the surface have profound meaning.

PERCEPTION KEY ARCHETYPES

1. You may wish to supplement the comments above by reading the third chapter of Northrop Frye's *Anatomy of Criticism* or the *Hamlet* chapter in Francis Fergusson's *The Idea of a Theater*. If you are able to read any sources that discuss archetypes in literature, try discussing the idea further with friends interested in the concept.

2. Whether or not you do additional reading, consider the recurrent patterns you have observed in dramas—include television dramas or television adaptations. Can you see any of the patterns we have described? Are there new patterns that seem to be showing up? Do the patterns you have observed seem basic to human experience? For example, do you tend to associate gaiety with spring, romance with summer, death with fall, and irony with winter? If so, what are the origins for these associations for you? Do you believe these origins are shared by all people?

3. Archetypes are very closely connected with myth. Can you think of any famous myths that have been alluded to in recent dramas? Consider myths like Jonah and the Whale, Cinderella, Hansel and Gretel, and Pinocchio. You may have a favorite myth or fairy tale that you have seen interpreted by a popular drama. Fairy tales can serve as archetypes, since they often explore issues of identity, the quest, and innumerable anxieties over basic moral issues central to the human condition.

Genres of Drama: Tragedy

Even today, people interested in drama often return to Aristotle's *Poetics* when they begin a discussion of tragedy. Aristotle developed a definition of tragedy by closely analyzing the plays of the Greeks, especially Sophocles's *Oedipus Rex*. We have profited from his analysis even though many critics have given up what they consider to be his narrowness of definition. He observed that tragedy has six elements: plot, character, diction, thought, spectacle, and music. By placing plot first, he gave priority to action as the essential ingredient for drama.

Some plays have tight plots, such as *Sleuth* or William Gillette's *Sherlock Holmes*; some have relatively loose plots, such as Luigi Pirandello's *Six Characters in Search of an Author*, which, because it emphasizes character so much, seems to have little plot. When Pirandello's play was first produced, the idea of characters wandering on stage looking for an author to use them in a drama seemed particularly strange. Its strangeness developed from its abandoning conventional plot, the cornerstone of drama for most theatergoers.

The term "plot" implies a sequence of incidents more or less tightly related to one another, often in a cause-and-effect pattern. One of the most common uses of tight, conventional plot is in detective mysteries. The mystery demands a sequence of incidents that needs unraveling, primarily by the detective, who, by discovering the underlying orderliness of events brings the drama to its inevitable conclusion. *Detective Story* and *Sherlock Holmes* use this kind of plotting. *Six Characters in Search of an Author* uses a looser plot. It presents characters on stage arguing with a stage manager and with each other about what seems to be an irrational quest: for an author to put them in a play. The argument seems directionless and almost casual. A rational conclusion seems unlikely. Edward Albee's recent experimental drama, *Listening* (1977, Figure 8-2), centers on a man and wife meeting where they fell in love. They talk to one another while their insane daughter listens. Their talk seems random and unfocused, though it apparently produces a suicide attempt on the part of the daughter. The plot is much too loose to be thought of as a sequence of events that would have resulted inevitably in such an attempt.

Tight plots are usually considered essential in tragedies. This is particularly true of those Greek and Shakespearian tragedies in which fate plays a dominant role. But for the best tragedies, according to Aristotle, the action must arise from character. The flaws and strengths of the protagonist's character must be factors contributing to the dramatic outcome. Aristotle may not have been fully convinced of this, however, since he tells us in the *Poetics* that "without action there could be no tragedy, whereas a tragedy without characterization is possible." Such an approach has often been taken by dramatists anxious to produce a hit on the popular stage and by television writers producing series dramas. But when we consider the great tragedies that

FIGURE 8-2 Angela Lansbury and William Prince in Edward Albee's *Listening*, directed by Edward Albee at the Hartford Stage Company. Photograph by Gerry Goldstein.

most define the genre, we think immediately of names of people: *Oedipus Rex; Agamemnon; Prometheus Bound; Hamlet; Macbeth; King Lear; Julius Caesar; Samson Agonistes.* In more modern tragedies, such as *Desire Under the Elms* and *Death of a Salesman,* the characters still remain at the center of the drama, although their titles may not confirm that. Modern tragedies do not always follow Greek or Elizabethan structures. Therefore, it is not a straightforward matter for us to explain what is and is not proper to the genre of tragedy. An enormous amount of energy has gone into defining tragedy, and much of it has been wasted. Modern drama tends to avoid traditional tragic structures because modern concepts of character, sin, guilt, death, and fate have been greatly altered. Modern psychology "explains" character in ways the ancients would not have understood. It has been said that there is no modern tragedy because there can be no character noble enough to be tragic. Moreover, the acceptance of chance as a force equal to fate in our lives has also reduced the power of tragedy for modern times. Even the myth—which some modern playwrights still understand as valid—has a diminished vitality in modern tragedy. It may be·that the return or development of a strong integrating myth—a world vision that sees the actions of humanity as tied into a large scheme of cosmic and religious events—is a prerequisite for producing a new dramatic structure that we can recognize as truly tragic.

PERCEPTION KEY CHARACTERISTICS OF TRAGEDY

Before going further in this discussion, you should try to establish what you mean when you talk about a tragedy. The everyday meaning of the word as applied to auto accidents, mishaps, and minor sadnesses is not at issue here. Rather, tragedy is a kind of drama that has certain characteristics or qualities we ought to be able to enumerate. Enumerate what characteristics you believe a tragedy has.

TRAGIC RHYTHM

From Aristotle, Kenneth Burke has devised a useful pattern for analyzing tragic structures. He establishes "tragic rhythm" as a movement or development on the part of the tragic hero or heroine throughout the drama. The pattern depends upon a noble or serious protagonist involved in a significant or unified action. The pattern of this tragic rhythm is:

Poiema: Purpose
Pathema: Passion
Mathema: Perception

Poiema implies a reason for searching out something, as, for example, Oedipus has a reason for trying to find the murderer of Laius, since the prophet Tiresias reveals that until Laius' murder is avenged, the land will remain plague-ridden. Oedipus' *pathema* represents the suffering he undergoes in trying to achieve his purpose. *Mathema* represents the terrifying perception that it was he himself who, unknowingly, had killed Laius, his own father, many years before. Once *mathema* has been achieved, Oedipus' tragic search is finished, and, with his own revenge upon himself by blinding and exile, he ends the tragedy. Most tragedies seem to have this pattern of *poiema*, *pathema*, and *mathema* to one extent or another, just as most tragedies depend on a high-born and exceptionally worthy protagonist for the central tragic figure. Modern tragedies have suffered most because generally democratic attitudes make it very hard for us to take high-born characters seriously in a modern setting. But, then, can ordinary characters be taken seriously as tragic? Arthur Miller's *Death of a Salesman* proved that this can happen (although not every critic will agree with us). The fall of Willy Loman, a very ordinary man, seems profoundly tragic. If Aristotle were analyzing tragedy now, he surely would have to revise some of his assertions about the character of the tragic protagonist.

Aristotle provides the basis for Burke's three terms when he cites three requirements of tragedy: reversal *(peripeteia)*, recognition *(anagnorisis)*, and suffering *(pathos)*. Aristotle's tragic rhythm is most specifically focused on plot. The reversal occurs when events turn from good to bad or bad to worse. Recognition is the protagonist's awareness of the reversal and its causes and, according to Aristotle, the best recognition occurs simultaneously with the reversal. Oedipus' suffering after his recognition of the truth is Aristotle's *pathos*. Aristotle describes *pathos:* "a fatal or painful action like death on the stage, violent physical pain, wounds, and everything of that kind." Tragedy, even for Aristotle, need not end in death but must end in an action that is painful and virtually as serious as death. Shakespeare ended his tragedies with death, so we have come to consider death the normal tragic fate. King Lear dies at the end of his play, and so does Cordelia, his virtuous maligned daughter. In the eighteenth century, which clearly possessed a very different world view from the seventeenth century, *King Lear* was usually produced with a different ending. It was still a tragedy, but the audiences felt Lear had suffered enough and that the death of his daughter was simply excessive. Usually she survived and married Edgar. *King Lear* was not generally played again as originally written until the nineteenth century.

THE TRAGIC STAGE

The great ages of tragedy have been Greek and Elizabethan. Some people have maintained that these two historical periods have shared certain basic ideas about the world: for instance that there is a "divine providence that shapes our ends," as Hamlet tells us, and that fate is immutable, as the Greek tragedies tell us. Both periods were marked by considerable prosperity and public power, and both ages were deeply aware that sudden reversals in prosperity could change everything. In addition, both ages shared ideas about the way a stage should be constructed. The relatively temperate climate of Greece permitted an open amphitheater, with seating on three sides of the stage. The Greek architects often had the seats carved out of hillside rock, and their attention to acoustics was so remarkable that even today in some of the surviving Greek theaters, a whisper on the stage can be heard throughout the audience. The Elizabethan stages, wooden structures jutting into a space enclosed by stalls in which the audience sat, also provided for the sight lines to come from three sides. Each kind of theater, in other words, was similar to a modified theater-in-the-round, such as is used occasionally even today. A glance will show that these theaters are very different from the standard theater of our time—the proscenium theater—as can be seen in comparing Figures 8-3, 8-4, and 8-5.

The proscenium acts as a "frame" to separate the action taking place on stage from the audience. The Greek and Elizabethan stage—

FIGURE 8-3 Greek Amphitheater. Athens Festival, Herod Atticus Theatre. Courtesy of the Greek National Tourist Office, New York.

while still separating the audience from the players by a space—operates without a frame and therefore involves the audience more directly, allowing the audience to perceive the action as a more immediate extension of human experience. Aristotle talks about the way in which the action of the tragedy can be directly involving when he describes the emotions that the tragic action evokes: fear and pity. Pity is the sympathy we have for the tragic hero or heroine. In order to feel it, we must respect the protagonist. This is one reason why the Greeks insisted upon a high-born tragic protagonist. The evocation of fear implies another reason for the necessity of a noble protagonist. If Oedipus the King can be brought down by a tragic flaw, then we ourselves can be brought down even more easily. Aristotle observed audiences of tragedies experiencing what he called a *katharsis*, a purging or washing out of the emotions of fear and pity as a result of participating with the tragedy. We do not know precisely what Aristot-

FIGURE 8-4 Modern rendering of DeWitt's 1596 drawing of the interior of an Elizabethan theater. Courtesy of the University of Utrecht.

FIGURE 8-5 Auditorium and proscenium, Royal Opera House, Covent Garden, London. Photograph by Clive Friend, FIIP, Woodmansterne Ltd.

le meant by *katharsis*. One possible interpretation is that in observing the terrible fall of others in a tragedy—especially those of higher station—we learn to place our own misfortunes in a clearer perspective. Our sympathy or pity is given wider range and sharper focus. In turn, we understand ourselves and our destinies better. We learn, among other things, that ultimately we share a common fate, and this enlightenment frees or purges us to some extent from the irrational and sickening burden of fear. In this sense pity purges fear.

PERCEPTION KEY THE PROSCENIUM STAGE

Test the preceding observations by examining your own experience in the theater. What is the effect of setting apart the dramatic action of a play by framing it with a proscenium? Do you know of any plays that seem to need a proscenium frame or that are weakened because of it?

Shakespeare's *Romeo and Juliet*

Romeo and Juliet may not be the simplest drama to use as a means of clarifying the nature of tragedy, but it has the virtue of being a bit more accessible than *Oedipus Rex*. For a contemporary audience, *Romeo and Juliet* is very instructive, because although its tragic hero and heroine are aristocratic, they are not a king and queen. Their youth and innocence add to their remarkable appeal while helping us see the possibilities of tragedy. The play presents the archetypal story of star-crossed lovers whose fate—partly because of the hatred their families bear one another—is sealed from the first. The archetype of lovers who are not permitted to love represents an even more basic struggle among archetypal forces that lie so deep in our consciousness that we need a drama such as this to help reveal them. It is the struggle between light and dark, between the world in which we live on the surface of the earth—enjoying the sun, the moon, the stars and all earthly luminaries—and the world of darkness, the underworld of the prehistoric gods that the Greeks relegated to Hades and the Christians to Hell. Young lovers represent life, the promise of human fertility, and the continuity of the human race. Most of us who are no longer in the bloom of youth were once such people, and we can both sympathize with and understand their situation. Few plot possibilities could be more potentially tragic than that of young lovers whose promise is plucked by death.

The play begins with some ominous observations by Montague, Romeo's father. He points out that when Romeo, through love of a girl named Rosaline (who does not appear in the play), comes home just before dawn, he "locks fair daylight out,"making for "himself an artificial night." In other words, Montague tells us that Romeo stays up all night, comes home, pulls down the shades, and converts day into night. These observations seem innocent enough unless one is already familiar with the plot, then it seems a clear and ironic observation: that Romeo by making his life's day a night is already foreshadowing his fate. After Juliet has been introduced, her nurse wafts her offstage with an odd bit of advice aimed at persuading her of the wisdom of marrying the man her mother wishes for her: Count Paris. "Go, girl, seek happy nights to happy days." At first glance, it seems innocent. But with knowledge of the entire play, it is prophetic.

Much of the play takes place at night, and the film version (Figure 8-6) by Franco Zefferelli (first produced on stage at London's Old Vic in 1960) was particularly impressive for exploiting dramatic lighting possibilities. This quality of the production is what Aristotle would have included in his term, "spectacle." Zefferelli's spectacle was also intensified by costuming, the simplicity of which broke with tradition, and the judicious use of music, one of Aristotle's six basic elements of tragedy. Spectacle includes all the visual elements of a production, which, in their richness or starkness, can combine to intensify the dramatic values of the play. Zefferelli's spectacle and music have a powerful emotional impact, one reason why this production was not only very successful, but also influential on other productions.

When Romeo first speaks with Juliet, it is not only night, but also it is in Capulet's orchard: symbolically a place of fruitfulness and fulfillment. Romeo sees her and imagines her not as chaste Diana of the moon, but as his own luminary sun: "But soft! What light through

FIGURE 8-6 *Romeo and Juliet.* Milo O'Shea as Friar Lawrence and Olivia Hussey as Juliet in Zefferelli's film. Copyright 1968. Paramount Pictures.

yonder window breaks? / It is the East, and Juliet is the sun!" He sees her as his "bright angel." When she, unaware he is listening below, asks, "O Romeo, Romeo! Wherefore art thou Romeo? / Deny thy father and refuse thy name," she is touching on profound things. She is, without fully realizing it, asking the impossible: that he not be himself. The denial of identity has often brought great pain in drama: as witness Oedipus who at first refused to believe he was his father's child. When Juliet asks innocently, "What's in a name? That which we call a rose / By any other name would smell as sweet," she is asking that he ignore his identity. The mythic implications of this are serious, and in this play totally fatal. Denying one's identity is rather like Romeo's attempting to deny day its sovereignty.

When they finally speak, Juliet explains ironically that she has "night's cloak to hide me" and that the "mask of night is upon my face." We know, as she speaks, that eternal night will be upon that face, and all too soon. Their marriage, which occurs offstage as Act Two ends, is also performed at night in Friar Lawrence's cell, with his hoping that the heavens will smile upon "this holy act." But he's none too sure. And before Act Three is well underway the reversals begin. Mercutio, Romeo's friend, is slain because of Romeo's intervention; Romeo then slays Tybalt, Juliet's cousin, and finds himself doomed to exile from Verona and Juliet, whose marriage is not public. Juliet, grieving for the dead Tybalt and the banished Romeo, misleads her father into thinking the only cure for her condition is a quick marriage to Paris. Upon that, Romeo comes to spend their one night of love together before he leaves Verona. Naturally, they want the night to last, and last—again an irony we are prepared for—and when daylight springs, Romeo and Juliet have a playful argument over whether it is the nightingale or the lark that sings. Juliet wants him to stay, so she defends the nightingale; he knows he must go, so he points to the lark and the coming light. Then both, finally, admit the truth. His line is, "More light and light—more dark and dark our woes."

Another strange archetypal pattern has begun here: the union of sex and death as if they were aspects of the same thing. In Shakespeare's time death was a metaphor for the sexual act, and when a singer of a love song protested, in pain, that he was dying, he expected everyone to understand that he was talking about sex. In *Romeo and Juliet* sex and death do go together, but not metaphorically. They are woven symbolically and literally together. The first most profound sense of this appears in Juliet's pretending death in order to avoid marrying Paris. She takes a potion from Friar Lawrence—who is himself afraid of a second marriage because of possible bigamy charges—and appears, despite all efforts of investigation, quite dead. (See Figure 8-7.)

When Romeo hears that she has been placed in the Capulet tomb, he determines to join her in death as he was unable to in life. The message Friar Lawrence had sent by way of another friar did not get through to Romeo explaining the counterfeit death. And it did not get through because genuine death, in the form of plague, had closed the roads to Friar John. Again, this is another reversal of the kind Aristotle approved. When Romeo descends underground into the tomb he must ultimately fight Paris, although he does not wish to. After killing Paris, Romeo sees the immobile Juliet, noticing how lifelike she seems. He fills his cup, a female symbol in the Tarot deck, with poison, and

FIGURE 8-7 *Romeo and Juliet.* E. H. Sothern and Julia Marlow. Courtesy of the Lincoln Center Library of the Performing Arts.

drinks it. When Juliet awakes from her potion and sees both Paris and Romeo dead, she can get no satisfactory answer for these happenings from Friar Lawrence. His fear is so great that he runs off as the authorities bear down on the tomb. This leaves Juliet to give Romeo one last kiss on his still warm lips, then plunge his dagger—a male sexual symbol in the Tarot—into her heart and die.

Earlier, when Capulet thought his daughter was dead, he exclaimed to Paris: "O son, the night before thy wedding day / Hath Death lain with thy wife. There she lies, / Flower as she was, deflowered by him. / Death is my son-in-law, Death is my heir." At the end of the play, both Juliet and his real son-in-law, Romeo, are indeed married in death. The metaphor of death and sex is ironically enacted in their final moments, which include the awful reversals that the audience beholds in horror: the misunderstandings that make Romeo and Juliet take their own lives for love of one another. And among the last lines of the drama is one that helps clarify one of the main themes: "A glooming peace this morning with it brings. / The sun for sorrow will not show his head." The world itself mourns for these young lovers. Theatergoers have mourned these deaths for generations, and the promise that these two families will now finally try to get along together in a peaceful manner does not seem to be strong enough to brighten the ending of the play.

PERCEPTION KEY TRAGEDY

1. If you have been fortunate enough to see a production of *Romeo and Juliet*, either live or on film, reflect about your experience. Did you perceive the archetypal patterns that we have mentioned? How fully were they developed? What about the struggle between light and dark? Was it dramatized in the spectacle of the play? Our discussion of the play did not treat the question of the tragic flaw: the weakness of character that permits the tragedy to befall the main characters. One of Romeo's flaws may be rashness—the rashness that led him to kill Tybalt and thus be banished. But he has other flaws as well. What might they be? What would you consider Juliet's tragic flaw or flaws?

2. You may not have been able to see *Romeo and Juliet*, but there are many other tragedies to see. Try to see any of the tragedies by Aeschylus, Sophocles, Shakespeare, or Ibsen's *Ghosts*, John Millington Synge's *Riders to the Sea*, or Arthur Miller's *Death of a Salesman*. Consider some of the issues of tragedy as we have suggested them. For example, decide whether the play is archetypal. Are there reversals and recognitions of the sort Aristotle observed? Are the characters important enough—if not noble enough—to excite your sympathy?

3. Aristotle identifies six basic elements in tragedy—plot, character, thought, diction, spectacle, and music. Are all of them essential? Could you have a tragedy without plot, for example? Which ones are the most important in the plays you analyze?

4. If you were to write a tragedy, what kind of tragic protagonist would you choose? What kind of plot or action? Why?

Genres of Drama: Comedy

If Aristotle composed a treatise on comedy, it has been lost. However, in his discussion of tragedy he observes that comedy is "an imitation of men who are inferior, but not altogether vicious." Thus, we do not expect comic protagonists to be kings and queens. He also points out that comedy need not, as with the best of tragedies, have a single plot or action, but can have multiple plots: a convention that is as common in today's comedy as it was in Aristotle's time. Comic dramatists such as William Congreve and Richard Brinsley Sheridan often employed subplots to achieve a dazzling contrast with the main line of development. The comic convention of multiple marriages (comedy is often related to the spring season, which we still celebrate with June weddings) is often possible because multiple plots give the dramatist time to develop interest in more than just one couple. The device of multiple plots is so completely connected with comedy that it is very difficult for dramatists of tragedy to employ it without risking unexpected comic effects. Some eighteenth-century critics complained about Shakespeare's use of the subplot for "comic relief," as in the clown parts of *King Lear* (wherein the Fool actually disappears after Act Three!). Shakespeare's multiple plots in *Much Ado About Nothing, Twelfth Night,* and numerous other comedies showed him to be a master of this invention.

OLD COMEDY AND NEW COMEDY

We know that the ancient Western comedies were performed at a time associated with wine making, thus linking the genre with the wine god, Bacchus, and his relative, Comus—from which the word "comedy" comes. We know, too, that some of the earliest comedies, along with satyr plays, were frankly phallic in nature. And we know that many of the plays of Aristophanes, the master of Old Comedy, were raucous and coarse. Plutarch was offended by plays like *The Clouds, The Frogs, The Wasps,* and *Lysistrata,* probably the world's most well-known phallic play, since it concerns a situation in which the women of a community withhold sex from the men until they decide not to wage any more war. At one point in the play, the humor devolves from the men walking around with enormous erections under their togas. Obviously, Old Comedy is old in name only, since it is still present in the routines of nightclub comedians and the bawdy entertainment halls of the world.

By contrast, the New Comedies of Menander, with titles such as *The Flatterer, The Lady From Andros, The Suspicious Man,* and *The Grouch,* his only surviving complete play, concentrated on the more common situations in the everyday life of the Athenian. It also avoided the brutal attacks on individuals, such as Socrates, which characterize much Old Comedy. Menander's critics credit him with having helped develop the comedy of manners, a form of drama that uses the manners of society as a basic part of its subject matter. For that reason, many of Menander's plots were useful for the Roman playwrights several centuries later, since, in general, their audiences were socially well-off, moneyed, powerful, and to some extent bored, just as were Menander's. Unfortunately, most of Menander's 105 plays have not survived. However, he was widely quoted and referred to by Roman critics, who saw in their own playwrights, especially Terence and Plautus, the continuing influence of Menander. We see Menander as important today because he represents the forerunner of much modern comedy that examines the foibles of society.

Old Comedy is associated with our modern farce, burlesque, and the broad humor and make-believe violence of slapstick. Each of these, in turn, is associated with satire, which is the kind of comedy that causes us to laugh at people and institutions in order to perceive their frailty and perhaps even correct them, at least in our thoughts. Just as the Greeks expected tragedy to be serious, they seem to have expected comedy to provoke thoughtful revelations of life. The best farces and satires—whether the plays of Aristophanes or the films of Charlie Chaplin—interpret beneath their surface important subject matter. For example, Chaplin became a model of the downtrodden common man in the early twentieth century. He became synonymous with modern man fighting the incredible forces of governments, machines, industries, and social stereotyping. Anyone who has seen Chaplin's *Modern Times*, for instance, will understand better the degrading effects of modern mass production assembly lines on laborers.

New Comedy is more suave and refined. Just as Old Comedy is rough and ready, with plenty of action and attacks on specific people, New Comedy tones down the broad humor. Concentrating from the beginning on manners, New Comedy developed the type character. Type characters play a fundamental role in comedy of manners because they help focus the qualities society is said to value and produce. Such characters can sometimes become stereotypes, although most dramatists try to maintain enough complexity so that the type characters do not become flat and predictable. When we discussed tragedy, we emphasized the archetypal action of tragedy. But despite a reliance on noble characters, tragedy does not depend on the portrayal of often-recurring type characters. Since the time of Plautus' interpretations of Menander, New Comedy developed type characters such as the famous *Miles Gloriosus*, or braggart warrior. Shakespeare's best known braggart warrior is Falstaff, in the *Henry IV* plays. The braggart warrior is the model Shaw uses in *Arms and the Man*. The prude, the gold digger, the hypocritical puritan, the hypochondriac, and other recognizable types, such as Oscar and Felix in Neil Simon's *The Odd Couple*, were brought to full development in New Comedy.

Farce and comedy of manners can be very serious in meaning. The forces that operate in comedy are usually human-made, and in comedy of manners they are directly related to the social order of which the characters are a part. Just as tragedy can make use of archetypal patterns that often point toward the death of an individual hero, comedy of manners has archetypal patterns of its own. Such patterns usually point toward marriage and the new life made possible by the hoped-for fruitfulness of such a union. The forces of society, personified often by a parent or controlling older person, are usually pitted against the younger characters who wish to be married. In this sense, one of comedy's most powerful archetypal patterns is a variant of the "generation gap." The "parents" or "parent" can actually be any older person who controls the younger people, usually by virtue of controlling their inheritance or their wealth. When the older person wishes to stop a marriage, he or she becomes the "blocking character." This character, for reasons that are usually social, philosophical, or sometimes simply mercenary, does everything possible to stop the young people from getting together. Naturally, the blocking character fails. But the younger characters do not merely win their own struggle. They usually go on to demonstrate the superiority of their views over those of the blocking character. For example, they may demonstrate that true love is a much superior reason for marrying than to merge two neighboring estates. One of the common patterns is for two lovers to decide to marry regardless of their social classes. The male, for instance, may be a soldier or a student but not belong to the upper class to which the female belongs. But usually at the last minute, through the means of a birthmark or the admission of another character who knew all along, the lower-class character will be shown to be a member of the upper class in disguise. Often the character himself will not know the truth until the last minute in the drama. This is a variant of Aristotle's recognition, although it is one that does not have unhappy consequences. In all of this, New Comedy is usually in tacit agreement with the standards of the society it entertains; all it really does is to stretch its limits in certain directions—creating a dramatic tension that is eventually resolved in the happiness of the lovers who are ultimately free to marry.

Blocking characters are often eccentrics whose behavior is characterized by an extreme commitment to a limited concept. They may be misers, for example, whose entire lives are devoted to mercenary goals, although they may not be able to enjoy the money they heap up. They may be malcontents, forever looking on the dark side of mankind, or they may be hypochondriacs whose every move is dictated by their imaginary illnesses. They may be very straight-laced and prudish, or they may be licentiates. But in any event, such characters are so extreme as to make their behavior virtually a form of a vice. The effort of the younger characters is often to reform the older characters, educating them away from their entrenched and narrow values toward accepting the idealism and hopefulness of the young people who, after all, are in line to inherit the world that the older people are reluctant to turn over to them.

Comedy of manners' archetypal pattern of the older generation blocking the way of the younger generation is both biological and sociological, since it is obvious that the younger generation cannot take over its place in the social power structure until the older generation gives way. Few societies give way without a struggle, and the archetypal struggle on the comic stage serves in many ways to give hope to the young when they most need it and to possibly help educate the old so as to make the real struggle less terrible.

PERCEPTION KEY OLD AND NEW COMEDY

1. Talking about comedy in the abstract is rather difficult. It is best for you to test what has been said above by comparing our descriptions and interpretations with your own observations. If you have a chance to see some live comedy on stage, use that experience, but if that is impossible, watch some television comedy and examine it for:
   a. Its criticism of society in general. Is it gentle? Savage? Absent altogether?
   b. Its use of the blocking character. Is it typical of what is described above? Is there a new twist you feel is noteworthy?
   c. Is there antagonism between the older characters and the younger characters? Does this antagonism imply a criticism of either group? Is it a fair criticism?
2. Do you observe examples of the generation gap? Are they similar to the archetypal pattern of the blocking character opposing the marriage of younger people? Do you observe any modern variations of this archetype?
3. Observe a few comedies. How many "type characters" can you identify? Is there an example of the dumb blonde? the braggart tough guy? the "big lover"? the poor but honest fellow? the dumb cop? We sometimes call these stereotypes, and they are usually hard to miss. How many such characterizations can you identify?

Molière's *Misanthrope:* Comedy of Manners with a Twist

Jean-Baptiste Poquelin—known as Molière—is acknowledged to be one of the greatest comic geniuses of all time. Like Shakespeare, he acted in his own plays, although unlike Shakespeare, he usually took the most important roles. Molière's plays are usually comedies of manners, and they often follow the archetypal pattern we just described so closely that they could be considered models for the genre. His blocking figures are often personifications of specific vices, and they always get their proper comeuppance at the end of the drama. His youths usually are worthy, obedient, and sympathetic enough for us to feel that they are unduly wronged by parents or parent substitutes who have either forgotten what it is like to be young or have chosen to act unreasonably.

The Misanthrope, however, is a very difficult and problematical play because it does not follow the usual pattern. For us it is all the more interesting because it seems to be a curious example of a play that incorporates some of the qualities of the Old Comedy with those of the New Comedy. Because it does so, it gives us a chance to see a line of development in drama that shows up again in modern dramatists like George Bernard Shaw—particularly in *Candida* and *Major Barbara*—and in the even more recent dramatist Edward Albee— particularly in *Tiny Alice.*

The Misanthrope follows one important pattern we find in the tradition of Old Comedy: It begins with a fantastic or extraordinary theme or idea, then works out the idea in successive scenes, showing what things are like when the idea is put into practice. Molière's idea is about being sincere in a society governed by ambition and founded on artificial politeness, artificial good manners, and all the insincerity such artificiality produces. Alceste has, as he tells us, been doomed "to be unfashionably sincere." As such, he has a reputation for being a misanthrope—a person who generally thinks the worst of people. Some of the ironies implied in such a situation are marvelous. For one thing, we would mostly agree that being sincere is a great virtue, but in *The Misanthrope,* it is quite the opposite. Alceste loses an important law case because he refuses to flatter the judges or bring special influence to bear on them. He tells Oronte that the sonnet he wrote is no good, only to end up with what seems to be a challenge to a duel. Alceste wants to deal with people not as they really are, but as they ought to be, and such a wish even leads him to discard his true love at the end of the drama.

Greek Old Comedy was very harsh on individuals. Such famous people as Socrates, playwrights, and governors would be attacked by name. But one thing that was not generally appreciated—nor generally tolerated by the producers of the dramas (called *archons*)—was an attack on humankind in general. In Greece the people were called the *demos,* and no matter how much a playwright might ridicule a rival, he rarely would attack the *demos.* On the other hand, Molière does not attack individuals in *The Misanthrope;* he attacks people in general, demonstrating in numerous ways how frail they are. However, the modern theatergoer may recall that Molière played the part of Alceste and his wife played the part of Célimène, the woman Alceste hoped to woo and win. Much of the talk has to do with fidelity and true love, and we know that Molière's wife was indeed unfaithful. Therefore, many of the lines each speaks may have had a very individual meaning for them and their original audience, and thus one of the usual qualities of Old Comedy might have been repeated in that sense.

Type Character

The Misanthrope has a very thin plot. Alceste is wooing Célimène (in whose house all the action takes place). But Célimène is a thoroughly modern young lady. She has many suitors and sees no reason why she should have to declare her love for one and therefore lose all the attention of the others. If Alceste is a type character, a misanthrope, or one who refuses to come to terms with society, then Célimène is also a type character, a coquette. As a coquette, she is perfectly able to manipulate all the men who are attracted to her. She prefers, or says she prefers, Alceste to the others, but no one can understand why Alceste is interested in her, since she possesses all the qualities of insincerity he hates. Among Célimène's many suitors are Oronte, who thinks of himself as a poet and who seems to be a characterization of sheer vanity, and Acaste and Clitandre, two empty-headed fellows who typify the shallowness of society. An important female character is Arsinoé, who, because she is older than Célimène, has given up coquetry for the appearance of being a prude. Prudishness gives her an

FIGURE 8-8 *The Misanthrope.* Fred Thompson as Acaste, Susanne Peters as Célimène, Guy Stockwell as Alceste, William Halliday as Clitandre. Directed by Terence Kilburn. The Meadowbrook Theater, Rochester, Michigan.

excuse for being single at an advanced age. She has her eye out for Alceste, and some characters think she would be a good match for him. Finally, there is a second romantic interest in the play: Philinte, a man who is Alceste's good friend, and Éliante, Célimène's cousin. Philinte is an optimist who counters all of Alceste's complaints about people with observations that suggest it is not so difficult to get along in society if one wishes. Philinte is, in other words, a foil or contrast to Alceste. We perceive them both more clearly because they offset each other. Éliante, on the other hand, is not so clear-cut a character. She seems to be sincere, as is Alceste, but her sincerity is not so unremitting that it becomes a fault. She can get along in society.

The romantic linking of a misanthrope who demands sincerity and honesty from everyone with a coquette who can thrive only as long as she can keep all her wooers dangling on the hook of insincerity is a fine example of comic irony. Alceste and Célimène are, in one sense, type characters. The fact that each can be summed up in a word or phrase, such as "misanthrope" and "coquette," gives us instant grasp of their nature. But Molière does not permit the characters to become stereotypes. He rounds out their portraits by characterizing them fully in order to maintain their complexity.

The dissection of the foibles of Molière's polite society is what most profoundly maintains the link with New Comedy. Molière describes a world in which it is thought to be normal to string along the hopes of young men and other suitors for as long as the fun lasts. It is a world in which gossip destroys reputations and in which personal influence is vastly more important than integrity or honesty. The law courts do not respect justice; they thrive on bribery and influence-peddling. People ask for criticism when they want flattery. They speak one way in front of a person, but in a totally different way when that person is absent. The entire society is basically hypocritical and vain. Alceste refuses to come to terms with it, and so he suffers. Célimène loves it because it entertains her so completely. Philinte sees its limits but has learned to live with it. Éliante is herself sincere, but she is so uncritical and accepting that she is hardly aware there is a problem.

CHARACTER: ARISTOTLE'S SECOND ELEMENT

Because the plot of this drama is slight, the emphasis Molière places on character makes up for the absence of action. Molière has some plot reversals, as we shall see, but his real delight is in exploring character, and it works because Molière gives us a revealing cross section of types we might find in any society similar to his. We realize our own society has much in common with Molière's. The fact that Molière's society, with all its faults, is portrayed so vividly helps us pay attention to his observations about character. And, finally, Molière depended on a popular literary device of his own day called a "character," a short, witty, verbal portrait, usually sarcastic, which is much like a cartoon.

FIGURE 8-9 *The Misanthrope*. Diana Rigg and Alec McCowen in Tony Harrison's National Theatre production. Courtesy of the Lincoln Center Library of the Performing Arts.

It is meant to be funny, but it also often rings true. In *The Misanthrope* most of the characters actually deliver a "character" of each other, Célimène's "character" of Alceste helps us understand him:

> he loves to make a fuss.
> You don't expect him to agree with us,
> When there's an opportunity to express
> His heaven-sent spirit of contrariness?
> What other people think, he can't abide;
> Whatever they say, he's on the other side;
> He lives in deadly terror of agreeing;
> 't would make him seem an ordinary being.[2]

By the same token, Alceste responds by characterizing people in general: "Men, Sir, are always wrong, and that's the reason / That righteous anger's never out of season; / All that I hear in all their conversation / Is flattering praise or reckless condemnation."

[2]Translated by Richard Wilbur.

When Philinte is given a chance to do a "character" of mankind, he admits that everything Alceste says is correct, but the very worst qualities provide the opportunity for philosophy. And philosophy is one of the noble inventions of the universe. So, for Philinte, everything balances itself out: "each human frailty / Provides occasion for philosophy, / And that is virtue's noblest exercise." The truth of Philinte's observation is basically established in the first four acts of the drama, with plenty of chance for the characters to be fully drawn and for the society to reveal itself. Once that is all taken care of, the plot resolves itself in Act Five. Like tragedy, comedy also depends often on reversal and recognition. In *The Misanthrope* the resolution takes place in the space of only a few stage minutes. It centers on Alceste's finally demanding that his sweetheart, Célimène, make up her mind. Will she choose him or not? She says, "I think it altogether too unpleasant / To choose between two men when both are present." Alceste replies, "I demand it. / The simple truth is what I wish to know, / And there's no need for softening the blow. / You've made an art of pleasing everyone, / But now your days of coquetry are done."

Alceste cannot force her to a choice until almost the last scene when Acaste and a group of others burst in with a letter of Célimène's. It contains a brilliant collection of short "characters"of each of her suitors, showing that she sees them all as possessing faults. Even Alceste, who she has permitted to think was her first choice, is described as "the greatest bore in the world." The outcome of the drama is in remarkable doubt at this point. We hardly know what to expect, even though, as we pointed out earlier, one archetypal pattern for comedy of manners includes the promise of a wedding at its close. When Célimène finally admits the truth about herself, we begin to think we have a possible ending for the drama. She says, "I've wronged you, I confess it." "My guilt toward you I sadly recognize. / Your wrath is wholly justified, I fear; / I know how culpable I must appear." Alceste makes a beginning at learning how to cope in society when he accepts her apologies. He even goes back on his own decision to speak frankly. He does not speak bluntly about what she did to him. "Woman, I'm willing to forget your shame, / And clothe your treacheries in a sweeter name; / I'll call them youthful errors, instead of crimes, / And lay the blame on these corrupting times." This is a big concession for Alceste, and we think all will end well with a proper marriage. He wants to take her off to some isolated spot away from the evils of their courtly society. But that is where the reversal comes in. She cannot renounce the world: "What! *I* renounce the world at my young age, / And die of boredom in some hermitage?" This shocks him. She begins to suggest a marriage arrangement that might work, and he rejects her totally. "No," he says, "I detest you now. I could excuse / Everything else, but since you thus refuse / To love me wholly, as a wife should do, / And see the world in me, as I in you, / Go! I reject your hand, and disenthrall / My heart from your enchantments."

FIGURE 8-10 *The Misanthrope*. Fred Thompson as Acaste, William Halliday as Clitandre, Elizabeth Orion as Arsinoé, Susanne Peters as Célimène. Directed by Terence Kilburn. The Meadowbrook Theater, Rochester, Michigan.

Alceste then explains to Éliante—who had been willing to play second-best to Célimène—that he could not marry her either. And that leaves Philinte and Éliante to get married, which they promise to do. But the drama ends with the two of them vowing to leave the stage and do everything possible to change Alceste's mind about Célimène. Will they do so? We will never know. The ending of the play makes it a great problem for critics of the drama. It clearly does not fit the archetypal pattern of comedy of manners that we have described, although it also clearly seems to be aiming at it. The fact that the play does not fully fit the pattern is one of its most delightful qualities. Its lack of resolution leaves us with a sense that the drama is ongoing. It also helps reveal some of the implications for a marriage of people with very different temperaments. Alceste and Célimène are really not very well suited, and it may be wrong of us to wish that Philinte and Éliante should succeed in their efforts to get them married.

In any event, *The Misanthrope* succeeds masterfully on many levels. It makes us laugh at foolish people and a foolish society; it helps us see our own faults and to laugh at them as well. And it offers some food for thought. Comedy, Old and New, always has a level of seriousness that gives it purpose. All drama, according to Aristotle, includes *dianoia*, thought. By thought he meant, in part, a significance or seriousness that made the play worthwhile when we were all done with it. Plays were not to be insignificant and trivial but to reveal insights into the human condition. *The Misanthrope* reveals the values of a certain kind of social order, the failures of people to come to terms with themselves and with others, and the self-delusions all people are heir to. Molière helps us see ourselves in relation to people who are enough like us for us to stop and take notice. In that sense, *The Misanthrope* has as much of the *dianoia* Aristotle found in the most serious tragedy. *The Misanthrope* helps us see that comedy may have an enormous reservoir of seriousness, even as it makes us laugh.

PERCEPTION KEY COMEDY

1. Read *The Misanthrope* and, if possible, see a production of it. Note how the observations above compare with your own experience. What are the relative emphases, for instance, between broad humor and social commentary? Do Alceste and Célimène become mere stereotypes, or are their characters fully developed?
2. Many comedies have extraordinarily complex plots, the degree of complexity often adding to the humor. Like *The Misanthrope*, many comedies have less complex plots but stress character. If you have seen a comedy lately, decide whether plot or character received more emphasis. What effect does that emphasis have on your response to the comedy?
3. What is the nature of the comment on society in the most recent comedy you have seen? Is society subtly "ribbed"? Is society openly criticized? Are the means by which society is treated similar to those used by Molière? Do you know of comedies that do not criticize society at all?
4. In the comedies you have seen are specific kinds of values stressed? Are these values economic, social, political, artistic, psychological, or religious? Is it possible to describe them in such direct terms? Do you find that comedies that stress *dianoia*, or serious thought, are more or less amusing to you?

Genres of Drama: Tragi-Comedy or the Mixed Genre

On the walls beside many stages we find two masks, the tragic mask with a downturned mouth, the comic mask with an upturned mouth. There is no third mask, although if there were, it would probably have a quizzical expression. The mask would be an expression of bewilderment, as if someone had just asked a totally unanswerable question. Mixing the genres of tragedy and comedy in a drama may give this kind of feeling. Audiences are often left with more questions than they had when they entered the theater. They are not always given resolutions that wrap things up neatly. Instead, tragi-comedy tends, more than either tragedy or comedy, to reveal the ambiguities of the world. It does not usually end with the finality of death or with the promise of a new beginning in marriage. It usually ends somewhere in between or sometimes with *both* a death and a marriage.

The reason tragi-comedy has taken some time to become established as a genre may have to do with the fact that Aristotle did not provide an analysis. However, another possibly stronger reason is that for a long time tragi-comedy was thought of as a mixing of two pure genres and thus inferior in kind. Critics from the Roman period through the Renaissance spent much of their time attempting to justify tragi-comedy as a genre in its own right. The Renaissance writer, Cinthio, talks about tragedies with happy endings and comedies with unhappy endings, suggesting that such plays, despite the interpreters of Aristotle, may be of great value. In the eighteenth century, Samuel Johnson described some of Shakespeare's plays as "mixing comick and tragick scenes," thus making them "compositions of a distinct kind."

Partly because of the work of earlier critics, we find the mixing of genres quite reasonable. Perhaps it is simply a way of making our drama truer to life. As Sean O'Casey commented to a college student: "As for the blending 'Comedy with Tragedy', it's no new practice—hundreds have done it, including Shakespeare. . . . And, indeed, Life is always doing it, doing it, doing it. Even when one lies dead, laughter is often heard in the next room. There's no tragedy that isn't tinged with humour, no comedy that hasn't its share of tragedy—if one has eyes to see, ears to hear." Much of our most impressive modern drama is mixed in genre so that, as O'Casey points out, it is rare to find a comedy that has no seriousness or sadness to it, or a tragedy that is unrelieved by laughter.

One result of the present domination of tragi-comedy over tragedy is that the modern playwright can emphasize dramatic irony, one of the most powerful literary techniques. Dramatic irony explores the disparity between the real outcome of a character's action and the outcome he or she anticipates. In turn, this irony plays against the expectations and sometimes the desires of an audience, thus building tension based on the audience's anticipation of the action. This tension is often built by giving the audience more information about a situation or a character than the characters in the drama have. The audience then can observe the ironic twists of the action. Irony exists in tragedy, as with Romeo and Juliet, who die ironically as a result of Friar Lawrence's plan to unite them happily. Irony is present in comedy, as we observed in Alceste, who ironically discovers the truth about what Célimène thinks of him. But by ranging through the great extremes of tragic and comic emotions, tragi-comedy may be able to exploit irony more than either of the "purer" genres. This is totally appropriate, since irony depends on ambiguity, and by its own dual nature, tragi-comedy is properly ambiguous.

Waiting for Godot

One of the more interesting modern tragi-comedies is Samuel Beckett's now-famous play, *Waiting for Godot* (Figure 8-11). It features two homeless, poverty-stricken men, Vladimir and Estragon. They are in an arid country waiting for Godot, who has apparently promised to meet them but whom they do not know. Their talk rambles on without apparent direction or meaning, except insofar as they seem to be talking about life and its meaningfulness. The plot is minimal. The action seems random. They meet Pozzo, a rich man who comes down the road beating his poor slave, Lucky. But Pozzo does not have any interest in Godot nor in Vladimir and Estragon. Pozzo leaves only to return in the second (and last) act, but when he returns, he is blind and does not recall having met Vladimir and Estragon before. Lucky gives a speech that is a marvelously humorous parody of the languages of philosophy and science. Nothing seems resolved. Finally, a small boy comes—the same boy who has been seen at the end of Act One. His message is the same as it was before: Mr. Godot is sorry, but he cannot come tonight. He will come tomorrow. Vladimir and Estragon have no choice; they must wait. And the play ends with our realization that the action of this drama is meant to be representative of our destinies. The characters are waiting for something to happen that will give meaning to all that has befallen them, and we are led to understand our own condition is essentially the same as theirs. We, too, are alone in the universe, waiting for something to give our lives meaning. Many of us wait for our own Godot, no matter what we may name it. Godot suggests God to us, but humankind worships many gods, so it is dogmatic to limit Godot to any one thing. The play reveals a modern kind of bafflement of the sort associated with Nietzsche's comment that "God is dead." Godot may not be God, but he is godlike, and he is

FIGURE 8-11 *Waiting for Godot.* Dana Elcar as Vladimir, Donald Moffat as Estragon, and Ralph Waite as Pozzo. Performed by the Los Angeles Actor's Theatre for the Public Broadcasting Service.

conspicuous by his absence. Beckett seems to be saying that we have much in common with Vladimir and Estragon.

Much of the dialogue of *Waiting for Godot* is ingenious for its capacity to reveal the uncertainty of Vladimir's and Estragon's situation. The very indirection and annoying repetitiousness may irritate the audience until they, too, seem to be participating with the strangeness of the circumstances. When Vladimir and Estragon try to figure out what they are doing waiting for Godot, we have this passage:

Estragon: What exactly did we ask him for?
Vladimir: Were you not there?
Estragon: I must not have been listening.
Vladimir: Oh . . . Nothing very definite.
Estragon: A kind of prayer.
Vladimir: Precisely.
Estragon: A vague supplication.
Vladimir: Exactly.
Estragon: And what did he reply?
Vladimir: That he'd see.
Estragon: That he couldn't promise anything.
Vladimir: That he'd have to think it over.
Estragon: In the quiet of his home.
Vladimir: Consult his family.
Estragon: His friends.
Vladimir: His agents.
Estragon: His correspondents.
Vladimir: His books.
Estragon: His bank account.
Vladimir: Before taking a decision.
Estragon: It's the normal thing.
Vladimir: Is it not?
Estragon: I think it is.
Vladimir: I think so too.
[*Silence.*]
Estragon: (anxious). And we?
Vladimir: I beg your pardon?
Estragon: I said, And we?
Vladimir: I don't understand.
Estragon: Where do we come in?
Vladimir: Come in?
Estragon: Take your time.
Vladimir: Come in? On our hands and knees.
Estragon: As bad as that?
[©1954 Grove Press, pp. 13-14.]

Much of the dialogue in the play is similar to the conversation here. It seems to be undirected and casual. Its apparent meaninglessness becomes a reflection of modern life. This is, again, an interesting case of Aristotle's mimesis. Some audiences, particularly when the play was first presented in the 1950s, resented its ambiguities and the unusual demands it made upon them. Some critics suggested that in an age that lay in the shadow of a holocaust, the meaninglessness of the play was a way of revealing the meaninglessness of modern life. In any case, the play makes great demands upon an audience. It does not simply tickle the audience's fancy as many frothy popular plays do. Such plays make people forget the troubles and uncertainties of life. Even the apparently more serious melodramas, such as *Sleuth*, *Gaslight*, *A Detective Story*, and *Dracula*—all highly successful plays—have a kind of seriousness that we realize is only temporary. Their seriousness applies to the matters within the play but not necessarily to the life we return to as we leave the theater. We know that the importance of all the suspense and action—based upon limited characterization and, in retrospect, predictable plot—will dissolve the moment we leave the theater. But in a play like *Waiting for Godot*, there is almost nothing that is stereotypical or predictable. We realize that the play is not an escape from, but an informing about, the experiences of life.

If we think again of Aristotle's elements of drama, we find that the plot of Beckett's play is of little importance. Moreover, the characters are restricted in their range—most of the audience would not know which character was Vladimir and which Estragon if asked later on. Although the diction is notable, there is no music and the spectacle is prosaic. Furthermore, the thought is such that critics still wonder what it is supposed to be. We sense that the play is both deeply philosophic and possibly religious, but it is not a simple task to decide on a direct and complete statement of what it means. It seems to mean both too much and too little at the same time.

The most profound difference between tragi-comedy and melodrama is most clearly evident in thought, the seriousness of the concerns of the drama. Once having been thrilled, concerned, worried, shocked, or alarmed in *Sleuth*, we are free of the play when the lights go on. It is no longer important to us despite the wide range of emotions it may have elicited. In *Waiting for Godot* we have a much narrower range of feelings to enjoy; virtually none of them are nameable. But once we leave the theater, we take the play and its problems with us. Its thought is "portable," and if we have participated fully with the drama, we are aware that a transformation has taken place within us. Such a transformation does not happen in melodrama: the form never evokes anything but a temporary effect.

Another successful tragi-comedian is Sean O'Casey, whose Dublin trilogy—*Shadow of a Gunman*, *Juno and the Paycock*, and *The Plough and the Stars*—has become justly famous. All these plays are about people in Dublin during the period of Ireland's struggle for independence from England beginning in 1916. O'Casey was a great comic genius, and the plays are filled with broad humor. In *Juno and the Paycock* Joxer Daly is a "stage Irishman" whose appearances in the play are marked by hilarious humor. Yet the play is profoundly sad. Juno is the long-suffering wife of the Paycock, Captain Boyle, who

FIGURE 8-12 *Juno and the Paycock.* Joseph Maher, Geraldine Fitzgerald, and Suzanne Lederer in the Long Wharf Theatre production, directed by Arvin Brown. Courtesy of the Long Wharf Theatre.

shirks work and struts around proudly through much of the play. Their son, Johnny, was wounded by the English as a Boy Scout in 1916, and around the time of the play itself—1922—lost his arm in a Civil War battle in O'Connell Street. Johnny is hounded by his own army buddies because he turned in a neighbor boy in the tenement, Robby Tancred. Captain Boyle becomes a strutting, drunken peacock when he thinks he is coming into a big inheritance that turns out to be a fluke. Their daughter Mary turns down a young man, Jerry, who says he loves her, for a fancy English solicitor who leaves her pregnant at the end of the play. Everyone else is in worse shape: Johnny is dead; the Captain is dead drunk, broke, and his wife has left him to forage for himself. As Juno and Mary leave the tenement, Mary bewails the fact that her child will be born with no father. Juno delivers one of the most memorable lines of the play, "It'll have what's far better—it'll have two mothers." When the play ends we realize we have laughed at people who have suffered a great deal and whose actions have caused others to suffer. And we know, too, that the kinds of vanity and stupidity and laziness we laughed at continue to cause enormous pain. There will always be strutting peacocks like Captain Boyle, just as there will always be young men like Johnny ready to go blindly off to war and young women like Mary ready to be used by men. Only Juno, despite her own strutting and her own vain qualities, comes through as a strong and possibly admirable character.

1. If you have a chance to see one of the tragi-comedies discussed above or a chance to see another tragi-comedy, examine it for its tragic and comic qualities. How do they develop? Is there a greater emphasis on one than the other? Consider the ways in which the two elements mix together. Are there tragic statements or tragic actions delivered in comic fashion?
2. Consider the importance of plot, character, thought, diction, and spectacle in a tragi-comedy you have recently seen. Are any of these elements specifically downplayed or specifically elevated in importance? The plays of Chekhov, such as *The Cherry Orchard* and *The Seagull*, are fine examples for study.
3. The characters in tragedy are usually more distinguished than ordinary people, while those in comedy are often less distinguished. How does tragi-comedy blend these two demands—if it does?
4. It would be useful to hold a discussion of why the genres of tragedy and comedy are of limited value for the modern playwright. What is it about our culture and these genres that seems to limit their usefulness?
5. Discuss with others who have experienced the same tragi-comedy what they believe is revealed by the play. Discuss the question of how the structural and textural qualities of the play contribute to its capacity to reveal values.

Experimental Drama

The last thirty years have seen widespread experimentation in drama in the Western world. Samuel Beckett, whose *Waiting for Godot* was considered experimental in his day, has gone on to write plays that have no words at all, as in *Acts Without Words*. One of his plays, *Not I*, has an oversize mouth talking with a darkened, hooded figure, thus reducing character to a minimum. In *Waiting for Godot*, plot was reduced in importance. In *Endgame* the characters are immobilized in garbage cans, thereby minimizing spectacle. Beckett's experiments have demonstrated that even when the traditional elements of drama are de-emphasized and reduced, it is still possible for drama to evoke intense participative experiences. Beckett has been the master of refining away. He seems to have subscribed to what the Bauhaus school of architectural design made into a catch phrase: "less is more." Even in drama this seems to have some validity.

Another important thrust of experimental drama has been to assault the audience. Some dramatic theoretical concepts, such as Antonin Artaud's "Theater of Cruelty," have regarded audiences as comfortable, pampered groups of privileged people. Peter Weiss' play, *The Persecution and Assassination of Marat as Performed by the Inmates of the Asylum at Charenton under the Direction of the Marquis de Sade* (or *Marat/Sade*), was influenced by Artaud's thinking. Through a depiction of insane inmates contemplating the audi-

FIGURE 8-13
Marat/Sade. The
Academy Theatre
production, Atlanta,
Georgia. Photograph by
Marty King.

ence at a very close range, it sought to break down the traditional comfort associated with traditional proscenium theater. *Marat/Sade* was not a proscenium piece; it was ideally performed in theater-in-the-round with the audience sitting on all sides of the actors and without the traditional fanfare of lights dimming for the beginning and ending of the drama. The audience is deliberately made to feel uneasy throughout the play. As Susan Sontag said:

> While the "cruelty" in *Marat/Sade* is not, ultimately, a moral issue, it is not an aesthetic one either. It is an ontological issue. While those who propose the aesthetic version of "cruelty" interest themselves in the richness of the surface of life, the proponents of the ontological version of "cruelty" want their art to act out the widest possible context for human action, at least a wider context than that provided by realistic art. That wider context is what Sade calls "nature" and what Artaud means when he says that "everything that acts is a cruelty."[3]

By describing the cruelty in *Marat/Sade* as ontological, Sontag means that the depiction of intense cruelty within the drama is there because cruelty underlies all human events, and the play attempts a revelation of that cruelty. She goes on to explain that the audience's own discomfort is a natural function of this revelation.

Just as Jean Genet's *The Blacks* and *The Balcony,* which both attacked the comfortable white, middle-class audiences that saw them,

[3]Susan Sontag, "Marat/Sade/Artaud," *Against Interpretation,* Farrar, Straus & Giroux, New York, 1965.

Marat/Sade was nonetheless performed on a stage. Even though it was not a proscenium, it was a space set apart from those watching the drama. Julian Beck and Judith Malina experimented early in the 1960s, in a play by Jack Gelber called *The Connection*, with reducing even further the distance between players and audience. The play was about a group of addicts waiting for their dealer to show up, and it was specifically designed to seem like a nonplay. Gelber was in the audience—clearly identified as the author—complaining about the way the production was distorting his play. In later Beck/Malina plays, such as *Paradise Now*, the distinction between players and audience grew even slighter, with relatively little distinction made between spaces for the players and spaces for the audience.

Richard Schechner's play *Dionysus in '69* broke down the distance almost entirely. The space of the theater was the entire space, with a design by Jerry Rojo that made audience and players indistinguishable (except to themselves, perhaps). The play demanded that everyone become part of the action; in some performances—and in the filmed performance—most of the audience and players ended the drama with a modern-day orgiastic rite. Such experimentation, indeed, seems extreme. But it is analogous with other dramatic events in other cultures, such as formal religious and celebratory rites. Moreover, it reflects a widespread reaction against a middle-class theater of pure creature comfort, in which nothing of real importance happens on stage and in which nothing is revealed to the audience. Such plays are rarely even remembered.

The theater of creature comfort is associated with the development in the nineteenth century of the "well-made play." Plays like William Gillette's *Sherlock Holmes* (revived in 1976), Bram Stoker's *Dracula*, and Alexander Dumas' *Camille* are representative of the kind. Usually each character is introduced in such a way as to excite our curiosity; each act ends with a note of suspense; the complications of the plot unfold rhythmically, building to a careful climax just before the end of the last act. All the complexities and difficulties are resolved surprisingly and delightfully moments before the final curtain. It was, in other words, a drama that thrived on formula. It was mostly form, with little or no content. Many contemporary plays still depend on the formula of the "well-made play," but it has become so predictable that it is uninteresting to the most serious dramatists of our time. Usually the only values that the "well-made play" reveal to us are those that have been revealed many times in the past. With experimental drama, at least, we run the risk of having something new revealed to us.

Another significant aspect of the contemporary experimental drama is the tendency to interpret freely the written text. The director tends to become more identified with the play than the author. Andrei Serban, the director of recent productions of *The Cherry Orchard* and *Agamemnon*, reinterprets these plays so freely that the authors, Chekhov and Aeschylus, hardly get a notice. When Brecht's *Three-*

penny Opera was performed recently, Richard Foreman, director of the highly experimental Hysteric-Ontological Theater in New York, dominated the play so much that the original text was almost ignored. The experimental theater of today is in the hands of such directors as Peter Brook of England, Jerzy Grotowski of Poland, Peter Schumann (of the Bread and Theater Puppets) of Vermont, and of Ann Halprin (see Chapter 10) of San Francisco, as well as those dramatists mentioned above.

Experimentation will doubtless continue in contemporary theater, although the initial shock of flaunting the traditions of the "well-made play" is past. Now the experimental drama concentrates more on the subtleties of mixing the media of dance and music with theater as well as experimenting with various emphases of Aristotle's elements of drama. We cannot know what the experimental theater will bring in the future, unless we simply say it will be something rather unlike what it has brought in the past.

PERCEPTION KEY EXPERIMENTAL DRAMA

Should you have the chance to experience a drama produced by any of the directors or groups mentioned above, try to distinguish its features from those of the more traditional forms of drama. What observations can you add to those made above? Consider the kinds of satisfaction you get as a participant. Is experimental drama as satisfying as traditional drama? What are the differences? To what extent are the differences to be found in the structure? In the textural details?

Summary

To a large extent, the subject matter of drama is the human condition as represented by action. By emphasizing plot and character as he describes the elements of drama, Aristotle helps us understand the priorities of all drama. Tragedy and comedy both have archetypal patterns that help define them as genres. Some of the archetypes seem related to the natural rhythms of the seasons and focus, in the case of tragedy, on the endings of things, such as death, and, in the case of comedy, on the beginnings of things, such as marriage. Comedy has several distinct forms. Old Comedy often abuses individual characters and revels in farce, burlesque, and slapstick humor. New Comedy emphasizes the comedy of manners, a social commentary that often depends on recognizable type characters. Tragi-comedy combines both genres to create a third genre. The ambiguity implied in tragedy joined with comedy makes this a particularly flexible genre, suited to the modern world view that emphasizes uncertainty. The experiments in modern drama have tried to break away from traditions, the comforts of which have assured audiences of being carefully treated rather than being involved in an intense and transforming dramatic experience. The human condition may shift from period to period in the history of drama, but somehow the constancy of human concerns has helped make Shakespeare and Molière our contemporaries. We see values revealed in their work that, perhaps, they saw as being less important than we do. But the truthfulness of their visions of their own world leads us to make our own interpretations no less truthful for being modern. The vigor of experimentation in our own time suggests a renewed vigor in our drama. There have been hints that a great age of drama is yet to come and may soon be upon us.

Chapter 8 Bibliography

Aristotle. *Aristotle's Theory of Poetry and Fine Art*, trans. S. H. Butcher. New York: Dover Books, 1951.

Bentley, Eric. *The Playwright as Thinker*. New York: Reynal and Hitchcock, 1946.

Cameron, Kenneth M., and Hoffman, Theodore. *A Guide to Theatre Study*, 2d ed. New York: Macmillan, 1974.

Fergusson, Francis. *The Idea of a Theater*. Garden City, N.Y.: Doubleday, 1953.

Frye, Northrop. *Anatomy of Criticism*. Princeton, N.J.: Princeton University Press, 1957.

Gassner, John. *Masters of the Drama*. New York: Dover Press, 1945.

———— and Allen, Ralph. *Theatre and Drama in the Making*, 2 vols. Boston: Houghton Mifflin, 1964.

Kernodle, George. *Invitation to the Theatre*. New York: Harcourt Brace & World, 1967.

Kerr, Walter. *Tragedy and Comedy*. New York: Simon & Schuster, 1967.

Nicoll, Allardyce. *The Theory of the Drama*. New York: Crowell, 1931.

Potts, L. J. *Comedy*. London: Hutchinson, 1949.

Steiner, George. *The Death of Tragedy*. New York: Knopf, 1961.

Wilson, Edwin. *The Theatre Experience*. New York: McGraw-Hill, 1976.

MUSIC

The Subject Matter of Music

If music has a revelatory capacity, it has, like the other arts, a content that is achieved by the form's transformation of some subject matter. However, some commentators have denied that music has a subject matter, while others have suggested so many different possibilities as to create confusion. Our approach suggests two kinds of subject matter for music: human feeling (emotions, passions, and moods) and sound. The complexities implied in such an approach require some discussion.

THE REFERENTIAL CAPACITY OF MUSIC

To begin with, it is difficult for music to refer to specific objects and events outside itself. Therefore, it is difficult to think of music as having the same kind of subject matter as a representational painting, a figurative sculpture, or a realistic novel. Nonetheless, composers have tried to circumvent this limitation by a number of means. One is to use sounds that imitate the sounds we experience outside music: birdsongs and clocks in Haydn's symphonies, a thunderstorm in Beethoven's Symphony No. 6, sirens in Charles Ives' works. Limited as this may be, it still represents one effort to overcome the abstract nature of music and to give it a recognizable subject matter.

Another means is a program—usually in the form of a descriptive title, a separate written description, or an accompanying narrative as in opera. *La Mer*, by Claude Debussy, has a program clearly indicated by its title—*The Sea*—and its subtitles: "From Dawn to Noon at Sea," "Gambols of the Waves," and "Dialogue Between the Wind and the Sea." Debussy tried to make *La Mer* refer to specific events that happen outside music. His success depends on our knowing the music's program and the relationship between the music and the events it is meant to interpret.

Yet, there is a problem involved with stating flatly that the sea is the subject matter of *La Mer*. The sea cannot be perceived in listening to *La Mer* in anything like the way it can be perceived imaginatively from a literary description or the way it can be perceived more directly in a painting. If *La Mer* were a work that used the actual sounds of the sea or closely imitated them—the crashing of waves, the roaring of winds, and similar sounds—the problem would be simplified. But *La Mer* uses much the same kinds of musical sounds we find in other symphonic compositions by Debussy that have nothing to do with the sea.

In light of this, it might be more reasonable to suggest that *La Mer* is an interpretation—using the medium of music—not of the sea but, rather, of our impressions of the sea. Since Debussy is often referred to as an Impressionist, many listeners seem to find this explanation plausible. In this sense the subject matter of *La Mer* can be said to be the feelings evoked by the sea. The music's content is the interpretation of those feelings. Given close attention to the program, this suggestion poses few difficulties. But most music has no program, and even *La Mer* can be enjoyed by those who are unaware of its program. Consequently, there may be some general feelingful character to the music that can be appreciated apart from any recognition that the swelling of a theme implies the swelling of a sea wind, that the crash of an orchestra suggests the crash of a wave, or that long, quiet passages suggest the stretches of the sea. Apparently those who do not know the program may still recognize general feeling qualities in these same passages despite the fact that they do not relate these qualities to their feelings about the sea. This suggests a general relationship between the structures of our feelings and the structures of music.

FEELING

Music seems to be able to interpret and thus clarify our feelings primarily because in some ways the structures of music parallel or are congruent with structures of feelings. A rushing, busy passage can suggest unease or nervousness so powerfully that we sense unease to be a quality of the music itself, even to the extent sometimes of feeling unease within ourselves. A slow passage in a minor key, such as a funeral march, can suggest gloom; a sprightly passage in a major key, such as a dance, can suggest joy. These extremes, and others like them, are obvious and easy for most listeners to comprehend. But there are innumerable subtleties and variations of feelings between these extremes, none of which is as nameable or as discussable as those mentioned. How can music interpret such feelings?

First of all, the power of sound to evoke feeling has been recognized by innumerable philosophers of art. John Dewey has said;

> Sounds *come* from outside the body, but sound itself is near, intimate; it is an excitation of the organism; we feel the clash of vibrations throughout the whole body. . . . A foot-fall, the breaking of a twig, the rustling of underbrush may signify attack or even death from hostile animal or man. . . . Vision arouses emotion in the form of interest—curiosity solicits further examination . . . or it institutes a balance between withdrawal and forward exploring action. It is sound that makes us jump.[1]

Second, feeling is aroused when a tendency to respond is in some way arrested or inhibited. Suspense is fundamental to a feelingful response. Musical stimuli activate tendencies that are frustrated by means of deviations from the expected, and then these frustrated tendencies are usually followed by meaningful resolutions. We hear a tone or tonal pattern and find it lacking in the sense that it demands other tones, for it seems to need or anticipate following tones that will presumably resolve its "needfulness." This is the basis of our discussion in the Appendix at the end of this chapter on "Tonality: Scales and Keys." According to Leonard B. Meyer, the stronger and more cumulative the tensions of these tonal needs and the more unexpected the resolutions, the more interesting the music. Furthermore:

> Musical experiences of suspense are very similar to those experienced in real life. Both in life and in music the emotions thus arising have essentially the same stimulus situation: the situation of ignorance, the awareness of the individual's impotence and inability to act where the future course of events is unknown. Because these musical experiences are so very similar to those existing in drama and life itself, they are often felt to be particularly powerful.[2]

Third, it may be that musical structures possess, at least at times, more than just a general resemblance to the structures of feelings. Susanne Langer maintains that

> the tonal structures we call "music" bear a close logical similarity to the forms of human feelings—forms of growth and attenuation, flowing and

[1]John Dewey, *Art as Experience*, Milton Balch and Co., New York, 1934, p. 237.
[2]Leonard B. Meyer, *Emotion and Meaning in Music*, The University of Chicago Press, Chicago, 1956, p. 20.

stowing, conflict and resolution, speed, arrest, terrific excitement, calm, or subtle activation and dreamy lapses—not joy and sorrow perhaps, but the poignancy of either and both—the greatness and brevity and eternal passing of everything vitally felt. Such is the pattern, or logical form, of sentience, and the pattern of music is that same form worked out in pure, measured sound and silence. Music is a tonal analogue of emotive life.[3]

Carroll C. Pratt, a psychologist, also maintains that the forms of music bear a close resemblance to certain characteristics of the forms of feelings. For example, the "staccato passages, trills, strong accents, quavers, rapid accelerandos and crescendos, shakes, wide jumps in pitch—all such devices conduce to the creation of an auditory structure which is appropriately described as restless."[4]

Our examples of music's capacity to clarify feelings are useful partly because they are extreme. Most listeners can agree that some music has become associated with funereal, gloomy moods. Some music, too, has become associated with joyous and gladsome moods. Naturally, much of this is the result of cultural conventions that we unconsciously accept. Vibrating string passages can sometimes suggest anxiety, just as a stentorian horn passage can suggest warlike alarms and uncertainties. In these cases it seems that the conventions have developed from the capacity of the music to bear the weight of associations with such specific feelings.

Once we push beyond convention, we can begin to appreciate the extraordinary richness of music's capacity to clarify the nuances of feeling. When we speak in terms of nuances or when we suggest that music can clarify subtle feelings, we then remove ourselves from the nameable feelings such as joy, sadness, uncertainty, anxiety, and security. Music is, perhaps, richest in its ability to clarify feelings for which we have no names at all. One reason why we return to listen to a favorite piece of music again and again may be that it, and it alone in many cases, can excite us and interpret for us feelings that we could not otherwise identify. One of the results of participating with such music is the revelation of the unnameable feelings that refine and enlarge our life of feeling. We can point to few arts that reach into our life of feeling as deeply as does music. By clarifying our feelings, music educates us to them; it explores feelings we may not have thought ourselves capable of experiencing.

Musical structures apparently not only evoke feeling in the listener but also reveal the structures of feeling. Presumably, then, the form of *La Mer* not only evokes feelings analogous to the feelings the sea arouses in us, but also the musical form interprets those feelings and gives us insight into them. The Formalists of music, such as

[3]Susanne Langer, *Feeling and Form*, Scribner's, New York, 1953, p. 27.
[4]Carroll C. Pratt, *The Meaning of Music*, McGraw-Hill, New York, 1931, p. 198.

Eduard Hanslick and Edmund Gurney[5]—just like Clive Bell and Roger Fry, the Formalists of painting (see pages 27–28)—deny this connection of music with nonmusical situations. For them, the apprehension of the tonal structures of music is by a unique musical faculty that produces a unique aesthetic effect, and they refuse to call that effect feeling since this suggests alliance with everyday feelings. For them, the grasp of the form or tonal interrelationships of music is so intrinsically valuable that any attempt to relate music to anything else is spurious. As Igor Stravinsky, certainly one of the greatest composers of our century, insisted. "Music is by its very nature essentially powerless to *express* anything at all. . . ."[6] In other words, the Formalists deny that music has a subject matter and, in turn, this means that music has no content, that the form of music has no revelatory meaning. We think the Formalists' theory is plainly inadequate, but the theory is an important warning against thinking of music as a springboard for nonmusical conceptions and sentimentalism. Moreover, much work remains—building on the work of philosophers of art such as Meyer, Langer, and Pratt—to make clearer the mechanism of how music's form may inform about feelings.

SOUND

Apart from feelings, sound might also be thought of as one of the subject matters of music, because in some music it may be that the form gives us insight into sounds. This is somewhat similar to the claim that colors may be the subject matter of some abstract painting (see pages 84–85). The tone C in a musical composition, for example, has its analogue in natural sounds, as in a birdsong, somewhat the way the red in an abstract painting has its analogue in natural colors. However, the similarity of a tone in music to a tone in the nonmusical world is rarely perceived in music that emphasizes tonal relationships. In such music, the individual tone usually is so caught up in its relationships with other tones that any connection with sounds outside the music seems irrelevant. It would be rare, indeed, for someone to hear the tone C in a Mozart sonata and associate it with the tone C of some birdsong. Tonal relationships in most music are based on scales that are mathematically structured (see Appendix) and thus are very different in their context from the tones of the nonmusical world. In turn, the individual tones are so tightly interwoven in their tonal relationships that as individual tones they have little or no relevance to the world outside. On the other hand, music that does not

[5]Eduard Hanslick, *The Beautiful in Music*, Gustav Cohen (trans.), Novello and Co., London, 1891, and Edmund Gurney, *The Power of Sound*, Smith, Elder and Co., London, 1880.
[6]Igor Stravinsky, *An Autobiography*, Simon and Schuster, New York, 1936, p. 83.

emphasize tonal relationships—such as that of John Cage—can perhaps give us insight into sounds that are noises rather than tones (see the definition of "noise" in the Appendix). Since we are surrounded by noises of all kinds—humming machines, people talking, and banging garbage cans, to name a few—we usually "turn them off" in our conscious mind so as not to be distracted from more important things. This is such an effective "turn-off" that we are surprised and often delighted when a composer introduces such noises into a musical composition. Then, for once, we listen *to* rather than listen *away* from them, and then we may discover these noises to be intrinsically interesting. It may be that one of the things Cage is doing is giving us insight into noises.

PERCEPTION KEY THE SUBJECT MATTER OF MUSIC

1. In discussing feeling as part of the subject matter of music, it is helpful to contrast emotion and passion with mood. We define emotion as a strong response to a specific and apparent stimulus. For instance, a given chord or a specific progression toward a tonic chord may excite in us an emotional response. Passion is emotion elevated to great intensity. Mood, on the other hand, is response that arises from no apparent stimulus as when one awakes with a feeling of lassitude or a general feeling of gloom. There is no apparent identifiable cause, and generally moods are not felt as strongly as emotions and passions. Mood is also a useful term sometimes to describe feelings that arise from emotions and passions and that mix in with them so thoroughly that we are not aware of their origin. This often seems to happen when we listen to music. For example, a great many chordal progressions or a great many thematic developments may produce a group of emotional responses that, taken in their entirety, have the character of, or evoke in the listener, a mood. Select two or three brief musical compositions and listen to them with the following questions in mind. Do these pieces have the character of or evoke feelings? Is it possible to identify passages that are dominated by emotion? Do any of the compositions seem to evoke or have the quality of moods? Are any of the compositions intense enough to be thought of as having passion as part of their subject matter? Are there any moments in which emotion, passion, and mood seem present together in the pieces you have selected?

2. In a small group, present a piece of music you think has feeling as part of its subject matter. What degree of agreement do you find from others' reactions to your selection? Is there general agreement on matters relative to emotion, passion, and mood? Can you perceive in the music qualities that would give grounds for agreement or disagreement? Try Tchaikovsky's *1812 Overture*; the "Tuba Mirum" from Berlioz's *Requiem*, Beethoven's *Grosse Fuge*, Op. 133, or "Der Erlkönig,"a song by Schubert.

3. Since the question of music's capacity to reveal feeling is extraordinarily complex, it would be of value to examine it in an open forum. One useful approach is to set up two panels, each of which takes a different stand on the question. One panel could discuss specific music that clearly reveals

one or more feelings. Another panel could discuss music that seems not to evoke or interpret feeling at all.

4. Try listening to a John Cage or a Spike Jones record that uses everyday sounds, such as barking dogs or car horns. With a group, discuss the value of such music for making one more aware of the characteristics and qualities of sounds we usually take for granted.

Tonal Music

Tonal music is based on scale systems that generate one tone—the tonic—around which all other tones are subordinated in varying degrees. Since the early Baroque period, around 1600, through the first decades of this century, tonality has been Western music's fundamental organizing principle. In recent decades, however, tonality has often been supplanted by atonal and nontonal systems in which no tonic is generated. However, tonality is still the most important force in popular music, including most rock and jazz. For purposes of simplification, we will begin by discussing only two of the scales available in tonal music: the C major scale, C-D-E-F-G-A-B-C, and the F major scale, F-G-A-Bᵇ-C-D-E-F. The B is flatted in the F major scale so as to lower that tone by a half step. If you refer to the piano keyboard (in the Appendix if not on a piano), you will see that the distance between each adjacent key and its touching black or white key is a half step. If there is no black key between two white keys (as in B-C), those white keys are a half step apart. The major scale is built with an established order of full and half steps. The pattern is always the same, so some notes may have to be flatted or sharped to maintain the pattern:

	full step	full step	half step	full step	full step	full step	half step
C major	C to	D to	E to	F to	G to	A to	B to C
F major	F to	G to	A to	Bᵇ to	C to	D to	E to F

By referring to Figure 9-29 in the Appendix, you will see that, if you begin with C, the piano keyboard is set up to have the right number of full and half steps to play a C major scale without resorting to any of the black keys. All other major scales, and almost all the minor scales, must use some of the black keys so as to keep the order of intervals of full and half steps that maintain the scale of a given key.

A composition that relies on a given key, such as C major, can use the expectancy of repetition of important tones, such as C, the tonic, and G, the dominant, to keep the audience's attention. Repetition of important tones rewards the audience's expectation. Avoiding the important tones can produce surprise, anxiety, and instability. Exploring the important tones and their relationship in a melodic or harmonic structure can help inform an audience about the tonal resources of that particular key and the tonal resources of the themes and harmonies with which a composer is working.

TONAL CENTER

A composition written mainly in one scale is said to be in the key that bears the name of the tonic or tonal center of that scale. A piece in the key of F major uses the scale of F major; although in longer, more complex works, such as symphonies, the piece may use other related scales in order to achieve variety and to explore the resources of melody and harmony in new keys. The tonal center of a composition in the key of F major is the tone, F. We can usually expect such a composition to begin on F, to end on it, and to return to it frequently to establish stability. Each return to F builds a sense of stability in the listener, while each movement away usually builds a sense of uncertainty or tension. Such movement conduces to producing an emotional response in the listener. The listener need not know what key the piece is in, since the tonal center is presented with emphasis as the piece is played. The listener perceives the tonic as the basic tone because it establishes itself as the point of reference for all other tones. The effect of this is clarified in the familiar melody of "Swing Low, Sweet Chariot" (Figure 9-1). After beginning with A, the melody immediately moves to F as a weighty rest point. The melody rises no higher than D' nor falls lower than C. For convenience, the notes are labeled above the notation in the figure.

Most listeners will sense a feeling of completeness in this brief composition. But the movement in the first four bars, from A downward to C, then upward to C, passing through the tonal center, F, does not suggest such completeness; rather, it prepares us to expect something new. If you sing or whistle the tune, you will see that the long tone, C, in bar 4 sets up an anticipation that the next four bars attempt to satisfy. In bars 5 through 8 the movement downward from D to C, then upward to A, and finally to the rest point at F suggests a temporary resting point. When the A sounds in bar 8, we are ready to move on again with a pattern that is similar to the opening passage: a movement from A downward to C, through the tonal center, back up through the tonal center to C, as in the opening four bars. Bar 13 is structurally repetitious of bar 5, moving from D downward but this time to A on the way to establishing the firm tonal center F in the last note of bar 13 and the first four tones of bar 14. Again, the melody continues downward to C, but when it returns in measures 15 and 16 to the tonal center, F, we have a sense of almost total stability. It is as if the melody has taken us on a metaphoric journey: showing us where we begin, where "home" is; showing us the limits of our movement away from "home"; then showing us the pleasures and the stability of

Swing Low, Sweet Chariot

FIGURE 9-1 "Swing Low, Sweet Chariot." Negro Spiritual.

returning to "home." Of course, the tonal center, F, is "home," and when the lyrics actually join the word "home" in bar 4 with the tone C, we are a bit unsettled. This is a moment of instability. We do not become settled until bar 8, and then again in bar 16, where the word "home" falls on the tonal center, F, which we have already understood —simply by listening—as the real "home" in the composition. This composition is simple, but it is also subtle. It points to the means by which our experiences in listening have helped us shape our sense of anticipation of stability and instability in tonal music.

PERCEPTION KEY "SWING LOW, SWEET CHARIOT"

1. What is the proportion of tonic notes (F) to the rest of the notes in the composition? Can you make any judgments about the capacity of the piece to produce and release tension in the listener on the basis of the recurrence of F?

2. Are there any places in the composition where you think F ought to be the next note but is not? If F is always supplied when it seems necessary, what does that signify for the level of tension the piece creates?

3. The ending of a piece such as this produces a high degree of finality. Yet the middle portions are phrases that also seem to have a sense of finality— though not so complete. How does the composition handle the differences

in demand? Compare measures 4, 6, and 10 with measures 8 and 16. Discuss the relative values of finality in these measures with others who have thought about this problem.

4. Does this music evoke feeling in you? What kind of feeling? Does the music interpret this feeling, help you understand it? If so, how does the music do this?

The notes in the scale of each key have special relationships to one another based upon their relative stability—which is to say their potential for consonance (see Appendix) when sounded with the tonic note of the key. The most important of the eight tones in the keys of C major and F major are:

Tonic: C	Tonic: F
Fifth (dominant): G	Fifth (dominant): C
Third (median): E	Third (median): A
Seventh (leading tone): B	Seventh (leading tone): E
Eighth (tonic): C'	Eight (tonic): F'

These five tones are not the only ones with names, though they are the tones that have the most basic and most perceptibly significant relationship to the tonic. They are especially important because they help establish the centrality of the tonic and guide our ear securely to recognize it when it is played. One procedure in tonal music is to establish the tonic solidly, veer away from it for a while, and then return to establish a secure "home base" feeling that constitutes much of the satisfaction listeners feel in such music. Consider the use of this procedure in a little minuet written by Wolfgang Amadeus Mozart's father, Leopold (Figure 9-3).

The minuet is symmetrical in structure. The first section is ten bars long, with the repeat sign, shown in Figure 9-2, indicating that the entire ten bars are to be played again. The second section is also ten bars long, with its repeat sign, shown in Figure 9-4, indicating that we return to the beginning of the repeat in bar 11, then play the second section again to the end. Thus, we have a composition of twenty bars with the following structure (A stands for section 1, B for section 2): A A B B. The function of the repetition, as in many complex works, is to help our ear grasp the shape and character of the piece. Since the material presented in A is very subtle in construction and since we cannot hope to recognize or grasp it immediately, as we can in "Swing Low, Sweet Chariot," the strategy of repetition can do much in helping us establish familiarity with the tonal center, observe the progress of the melodic line, and clarify the limits of our expectation.

If you can have someone play this piece, you will see that the A section, although it begins on the tonic C' in the G clef and C in the bass clef, also begins a movement that takes us away from the tonic,

From Leopold Mozart's
"Notebook For Nannerl"
(1759)

FIGURE 9-2 A repeat sign.

FIGURE 9-3   Minuet.
From Leopold Mozart's
"Notebook for Nannerl"
(1759).

FIGURE 9-4   Beginning
of a repeat.

and brings us to an uncertain rest point in bar 10 on the dominant G in the bass clef. The immediate repetition of the A section helps resolve this instability by bringing the statement of tonic C in bar 1 to our ears again. The tonic C is clearly audible in bars 1, 4, and 5, but its appearance is rare and not clearly audible in bars 6 through 10, since other, distracting tones command our attention. But this mild uncertainty is dissolved away by the expectation built in the three-note patterns of bars 11, 12, and 13. Their pattern—D-B-G, E-C-G, F-D-B— is three descending broken chords, the first of whose tones rises in pitch steadily, raising our own sense of anticipation. It is with mild relief that we hear our anticipation rewarded in the last note of bar 14 with the tonic C in the bass clef. But as if he realized he had satisfied our anticipation and held our attention securely, Mozart then moves back to exploring a rhythmic pattern in bars 16 and 18 that sounds like a hesitation (Figure 9-5).

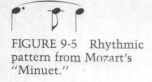

FIGURE 9-5 Rhythmic pattern from Mozart's "Minuet."

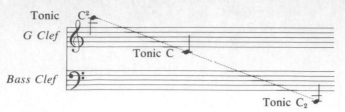

FIGURE 9-6 Movement to tonic in bar 20.

The security of the tonic in bars 16, 17, and 18 is minimal because the tonic is barely audible in the bass clef. The final movement downward to the tonic in bar 20 confirms the movement of the entire piece (Figure 9-6). The structure of the piece is elegantly simple: a descent from the high treble tonic to the deep bass tonic. The structure could work in reverse, too, moving from the bass to the treble, but there is a question of how complete the listener's sense of having achieved stability might be. Moving downward in pitch, as this piece does, guarantees the achievement of closure and rest.

The uncertainties that are developed in this piece are actually quite slight. Listening to the piece reveals it to be light, pleasant, and restful despite the minimal repetitions of tonic C. The reason that the tensions are so slight is partly because Mozart has provided us with numerous reference points in his repetition of the dominant G and mediant E tones. These tones, with the tonic C, constitute the most fundamental triad in the key of C major—the C major chord C-E-G. Mozart is exploring the resources of the key and educating our ear to the perhaps otherwise unanticipated complexities and delights of its basic chord. Another reason why the piece seems so unassuming and airy is that the melodic line is very simple and moves, with only a few exploratory distractions, reliably downward on its journey to the C_2 tonic. Moreover, its rhythmic character, even for a minuet—a courtly dance—is almost unrelievedly simplified. The tempo, *allegretto*, means "a little fast," suggesting a lightness of touch. The time signature, ¾ means each bar should have the duration of three quarter notes. In fact, most bars do have only three notes or a dotted half note (as in the G clef in bar 4), which is equivalent in time to three quarter notes. The "hesitation" pattern (Figure 9-5) is the only relief the piece has from the steady pattern of three quarter-notes per bar. A comparison of the music for "Swing Low, Sweet Chariot" will show how much more complex that piece is rhythmically than the minuet.

PERCEPTION KEY LEOPOLD MOZART'S "MINUET"

1. How do these first four bars help establish the tonal center? To what extent do these bars generate what follows in the rest of the piece?
2. Listen to the piece being played and follow the notes in the score. Which bars make you feel most uncomfortable? Which most comfortable? Which

bars are most interesting to you? Which are the least interesting? Is there a correlation between what interests you and what makes you feel comfortable? Or is there an inverse correlation?

3. Have someone play the piece using this structure: A-B-A. This can be accomplished by repeating bars 1 through 10 after the normal ending. If possible, listen to this "adaptation" with others and discuss the effect of listening to it this way. If you listen to it alone, ask yourself what the effect is on you. Does it satisfy you as much as the normal structure, A-A-B-B, does?

4. Does the difference in frequency of tonic notes in the G clef as compared with the bass clef help you decide which clef is more important in the composition? In what ways might one clef be more or less important? How might their relative importance affect your sense of satisfaction with the composition?

ATONALITY

Atonal music abandons the tonal center. All twelve tones (including the sharps and flats—the black keys on the piano) are equal in value; thus, the other name for the music—twelve tone music. No tone is returned to more frequently than any other, for if a system were not worked out to ensure that no tone was more frequently used than any other, the old phenomenon of the tonal center would take effect. Therefore, Arnold Schoenberg devised a tone row: a sequence of twelve tones, which was the melodic line. This tone row then constituted the basic component of the music; it was arranged in a variety of sequences to form all melodic and harmonic material. Schoenberg's *Pierrot Lunaire* and his String Quartets Nos. 1 and 3 are good examples of atonality. It is still a technique contemporary composers use, and it is appearing in jazz and other popular music, though sparingly.

POLYTONALITY

Polytonal music has melodies in different keys played simultaneously. The result is a curious kind of instability and, sometimes, mild confusion that composers can resolve or not as they choose. Sometimes polytonal music enables us to hear more distinctly two or more melodies being played simultaneously. The key separations help us hear the melodic separations. This technique has been used by composers as different as Maurice Ravel and Charles Ives. Igor Stravinsky's *History of a Soldier* is an exceptionally interesting example of the successful use of polytonality.

NONTONAL MUSIC

Some electronic composers, such as Milton Babbitt and Karl-Heinz Stockhausen, have been avoiding tonality most of the time. Their compositions usually depend to a large extent on other techniques for developing structure. Although tonal music can depend on our sense of the impending tonic to give "shape" to a musical composition, the electronic composers depend on repetition, loudness and softness, variations of speed and pitch, and sometimes silence. Often when they do produce tones—as they frequently do—the tones are pure; that is, the familiar overtones, or partials (see Appendix), which identify tones for most of us, are absent. The novelty of hearing an absolutely pure tone is something that many listeners are not prepared to accept. Consequently, electronic music is sometimes shunned by listeners who prefer the traditional timbres of musical instruments.

John Cage has experimented in his music with breaking panes of glass, dropping objects, dripping water, turning on and off household appliances such as the radio, and even total silence. He is committed, at times, to an exploration of the noises of the everyday world. And he achieves some success by organizing them into structures that reveal the characteristics and qualities of these sounds. For instance, have you really listened to breaking glass? The fact that we are used to thinking of music only as organizations of tones makes it difficult sometimes for us to take Cage's work seriously. But if we think of music as organized sound rather than just as organized tones, the problem of acceptance is eased. Since it is the opinion of many young composers that nontonal music will be preferred more and more in composition for some time, it may be useful for us to broaden our personal conceptions of music.

Musical Structures

The most familiar musical structures are based, in one sense or another, on repetition—of rhythm, melody, timbre, harmony, and dynamics (see "Some Basic Elements of Music" in the Appendix). Even the refusal to repeat any of these will be effective mainly because repetition is usually anticipated by the listener. Repetition in music is of particular importance because of the serial nature of the medium. The ear cannot retain sound patterns for very long, and thus it needs repetition to help hear the musical elements and their relationships.

THEME AND VARIATIONS

Theme and variations of that theme constitute a favorite structure for composers from the seventeenth century to the present. We are usually presented with a clear statement of the theme that is to be varied. The theme is sometimes repeated so we have a full understanding of it; then modifications of the theme follow. We can identify the process schematically in this fashion, with A being the original theme: $A\text{-}A^1\text{-}A^2\text{-}A^3\text{-}A^4\text{-}A^5$ . . . and so on, to the end of the variations. Some marvelous examples of structures built on this principle are Bach's *Art of Fugue*, Beethoven's *Diabelli Variations*, Brahms's *Variations on a Theme by Joseph Haydn*, and Edward Elgar's *Enigma Variations*.

If the theme is not carefully perceived when it is originally stated, the listener will have little chance of hearing how the variations relate to the theme. Furthermore, unless one knows the structure is theme and variations, much of the delight in the composer's ingenuity will be lost. Interestingly enough, theme and variations is a structure that many arts can employ, as in successive treatments of the same subject matter in successive paintings. Impressionist Claude Monet painted Notre Dame Cathedral in Rouen at different hours of the day. He would paint on one canvas beginning at 10 A.M. Then, when the clock had moved ahead an hour, he removed that canvas and worked on the next, and so on. In architecture we might think of the churches of the world as theme and variations, although it is clear that in music we are not talking about a collection of structures but, rather, a collection of structural details that add up to a structure.

RONDO

There are many rondo forms, but all have a similar approach to the question of repetition. The refrain or first section will include a theme or melody and may include a development of that theme. Then, after a contrasting section or episode with a different theme, the refrain is repeated. Occasionally, early episodes are also repeated, but usually not so often as the refrain. It can be described: A-B-A-C-A—either B or D—and so on, ending with the refrain, A. Sometimes composers will end on an episode instead of a refrain, although this is an unusual procedure. The rondo may be slow, as in Mozart's *Haffner Serenade*, or it may be played with blazing speed, as in Weber's *Rondo Brilliante*. The rondo may also suggest a question-answer pattern, as in the children's song, "Where is Thumbkin?" Sometimes the treatments reverse the A-B form, so the refrain comes second each time. The fast first and third movements of Vivaldi's *Seasons*, Haydn's *Gypsy Rondo*, Johann Pachelbel's popular *Dance Rondo*, and the slow second movement of Beethoven's Symphony No. 4 are all interesting examples of the rondo.

Fugue

One specialized form of counterpoint (see Appendix) is called the fugue. It was developed in the seventeenth and eighteenth centuries and is closely connected with the name of J. S. Bach, whose monumental *Art of Fugue* ranks as one of the most exhaustive explorations of a melodic line in the history of music. Most fugues feature a melody—called the "statement"—which is given clearly in the beginning of the composition and usually begins with the tonic note of its key. Then that same melody more or less—now called the answer—appears

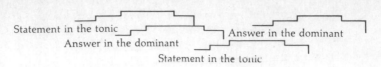

FIGURE 9-7 The fugue.

again, usually beginning with the dominant note (the fifth note) of that same key. The textural quality of the fugue—with the melodic lines of the statements and answers rising to command our attention, and then submerging into the background as episodes of somewhat contrasting material intervene to attract our notice—is complex but delightful. Consider the following diagram shown in Figure 9-7 as a suggestion of how the statements and answers of a fugue might interact; they compete for attention fiercely.

The fugue is often referred to as an imitative form, which means that statements and answers are usually very similar to each other in structure. Sometimes they share the same pattern of ascending or descending tones. Often they adapt similar rhythmic patterns. In some cases they may mirror each other, and in other cases the statement may reappear upside down as an answer. Sometimes fugues exist not as compositions set apart, but as part of another composition. Many symphonies, for example, have brief fugal passages as a means of achieving contrast. Sometimes those fugal passages become the basis for independent fugues. Thus, Beethoven's *Grosse Fuge* in B♭ was originally composed as a part within a string quartet. But whether it is by itself or part of something else, the fugue can have many different characters. When it is played fast and dancelike, it is often called a *canzona*. When it is played slowly, with a stateliness or seriousness associated with it, it is called a *ricercar*. One of its most effective devices is called the *stretto*: one voice coming in before the previous voice has finished.

SONATA FORM

The eighteenth century brought the sonata form to full development, and contemporary composers still find it a useful structure. Its simplest version is described as A-B-A, with these letters representing the main sections of the composition and not just themes, as the letters represent in the rondo. The first A is the exposition, with a statement of the main theme in the tonic key of the composition and usually a secondary theme or themes in the dominant key: the key of G, for example, if the tonic key is C. In the A section, the thematic material may be restated, but it is usually not developed. This occurs in the B or development section, with the themes usually in new but closely related keys. The development section usually explores contrasting dynamics, timbres, tempos, rhythms, and harmonic possibilities inherent in the material of the exposition. In the third section or recapitulation, the basic material of the first section or exposition is repeated, usually in the tonic key. After the contrasts of the development section, this repetition in the home key has a quality of return and finality.

The sonata form is ideal for revealing the resources of thematic material. For instance, the principal theme of the exposition when contrasted with a very different second theme, as in the opening movement of Beethoven's *Eroica* Symphony, takes on a new and surprising quality. We may even feel we did not fully hear the principal theme the first time. This is one of the major sources of satisfaction for the careful listener. Statement, contrasting development, and restatement is a useful pattern for revealing the resources of almost any basic musical material, especially the thematic.

The symphony is usually a four-movement structure often employing the sonata form for its opening and closing movements. The middle movement or movements normally are contrasted in dynamics, timbres, harmonics, and thematic materials, and most obviously in tempos with the first and last movements. Listeners' ability to perceive how the sonata form functions within most symphonies is essential in helping them sense the unified quality of the total composition.

PERCEPTION KEY SONATA FORM

1. Examine closely the first movement of a symphony by Haydn, Mozart, Beethoven, or Brahms. Identify the exposition section—which will come first—and the beginning of the development section. When you can do this, examine the movement until you can identify the end of the development and the beginning of the recapitulation section. You should perceive some change in dynamics and tempo at each of these points, just as you will perceive changes in key, from home key or tonic to contrasting key and back to home key or tonic. You need not know the names of those keys in order to be aware of the changes. They are usually fairly perceptible.

2. Once you have developed the capacity to identify these sections of the sonata form, describe the qualities of each of them that make them different. Be sure to describe the qualities of melody, harmony, timbre, dynamics, rhythm, tempo, and contrapuntal qualities if any. You may also wish to describe the sections in other terms, such as the qualities of feeling you might sense in them.

3. When you have confidence in your perception of the sonata form, do some comparative studies. Take the first movement of a Haydn symphony—Symphony No. 104 in D major, the *London*, would be useful—and compare each of the sections of the first movement with those of the first movement of any of Brahms' four symphonies, the first movement of Symphony No. 7, *Antarctica*, by Ralph Vaughan Williams, or the first movement of Dmitri Shostakovich's Symphony No. 9. Is such a composition useful for developing an understanding of the resources of the sonata

form? Can you make any useful critical evaluations among these works by this means?

4. Do the various sections of the sonata seem particularly suited to evoking feelings? Can you describe them?

FANTASIA

Romantic composers (roughly, the period of 1800 to 1900) began working with looser structures than the demanding sonata form. We find compositions with terms identifying—presumably—their structures, such as rhapsodies, nocturnes, aubades, and fantasias. They are all somewhat impressionistic in nature, suggesting moods as their subject matter. The fantasia may be the most helpful of these to examine, since it is to the sonata form what free verse is to the sonnet. The word "fantasia" implies imagination, which suggests, in turn, the unexpected and the innovative. It is not a stable structure, and its sections cannot be described in such conventional terms as A-B-A. The fantasia usually offers some stability by means of a recognizable melody of a singable quality, but then it shifts to material that is less identifiable thematically, less tonally certain, and less harmonically secure. The succession of musical motifs is presented without regard for any predetermined order. However, there are controls in terms of pacing, the quality of themes and their duration, the harmonic coloring, and the dynamics. Sometimes the fantasia will explore a wide range of feelings by contrasting fast and slow, loud and soft, richly harmonic and harmonically spare passages, and singable themes with themes that are less singable or appealing.

Many of Robert Schumann's best works are piano pieces he called fantasias. Mozart's Fantasia in C minor is an excellent example of the mode, but probably most of us are more familiar with Moussorgsky's Fantasia: *A Night on Bald Mountain*, which was used in Walt Disney's *Fantasia*, a 1940 film.

PROGRAM MUSIC

Another structure, and one related to the fantasia, is program music, in which the nature of the musical material is shaped in part according to the predetermined program for the composition. *A Night on Bald Mountain* is a good case in point because it interprets the program of a terrible storm and the calmness of the following morning, while also interpreting the terror and fright—in relation to the storm—and gratitude and calm as the sun rises and the birds sing. Often in program music it seems that what is interpreted is not objects or events but the feelings evoked by objects or events. Were we present on Bald Mountain during the storm, we might indeed feel terror—as well as the gratitude that comes when the source of terror is removed. Moussorgsky's music interprets these feelings and reveals them to us partly because we are not distracted—as we would be if we were on the mountain—by actually being terrorized or grateful. Thus, through the music, we can understand something of the structures and qualities of these feelings without being threatened by them.

Program music reveals feelings associated with specific objects and events that lie outside music. Some musicologists suggest that, by interpreting feelings, music—including program music—expands and develops our life of feeling. This is thought to be the reason that people who know little about the technical aspects of music can respond excitedly to program music—since we already have some awareness of objects and events outside of music and can relate meaningfully to references to that awareness. Responding to the more generalized interpretation of feelings in nonprogrammatic music—which does not interpret feelings related to specific objects and events—may be more difficult for most listeners. Without the specificity of a program, we may find the interpretation of feeling by such music less discernible and less comprehensible. To comprehend such interpretations, one must be more acutely aware of the character of the musical elements— rhythm, tempo, melody, timbre, harmony, and dynamics—and their structure. In short, program music reveals feelings associated with specific situations in life. Nonprogrammatic music reveals feelings of a more general character, such as moods, unrelated to specific objects or situations. In this respect, the distinction between program and nonprogrammatic music is analogous to the distinction between representational and abstract painting (see Chapter 4).

PERCEPTION KEY PROGRAM MUSIC

1. After reviewing the program of the music, listen to one of the following: Moussorgsky's *Pictures at an Exhibition* or Fantasia: *A Night on Bald Mountain*; Tchaikovsky's *1812 Overture* or Fantasia, *The Tempest* (particularly if you have recently read Shakespeare's *Tempest*); Debussy's *La Mer*; Ralph Vaughan Williams's Symphony No. 7, *Antarctica*; Charles Ives's *Three Places in New England* or Symphony: *Holidays*. Does the music evoke in you feelings similar to those that might be evoked by the situations referred to in the program? Does the music reveal these feelings—give you a better understanding of them? If so, how?

2. If you have friends who have also listened to the composition you chose, ask them if they were able to identify any feelings revealed or evoked by the music. Is there considerable variety of answers among you and your friends to the above question? What might this mean?

3. Examine the musical elements of your composition for the means by which feelings are revealed or evoked in you or in your friends. Refer to the section entitled "The Basic Elements of Music" to be sure you are considering as many of the basic elements as possible. Are the techniques you can isolate usable in nonprogrammatic music to reveal or evoke feelings, or do you think these techniques are strictly limited to program music? Explain your reasons.

4. Is it possible for you to recognize that music has a feeling quality without

that feeling being aroused in you? For instance, the second movement of Beethoven's Symphony No. 3, the *Eroica*, is almost universally described as being sad music, that in some way sadness is a characteristic or quality of the music. Does that mean you should feel sad when you listen to that music? Furthermore, is it possible for that music to interpret sadness, make it more understandable to us, without our feeling that sadness? If we do feel sadness when we listen to music, is it the same kind of sadness we feel in nonmusical situations? These are extremely complex and difficult questions that have been perplexing philosophers of music for over a century. Thinking about them carefully will help you begin to understand the nature of music.

The Symphony

The development of the symphony marks one of the highest points in the history of Western instrumental music. The symphony has proved to be flexible enough a structure that it has flourished in every musical era since the early eighteenth century, where we perceive its beginnings in the Baroque period with the sinfonias of Handel and the symphonies of C. P. E. Bach, Francesco Rosetti, and others. The word "symphony" suggests a "sounding together." From its beginnings, through its full and marvelous development in the symphonies of Haydn, Mozart, Beethoven, and Brahms, the symphony was particularly noted for its development of harmonic structures (see the Appendix). Harmony is the sounding together of tones that have an established relationship to one another. Because of its complexity, harmony is a subject many composers must study in great depth during their apprentice years. The symphony as it existed in the early eighteenth century, in the Classic period of the late eighteenth and early nineteenth centuries, in the Romantic period of the middle and late nineteenth century, and in the twentieth century has undergone many subtle changes. These changes can be traced to varying concepts of harmonic structure, most of which are extremely complex and not fully intelligible without considerable analysis. Triadic harmony (which means the sounding of three tones of a specific chord, such as the basic chord of the key C major, C-E-G, or the basic chord of the key F major, F-A-C) is common to most symphonies, although such satisfying harmonies are not as commonly found in modern symphonies as in classic symphonies. Even in classic symphonies, the satisfaction that the listener has in hearing distinct triadic harmony is often withheld by the composer in order to develop musical ideas that will resolve themselves and their tensions in a full, resounding chordal sequence of triads.

The symphony is also notable for its interest in melodic development. All of the forms that we have mentioned—theme and variations, rondo, fugue, and sonata—develop melodic material. Because it is a larger structure usually with four movements, the symphony can develop melodic ideas much further than any of these forms ordinarily can. Indeed, the symphony often includes many—sometimes all—of these forms. In general, as the symphony evolved into its conventional structure in the time of Haydn and Mozart, the four movements were ordered as follows: first movement, sonata form; second movement, A-B-A or rondo form; third movement, minuet; fourth movement, sonata form or rondo. There were exceptions to this order even in Haydn's and Mozart's symphonies, and in the Romantic and following periods the exceptions increased as the concern for conventions decreased.

The relationship between the movements of a symphony is a subject of controversy. It is by no means true that the same melodic material or the same key or harmonic approach will prevail in all the movements. For some listeners the sequence of the four movements in a symphony will seem arbitrary. On the other hand, there are some symphonies that do make an effort to develop the same or similar melodic material through all four movements. This is relatively uncommon because four movements can rapidly exhaust all but the most sustaining and profound of melodies. One's ear can get tired of hearing the same tunes through four movements. The preferred method has been to follow the conventional patterns of tempo in the four movements, using appropriate melodic ideas in each movement, which is to say themes that seem to be best suited for fast or slow tempos. There can never be uniform agreement on such a point, so critical discussion often centers on the appropriateness of the melodic material for a given movement of the symphony.

A comparison of the tempo markings of several symphonies by important composers shows several similarities: fast opening and closing movements with contrasting slower middle movements. One of the most important connecting devices holding the four movements of a symphony together is the convention of altering the tempo in patterns similar to those that follow. An alteration of tempo can represent a profound alteration in mood in a movement. The predictable alteration of tempo is one of the things our ear depends upon for finding our way through the whole symphony. In such large structures, we need all the sign-posts we can get, since it is easy to lose one's way through a piece of music that may last almost an hour. The tempo markings below are translated loosely so as to be helpful and descriptive.

Haydn, Symphony in G major, No. 94, the *Surprise*
1. *Adagio, vivace* (slowly, very lively)
2. *Andante* (moderately slow)
3. *Minuet* (not fast, the dance tempo of the minuet)
4. *Finale, allegro molto* (final movement, very fast)

Mozart, Symphony in C major, No. 41, the *Jupiter*
1. *Allegro vivace* (fast and lively)

2. *Andante cantabile* (slow and songlike)
3. *Minuet and trio, allegretto* (dancelike, then a little fast)
4. *Finale, allegro molto* (final movement, very fast)

Beethoven, Symphony in C minor, No. 5
1. *Allegro con brio* (fast, breezy)
2. *Andante con moto* (slowly, with motion)
3. *Allegro, scherzo* (fast, with dance rhythm)
4. *Allegro, presto* (fast, very quick)

Brahms, Symphony in E minor, No. 4
1. *Allegro non assai* (fast, but not very)
2. *Andante moderato* (moderately slow)
3. *Presto giocoso* (fast and jolly)
4. *Allegro energetico e patetico* (fast, with energy and feeling)

The tempo markings in these and other symphonies, including those of modern composers such as Gustav Mahler, Benjamin Britten, and others, suggest that each movement is designed with other movements in mind. That is, each movement offers a contrast (see the Appendix) to those that come before or after it. Composers of symphonies have many means at their disposal to achieve contrast. The first, as we have said, is variation in tempo. This is clear in the time markings of fast and slow, but it is also present in other ways. The sonata movements are usually written in 4/4 time, which means that there are four quarter notes in each measure, with the first and third usually getting a slight accent. Minuet movements, like many other dance movements, are in 3/4 time, three quarter notes to a measure, with the first receiving the accent. March time, used in many middle movements is usually either 6/8 time or 2/4 time. In 6/8 time there are six eighth notes to a measure, with the first and fourth receiving the accent. In 2/4 time the first of the two quarter notes receives the accent. Sometimes this produces the "oompah" sound we associate with marching bands.

Contrast is also achieved in dynamics (see the Appendix), with loud and soft passages likely to be found in any movement. Naturally, we might expect the middle movements, which are often shorter than the first and last, to use less dynamic shifting. We usually expect the last movement to build to a climax that can often be a smashing, loud finale. Variations in the length of movements, in their range of loud and soft passages, and in their suddenness of dynamic changes all add to contrast. And since the symphony is usually played by a large orchestra, the composer has a variety of instrumental families to depend on for adding contrast. A theme, for instance, can be introduced by the violins, passed on to the woodwinds, then passed on to the horns, only to return to the violins. Second subjects (second themes in a movement) can be introduced by flutes or piccolos so as to contrast with the thematic materials developed by other families of instruments. The second subject itself is often very different in length, pitch, and rhythmic character from the first theme, thus achieving further contrast. Sometimes a theme or developmental passage can be carried by a single instrument in a solo passage; it may return later with all the instruments in that family playing together. Once the theme has been introduced, then slated by different instruments, it may be played by the entire orchestra. The resultant contrast increases our attentiveness, helping us grasp the melodic material by showing us how it sounds in different ranges of pitch (higher in the flutes, lower in the cellos), and permits us to see how composers' inventiveness exploits the power of the entire ensemble at their disposal. The possibilities for achieving contrast in the symphony may account, in part, for its sustaining popularity and success over the centuries.

Contrast in tempo, time signature, dynamics, and instrumentation are all readily perceived by our ear, even if we are not trained and do not have access to the score of the composition. But there are more subtle means of achieving contrast that are also worth observing. For one thing, our discussion of tonality in music should help us appreciate the fact that, even within a specific movement. a composer will probably use a number of different keys. Usually they are related keys, such as a subsequent key based on the dominant tone of the previous key (C major followed by G major, or F major followed by C major). The dominant tone is the fifth tone, and one of the most convenient ways of moving from key to key is to follow the cycle of fifths, confident that each new key will clearly relate to the key that precedes it. Distant keys, A major to, say, D minor, can produce a sense of incoherence or uncertainty. Sometimes such motions between keys are used to achieve such effects. The average listener cannot always tell just by listening that a passage is in a new key, although practiced musicians can tell immediately when a new key is introduced. The exploration of keys and their relationship is one of the more interesting aspects of the development portions of most symphonies. The very concept of development, which means the exploration of a given material, thematic and/or harmonic, is sometimes best realized by playing the same or similar material in different keys, finding new relationships among them. Our awareness of special effects or of haunting and moving passages is often due to the subtle manipulation of keys or related tonal structures that analysis with a score might help us better understand. For the moment, however, let us concentrate on what the average listener can detect in the symphony.

PERCEPTION KEY THE SYMPHONY

Listen to a symphony by C. P. E. Bach, Haydn, Mozart, Beethoven, Brahms, or a more modern composer. As you listen, jot down some notes on each movement. Try to deal with the following questions:

1. Is the tempo fast, medium, or slow? Is it the same throughout? How much contrast is there in tempo within the movement? Between movements?

2. Can you hear differences in time signature—4/4 time, 2/4 time, 3/4 (waltz or dance time), 6/8 (march time)?
3. How much difference in dynamics is there in a given movement? How much difference is there from one movement to the next? Are some movements more uniform in loudness than others?
4. What variations do you perceive in instrumentation? If you have a difficult time distinguishing among instruments, use this guide for families of instruments, from the highest pitches to the lowest pitches:
   woodwinds: flutes, oboes, clarinets, bassoons
   brass: trumpets, horns, trombones
   strings: first violins, second violins, violas, violincellos, contrabasses
   percussion: tympani, snare drum, tam-tam (melodic material is treated, if at all, by xylophone, bells, celeste, and similar instruments in the percussion family).
5. Is thematic material treated by single instruments, groups of instruments, or by the entire orchestra?
6. Are you aware of thematic material establishing the tonal center, moving away from it in the movement, then returning? (This may only be answerable by a highly practiced listener.)
7. Are you surprised by any passage within a movement? Why?
8. As a movement is coming to an end, is your expectation of the finale carefully prepared for by the composer? Is your expectation frustrated in any fashion? Are you surprised by any passages within a movement?

Beethoven's Symphony in E♭ Major, No. 3, *Eroica*

Beethoven's "heroic" symphony is almost universally acclaimed by musicians and music critics as a masterpiece of the symphonic form. It has some of the most daring and imaginative textures and structures we will find in any symphony, and it succeeds in unifying its movements by developing similar thematic material throughout. It was finished in 1804 and originally intended to celebrate the greatness of Napoleon, whom Beethoven regarded as a champion of democracy and the common man. But when Napoleon declared himself emperor in May, 1804, Beethoven, feeling his faith in Napoleon was betrayed, was said to have been close to destroying the manuscript of the entire symphony. However, the surviving manuscript reveals he simply tore off the dedication page and substituted the general title, *Eroica*, instead of celebrating a specific hero.

The four movements of the symphony follow the tempo marking we would expect of a classic symphony, but there are a number of important ways in which the *Eroica* is distinct and important in the history of the form. The first movement, marked *allegro con brio* (fast) is in the sonata form, with an opening statement of thematic material based in a simple chord in the key of E♭ major. Its development section introduces various other related keys, and the recapitulation returns to the principal thematic material in the original home key. But the movement is twice as long as the usual first movements of earlier

FIGURE 9-8 Portrait of Beethoven. The Bettman Archive.

symphonies. Its size, as well as the fusion of themes and their development into such a large structure, was enormously influential for later composers. The feelings that are evoked by the movement are profound and sometimes enigmatic, but it is clear that Beethoven raised and frustrated numerous expectations as he worked through his material, building to a sense of conclusion only to retreat, rebuild, and retreat again until he felt he had thoroughly worked through his musical ideas. The conclusion of the movement is massive and overwhelming, impressing us with tremendous force and energy.

The slow second movement is dominated by a funeral march in

2/4 time, with a very plaintive melody, a painfully slow tempo (in some performances), and a generally tragic mood sustained throughout. We cannot say what might have been in Beethoven's mind in composing this movement, but it is clear that in contrast with the dramatic and vivid first movement, the second movement is a sobering qualification to the reaches of power explored in such depth in the first movement. The second movement uses a fugue in one of its later sections, even though the tempo of the passage is so slow as to seem to "stretch time." Despite its exceptional slowness, the fugue, with its competing voices and constant, roiling motion, seems appropriate for suggesting a heroic, warlike character. The entire movement is characterized by a constant return to the theme of the funeral march, so that the structure can be designated a rondo: A-B-A'-C-A". In each case, the A represents a section built on the theme of the funeral march. The other material, including the fugue in C, offers some contrast, but because it is of a similar character with the march theme, it offers no relief.

The relief comes in the third movement, marked *scherzo*, which is both lively (scherzo means a joke) and dancelike. The thematic material developed in this movement is suggestive of the material in the first movement, therefore linking the two movements in ways that are not as common in the symphony form as they might be. The time signature is 3/4, the same as the opening movement. Much of the thematic material is built on a simple chord as in the first movement. And, finally, it is distributed rapidly from one group of instruments to another, as also happens in the first movement. But the third movement is much briefer than the first, while only a little briefer than the last.

The finale is marked *allegro molto* (very fast). A theme-and-variation movement, it is a virtual catchall. It includes two brief fugues, a dance using a theme similar to the main theme of the first movement, which is itself not introduced until after a rather decorative opening, and a brief march as well. Fast and slow passages are contrasted in such fashion as to give us a sense of a recapitulation of the entire symphony. As critics have said for more than a century, the movement brings us "triumphantly" to a conclusion that, as we can perceive from our own responses, is profoundly stable. At this point, we can most fully appreciate how intense the progression of feeling has been from listening to the first theme, to its transformations, its returns, its approximations in similar themes, and its final return at the end of the symphony, showing us just how rich even a simple chord-based theme can be in the hands of a master.

This discussion is of limited use without your hearing the symphony and following it with the score. Such a project is not as difficult as it may sound at first, particularly if you have a guide to help you through and the opportunity to go over it a few times. Our discussion below, movement by movement, is meant to be a guide to what you can expect to hear as you listen to each movement.

Movement I: *Allegro con brio.* Fast, breezy.

The first two chords are powerful, staccato, and compressed. They are one of the basic chords for the home key of E♭ major: G-E♭-B♭-G, proceeding from the lowest tone to the highest. This chord is shown in Figure 9-9.

Violino I

FIGURE 9-9   Opening chord in E-flat major.

Then, at the third measure (Figure 9-10) the main theme of the symphony is introduced.

Violoncello

FIGURE 9-10   Main theme, first movement, *Eroica* Symphony.

Because it is stated in the cellos, it is low in pitch and somewhat portentous, although not threatening. Its statement is not quite complete, for it unexpectedly ends on a C#, which prepares us to expect something further. The horns and clarinets take the theme at bar 15, only to surrender it at bar 20 to a group of ascending tones closely related to the main theme.

The second theme is in profound contrast to the first. It is a very brief pattern of three descending tones that is moved from one instrument to another in the woodwinds, beginning with the oboes at bar 45 (Figure 9-11). This theme is basically unstable since it is like a gesture that needs something to complete its meaning. Even the next thematic passage of dotted eighth notes at bars 60 through 64 seems to be incomplete as stated by flutes and bassoons (Figure 9-12).

Ob.

FIGURE 9-11   Second theme, oboes at bar 45.

FIGURE 9-12   Flutes and bassoons at bars 60 through 64.

The next bars (to 83) are marked by a rugged rhythmic passage primarily audible in the violins. This passage suggests a preparation for something and not a theme in and of itself. What it prepares us for is a further incomplete thematic statement at bar 83, a very tentative, delicate interlude. The violin passage which preceded it—shown in Figure 9-13—is important because it often acts as a link in the

FIGURE 9-13   Violin passage preceding bar 83.

movement between differing material. Getting this passage firmly in your memory will help you follow the score, for it returns dependably.

Many passages have several unsettling fragments, such as the dark and brooding quality of the cello and bass motive shown in Figure 9-14,

FIGURE 9-14   Cello and bass motive.

which seems to sound as a kind of warning, almost as if it were preparing us for the funeral march of the second movement. It repeats much later in variation at bar 498, acting again as both an unsettling and retarding passage. Many other passages also appear to be developing into a finished statement only to trail off. Commentators have frequently described these passages as digressions, but this is misleading, because these passages direct us to new and relevant musical material.

The exposition begins to end at bar 148, with a long passage in B♭, a key closely related to E♭. The measures from 148 to 152 hint at the opening theme, but they actually prepare us for a dying-down action that joins with the development. In most recordings, the repeat sign at 156 is ignored. Instead, the second ending (bars 152–159) is played, and this passage tends to stretch and slow down, only to pick up when the second subject is played again in descending patterns from the flutes through all the woodwinds.

The development section is colossal, from bars 156 to 394. The main theme is suggested first at 178 in a different key in the cellos, then played again in B♭ from 186 to 194, with the effect of being very slow and drawn out. This underlies the rest of the activity of the orchestra, so unless it is emphasized, our ear may not pick it up immediately. The momentum speeds up around bar 200, where the main theme is again played in an extended form in the cellos and the contrabasses. The fragmented motives contribute to a sense of incompleteness and instability. We do not usually have the fullness of the main theme to hold on to, and the second theme's own fragmentary character is everywhere emphasized, as we can see between bars 220 and 230. When we reach the crashing discords at bar 275, the following quieting down becomes a welcome relief. The subsequent passage seems very peaceful and almost without direction until we hear again the main theme in B♭ at bar 300, then again at 312 in the cellos and basses. The passage builds again in loudness, then quiets down, and then the main theme is stated clearly in the bassoons, preparing for an extended passage that includes the main theme in the woodwinds, building to a mild punctuation in the strings at bar 369 (Figure 9-15).

FIGURE 9-15   Strings at bar 369.

The remainder of the development passage is marvelously mysterious, with the strings maintaining a steady tremolo and the dynamics brought down almost to a whisper. This is in preparation for the horn introduction of measures 394 to 395, where the main theme is suggested in virtually a solo passage. These measures are, perhaps, the most significant two measures of the movement because of the way in which they boldly announce the beginning of the recapitulation. The horns pick the theme up again at bar 408, loud and clear, and begin a restatement of most of the exposition section. The recapitulation, which extends to bar 556, leads into a brief second development passage, treating the main theme in several unusual ways, such as the tremolo statement in the violins at bars 559 to 565 (Figure 9-16).

FIGURE 9-16   Violins at bars 559 through 565.

The long, slow, quiet passages after bar 575 prepare us for the incredible rush of power that is the coda—the "tail" or final section of the movement.

The triumph in the movement is most perceptible, perhaps, in the juxtaposition of a delightful, running violin passage fom bar 631 to bar 639, with the main theme and a mild variation played in the horns. It is as if Beethoven is telling us that he has perceived the musical problems that existed with his material and that since he has now worked them out, he can celebrate with a bit of simple, passionate, and joyous music.

1. Describe the first movement's main theme, in comparison with the second theme. What are their principal qualities of length, "tunefulness," range of pitch, rhythm, and sense of completeness? Could either be feasibly presented as a separate tune? Which is easier to whistle or hum?

2. What are the effects of hearing the main theme played in different keys, as in bars 3 to 7, bars 184 to 194, and bars 198 to 206? All these passages present the theme in the cellos or contrabasses. What are the effects of the theme's appearance in other instrumental families, such as the bassoons at bar 338 in the development section and the horns at bar 408 in the recapitulation section? Does the second subject appear in a new family of instruments in the development section?

3. How clearly marked do you find the exposition, development, and recapitulation sections? Can you describe the feelings you find evoked by the music? Are they different in each of the sections? What specific qualities in the music produce the feelings you have?

4. The structure of the movement—exposition, development, and recapitulation—presents thematic and harmonic material, works with it in inventive ways, then restates the original material in order to permit us to understand its nature better. The recapitulation should help us grow more aware of the resources of the musical ideas that allowed for the inventiveness of the development. Does this happen in your experience? What effects do you sense as a result of hearing the recapitulation return with its direct statements of the main theme and the second subject (as well as other motives and materials from the opening section)?

5. Many symphonies lack a coda. Do you think Beethoven was right in adding a coda? If so, what does it add?

6. If possible, record the movement on a tape recorder, but begin with the development section, then follow with the recapitulation and exposition sections. Does listening to this "reorganization" help clarify the function of each section? Does it offer a better understanding of the movement as it was originally structured? Does this "reorganization" evoke significantly different feelings?

Movement II: *Marcia Funebra. Adagio assai.* Funeral march, very slow.

A funeral march in 2/4 time, the movement begins with its first theme in the opening bars shown in Figure 9-17.

FIGURE 9-17   Second movement opening bars, funeral march.

The opening is slow, quiet, and brooding. The rhythm seems to limp. The second theme, a plaintive descending passage in the violins at bar 17 (Figure 9-18), is no less unrelieved in its sadness. Its very limited

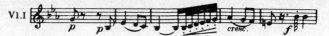

FIGURE 9-18   Violins at bar 17.

range, from B♭ to E♭, then back down to B♭, gives to that sadness a closed-in quality. At bar 69, the second, or B, section begins, ending at bar 105, when the funeral theme is restated very quietly in the violins. This is the A′ section, ending at bar 113. A brief fugue appears at bar 114, beginning the C section with the material from bar 17 inverted in the second violins (Figure 9-19).

FIGURE 9-19   Beginning of a brief fugue at bar 114.

The tempo picks up considerably at this point, with many passages echoing the full orchestral qualities of the first movement. The flutes contribute an interesting contrast in sixteenth notes in a descending pattern beginning with bar 168, continuing through the beginning of the recapitulation, or A″ section, which is announced by a restatement of the funeral theme at bar 172, but this time in the bassoons, horns, cellos, and contrabasses. The second theme is restated totally, beginning at bar 182. The coda, or ending section, begins at bar 211 with a surprise, a new melody in the violins seen in Figure 9-20.

FIGURE 9-20   Coda and new melody. Violins at bars 211 through 217.

It is not as plaintive as the other themes but suggests some brightness and new potential for relief. As if to emphasize that point, Beethoven brings back the funeral theme at bar 238 but in fragmented form. The funeral theme has lost some of its power. The movement ends with no dramatic finale, but rather a simple pair of rising passages at bars 246 and 247. It is the end of the movement, but it is not totally conclusive. We anticipate immediately the opening passage of the next movement.

PERCEPTION KEY MOVEMENT II

1. Compare the dynamics of the second movement with the first. Given the differences in length, are the dynamics handled very differently?

2. The use of contrast in the second movement is much more restricted than in the first movement. What is the effect of this difference?
3. Are the sections: A-B-A'-C-A"-coda as clearly defined as the exposition, development, recapitulation, and coda sections of the first movement? What effects does Beethoven achieve by bringing the funeral theme back again and again? Do you begin to anticipate its return?
4. Do you feel as satisfied at the end of the second movement as you did at the end of the first? How does the difference in the sense of completion achieved by each movement contribute to your feelings upon hearing these movements?

Movement III: *Scherzo. Allegro vivace.* **Fast and lively.**

The third movement begins softly but at a rapid pace, with the theme at bar 7 in the violins, the oboes, and then in the other woodwinds (Figure 9-21).

FIGURE 9-21   Beginning of third movement. Oboes at bar 7.

It is an agreeable, uplifting theme that repeats with some regularity, as in bars 85 to 88, 265 to 268, and 299 to 302. The sonorities achieved here remind us of the first movement, as in bars 100 to 115, and the passage from bar 150 to the beginning of the trio at 165. The trio itself (named for the tradition of having three voices play in harmony) begins with a horn passage that states the principal theme shown in Figure 9-22.

FIGURE 9-22   Horn passage stating the principal theme of the trio.

The rhythmic pattern of the theme is not reminiscent of the main theme of the first movement, but the fact that the horns play it alone and the fact that the notes G-C-E-G are shared by the main theme combine to remind us of the opening movement. Then, after the contrasting woodwind interlude from bar 205 to bar 216, fanfarelike passages dominate the horns. The passage at 255 begins a hard-driving buildup of staccato quarter notes. The contrasting theme in the violins and woodwinds (bars 265 to 268) is a restatement of the first theme (see Figure 9-20) from bars 7 to 10 (Figure 9-23).

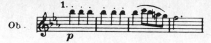

FIGURE 9-23   Woodwinds at bars 265 through 268.

The full orchestral passages that follow contain many allusions to the full orchestral passages of the first movement. Furthermore, they sound satisfying and familiar to us because they repeat the beginning of the third movement. They are also more solid harmonically than the immediately preceding passages, relying much more on the main key, E♭. The finale of the movement with its coda is a steady rhythmic passage that builds in fullness to the conclusion.

PERCEPTION KEY MOVEMENT III

1. Examine the principal themes in this movement. Do they contrast with each other as much as do themes in other movements?
2. The movement is marked *scherzo*, a dancelike rhythm. Do you sense dancelike passages here? Does the movement suggest a dance to you?
3. What is the effect of having the opening scherzo repeat itself entirely from bars 256 to the coda? Are there many audible differences between the two versions. You might listen to them, one right after another, without the trio section to make your comparison.

Movement IV: *Finale. Allegro molto.* **Very fast.**

The opening passages in the strings are quite different from anything we have heard earlier. They are both mysterious and suggestive of things to come, particularly as they build up to almost silence—followed by the plucking of single notes in the strings. The pattern of these notes looks and sounds like a cross between the main theme of the first movement and the first theme of the third movement (Figure 9-24).

FIGURE 9-24   Fourth movement. Opening passage for violins.

This passage sounds playful, as if it were designed to suggest toy soldiers.

But this theme, called the bass theme, is countered by another more important theme, the melody theme, which begins at bar 76, stated in the woodwinds (Figure 9-25).

FIGURE 9-25   Melody theme at bar 76.

The violins restate this melody theme completely at bar 85, then again at bar 103. We call one theme the melody theme and the other the bass theme because Beethoven has used an extraordinary bit of ingenuity here. He has taken the melody line and bass line from one of his contra-dances, varied them slightly, and separated them for use as the two distinctive themes of the movement (Figure 9-26).

FIGURE 9-26   Melody and bass line of the contra-dance.

Beethoven uses a fugue shortly thereafter, beginning at bar 117 in the cellos, with a repeat of the fugal theme in the clarinets and bassoons (Figure 9-27).

FIGURE 9-27   Cellos at bar 117.

Both the bass theme and the melody theme are clearly audible as the bass theme takes over in a marchlike passage. This passage builds up energy and anticipation, with rhythms that are reminiscent of the ending of the first movement. When the melody theme takes over at bar 256, we hear it clearly in the violins and the flutes. Another fugal passage begins at bar 277, using both themes, either entirely or in part. The thematic material is quite audible as it moves from one family of instruments to another. The effect of this passage, even though the themes are in the home key, is to build anticipation for something that is coming later. The andante or slow passage that follows, at bar 348, is marked *con expressione*, with expression, meaning that the passage should be played lyrically. But it is not quite what might be anticipated by the fugue preceding it. We find that the slow, songlike quality of this passage is something of a surprise. The melodic quality, we realize, stands out in distinct contrast to most of what we have been hearing, especially to the marches and the fugues that perhaps more properly belong to a symphony celebrating the heroic. Marches, driving orchestral passages, warlike fugues, and intense rhythms seem almost appropriate to a symphony inspired by Napoleon. But, quite possibly, this last songlike passage hints at a romantic quality the hero should also have. Even Napoleon had his Josephine. But this mood breaks rapidly with the descending violin passage at bar 380. The second theme returns in the horns, and although the pace does not pick up quickly, the entire orchestra builds steadily throughout the passage, moving in a stately fashion, suggesting an official ceremony. A number of brief interludes treat the themes we have heard earlier, although the fragmentary quality of these interludes and the steady building of rhythmic intensity and pitch by the entire orchestra suggest that we are coming to a conclusion. Yet we hardly know when to expect it. When we hear the opening passages of the movement begin a repetition at bar 431, with an increase of the tempo to *presto,* extremely fast, we realize that we are coming to the end of the entire symphony. Even when the very last presto passages are played considerably slower than marked—as you will hear in many recordings—the straightforwardness and the openness of the finale are impressive. Careful listening has brought us a great distance, and the frankness of the symphony's ending convinces us that what we have heard is musically fully realized.

PERCEPTION KEY MOVEMENT IV

1. Much of the contrast in this movement is achieved by using fugue, march, and dance forms to work and rework two basic themes. Is this contrast effective? Is is clearly audible as you listen to the movement?
2. Compare the melody and bass themes for their relative qualities of length, "tunefulness," range of pitch, rhythm, and their sense of completeness. What do you discover? If you did the perception key for the first movement, you will have a basis of comparison already in your mind. What are the differences between your observations comparing themes in this the fourth movement as opposed to the first movement?
3. Compare your sense of closure and finality at the end of the fourth movement with your sense of finality at the end of the first movement. Is there a profound difference?

The experience of listening to the *Eroica* symphony and responding to our observations and questions above is best carried out with a score. We suggest that for the most responsive listening, you mark the score to observe where the themes we have noted by bar and number appear. This will help you keep track of where you are, particularly if you are not used to reading orchestral scores (as most people are not!). But even without a score the careful listener can use the themes as we have marked them out in these pages as a guide to listening well. Going over each movement once or twice will help guide your ear through the experience. Then, once you have done this, sit back and listen to the entire symphony again.

PERCEPTION KEY THE *EROICA* SYMPHONY

1. In what ways has Beethoven tried to relate the four movements of the symphony together? Does a sense of relatedness develop for you?
2. Is the symphony properly named? What qualities do you perceive in it that seem "heroic" to you?
3. Comment on Beethoven's use of dynamics in the whole symphony. Comment on his use of contrast and variations in rhythm.
4. Are you aware of a variety of feeling qualities in the music? Does there seem to be an overall "plan" to the changes in these qualities as the symphony unfolds?
5. Is there a consistency in the thematic material used throughout the symphony? Are there any inconsistencies?
6. Do you find that fatigue affects your responses to the last movement or any other portion of the symphony? The act of creative listening can be very fatiguing. Could Beethoven have taken that into consideration?
7. In what particulars have you found yourself agreeing with our observations regarding the symphony? In what ways have you found yourself disagreeing?

A Brief Glossary of Styles and Genres—with Suggestions for Listening

Our discussion and analysis of the symphony is meant to be a model for both close analysis and creative listening. We cannot expect to analyze as carefully all the music we hear. But we can expect to listen closely and to participate as much as possible with the music that we find interesting. As a way of helping interested listeners, this glossary of musical styles should serve as a guide to different styles of music. All the compositions that are named are available on record and are in the *Schwann Record Guide*. No specific recording is suggested, since recordings come into and go out of print with such rapidity that such suggestions often become obsolete.

RENAISSANCE: 1300–1600

Guillaume Dufay (1400–1474), hymns and songs. Josquin Des Pres (ca. 1440–1521), *Missa Pange Lingua*, *Missa L'Homme Arme*, motets.

Giovanni Palestrina (1525–1594), Magnificat, *Missa Sine Nomine*, motets. Roland de Lassus (1532–1594), *St. Matthew Passion*, motets, and madrigals. Giovanni Gabrieli (1551–1612), assorted canzoni for brass instruments, madrigals, and motets. Carlo Gesualdo (1560–1613), madrigals and motets.

Much of the instrumental music of the Renaissance was composed for dancers, although some was also composed for use in the church. The dance pieces of the Renaissance are still among the most delightful of any period. The slow pavanne, the more frenetic morris dance, and the speedy galiard are still being danced. The music composed for such dances naturally correlates with the needs—in terms of tempo and contrast—of the dances themselves. Some of the composers named above wrote music for the dance, and the best way to listen to it is to find an anthology record such as *Dance Music of the Renaissance* (Musical Heritage Society, Inc., Tinton Falls, N.J.).

The instrumental music composed for religious purposes seems designed for churches—such as Giovanni Gabrieli's antiphonal (meaning sounds opposite or answering one another) pieces for brass, in which one brass chorus in one cross section of a church would answer another chorus in the opposite section. The resounding echoes from the church stonework, with the persistence of partials as well as primary tones, produced unexpected timbres and unexpected consonant-dissonant combinations. This music is still played today and is still exciting to hear.

But the music written for the voice in the Renaissance probably seems more significant to us now than that written for instruments, brilliant as the instrumental writing is. The masses of Des Pres and Palestrina—as well as those by Dufay, whose *Missa L'Homme Arme* is almost as well known as Des Pres' on the same theme—are the most ambitious compositions of the period. Setting the words of the mass to music involves a careful attention to the meaning of those words and a careful interpretation in musical terms of that meaning. Consequently, it is always wise to read the words of the mass before listening to a mass of any period.

Madrigals—songs written in the native or vernacular language rather than in Latin—were immensely popular throughout the entire Renaissance. Roland de Lassus' madrigals are exceptionally influential and beautiful. Most important Renaissance composers wrote madrigals, and many contemporary singing societies include them in their repertory—consequently many may sound familiar. Motets were also words set to music but usually Latin words. The form was contrapuntal, with an organon bass line and the words sung in the upper registers.

Listen For:

1. Smooth consonance and very little dissonance except for occasional accent.

2. Careful attention paid to the text, with the music, especially its rhythms, usually imitative to some extent of the words.
3. Relatively conservative and restricted use of dynamics except occasionally in some instrumental music.
4. A smooth, sonorous quality to the voices, with careful distinctions between soprano, alto, tenor, and bass, emphasizing the beauty of the voices, their contrasts, and their blending.
5. Relatively slight tension building, with very quick release in treatment of themes—theme one, usually a few measures, will come to a resting point just as theme two, often very similar in quality, begins. This pattern repeats throughout.
6. Slight use of contrasts, relatively restricted range of pitch.

PERCEPTION KEY RENAISSANCE MUSIC

1. Listen to a Renaissance composition for instruments and one for voices. Compare them by means of descriptive analysis for their uses of musical elements. Which seems to you to be more imaginative or successful in the handling of timbres, tempos, contrasts, dynamics, and musical tension?
2. Listen to a song written by Byrd (1540–1623), Morley (1557–1602), or Dowland (1560–1626). How carefully integrated is the music with the text? What techniques were used by the composer to make the music congruent with the words? Was he successful? Be detailed in your discussion.

BAROQUE: 1600–1750

Claudio Monteverdi (1567–1643), *Carnival Songs, Vespers for the Blessed Virgin, Moral and Spiritual Pieces,* madrigals and incidental songs. Henry Purcell (1659–1695), *Masque: The Faerie Queene, King Arthur,* songs. Antonio Vivaldi (1675–1741), *The Four Seasons;* concertos for lute, flute, and many combinations of instruments. J. S. Bach (1685–1750), the Brandenburg Concertos, Mass in B Minor, *Art of Fugue, St. Matthew Passion, Well-tempered Clavier,* cantatas, fugues and concertos for various instruments. G. F. Handel (1685–1759), *Messiah, The Creation,* Concerto Grosso in D Major.

Madrigals and songs, as well as larger compositions for voice and instruments, continue to be important for the composers of this period. Most of these have a religious subject matter, but many do not. Purcell's writing is conspicuous for its treatment of secular English and Irish traditional material. Yet, masses and religious cantatas—as well as such church instrumental compositions as Bach's organ preludes—are consistently popular. The church's influence is all but imperceptible in the concertos of Vivaldi, Bach, and Handel, in which the subject matter is certainly not religious but much more the kind of subject matter we associated with pure music, that of feeling abstracted from specific objects or events.

Purcell, Bach, and Handel are products of the Reformation, the splitting away of the Protestant churches from Catholicism. The Protestants needed religious music, although they wanted it to be of a less gaudy nature than Catholic music. Yet, Protestant church music sounds very much the same to our ears as Catholic music even though much Protestant music was based on religious hymns written by such men as Martin Luther. The rapid increase of wealthy families in this period made it possible to support a secular music designed not to uplift the audience in a religious sense but simply to entertain its sensibilities. The more purely instrumental music, as well as Monteverdi's songs and the vocal works of Purcell, were often designed to attend to the needs of a nonchurchly audience.

As a consequence, Baroque music tends to be more richly ornamented, brilliant, and vigorous than the simpler—relatively speaking—Renaissance compositions. It is also more ambitious and sometimes more superficial.

Listen For:

1. Considerable tension in the drive of tempos, although not necessarily much variety in tempos within a composition.
2. Virtuosity in melodic lines, with ingenious counterpoint and carefully sustained melodic tension developed by the constant playing of one melodic line against another.
3. Considerable contrast achieved through varieties of pitch in a composition—though most Baroque music emphasizes the upper registers—and through varieties in timbres.
4. Contrast achieved through the pitting of one instrument against the orchestra, the concerto; or contrast achieved by pitting a small group of instruments against the orchestra, the concerto grosso.
5. Attention to structures such as rondo and theme and variations, indicating an attempt to explore the resources of thematic material.
6. Interesting uses of harmony, particularly in the passions and cantatas of Bach and in the oratorios of Handel (dramatic musical compositions closely related to opera, but without the addition of the spectacle of acting).
7. Greater tolerance of dissonances, particularly those that involve more than two dissonant tones.

PERCEPTION KEY BAROQUE MUSIC

1. Listen to two compositions, one religious, such as Bach's *St. Matthew Passion* or Monteverdi's *Vespers for the Blessed Virgin*, and one which is secular, such as Vivaldi's *The Four Seasons*, or Purcell's *Masque: The Faerie Queene*. Begin by describing the general impressions they give you. Do you detect a religious subject matter in the religious composition? Do

you detect the secular nature of the nonreligious composition? What uses of tempos, dynamics, timbres, and contrasts do the compositions share? What uses seem more peculiar to each? Can secular music be distinguished from religious music by reference to their use of musical elements?

2. Listen to at least one concerto or concerto grosso. Describe it as carefully as possible in terms of its use of melodic material, its concerns for counterpoint, its interest in harmony, and the means by which it achieves contrast and tension. Is tension relieved at the points of arrival—the endings of musical phrases or sections of the composition—by means of the cadences we described in discussing a sense of ending in Question 3 of the perception key (page 309) on "Swing Low, Sweet Chariot"?

CLASSIC: 1750–1830

Franz Josef Haydn (1732–1809), Symphony in G major, No. 94, the *Surprise;* Symphony in D major, No. 101, the *Clock;* String Quartet No. 2 (Opus-76–which contains six fine quartets); *The Seven Last Words of Christ.* Wolfgang Amadeus Mozart (1756–1791), *Requiem,* Symphony in C major, the *Jupiter;* Concerto for Piano, No. 21 in C major; *Eine Kleine Nachtmusik* (or Serenade in G major). Ludwig van Beethoven (1770–1827), Symphony No. 5 in C minor; Symphony No. 6 in F major, the *Pastorale;* Symphony No. 9 in D minor, the *Chorale;* the Rasumovsky Quartets (Nos. 1, 2, 3).

Although most of the classic composers produced some religious music, it was not their principal activity. Haydn's Mass in D minor, for Lord Nelson, may be as political as it is religious. Yet, Mozart's *Requiem* may be the greatest ever written, and Beethoven's *Missa Solemnis* compares well with the masses of the great ages of religion. But these are limited examples. Haydn's 104 symphonies were written to amuse a small courtly audience that demanded new musical material for its weekly concerts. Mozart wrote for a broader musical audience that included the bourgeosie, not just the aristrocrats. Their taste was not for religious music.

Classic composers built on the tonal experiments of the Baroque. They developed, for example, the sense of keyness and key interrelationship that Bach clearly valued. They also developed the vertical chordal texture that is usually lacking in most Baroque music, which emphasized counterpoint. Their harmony is basically triadic, as described in the section on tonal music, which builds on three-note chords and their variants—such as C-E-G in the key of C. The classic composers also developed the larger structures with predetermined repetitive structures, such as the sonata form, the rondo, and the minuet.

The melodic lines in classic compositions are often long and sustained, and they have a highly distinct quality to them that makes them more recognizable than most Baroque melodies. In Bach's Brandenburg Concerto No. 2 you will hear many melodies, but you will tend to be attracted to the texture of the sounds: the tone colors, dynamics, and contrapuntal effects. A classic composition calls attention to its structural qualities, since the textural elements of harmony and dynamics are controlled by the demands of strong key-based chords to "back up" the melodies as prescribed by the structure.

The texture of Beethoven's Symphony No. 5 does not closely resemble that of the *Brandenburg Concerto No. 2*. For one thing, our ear hears elements in the Beethoven that are clearly building blocks. The most famous motif in the symphony (Figure 9-28) is stated first by

FIGURE 9-28   Beginning motif from Beethoven's Symphony No. 5.

all the strings and the clarinets, then by second violins alone, then first violins, then violas, and on and on until another motif based on this first one appears. Then the original motif finds its way into the background sounds, which we have to strain to listen for until we begin to understand the motif is not there just to be listened to in isolation: It is there as a clearly identifiable unit that helps build the structure.

Listen For:

1. A dramatic variety in use of tempos, even within a small section of a composition.
2. Strong, well-highlighted melodies that are sometimes sustained for a relatively long time.
3. Melodic material, such as the beginning motif in Beethoven's Symphony No. 5, that contributes as a building block to the structure of the work.
4. Contrast achieved by means of opposing timbres of different families of instruments: strings, brasses, woodwinds, and percussion all taking clearly identifiable roles in a piece for orchestra.
5. Great dynamic range, particularly in Beethoven and the music of the later part of the period; less of a dynamic range in Haydn, although his experiments—in the *Surprise* Symphony, for instance —are interesting.
6. Full development of forms such as the rondo, the sonata form, theme and variations.
7. Full triadic harmony, with emphasis on exploiting the "keyness"

of the scale employed; dependence on a strong tonic center and the exploitation of the contrast of related keys.

8. Strong dissonant passages preparing for powerful resolutions of cadential consonance; dissonance for emphasis and dramatic purposes.

PERCEPTION KEY CLASSIC MUSIC

1. Listen closely to a symphony of Haydn. Describe each movement of the symphony in terms of its uses of basic musical elements. Can you determine the kinds of general feelings that might be revealed and evoked by each of the movements? Are they contrasted from movement to movement? What are the principal means of contrast used from movement to movement? Which movements seem to have the most in common in their uses of musical elements?

2. Listen to the last movement of Haydn's *Clock* Symphony, Mozart's *Jupiter* Symphony, and Beethoven's *Pastorale* Symphony. Which of these seems most clearly to have feeling as part of its subject matter? Is the sound of the clock a part of the subject matter of the Haydn symphony? Are the sounds of nature part of the subject matter of the Beethoven symphony? What kinds of insight, if any, are revealed to you by each of these works? In answering this question, refer to the musical elements that influence your conclusions.

ROMANTIC: 1800–1900

Hector Berlioz (1803–1869), *Symphony Fantastique, Romeo and Juliet, Roman Carnival Overture, Requiem.* Felix Mendelssohn (1809–1847), Concerto in E minor for Violin, *Incidental Music for A Midsummer Night's Dream;* Symphony No. 4, the *Italian.* Frederick Chopin (1810–1849), preludes or waltzes for piano. Johannes Brahms (1833–1897), Symphony No. 1 in C minor; *Variations on a Theme by Haydn;* Concerto for Violin and Orchestra; Double Concerto for Violin, Cello, and Orchestra; *Hungarian Dances.* Peter Tchaikovsky (1840–1893), *Swan Lake, The Nutcracker Suite,* Concerto No. 1 in B^b minor for Piano, *Romeo and Juliet,* Symphony No. 4 in F minor.

The careful work of the classic composers in establishing cadential patterns, leading to strong rest points and even stronger ending points at the conclusion of compositions, is modified in the romantic style—particularly the later music of Wagner (his works are suggested for listening in the section on opera). In some of Wagner's music, the horizontal line of the melody seems to have no rest points at all. The melodies seem almost interminable, though some are clearly shaped and recognizable as they return again and again. Wagner also often used building-unit motifs—somewhat similar to those used by Beethoven in his Symphony No. 5—for example the "look motif" from *Tristan und Isolde*, and the "sword motif" from *The Ring of the Niebelungs.*

Unlike Beethoven's, Wagner's motifs are associated with specific objects or events and are used to refer to or interpret them.

Reference to specific objects and events in romantic music is much greater, in general, than in classic music. In works such as the *Pastorale* Symphony, Beethoven begins the trend toward such reference. But romantic composers are vastly more ambitious in this regard than those who went before them. Berlioz and Tchaikovsky were not the only composers to dedicate a work to one of Shakespeare's plays or to try to make their musical composition refer to and interpret a piece of literature. The occasional marriage of music, literature, and dance, as in Tchaikovsky's *Swan Lake* (see pages 377–379), seems entirely easy and natural in the romantic period.

Some of the classic structures—such as the sonata form and the larger structure built on it, the symphony—persist in the works of Mendelssohn, Brahms, and Tchaikovsky in particular. But the expansion of the orchestra, with sometimes more than a hundred pieces, helped the romantic composer build the classic structures into something enormously expansive, with huge waves of sound that were all but impossible for classic composers who rarely had or needed huge orchestras. The size of the orchestra seems also to have affected the character of the concerto, with the solo instrument concentrating on extraordinary virtuosity as a help in balancing the relationship between a piano or violin, say, and the entire orchestra.

Listen For:

1. Careful use of tempos, particularly those that are extreme in speed, or, more frequently, extreme in slowness.
2. Melodic lines that are lengthy, often growing into new melodic lines without clear transitions.
3. Greater contrasts of dynamics than found in classic music, occasional bombast as in certain works of Berlioz and Tchaikovsky.
4. Interest in varieties of timbres on a grand scale, with choruses of instruments of a different family.
5. Appearance of less predetermined structures such as the nocturne, the aubade, the serenade, the capriccio, etudes, and sonatas that are not sonata-form compositions.
6. Harmonic texture strong, noticeable, and sustained; harmonies generally much more significant than in classic music in the sense that they are more obvious, more in competition with the melodic line for attention.
7. Greater emphasis and reliance on dissonances and a lesser interest in consonance as a means of relieving tension.
8. Growing interest in exploring the capacities of music to refer to specific objects and events, and thus emphasis on program music and opera.

1. After having read Shakespeare's *Romeo and Juliet*, listen to Berlioz's and Tchaikovsky's compositions of the same title. Is there a perceptible connection between the musical compositions and the play? Can you conclude that the compositions are interpretations of the play? Is it possible to decide which of the musical compositions is more faithful to the play, or which is more successful in its effort at interpretation?
2. Analyze the use of musical elements in a nonprogrammatic piece of Romantic music such as a concerto or a symphony. Describe carefully the use of tempos, melodic lines, harmonic qualities, dynamics, and anything else you believe is relevant. Does your description correlate with descriptions of the same piece made by other listeners?
3. Having performed the analysis in Question 2 above, do you feel confident in holding an opinion about the success of the composition? How do your opinions relate to those of others who have performed the same analysis? How do they relate to those who have not performed the analysis at all?

MODERN: 1900–PRESENT

Gustav Mahler (1860–1911), *Kindertotenlieder, Das Lied von der Erde,* Symphony No. 8 in E♭, *Symphony of a Thousand*; Symphony No. 9 in D major. Claude Debussy (1862–1918), *La Mer, Nocturnes, Clair de Lune, Children's Corner Suite*. Richard Strauss (1864–1949), *Death and Transfiguration, Don Quixote, Till Eulenspiegel, Thus Sprach Zarathustra*. Ralph Vaughan Williams (1872–1958), Mass in G minor; Symphony No. 1, *Sea*; Symphony No. 7, *Antarctica*. Arnold Schoenberg (1874–1951), *Transfigured Night, Pierrot Lunaire*. Charles Ives (1874–1954), *Three Places in New England, Holidays* Symphony. Maurice Ravel (1875–1937), *Bolero*, Concerto in D major for the Left Hand (piano), *Rhapsodie Espagnole*. Ernest Block (1880–1959), *Schelomo*, Rhapsody for Cello and Orchestra. Bela Bartók (1891–1945), *Concerto for Orchestra; Miraculous Mandarin Suite; Music for Strings, Percussion, and Celesta*. Igor Stravinsky (1882–1971), *Firebird: Suite, Petrouchka, The Rites of Spring, Oedipus Rex, Symphony of Psalms*. Edgar Varese (1885–1965), *Deserts, Ionization*. John Cage (1912–   ), *Variation IV, Indeterminacy*. Benjamin Britten (1913–1976), *Young Person's Guide to the Orchestra, War Requiem*. Karl-Heinz Stockhausen (1928–   ), *Mikrophonie I for Tam-tam, 2 Microphones, & Filters, & Potentiometers*. Krzysztof Penderecki (1933–   ), *Threnody for the Victims of Hiroshima, Dies Irae* (Auschwitz Oratorio).

Much of the music of the older composers of the modern period, such as Mahler, is close to the Romantics, continuing similar attitudes toward dissonance, rich harmonics, and program music. The younger composers often moved away from a tonal center. Like Schoenberg, they used atonality, an approach that treats all notes of a scale as equal in value, with no tonic, dominant, or mediant notes. Others, like Charles Ives, sometimes employed polytonality, in which melodic lines written in different keys were sounded together. The effect of having two strong key-based lines operating simultaneously can be very exciting. "July 4th" in Ives' *Holidays* Symphony is an interesting example, as one seems to hear two marching bands playing two different tunes marching toward, then through, one another. This actually was something Charles Ives once saw when he was a child watching his father's marching bands entertaining an audience in Danbury, Connecticut, on July fourth.

Some composers, such as Bartók, Stravinsky, and Paul Hindemith (1895–1963), developed a neoclassicism that tried to combine classic formal structures with the expansiveness of the Romantic approach to the use of mythic inspiration and literary sources. Their music has generally been well received, helping us to reevaluate the achievement of the classic composers.

Composers such as Luciano Berio (1925–   ) and Stockhausen have been working in the medium of electronic music and, sometimes, nontonal sounds or noises. Their work has been difficult for contemporary audiences to appreciate because it breaks so sharply with the traditions of the past. Some audiences treat their works as if they were not music at all. The absence of a strong tonal center and the use of noises have been enough to make it very difficult for some audiences to respond positively. The timbres achieved by electronic synthesizers have also been difficult for audiences used to the sounds of traditional musical instruments. One of the positive virtues of electronic music is the calling into question the perhaps dogmatic conception of music as having organized tones as its medium. When all sound is at the disposal of composers, their limits and their ambitions must be considerably different from those of their predecessors, who generally relied upon clearly defined scales and predetermined structures.

Listen For:

1. Wide variety of tempos, with strong accents and dramatic emphasis; sudden shifts and stops.
2. Melodic lines that resemble, in many cases, those of the Baroque —continuous, restless—and, in fewer cases, those of the classic period.
3. Fragmentation of melodic material in some cases, with themes that do not have the clearly perceptible beginning, middle, and end of traditional music; melodic lines that seem bits and pieces of sound, almost randomly organized, yet obviously linear—or horizontal—in their progress.
4. Considerable interest in timbres, even in the more traditional-sounding compositions, but extraordinary interest in electronic

timbres and timbres of objects not ordinarily thought of as musical instruments.

5. Wide variety of structures borrowed from traditional music, but also structures that are not predetermined, that seem to develop and grow in accord with the musical potentialities.
6. Harmonies often similar to those of the Romantics, but much less concern for harmony as such—less reliance on harmony for overall orchestral color or for emphasis and ending.
7. Wide range of dynamics, but a tendency to be more abrupt, to shift dynamics without warning.
8. Preference for percussive effects and an expanded use of percussion instruments in all kinds of compositions.
9. More tolerance for dissonances, even to the extent of using them for the ending points of compositions; consonance does not necessarily resolve tensions nor dissonance create them.
10. Interest in nontonal sounds or noises.

PERCEPTION KEY MODERN MUSIC

1. Choose a piece of music such as the *Firebird: Suite, Ionization,* or *Threnody for the Victims of Hiroshima* and analyze it for its capacity to create, sustain, and resolve tension. What seem to be its resources, in terms of musical elements, for producing tension? Are they vastly different from those of traditional music, or are they much the same?
2. Listen to a piece of music by any two composers listed as modern. Be sure their birth dates are a generation apart. Compare their treatment of specific musical elements—tempo, melody, harmony, dynamics, timbres, etc. How different are they? How do the chief differences affect your comparative evaluations of their works?
3. Choose a piece of electronic music and describe its use of musical elements. Are there any musical elements possessed by electronic music that are absent from traditional music? Explain the relative importance of each element used in the composition. Do others agree with your judgments?

OPERA

Claudio Monteverdi (1567–1643), *Orfeo.* W. A. Mozart (1756–1791), *The Marriage of Figaro, Don Giovanni, The Magic Flute.* Gaetano Donizetti (1797–1848), *Don Pasquale, Lucia di Lammermoor, Robert Devereux.* Vincenzo Bellini (1801–1835), *Norma, La Sonnambula.* Richard Wagner (1813–1883), *Tristan and Isolde, The Flying Dutchman, Tannhäuser, Lohengrin,* the "Ring" cycle—*Das Rheingold, Die Walküre, Siegfried, Götterdammerung.* Guiseppe Verdi (1813–1901), *Aida, Macbeth, Rigoletto, La Traviata, The Force of Destiny, Otello, Falstaff.* Georges Bizet (1838–1875), *Carmen.* Giacomo Puccini (1858–

1924), *La Bohème, Madame Butterfly, Turandot.* Richard Strauss (1864–1949), *Der Rosenkavalier, Salome.* Scott Joplin (1868–1917), *Treemonisha.* George Gershwin (1898–1937), *Porgy and Bess.* Kurt Weill (1900–1950), *Threepenny Opera.* Gian-Carlo Menotti (1911–   ), *Amahl and the Night Visitors, The Medium.* Benjamin Britten (1913–1976), *Peter Grimes.* Krzysztof Penderecki (1933–   ), *The Devils of Loudun, Paradise Lost.* The Who, *Tommy* (1969).

Because opera depends on a dramatic narrrative, which is usually called the "libretto" (little book), it refers to specific events. In a way, the music has a program, but the program is not separate from the composition, as it would be with *La Mer* or any other wordless piece of program music. Opera's program is its story line, which is acted, sung, and sometimes spoken. Most operas are not written in English, so many Americans have trouble following the narratives of Wagner, Verdi, or Bizet, for example. But even operas in English are sometimes difficult to follow, since the musical demands occasionally make clear articulation difficult. The problem can be solved, usually, only by acquainting oneself with the libretto—just as one must acquaint oneself with the program of a piece of program music.

The subject matter of opera is more obvious than the subject matter of a piece of nonprogrammatic music. Opera still uses all the basic elements of music, but those elements are closely wedded to the needs of the unfolding drama. Opera usually interprets highly dramatic situations, such as the resolution in face of torture that Grandier displays in Penderecki's *Devils of Loudun* or the heroism Treemonisha displays when she is challenged by voodoo forces in Scott Joplin's

FIGURE 9-29 Verdi's *Aida,* Rome: Baths of Caracalla. Photo by Jacobus.

ragtime opera, the first opera by a black American. The musical character of great arias often becomes much clearer when one knows the dramatic necessities they are serving—which is to say that the significance of the aria is clearer when we have heard it in the total context of the opera's dramatic spectacle.

The Who's recent success with the rock opera *Tommy*—not to mention similar successes with *Jesus Christ Superstar* and *Godspell*—should serve to remind us that opera is a highly popular art and not something reserved for esoteric tastes. In many European cities opera stars such as Montserrat Caballé, Jon Vickers, Joan Sutherland, Sherrill Milnes, and Luciano Pavarotti are cheered like soccer or film stars. Non-European audiences also usually react warmly to opera when they are thoroughly acquainted with the story. That should always be a listener's first step before hearing an opera: read the libretto.

Listen For:

1. Uses of musical elements such as tempo, melodic lines, timbre, harmony, and dynamics that are characteristic of the periods in which the operas are written.
2. Efforts to fuse the musical materials to the text being sung, as in the masses of the late Renaissance and the early Baroque—but now with secular material of a highly dramatic nature in motets and madrigals.
3. Frequent use of orchestral dynamics to help evoke an emotional response to the dramatic situation on stage or, if not to evoke the response, to suggest it or interpret it on behalf of the characters.
4. Vocal coloration to express dramatic emotion on the part of the character.
5. Occasional exaggeration of the dramatic situation as an effort to highlight emotional values—sometimes called melodrama (literally, drama with music).
6. Featuring the human voice at its most beautiful, sometimes at the expense of the narrative, as a way of demonstrating the virtuosity of opera's principal musical instrument: the voice.
7. Means of creating tension musically, particularly as moments of tension are timed to the needs of the narrative.
8. Because of the reference to specific events as the cause of feeling, emphasis on feeling as emotion and passion.

PERCEPTION KEY OPERA

1. Choose an opera in English: *Peter Grimes*, Ralph Vaughan Williams' *Pilgrims' Progress*, *The Medium*, or the last act of *Treemonisha*. Acquaint yourself with the libretto. After listening to the opera, identify the kinds of emotions and passions interpreted by the singers. How successful is the opera in clarifying these feelings?

2. In the opera you have chosen, what are the most basic means used to build tension? Compare them with the tension-building means you have discovered in nonoperatic music.
3. After acquainting yourself with the libretto or synopsis of a non-English-language opera, such as an opera of Wagner or Verdi, listen for the ease or difficulty with which it establishes and interprets feelings—in comparison with an English-language opera. Do you find the foreign language an insurmountable difficulty in understanding the emotional interpretations even after you have studied the libretto?
4. Take an opera of a given period—Renaissance, Classic, Baroque, Romantic, or modern—and evaluate the ways in which it has used the stylistic resources of that period for the purposes of interpreting a dramatic narrative. Do the resources of that stylistic period lend themselves to the purposes the opera puts them? Does the opera do those resources an injustice? Explain and be specific in referring to the resources in question.

CONTEMPORARY POPULAR MUSIC

This category includes folk, jazz, soul, Latin, calypso, rock, and country and western. Since popular music changes very rapidly, our suggestions for this section avoid naming specific groups or albums. The genres of popular music are primarily those named above, but even those are subject to change, as the periodic surfacing and disappearance of rhythm and blues would suggest. It is noteworthy that popular music, like most folk arts, tends to be conservative in its use of the basic elements of music. Most of the music we hear on the radio, for instance, is strong in establishing a tonal center and respecting the implications of a key-based scale. It is also conservative in its use of steady tempos—with some halving and doubling of tempo permitted but little variation of a radical sort. Even the strongly rhythmic Latin music usually establishes a complex rhythmic pattern at the outset and maintains it to the end of the piece. The structure of most popular pieces is also conservative, with precise limits to the number of measures permitted in the verse and chorus of the piece. Building a piece on twelve- or sixteen-bar (measure) units is normal. The result of this is somewhat akin to the result of writing sonnets: sometimes the form will strangle inspiration, sometimes it will intensify inspiration and permit the artist to create "better than he knew."

Listen For:

1. Powerful tonal center with clear and intense cadences leading to rest points and conclusions.
2. Usually a distinct melodic line with a clear and recognizable principal melody and a strongly contrasting secondary melody.
3. Reliance on the A-B-A' form in which the first section is

contrasted with the second section, then repeated as a means of reinforcing the conclusion.

4. Occasional disregard for melodic line—as in some modern jazz and "hard" rock—in which the line is not clearly shaped or "memorable," but is reminiscent of the texture of Baroque counterpoint: the melodic line pushes onward with vigor, but without much clarity.

5. Various approaches to dynamics, with some pieces totally unchanging and others changing in response to the text being sung or in hopes of offering a contrast to an earlier section.

6. Relatively simple harmonies, usually based on the most clearly delineated chords of the basic key, such as the major triad and the seventh and ninth chords.

7. Various approaches to dissonance—sometimes following the lead of the Classic period and sometimes that of the modern period of music.

8. Reliance on repetition of theme, lyrics, and entire sections.

9. Use of electronically amplified volume as a significant element of the musical experience.

10. Exploration of feelings related to high energy, tension, restlessness, and moods such as those associated with the blues.

PERCEPTION KEY CONTEMPORARY POPULAR MUSIC

1. Select a piece of music from a popular style you admire—folk, jazz, soul, or whatever. Clarify its use of basic musical elements in such a way that you are satisfied you are describing the essential characteristics of that particular style.

2. Compare two different popular styles. How do they use rhythm, tempo, melody, timbre, harmony, dynamics, and dissonance? Are the two styles very different from one another, or are they more similar than might first be thought?

3. What kinds of feelings might be considered the subject matter of the pieces you have chosen to discuss? How does the music help reveal those feelings? Do other listeners agree with you?

Summary: The Content of Music

We began this chapter by suggesting that feelings and sound are the primary subject matters of music. This implies that the content of music is a revelation of feelings or sound and that music gives us a more sensitive understanding of them. However, as we indicated in our opening statements, there is considerable disagreement about music's subject matter, and therefore, there is disagreement about music's content. If music does reveal feelings or sound, the way it does so is still one of the most baffling problems in the philosophy of art.

Even a brief survey of the theories about the content of music is beyond our scope here, but given the basic theory of art as revelation, as we have been presupposing in this book, a couple of examples of how that theory might be applied to music are relevant. In the first place, some music apparently clarifies sounds as noises. For example, John Cage, at times, uses devices such as a brick crashing through a glass. Normally when we hear such noises, we listen away from them to what they signify, such as an accident or theft or riot. In everyday life it would be strange indeed to listen to such noises for their own sake, for their intrinsic values. But by putting such noises into a composition, Cage brackets out the everyday situation and helps us "listen to" rather than "listen through" such noises. In this way he clarifies those noises. His musical form organizes sounds and sometimes silences before and after the noise of the breaking glass in such a way that our perception of the noise of breaking glass is made more sensitive. Similar analyses can be made of the sounds of musical instruments and their interrelationships in the structures in which they are placed.

Second, there seems to be some evidence that music gives us insight into our feelings. It is not ridiculous to claim, for example, that one is feeling joy like that of the last movement of Mozart's *Jupiter* Symphony, or sadness like the second movement—the funeral march—of Beethoven's *Eroica* Symphony. In fact, joy and sadness are general terms that only very crudely describe our states of feeling. We experience all kinds of different joys and different sadnesses, and the names language gives to these are imprecise. Music, with its capacity to evoke feelings, and with a complexity of texture and structure that in many ways is greater than that of language, may be able to reveal or interpret feelings with much more precision than language. Perhaps the form of the last movement of the *Jupiter* Symphony—with its clear-cut rising melodies, bright harmonies and timbres, brisk strings, and rapid rhythms—is somehow analogous to the form of a certan kind of joy. And if so, then perhaps we find revealed in that musical form a clarification or insight about joy. Such explanations are highly speculative. However, they are not only theoretically interesting but may also intensify one's interest in music. There is mystery about music, unique among the arts, that is part of its fascination.

Appendix

We begin with some definitions, proceed to questions regarding music notation, then consider the basic musical elements of rhythm, melody, counterpoint, harmony, dynamics, and contrast. We present this material in the hopes that we can have a common language and a common understanding in the discussion of music. Much of what follows will be of even more value if you play an instrument.

NOISE

Noise, like all sound, is a result of the movement of air in the form of waves. The more physical space between the crest of the waves, the lower the pitch of the sound; the closer the crest of the waves, the higher the pitch. Noise is a conglomerate of sounds with a variety of pitches—none distinguishable by the ear. For an example of "white noise"—noise with sounds of all pitches at once—listen to the noise between stations on an FM radio band.

TONE

A sound that has one definite frequency or that is dominated by one definite frequency is a tone. Music is usually made up of a succession of tones. Songs unfold by virtue of our ability to hear tones and remember them as they are played in succession. Tones on a musical instrument will have other related tones, or partials, sounding simultaneously, although not as loudly as the primary tone. Our ear is used to hearing a primary tone with fainter partials; therefore, when electronic instruments produce a pure tone—that is, with no partials—of any frequency, it may sound very odd to us.

TIMBRE, OR TONE COLOR

All instruments produce a primary tone and a series of partials, such as—to name only two—tones of a fifth and an octave higher. But all instruments are different in the intensity or loudness of each of the partials. Consequently, a trumpet or a piano playing C will each have its distinctive quality of sound. Each instrument and group of instruments has a distinctive timbre, or tone color, because of the variation in intensity of the simultaneously sounding partials that accompany the primary tone. (Figures 9-30 and 9-32).

CONSONANCE

The sounding of partials implies that tones of different but related frequencies have a tendency to sound soothing and pleasant together. When two or more tones are sounded simultaneously and the result is pleasing to the ear, the resultant sound is termed consonant. The phenomenon of consonance may be qualified by several things. For example, what sounds dissonant or unpleasant often becomes more consonant after repeated hearings. Thus, the sounds of the music of a different culture may seem dissonant at first but consonant after some familiarity develops. Also, there is the influence of context: a combination of notes may seem dissonant in isolation or within one set of surrounding notes and consonant within another set. In the C major scale, the strongest consonances will be the eighth (C + C') and the

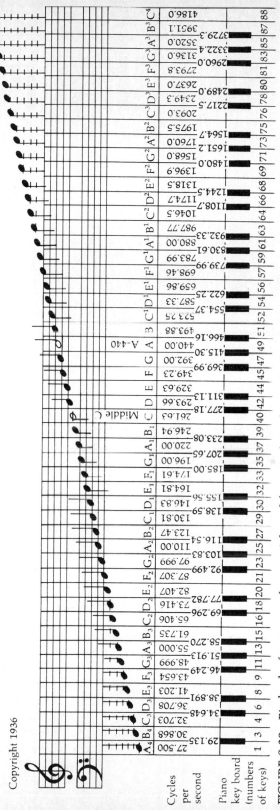

FIGURE 9-30 Pitch: the frequency of notes. Adapted from Carl Seashore, *The Psychology of Music*, 1938, McGraw-Hill, New York, p. 73.

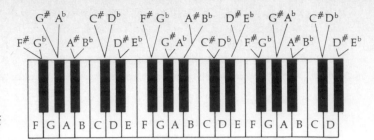

FIGURE 9-31 Notes of
the piano keyboard.

fifth (C + G), with the third (C + E,) the fourth (C + F), and the sixth (C + A) being only slightly less consonant. See the graph in Figure 9-32, based on research by Helmholtz.

In this experiment one violin held the note C' (the C above middle C—check Figure 9-31), while a second violin went up two octaves. The greater the distance of the curved line from the horizontal straight line, the greater the dissonance; the closer the lines, the greater the consonance. The degree of consonance is not directly related to the interest level of a given interval. An interval of a sixth may sound much more intriguing than the perfect consonance of the octave.

DISSONANCE

Just as some notes sounding together tend to be soothing and pleasant, other notes sounding together tend to be rough and unpleasant. This is a result of wave interference and a phenomenon called "beating," which accounts for the roughness we perceive in dissonance. The most powerful dissonance is achieved when notes close to one another in pitch are sounded simultaneously. The second (C + D) and the seventh (C + B) are both strongly dissonant. Dissonance is important in building musical tension, since the desire to resolve dissonance with

FIGURE 9-32 Graph of relative dissonance. From Alexander Wood, *The Physics of Music*, 2d ed., 1944, Methuen, London, p. 157.

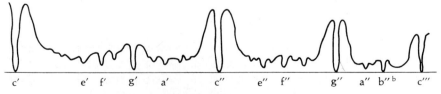

consonance is strong in most listeners. There is a story that Mozart's wife, for example, would retaliate against her husband after some quarrel by striking a dissonant chord on the piano. Wolfgang would be forced to come from wherever he was to play a resounding consonant chord to relieve the unbearable tension.

PERCEPTION KEY DEFINITIONS

1. Tone color: experiment by listening to a given note or series of notes played by different instruments, such as the piano, guitar (nylon and steel strings produce different tone colors), harmonica, kazoo, accordion, etc. Is it difficult to tell one instrument from another? Do any of the instruments tend to group into "families" by virtue of similarities of tone color? Do you find that people have developed preferences among tone colors?

2. Consonance and dissonance: using a piano or a guitar, strike the note C, then the note C' an octave higher. Use this combination as the standard for what is consonant. Then strike every combination of C plus another note and identify the consonant combinations. Also identify the most interesting combinations. What is their relationship to consonance or dissonance?

3. Dissonance: have someone with a good voice sing a note that he or she can hold for a few moments. Try to sing a note simultaneously that is definitely dissonant with the first note. Is this difficult to do? If you yourself cannot sing, listen to two other people perform the experiment and decide how difficult it is to create dissonance. Does the ease or difficulty of producing dissonance surprise you in any way? What might it mean for our experiences in listening to music?

4. Experiment in listening: by paying close attention to tone color, begin trying to name the instruments you hear in the next piece of music you listen to. Listen with others until you are confident that, along with them, you can tell a trumpet from a trombone, a violin from a cello. If you have difficulties, Benjamin Britten's *Young Person's Guide to the Orchestra* is an especially interesting and helpful work.

5. Experiment in listening: listen closely to one of your favorite pieces of music. Where do the strongest consonances occur in the piece? Are they strong and well defined? Are they satisfying? Are they as interesting as the strongest dissonances? Do the consonances and dissonances seem to need each other? Why? Take a piece of music of a kind you do not usually listen to. How does it compare in terms of its level of consonance and dissonance with your favorite? Does this give you any clue as to why you prefer your favorite?

The Basic Elements of Music

RHYTHM

"Rhythm" is a term referring to the temporal measurement of organized sounds. Rhythm measures the time it takes to play a given note (its duration) and the time when a given note is to be played. Our perception of rhythm in a composition is also affected by accent or stress on given notes. In the waltz, the accent is heavy on the first note (of three) in each musical measure. In most modern jazz, the stress falls on the second and fourth notes (of four) in each measure. Most marching music, which has six notes in each measure, emphasizes the first and fourth note. (See Figure 9-33.)

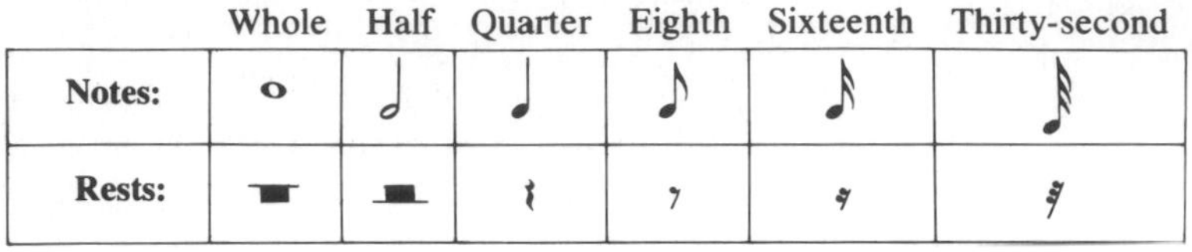

	Whole	Half	Quarter	Eighth	Sixteenth	Thirty-second
Notes:	o	♩	♩	♪	♪	♪
Rests:	▬	▬	𝄽	𝄾	𝄿	𝅀

FIGURE 9-33   Note and rest values.

TIME SIGNATURES

FIGURE 9-34   Time signatures.

DOTS AND TIES

A dotted note (Figure 9-35) means the original note is to be held for an additional half of its time value. This dotted half note, then, would be held for the duration usually assigned to three quarter notes. Two notes connected by a curved line (Figure 9-36) are played as if they were only the first note; the value of the second note is simply added to the first, so these two half notes would sound for the same duration as a whole note.

♩.

FIGURE 9-35   A dotted half note.

♩ ♩

FIGURE 9-36   Tied half notes.

TEMPO

The speed at which a composition is played is its tempo. We perceive tempo in terms of beats, just as we perceive the tempo of our heartbeat as seventy-two pulses per minute, approximately. Many tempos have descriptive names indicating the general time value for the basic note of a musical measure. *Presto* means "very fast"; *allegro* means "fast"; *andante* means "at a walking pace"; *moderato* means "at a moderate pace"; *lento* and *largo* mean "slow." Sometimes metronome markings are given in a score, but musicians rarely agree on any exact time figure. Tension, anticipation, and one's sense of musical security are strongly affected by tempo.

MELODY

"Melody" or "theme" is usually defined as a group of notes played one after another having a perceivable shape. The shape of a melody has, more or less, a beginning, middle, and end, and it is recognizable when replayed. Vague as this definition is, we rarely find ourselves in doubt about what is or is not a melody. We not only recognize melodies easily but can say a great deal about them. Some melodies are brief—only a few notes; whereas others seem extensive and are composed of a great many notes. Some melodies are slow, others fast; some are bouncy, others more somber; some are catchy, others less immediately interesting (although they may bear more relistening than catchy melodies); some seem very simple, others considerably more complex. Since melodies can be described in many ways, it is helpful to begin developing your own vocabulary for communicating what you perceive about melodies and comparing your perceptions with others.

PERCEPTION KEY RHYTHM AND MELODY

1. With a small group of listeners, examine the rhythm and melody of a popular recording you feel has some musical interest. Have each listener describe the rhythm and the melody as carefully as possible and compare descriptions. How difficult is it to perceive rhythmic and melodic qualities? You might consider the following questions: Is the melody easy to remember? Is the tempo slower or faster than your heartbeat? Is the rhythm more noticeable than the melody? Is the rhythm more complex, more imaginative, or more interesting than the melody? Which is more important to you, the melody or the rhythm? Or are they equal in importance?
2. Listen to one or all of the following kinds of music:
   a. Indian music—Uday or Ravi Shankar
   b. Jazz, traditional or modern
   c. Latin American music, Reggae
   d. Country and Western, Blues
   e. A movement of a symphony by Mozart or Beethoven
   f. A song by Strauss, Schubert, or Schumann
   g. Soul
   h. A hymn
   What are the similarities in terms of rhythmic and melodic qualities between these kinds of music? What are the differences? If you have preferences among these musics, are they based on your perception of their rhythmic and melodic qualities? Be as candid as possible about your preferences and discuss them with others who may hold different views.

COUNTERPOINT

In the Middle Ages the monks composing and performing church music began to realize that powerful musical effects could be obtained by singing or playing two or more melodic lines at the same time. They may be different melodies, or the same melody staggered like "Row, Row, Row, Your Boat." This is called "counterpoint"—a playing of two or more melodies against each other. It implies an independence of

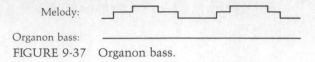

Melody:

Organon bass:

FIGURE 9-37   Organon bass.

simultaneous melodic lines each of which can, at times, be the dominant melody. The opposition of melodic lines creates tension by virtue of their competition for our attention. Seventeenth- and eighteenth-century counterpoint became incredibly complex, although its origins were relatively simple. The basis for counterpoint began in the Middle Ages with the organon bass—bass voices droning a sustained tone—above which the tenor voices sang or chanted the melodic line. Diagrammed, it might look something like Figure 9-37.

The Scotch bagpipe and the organ are instruments especially adaptable for exploiting the organon bass. Even modern rock bands have picked up the idea—possibly influenced by the chanting of Tibetan monks—and have discovered its potential for building tension.

As the bass line grew more complex, it began to develop as a melody in its own right. Once this second melody was freed from its restrictions of pitch (being limited to the bass notes), the possibilities of interaction of the contrapuntal lines became enormous. Some typical situations are diagrammed below. The higher the melodic line, the higher the pitch of the melody.

See Figure 9-38. In example A, melody 2 will probably remain subservient to melody 1 except at the moment when it rises in pitch above melody 1—assuming that the relative loudness of each melody remains the same. In example B, melody 1 will probably remain the dominant melody and receive most of our attention. In example C, melody 2 gradually wrests dominance from melody 1. In all examples this assumes not only that the loudness of each melody is relatively equal but also that the tone colors and rhythmic qualities are similar.

FIGURE 9-38   Counterpoint.

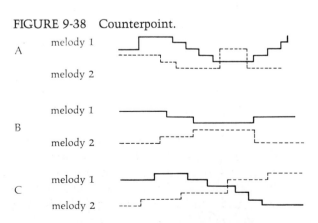

1. Listen to a contrapuntal piece of music such as one of Bach's *Brandenburg Concertos*, a piece from his *Well-Tempered Clavier*, or a concerto of Vivaldi. Identify as best you can each of the melodies you can hear distinctly and describe them carefully. Compare your descriptions with those of other listeners. Describe, too, the rhythmic character of the piece and the kinds of tone colors that are employed. Identify the instruments as they take turns playing the melodic lines.

2. Take a small section of a contrapuntal composition—a half minute or so—and see if you can diagram the melodic lines in the manner we have suggested above. Compare your diagram with those of others and listen again to those sections on which you may disagree. Do other listeners help you find melodies you did not know were there?

3. If you have access to one of Bach's organ fugues on a recording, listen closely to the first melodic statement. Trace it from the beginning of the composition to the end. Probably the simplest and best fugue for this would be Bach's Fugue in G minor, the "Little Fugue." The first subject is shown in Figure 9-39.

FIGURE 9-39   First subject of Bach's *Little Fugue* in G minor.

4. In the event no contrapuntal music is available, you can sense the intricacy and pleasure of counterpoint by singing a round like "Frère Jacques" or "Row, Row, Row Your Boat" with a group of friends. In a round, one singer starts the melody, then at a selected point the next singer starts the same melody before the first singer has finished, etc.

HARMONY

Harmony is the sounding of tones simultaneously. The harmony that most of us hear is basically chordal. A chord is a group of notes sounded together that has a specific relationship to a given key: the chord C-E-G, for example, is a major triad in the key of C major. At the end of a composition in the key of C, it will emphasize the sense of arrival—or the sense of finality—more than almost any other technique we know.

Chords are particularly useful for establishing cadences: progressions to resting points that release tensions. Cadences move from relatively unstable chords to stable ones. You can test this on a piano by first playing the notes C-F-A together, then playing C-E-G (consult Figure 9-31 for the position of these notes on the keyboard). The result will be obvious. The first chord establishes tension and uncertainty, making the chord unstable, while the second chord resolves the tension and uncertainty, bringing the sequence to a satisfying conclusion. You will probably recognize this progression at once as one you have heard in many compositions, for example, the "A-men" that closes most hymns. The progression exists in every key with the same sense of stability.

Every interval has a degree of stability or instability that composers rely on when constructing harmonic passages. If they wish to emphasize instability, they will prefer intervals that are seconds (C + D) or sevenths (C + B). If they wish to emphasize stability, they will choose intervals of the octave (C + C') or the fifth (C + G). The thirds (C + E) and sixths (C + A) are fairly stable. The stability of these intervals is related to their approach toward consonance, and your earlier experiments should clarify the nature of stability in relation to consonance and dissonance. The more consonant an interval, the more stable it is.

When we speak of harmony, we speak of the vertical element of music. Melody is the horizontal element, as can be seen at a glance from Figure 9-40. These are the opening notes of the chorus of "Battle Hymn of the Republic": the octave C interval in the bass clef and the third plus the fifth interval (E and G) in the treble clef.

G or treble clef

F or bass clef

FIGURE 9-40 Harmony—the vertical element.

Clearly these are the most stable intervals in the composition, with only the third, E, being slightly less than optimum in stability. The piece then establishes a powerful stability through its harmony at the outset. Whatever may happen in the middle of the composition, we will expect the end to be just as stable. A glance at the last measure of the piece (Figure 9-41) will show this to be quite true. Whereas the opening included two C's, an E, and a G, the final harmony dispenses with the G and substitutes another C, adding even more stability to the ending.

PERCEPTION KEY HARMONY

1. If possible, have someone play this piece on the piano. Can you identify any points in which the harmony achieves more stability than in the opening notes? Are there any unstable harmonies in the piece?
2. Since this is just the chorus, have the entire piece played. Ask youself the same questions as in question 1 above.
    Note: In lieu of the piano, the experiment may be conducted with voices or with other instruments.

Battle Hymn of the Republic

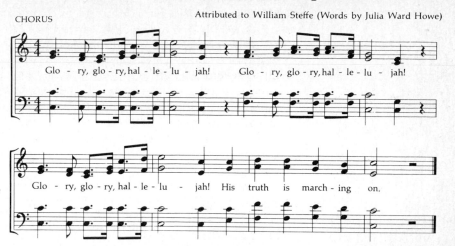

CHORUS

Attributed to William Steffe (Words by Julia Ward Howe)

Glo - ry, glo - ry, hal - le - lu - jah! Glo - ry, glo - ry, hal - le - lu - jah!

Glo - ry, glo - ry, hal - le - lu - jah! His truth is march - ing on.

FIGURE 9-41 "Battle Hymn of the Republic." Attributed to William Steffe (Words by Julia Ward Howe).

The experiment with "Battle Hymn of the Republic" is important, but it reveals only some of the powers and significance of harmony. Harmonic techniques did not grow up overnight, nor are they common to music of all cultures. Rhythm and melody have enough power to sustain attention by themselves, so that what is supplied by harmony in Western music is not missed by those who do not have it in their own music. However, once non-Westerners absorb the techniques of harmony, they often incorporate it in their own music.

Harmony is based on apparently universal psychological reactions. The smoothness of consonance and the roughness of dissonance seem to be just as perceptible to the non-Western as to the Western ear. The effects will be somewhat different in each case due to cultural conditioning, but there is a generally predictable effect within a limited range. One anthropologist, when told about a Samoan ritual in which he was assured he could hear original Samoan music—as it had existed from early times—hauled his tape recorder to the site of the ceremonies, waited until dawn, and when he heard the first stirrings turned on his machine and captured the entire group of Samoans singing "You are my sunshine, my only sunshine." Their harmony was relatively simple, but it was clear they liked the song and responded to its harmonic qualities. The anthropologist was disappointed, but his experience underscores the universality of music.

Approaches to harmony have varied greatly in different periods of the history of music. Contrapuntal music of the seventeenth and eighteenth centuries does not usually emphasize harmony. From Bach, through Mozart, and to Beethoven, harmony begins to develop enormous complexities and interesting subtleties. We cannot talk about them here, although you might wish to consult a history of Western music, which will give you more technical details. We should note, however, that in the late eighteenth century harmony began to be "featured" in musical compositions. The harmony helped clarify the structure of the melodic lines as well as beginning to attract attention to its own qualities. By the middle of the nineteenth century—in the works of Wagner particularly—harmony began to be as obvious and important as melody and rhythm. Large expansive chords were developed and sustained. In extreme cases some critics felt the delights of melody were being sacrificed for what seemed a technical examination of harmonic effects.

PERCEPTION KEY HARMONY

Choose a musical composition from Haydn, Mozart, or Beethoven; choose another by Wagner, Richard Strauss, or Ralph Vaughan Williams. Compare them for their use of harmony. Ask yourself the following questions:
1. How important is the harmony in comparison with rhythm and melody?
2. What specific effects seem to be achieved by the harmony?
3. Which moments seem to be the most satisfying or dissatisfying in terms of harmony?
4. Are there moments that seem all harmony—when rhythm and melody seem to disappear? When? Can you discuss the importance of these moments to the overall success of the composition?
5. Is there agreement among other listeners and yourself about which harmonic moments are pleasing and which are not? Is there agreement about which are effective and which are not?
6. Can you detect any preference in yourself for the use of harmony? How does your preference compare with the preferences of other listeners? What does your preference seem to be based on?

DYNAMICS

One of the most easily perceived elements of music is dynamics: the music's loudness and softness. Composers vary their dynamics—as they vary keys, timbres, melodies, rhythms, and harmonies—to achieve variety, to establish a pattern against which they can play, to build tension and release it, to feature various moments of the composition, and to provide the surprise which can delight an audience. Two terms, *piano* ("soft") and *forte* ("loud"), with variations such as *pianissimo* ("very soft") and *fortissimo* ("very loud"), are used by composers to identify the desired dynamics at a given moment in the composition. A gradual building up of loudness is called a *crescendo*, whereas a gradual building down is called a *decrescendo*. Most compositions will have some of each, as well as passages that sustain a dynamic level.

The capacity of dynamics to emphasize segments of a composition and to clarify the relationship of one textural element to another—or to the total structure—is basic to the composer's means. Yet dynamics can be easily abused with too much shifting from loud to soft or simply too much loudness without relief or contrast. The subtlety of musical judgment almost always shows up in the subtle use of dynamics.

PERCEPTION KEY DYNAMICS

Listen closely to two different compositions. Choose one from a popular band like Chicago, Santana, Yes, Bob Dylan. Choose another from Charles Ives, Igor Stravinsky, Dmitri Shostakovich, or Pierre Boulez. Compare them for:

1. Variations in dynamics
2. Effective use of dynamics
3. Value of dynamics in relation to other musical elements, such as melody, rhythm, or harmony

CONTRAST

Clearly, one thing that helps us value dynamics in a given composition is the composer's use of contrast. But contrast is of value in other ways, too. When more than one instrument is involved, the composer can contrast timbres. The brasses, for example, may be used to offer tonal contrast to a passage that may have been played by the strings. The percussion section, in turn, can contrast with both those sections, with high-pitched bells and low-pitched kettledrums covering a wide tonal range. The woodwinds offer yet another range of tone color, and the composer writing for a large orchestra often will use all of the families of instruments in ways designed to exploit the difference in the way these instruments sound even when playing the same music.

Composers may approach rhythm and tempo with the same attention to contrast. Most symphonies begin with a fast movement (usually labeled *allegro*) in the major key, then a slow movement usually follows in a related or contrasting key, then a third movement with bright speed, and a final movement that resolves to some extent all that has gone before—again at a fast tempo, although sometimes with some contrasting sections within it. Such a symphony, examined in great detail in this chapter, is Beethoven's *Eroica.*

PERCEPTION KEY CONTRAST

1. Select a recording that you like and know well. Listen to it carefully for the presence of contrasting elements. Point out the kind of contrast you perceive to other listeners. Do they perceive the contrast as well as you do? Do they perceive some kinds of contrast you do not?
2. Can you tie in the nature of the contrasting elements with the overall

success of the piece? How does contrast or the lack of it contribute to that success?

3. Can you identify all the kinds of contrast we mentioned above? Can you find other kinds of contrast?

Chapter 9 Bibliography

Abraham, Gerald. *The Concise Oxford History of Music.* New York: Oxford University Press, 1979.

Bukofzer, Manfred. *Music in the Baroque Era.* New York: Norton, 1947.

Chase, Gilbert. *America's Music.* New York: McGraw-Hill, 1955.

Dalhaus, Carl, tr. William Austin. *Esthetics of Music.* Cambridge: Cambridge University Press, 1982.

Debussy, Claude et al. *Three Classics in the Aesthetics of Music.* New York: Dover, 1962.

Erickson, Robert. *The Structure of Music.* New York: Farrar Straus & Giroux, 1955.

Grout, Donald. *A History of Western Music.* New York: Norton, 1960.

Grove's Dictionary of Music and Musicians. New York: St. Martin's Press, 1955.

Haydon, Glenn. *On the Meaning of Music.* Washington, D.C.: Library of Congress, 1948.

Hindemith, Paul. *Composer's World.* Cambridge, Mass.: Harvard University Press, 1952.

Lang, Paul Henry. *Music in Western Civilization.* New York: Norton, 1941.

Meyer, Leonard B. *Emotion and Meaning in Music.* Chicago: University of Chicago Press, 1956.

———. *Explaining Music.* Berkeley: University of California Press, 1973.

Ratner, Leonard G. *Harmony: Structure and Style.* New York: McGraw-Hill, 1962.

Rosen, Charles. *The Classic Style.* New York: Viking Press, 1971

Sachs, Curt. *The Wellsprings of Music.* New York: McGraw-Hill, 1965.

Stravinsky, Igor, and Craft, Robert. *Expositions and Developments.* Garden City, N.Y.: Doubleday, 1962.

Tovey, Donald F. *Beethoven.* New York: Oxford University Press, 1945.

———. *Essays in Musical Analysis.* New York: Oxford University Press, 1944.

Zuckerkandl, Victor. *Sound and Symbol.* Princeton, N.J.: Princeton University Press, 1956.

DANCE

10

All dance has the subject matter of bodies and shapes in space, and, in this sense, it has common ground with sculpture. Further, dance has the additional dimension of motion—as does kinetic sculpture—which also becomes part of its subject matter. The motion of bodies and shapes and the modulation of spaces between them constitute the primary subject matter of all dance.

Most dances, however, have an added subject matter. Thus, the dance may portray a narrative, as does most dramatic literature, which informs us about a human situation. Robert Helpmann's ballet *Hamlet* can be interpreted as having Shakespeare's *Hamlet* as its subject matter. For viewers of the dance who know the play *Hamlet*, this might be very important; but for viewers who do not, the subject matter of the dance will be the human situation explored by the dance narrative of Hamlet's struggle. Whether or not we know the play, our insight into the situation will be deepened by the dance itself.

Like music, dance may have feelings as part of its subject matter. But more than music, dance may have states of mind as part of its subject matter. Feelings are relatively transient, such as pleasure and pain, and can usually be easily superseded. But states of mind involve attitudes, tendencies that engender certain feelings on the appropriate occasions. A state of mind is a disposition or habit that is not easily superseded. For example, jealousy usually involves a feeling so strong that it is best described as passion. Yet jealousy is more than just a passion, for it is an orientation of mind that is relatively enduring. Thus, José Limón's dance *The Moor's Pavane* explores the jealousy of Shakespeare's *Othello*. In Limón's version, Iago and Othello dance around Desdemona and seem to be directly vying for her affections. Thus, *The Moor's Pavane* represents an interpretation of the states of mind Shakespeare treated, although it can stand independently of the play and make its own contribution to our information about jealousy as it was felt by Othello.

The dramatic narrative—the portrayal of a story—is often subordinated in modern dance. Then a more direct attempt to represent and interpret feelings through bodily movement is possible, as in Paul Sanasardo's *Pain*, in which the dance clearly focuses on a basic feeling until some of the audience—so it has been reported—virtually begins to feel the pain itself. The still photograph (Figure 10-1) clearly indicates the character of the depiction of emotion.

The dance is a serial structure unfolding in time and thus cannot be held still for contemplation. The serial character of both dance and music may be one of the reasons that dance is almost always performed to music. Even silence in some dances seems to suggest music, since the dancer exhibits visual rhythm, the rising and falling of stress that we perceive in music. But the interpretation of states of mind is achieved only partly through the elements dance shares with music. The interpretation is achieved more importantly by the motion of the dancing bodies.

By way of experiment, to demonstrate how much most of us know about how body movements can represent and reveal states of mind, the following perception key should be illuminating.

PERCEPTION KEY DANCE AND STATES OF MIND

1. Using as little bodily motion as possible, try to represent a state of mind to a group of onlookers. Ask them to describe what you have represented. How closely does their description match your intention?
2. Represent one of the following states of mind by bodily motion: love, jealousy, self-confidence, pride, horror. Have others do the same. Do you find such representations difficult to perceive when others do them?
3. Comment on one of the performances in the suggestions above. What were the motions your group used for the above representations? Discuss the distinctive capacity bodily motion has for representing states of mind.
4. Try to move in such a way as to represent no state of mind at all. Is it possible? Discuss this with your entire group.
5. Representing or portraying a state of mind allows one to recognize that state. Interpreting or revealing a state of mind gives one insight into that state, a deeper understanding. In any of the experiments above, did you

FIGURE 10-1 Judith Blackstone and Paul Sanasardo in *Pain*. Photograph courtesy of Paul Sanasardo Dance Company, New York.

find any examples that went beyond representation and involved revelation? If so, what made this possible? What does artistic form have to do with this?

6. Is it possible for you to recognize a state of mind such as jealousy being represented without having that state of mind being evoked in yourself? Is it possible for you not only to recognize but also to gain insight about a state of mind without the state of mind being evoked in yourself?

Form and Dance

If the subject matter of dance can be bodies in motion, works of art, human situations, feelings, and states of mind, the form of the dance—its textural elements as they function together to organize the structure—gives us insight into the subject matter. But the textures and structures of the dance are not as clearly perceptible as they usually are in painting, sculpture, or architecture. Sculptures, paintings, and buildings normally "sit still" long enough for us to reexamine details. We have time and opportunity to perceive fully and comprehend the textures and their relationships to the structure. But the dance moves on relentlessly, like poetry in recitation, drama, and music, preventing us from reexamining its parts. We can only hope to hold in memory a part for comparison with a new part, and those parts as they help create the structure. Therefore, one prerequisite for a thorough enjoyment of the dance is the development of a memory for dance movements. The dance will usually help us in this task by the use of repetitive movements and variations on them. It can do for us what we cannot do for ourselves: present once again textural elements for our renewed consideration. Often the dance builds tension by withholding movements we want to have repeated; sometimes it creates unusual tension by refusing to repeat any movement at all. Repetition or the lack of it—as in music or any serial art—becomes one of dance's most important structural features.

Part of our attention will be directed toward the varieties of dance modes—primitive, folk, social, ballet, and modern—to see how those modes are related to each other and to musical accompaniment. Part of our attention will be directed toward the varieties of textural modes—more specifically, individual dance movements and their character—that constitute a basic "vocabulary" for all dances. We consider first several important kinds of dance, beginning with its origins as perhaps the earliest art form.

Primitive Dance

It has become commonplace to point out that dance is the most original art of all peoples. Since the only requirement for a dance is a body in motion and since all cultures have this basic requirement, dance, it has been reasoned, probably precedes all other arts. In this sense dance is truly primitive: It comes first.

The origins of dance are probably not strictly artistic (revelatory), in that most primitive dances are connected with either religious or practical acts. Often primitive dance religiously celebrates some tribal achievement. At other times the dance, although still religious, is expected to have a more or less immediate and specific practical effect. In this kind of dance—the Zuni rain dance or the ghost dance of the Sioux, for instance—the movement is ritually ordered and expected to be practically effective as long as the dance is performed properly.

Some primitive dance has sexual origins and often is a ritual of courtship. Since this phenomenon has a correlative in nature—the courtship "dances" of birds and some other animals—it may well be that primitive peoples occasionally imitated them. Certain movements in Mandan Indian dances, for instance, can be traced to the leaps and falls of western jays and mockingbirds who, in finding a place to rest, will stop, leap into the air while spreading their wings for balance, then fall suddenly, only to rise into the air again. Even modern dancers like Ann Halprin of the San Francisco Dancers Workshop, in preparing for her recent dance *West/East Stereo*, sent her dancers to the San Francisco Zoo to observe birds, leopards, and other animals in order to represent them onstage. In that sense that particular dance might be thought of profitably in terms of its connection with the origins of dance.

PERCEPTION KEY PRIMITIVE AND SOCIAL DANCE

1. Critics of the social dances of young people occasionally complain that those dances are primitive and therefore unhealthy. Is this reasonable?
2. Condemning or praising current social dances as primitive implies a value judgment. What are the implications of using the concept of primitive as a basis for making such evaluative criticisms?

Ann Halprin's sending her dancers to the zoo for inspiration points up another interesting fact about dance, whether primitive or not. Dance of all kinds draws much of its inspiration from nature: the motion of a stalk of wheat in a gentle breeze, the scurrying of a rabbit, the curling of a contented cat, the soaring of a bird, the falling of a leaf. These kinds of events have supplied dancers with ideas and examples for their own movement. But there is another level of inspiration that comes from the natural shapes of things.

A favorite shape for the dance is that of the spiral nautilus, so often seen in shells, plants, and insects:

This form is apparent in individual movement (see Figures 10-1 and 10-5a), just as it is in the movement of groups of dancers whose floor pattern may follow the spiral pattern (see Figure 10-2).

The circle is another of nature's most pervasive and fascinating shapes. The movements of planets and stars suggest circular motion, and, more mundanely, so do the rings working out from a stone dropped in water. The circle and circular motion have been compelling for the primitive dancer, the court dancer in Elizabethan times, and the ballet and modern dancers in our time.

FIGURE 10-2 Spiral plan from *Tanzsynfonia*, 1973. From Lincoln Kirstein, *Movement and Metaphor*, Praeger Publishers, New York.

In a magical-religious way, circular dances have been thought to bring the dancers—and therefore humans in general—into significant harmony with the divine forces in the universe. The planets and stars are heavenly objects in circular motion, so it was "reasonable" for primitive dancers to feel that they could make themselves congruent with these divine forces by means of the circular dance. Dance teachers in the Renaissance were thought to have a moral function principally because they helped people put themselves into the requisite harmony with the motion of the most divine objects. It should be noted, furthermore, that the circular form is powerful in many arts. Many of the illustrations in this book of painting, sculpture, and architecture are evidence of this. Consider also structures in music and in literature, ending where one began often has an enormous satisfaction to it, acting as a profound release of tension.

THE GHOST DANCE

One of the most fascinating primitive dances we know of was the ghost dance of the Sioux in the late nineteenth century. It was a circle dance performed by men and women lasting for twenty-four hours. Its purpose was to raise the spirits of dead Indians in order to finish off the white man and to reclaim the land for the Indians who remained. In the 1880s a variety of tribes banded together in religious association and began the dancing. A prophet-seer named Wovoca—or Black Elk—declared that if the dance was done properly, the dead Indians would rise.

The dancers, about two hundred at a time, formed a relatively compact circle and chanted as they danced, moving sideways to their left around a center pole. They wore bead-and-bone vests, which were called ghost shirts and thought to be impenetrable by the white man's bullets. One of the results of the dancing and chanting for hours at a time was a trancelike state resembling death. Dancers felt they were making communion with the spirit world. Unfortunately, one of the end results of the faith in the rising of the dead Indian armies was the famous massacre of Wounded Knee in 1890. The dancing unnerved white officials and was disapproved of, but it continued secretly. And those who died at Wounded Knee—at least some of them—fully expected to be invulnerable and to be joined by their spiritual forebears in their struggle. The ghost dance was a visible testament of belief and an instrument of action.

THE ZUNI RAIN DANCE

The rain dance is also a religious-practical dance, but its results have not been so unfortunate as those of the ghost dance. Tourists can see rain dances in the American Southwest even today. The floor pattern of the dance is not circular but a modified spiral, as can be seen from Figure 10-3. The dancers, properly costumed, form a line and are led by a priest, who at specific moments spreads corn meal on the ground, symbolizing his wish for the fertility of the ground.

The ritual character of the dance is clearly observable in the diagram, with dancers beginning toward the north, then turning west, south, east, north, west, south, and ending toward the east. The gestures of the dancers, as with the gestures in most rituals, have definite meanings and functions. For example, the dancers' loud screams are designed to awaken the gods and arrest their attention, the drumbeat suggests thunder, and the rattles the dancers sound suggest the sound of rain the dancers hope for.

PERCEPTION KEY PRIMITIVE DANCE AND CONTEMPORARY RITUALS

1. Contemporary rituals such as some weddings and funerals involve motion that can be thought of as dance motion. Can you think of other contemporary rituals that involve dance motion? Do we need to know the meanings of the ritual gestures in order to appreciate the motion of the ritual?
2. How much common ground do we share with primitive dancers with reference to our trying to give meaning to our gestures, either in a generally accepted "dance situation" or out of it? Enumerate instances.
3. Do we have dances that can be considered as serving functions similar to those of the primitive dances we have described? Consider, for instance, the dancing in the streets that followed the end of World War II. Are there other instances?

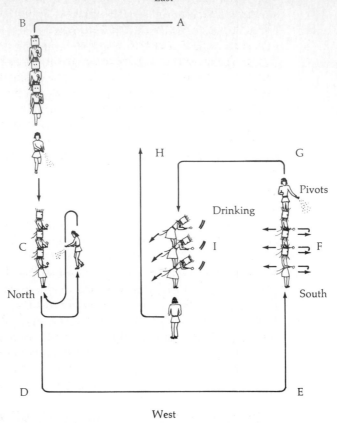

East

A

B

H

G

Pivots

Drinking

I

F

C

North

South

D

E

West

FIGURE 10-3 Spiral plan of the Zuni rain dance. From John L. Squires and Robert E. McLean, *American Indian Dances*, copyright © 1963 by the Ronald Press, New York; illustrations by R. McLean.

Social Dance

Social dance is not specifically theatrical, as are ballet and modern dance. Folk and court dances are often done simply for the pleasure of the dancers. Because we are more or less familiar with square dances, round dances, waltzes, and a large variety of contemporary dances done at parties, we have some useful points of reference for dance in general.

COUNTRY AND FOLK DANCE

Unlike primitive dance, social dance is not dominated by religious or practical purposes, although it may have secondary practical purposes that are important to the dancer, such as meeting people or working off excess energy. More important, it is a form of recreation and social enjoyment. Country dance—for example, the English Playford dances —is a species of folk dance that has traces of primitive origins, because country people tended to perform dances in specific relationship to special periods in the agricultural year, such as planting and harvesting. The connection now is tenuous, however, since contemporary dancers rarely relate to any specific agricultural subject matter. Now the subject matter seems to be mainly energy and celebration.

Most of the many forms of folk dances that have arisen in Western countries have survived to one degree or another. Folk dances are the dances of the people—whether ethnic or regional in origin—and they are often very carefully preserved in our time, sometimes with contests designed to keep the dances alive. When they perform, the dancers often wear the peasant costumes of the region they represent. Virtually every European nation, as well as Asian and African nations, has its own folk dance tradition. (See Figure 10-4.)

THE COURT DANCE

The court dances of the Middle Ages and the Renaissance developed into more stylized and less openly energetic modes than the folk dance, for the court dance was performed by a different sort of person and served a different purpose. Some of the favorite older dances were the volta, a dance that was a favorite at Queen Elizabeth's court in the sixteenth century, and that involved the male dancer hoisting the female dancer in the air from time to time; the pavane, a stately dance popular in the seventeenth century; the minuet, popular in the eighteenth century, performed by groups of four dancers at a time; and the allemande, apparently German in origin, also of the eighteenth

FIGURE 10-4 Pieter Breugel the Elder, *The Wedding Dance.* Oil on panel, 47 by 62 inches. The Detroit Institute of the Arts. Purchase, city appropriation.

century—a dance performed by couples who held both hands, turning about one another without letting go. These dances and many others were favorites at courts primarily because they were enjoyable to do—not because they performed a religious or practical function. Because the dances were also pleasurable to look at, it very quickly became a commonplace at court to have a group of onlookers as large as or larger than the group of dancers. Then it was not long before professional dancers came into demand for more significant court functions, such as the sixteenth-century masques, which were mixed-media entertainments in which the audience usually took some part—particularly in the dance sequences.

PERCEPTION KEY SOCIAL DANCE

1. How would you evaluate rock dancing? Why does rock dancing demand loud music? Does the performing and watching of spontaneous and powerful muscular motions account for some of the popularity of rock dancing? If so, why? Why do you think the older generations generally dislike both rock music and rock dancing? Is rock dancing primarily a mode to be watched or danced? Or is it both? Explain what the viewer and the dancer, respectively, might derive from the experience of rock dancing.
2. If you know any authentic folk dance, arrange a performance. How does the group that watched the performance regard the dance? Discuss the problems involved in doing the dance, and then discuss what might inhibit a full appreciation in viewing the dance.

Ballet

The origins of ballet usually are traced to the early seventeenth century, when dancers performed interludes between scenes of an opera. Eventually the interludes grew more and more important, until finally ballets were performed with no operatic accompaniment. In the eighteenth century, the *en pointe* technique was developed, with female dancers elevated on their toes to emphasize their airy, floating qualities. This has remained the technique to this day and is one of the important distinctions between ballet and modern dance, which avoids *en pointe* almost entirely.

Certain kinds of movements gradually began to be developed and taught for the ballet. Today there is virtually a vocabulary of movements that all ballet dancers must learn, since these movements constitute the structural details of every ballet. In this sense they are as important as the keys and scales in music, the vocabulary of tones constantly employed in musical composition. Figure 10-5 shows a number of the more important ballet positions. There are many more, but these are the basic ones with which we may begin.

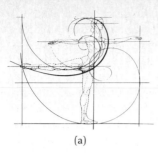

(a)

FIGURE 10-5   Drawings by Carlus Dyer of some important ballet positions. (a) The arabesque spiral. (b) Basic positions of the body. (c) Entrechat quatre. (d) Grand Plié.

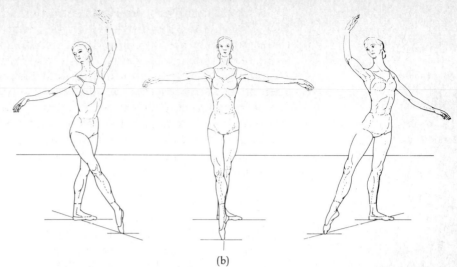

(b)

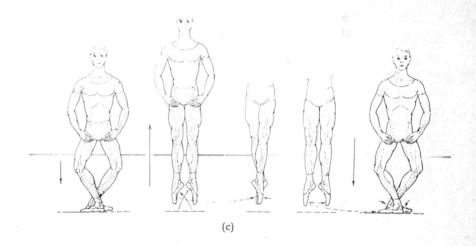

(c)

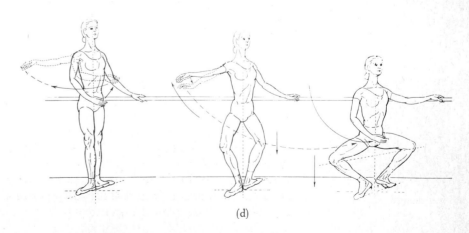

(d)

A considerable repertory of ballets has been built up in the last 270 years, with many more ballets lost to us entirely through the lack of an adequate system of notation with which to record them. The same was true of music until an adequate system of music notation was adopted. Today most dance is recorded on motion picture film or videotape, although there is a system—Labanotation—that can be used effectively by experts for recording a dance. Some of the ballets many of us are likely to see are Lully's *Giselle; Les Sylphides*, with music by Chopin; Tchaikovsky's *Nutcracker, Swan Lake*, and *Sleeping Beauty; Coppelia*, with music by Delibes; and *The Rites of Spring*, with Stravinsky's music.

All these ballets—like most ballets—have a program, which is often called the pretext. The pretext is a narrative line or story around which the ballet is built. In this sense, the ballet tells a story in the medium of bodily motion. The ballet has as its subject matter a story that is interpreted by means of stylized movements such as the arabesque, the bourrée, and the relévé—to name a scant few. Our understanding of the story line is basically conditioned by our perception of the movements that present the story to us. We have little else to respond to, except, perhaps, a printed statement of what the dance represents. It is astounding how, without having to be obvious and without having to resort very often to everyday gestures, ballet dancers can present a story line to us in an intelligible fashion. Yet it is not the story nor the performance of specific movements that constitutes the content of the dance; it is the meld of narrative and movement.

PERCEPTION KEY NARRATIVE AND BODILY MOVEMENT

1. Without training we cannot perform ballet movements, but all of us can perform *some* dance movements. By way of experiment and simply to increase understanding of the meld of narrative and bodily movement, try representing a narrative by bodily motion to a group of onlookers. Choose a narrative poem from our chapter on literature, or choose a scene from a play that may be familiar to you and your audience. Let your audience know the pretext you are using, since this is the normal method of most ballet. Avoid movements that rely exclusively on facial expressions or simple mime to communicate story elements. After your presentation, discuss with your audience their views about your success or failure in presenting the narrative. Discuss, too, your problems as dancer and what you felt you wanted your movement to reveal about the narrative. Have others perform the experiment, and discuss the same points.

2. Even the most rudimentary movement attempting to reveal a narrative will bring in interpretations that go beyond the narrative alone. As a viewer, discuss what you felt the other dancers added to the narrative.

Our understanding of what is going on before our eyes in ballet, as in opera, is often conditioned by our knowledge of the pretext or narrative line. Only when we have that knowledge can we be expected to be aware of the meld of narrative and movement that is crucial to ballet. Without that knowledge, our understanding of the dance is restricted to such things as observing the technical exactness of the execution of specific movements or the qualities of the succession of those movements abstracted from reference to specific objects and events. That kind of understanding, of course, has its rewards, as is obvious in the cases of abstract painting and sculpture, and music which has no program; but that kind of understanding is related to only a portion of the ballet's perceptible qualities.

SWAN LAKE

One of the most popular ballets of all time is Tchaikovsky's *Swan Lake (Le Lac des Cygnes)*, composed from 1871 to 1877 and first performed in 1894 (Act II) and 1895 (complete). The choreographers were Leon Ivanov and Marius Petipa, both significant in the history of ballet. Tchaikovsky originally composed the music for a ballet to be performed for children, but its fascination has not been restricted to young audiences. With Margot Fonteyn and Rudolf Nureyev the reigning dancers in this ballet in our time, *Swan Lake* has been a resounding popular favorite on television and film, not to mention repeated sellout performances in dance theaters the world over.

Since the chances of seeing a performance—live or on film or television—are good, we will offer a brief description of the dance, with a representative photograph (Figure 10-6), as a means of providing some access to the dance experience.

Act 1 opens with the principal male dancer, the young Prince Siegfried, attending a village celebration. His mother, the Queen, finding Siegfried sporting with the peasants, decides that it is time for him to marry someone of his own station and settle into the nobility. After she leaves, a pas de trois—a dance with three dancers, in this instance Siegfried and two maids—is interrupted by the prince's slightly drunk tutor, who tries to take part in some of the dancing but is not quite able. When a flight of swans is seen overhead, the prince resolves to go hunting.

The opening scene of Act 2 is on a moonlit lake, with the arch magician, Rothbart, tending his swans. The swans, led by Odette, are maidens he has enchanted. They can return to human form only at night. Odette's movements are imitated by the entire group of swans, movements that are clearly influenced by the motions of the swan's long neck and by the movements we associate with birds—for example, an undulating motion executed by the dancers' arms and a fluttering executed by the legs. Siegfried comes upon the swans and restrains his hunters from shooting at them. He falls in love with Odette, all of whose motions are characterized by the softness and grace of the swan. Siegfried learns that Odette is enchanted and that

FIGURE 10-6 Margot
Fonteyn and Rudolf
Nureyev in *Swan Lake*.
Dance Collection, New
York Public Library.

she cannot come to the ball at which the Queen has planned to arrange
the marriage of Siegfried. He also learns that if he vows his love to her
and keeps his vow, he can free her from the enchantment. She warns
him that Rothbart will do everything to trick him into breaking the
vow, but Siegfried is determined to be steadfast. As dawn arrives, the
lovers part and Rothbart retrieves his swans.

Act 3 commences with the ball the Queen has arranged for
presenting to Siegfried a group of princesses from whom he may
choose. Each princess, introduced in lavish native costume with a

retinue of dancers and retainers, dances the dance of her country, such as the allemande, the czardas, the tarantella. But suddenly Rothbart enters in disguise with his own daughter, Odile, who looks exactly like Odette. Today most performances require that Odette and Odile be the same dancer, although the parts were originally written for two dancers. Siegfried and Odile dance the famous Black Swan pas de deux, a dance that is notable for its virtuosity. It features almost superhuman leaps on the part of Siegfried, and it also involved thirty-two rapidly executed whipping turns (fouettés) on the part of Odile. Her movement is considerably different in character from that of Odette. Odile is more angular, less delicate, and in her black costume seems much less the picture of innocence Odette had seemed in her soft white costume. Siegfried's movements suggest enormous joy at having Odette, for he does not realize that this is really Odile, the magician's daughter.

When the time comes for Siegfried to choose among the princesses for his wife, he rejects them all and presents Odile to the Queen as his choice. Once Siegfried has committed himself to her, Rothbart exults and takes Odile from him and makes her vanish. Siegfried, who has broken his vow to Odette, realizes he has been duped and ends the act by rushing out to find the real Odette.

Like a number of other sections of the ballet, Act 4 has a variety of versions that interpret what is essentially similar action. Siegfried, in finding Odette by the lake at night, sacrifices himself for her and breaks the spell. They are joined in death and are beyond the power of the magician. Some versions of the ballet aim for a happy ending and suggest that though Siegfried sacrifices himself for Odette, he does not die. Through their sacrifice for one another and through their mutual love, Siegfried and Odette break the evil spell Rothbart has cast over them. In this happy-ending version, Odette, upon realizing that Siegfried had been tricked, forgives him. Rothbart raises a terrible storm in order to drown all the swans, but Siegfried carries Odette to a hilltop, where he is willing to die with her if necessary. This act of love and sacrifice breaks the spell and the two of them are together as dawn breaks.

In the version that does not specifically aim at a happy ending, Act 4 concentrates on spiritual victory and reward after death in a better life than that which was left behind. Odette and the swans dance slowly and sorrowfully together, with Odette rising in a stately fashion in their midst. When Siegfried comes, he begs her to forgive him, but nothing can break the magician's spell. Odette and he dance, they embrace, she bids him farewell and casts herself mournfully into the lake, where she perishes. Siegfried, unable to live without her, follows her into the lake. Then, once the lake vanishes, Odette and Siegfried are revealed in the distance, moving away together as evidence that the spell was broken in death.

The late John Cranko produced an even more tragic version with the Stuttgart Ballet. Siegfried is drowned in the rising of the lake—presented on stage most dramatically with long bolts of fabric undulating across the stage. Odette is whisked away by Rothbart and condemned to keep waiting for the hero who can be faithful to his vow. This version is particularly gloomy, since it reduces the heroic stature of Siegfried and renders his sacrifice useless. The hero who can rescue Odette will have to be virtually superhuman.

Clearly, the story of *Swan Lake* has archetypal overtones much in keeping with the Romantic age in which it was conceived. John Keats, who wrote fifty years before this ballet was created, was fascinated by the ancient stories of men who fell in love with supernatural spirits, which is what the swan-Odette is, once she has been transformed by magic. Likewise, the later Romantics were fascinated by the possibilities of magic and its implications for dealing with the forces of good and evil. In his *Blithedale Romance*, Nathaniel Hawthorne wrote about a hypnotist who wove a weird spell over a woman. The story of Svengali and his ward Trilby was popular everywhere, seemingly attesting to the fact that strange spells could be maintained over innocent people. This interest in magic and the supernatural is coupled with the Wagnerian interest in heroism and the implications of the sacrifice of the hero for the thing he loves. Much of the power of the idea of sacrifice derives from the sacrifice of Christ on the cross. But Tchaikovksy—like Wagner, whose hero in the *Ring of the Niebelungs* is also a Siegfried whose end with Brunnhilde is similar to the ending in *Swan Lake*—concentrates on the human valor of the prince and its implication for transforming the evil of this world into good.

PERCEPTION KEY SWAN LAKE

1. It may be possible for you to see a production on stage, television, or film of *Swan Lake*. If so, focus on a specific act and comment in a discussion with others on the suitability of the bodily movements for the narrative subject matter of the act.
2. If you cannot see the ballet, phonograph records are easily available; and you should be able to comment on the possibilities for movements that would be effective for specific portions of the dance. For instance, how should Odette and the swans move at the opening of Act 4? How should Siegfried move in his last pas de deux in the same act?
3. Whether or not you have a chance to see the ballet, try to move in such a way as to present your interpretation of a specific moment in the ballet. You might try something as simple as Odette fluttering with the swans in Act 2 or as complicated as Siegfried or Odette casting himself or herself into the lake in Act 4.
4. If someone who has had training in ballet is available, you might try to get him or her to present a small portion of the ballet for your observation and discussion. What would be the most important kinds of questions to ask such a person? This could be the subject of valuable research.

Modern Dance

The origins of modern dance are usually traced to the American dancers Isadora Duncan and Ruth St. Denis. These women rebelled against the stylization of ballet, with ballerinas dancing on their toes and executing the same basic movements in every performance. Isadora Duncan insisted on natural movement, often dancing in bare feet with gossamer drapery that showed her body and legs in motion. She felt that the emphasis ballet places on the movement of the arms and legs was wrong. Her insistence on placing the center of motion at the solar plexus—just below the breastbone—was based on her feeling that the torso had been neglected in the development of ballet. She felt, too, that the early Greek dancers, whom she wished to emulate, had placed their center of energy at the solar plexus. Her intentions were to return to natural movement in dance, and this was one effective method of doing so.

The developers of modern dance who followed Isadora Duncan (she died in 1927) built on her legacy. In her insistence on freedom with respect to clothes and conventions, she infused energy into the dance that no one had ever seen before. Although she was a native Californian, her successes and triumphs were primarily in foreign lands, particularly in France and Russia. Her performances differed greatly from the ballet. Instead of developing a dance built on a pretext of the sort that underlies *Swan Lake*, Duncan took more abstract subject matters—especially moods—and expressed her understanding of them in dance. Her dances were lyrical, personal, and occasionally extemporaneous. Her movements were not stylized, as in ballet, nor were they always predictable. Since she insisted that there were no angular shapes in nature, she would permit herself to use none. Her movements tended to be ongoing and rarely came to a complete rest. An interesting example of her dance, one in which she does come to a full rest, is recounted by a friend. It was performed in a salon for close friends, and its subject matter seems to be human emergence on the planet:

> Isadora was completely covered by a long loose robe with high draped neck and long loose sleeves in a deep muted red. She crouched on the floor with her face resting on the carpet. In slow motion with ineffable effort she managed to get up on her knees. Gradually with titanic struggles she rose to her feet. She raised her arms toward heaven in a gesture of praise and exultation. The mortal had emerged from primeval ooze to achieve Man, upright, liberated, and triumphant.[1]

Figure 10-7 shows Duncan in *La Marseillaise*.

[1]From Kathleen Cannell, "Isadorable Duncan," *Christian Science Monitor*, December 4, 1970. Reprinted by permission from The Christian Science Monitor. © 1970 The Christian Science Publishing Society. All rights reserved.

FIGURE 10-7   Isadora Duncan in *La Marseillaise*. Dance Collection, New York Public Library.

Martha Graham, José Limón, Doris Humphrey, and other innovators who followed Isadora developed modern dance in a variety of directions. Graham, who was also interested in Greek origins, created some dances on themes of Greek tragedies, such as her *Medea*. In addition to his *Moor's Pavane*, Limón is well known for his interpretation of Eugene O'Neill's play *The Emperor Jones*, in which a black slave escapes to an island only to become a despised and hunted tyrant. These approaches are somewhat of a departure from Duncan, as they tend to introduce the balletic pretext into modern dance. Humphrey, who was a little older than Graham and Limón, was closer to the original Duncan tradition in such dances as *Water Study*, *Life of the Bee*, and *New Dance*, a 1930s piece that was successfully revived in 1972.

Modern dance can be any one or all of these approaches simultaneously. Today's more innovative dancers, like Twyla Tharp and Meredith Monk, sometimes shock and surprise audiences with dances that often seem to have only bodily motion as their subject matter. Such dances have no recognizable pretext or any recognizable "official dance movements." Both Tharp and Monk are experimenting with abstract movement—as did Duncan—that is not always thought of as appropriate to the dance. However, Monk's ten- or fifteen-acre large-scale panoramic dance entitled *Needle Brain Lloyd and the Systems Kid* (Figure 10-8) does have a general pretext—the settling of America.

FIGURE 10-8   Meredith Monk's *Needle-Brain Lloyd and the Systems Kid*. Photograph by Peter Moore.

Dancers enter rowing a boat across a lake, haul the boat out, turn it upside down, and sit in front of it for the entirety of the dance. Meanwhile others dancers play croquet, pitch tents, ride horses and motorcycles, and perform innumerable other movements. Isadora's legacy to modern dance is freedom of imagination and invention. Today's dancers have clearly accepted that legacy, and today's modern dance can be virtually anything a choreographer can imagine.

PERCEPTION KEY PRETEXT AND MOVEMENT

1. Try a half-minute experiment. Devise a series of movements that will take about thirty seconds to complete and that you are fairly sure do not tell a story. Then "perform" these movements for a group and question them on what they think the pretext of your movement is. Do not tell them in advance that your dance has no story. As a result of this experiment, you might ask yourself and the group whether it is possible to create a sequence of movements that will not suggest a story line to some viewers. What would this mean for dances which try to avoid pretexts? Can they?
2. Without explaining that you are not dancing, represent a familiar human situation to a group by using movements that you believe are not dance movements. Is the group able to understand what you represented? Do they think you were using dance movements? Do you believe it possible to have movements that cannot be included in a dance? Are there, in other words, nondance movements?

ALVIN AILEY'S *REVELATIONS*

One of the classics of modern dance is Alvin Ailey's *Revelations* (Figure 10-9), based largely on black American spirituals and the black American experience. It was first performed in January 1960, and hardly a year has gone by without its having been performed to highly enthusiastic crowds. Ailey, who no longer dances but choreographs for the New York City Center Ballet—as well as for his own company—has refined *Revelations* somewhat over the years, but its basic impact has remained. Favorable response to this dance was heightened considerably in its early years by the presence of Judith Jamison, a striking dancer who took the lead role. But even in her absence it has retained its power to bring audiences to their feet for standing ovations at almost every performance.

Some of the success of *Revelations* stems from Ailey's choice of the deeply felt music of the black spirituals to which the dancer's movements are closely attuned. But, then, this is also one of the most noted qualities of a ballet like *Swan Lake*, which is said to have the richest orchestral score of any ballet. Music, unless it is program music, may not correctly be thought of as a pretext for a dance, but there is certainly a perceptible connection between, say, the rhythmic

FIGURE 10-9   The Alvin Ailey City Center Dance Theater, New York. *Revelations*, "Wading in the Water," with Judith Jamison. Photograph by Fred Fehl.

qualities of a given music and a dance that might be composed in such a way as to take advantage of those qualities. Thus, in *Revelations* the energetic movements of the dancers often appear as visual, bodily transformations of the rhythmically charged music.

Although it is not possible to describe the entire dance in these pages, we will try to point out certain general qualities of which an awareness—should there be a chance to see this dance in actual performance or on film—may prove useful for refining one's experience of modern dance in general. *Revelations* has a general pretext—that of black experience as related by the spirituals—and each of its separate sections has its own pretext. But no pretext is as tightly or specifically narrative as is usually the case in ballet. It is usually the generalized situation that acts as pretext.

The first section of the dance is called "Pilgrim of Sorrow," with three parts: "I Been Buked," danced by the entire company (about twenty dancers, male and female); "Didn't My Lord Deliver Daniel," danced by only a few dancers; and "Fix Me Jesus," danced by one couple. The general pretext is the suffering of blacks at the hands of their tormentors, like the Israelites of the Old Testament, but taking refuge in their faith in the Lord. The most dramatic moments in this section are in "Didn't My Lord Deliver Daniel," a statement of overwhelming faith characterized by close ensemble work. The inline dancers parallel the rhythms of the last word of the hymn: "Daṅ-i-eĺ," accenting the first and last syllables with powerful rhythmic movements.

The second section, titled "Take Me to the Water," is divided into "Processional," danced by eight dancers; "Wading in the Water," danced by six dancers; and "I Want to Be Ready," danced by a single male dancer. The whole idea of "Take Me to the Water" is centered on the concept of baptism, linking the dancers with the Baptist faith and asserting the faith in God that characterizes the source of energy of the black spirituals. "Wading in the Water" is particularly exciting, with dancers holding a stage-long bolt of light-colored fabric to represent the water. The dancers shimmer the fabric to the rhythm of the music and one dancer after another crosses over the fabric, which symbolizes at least two things: the waters of baptism and the Mosaic waters of freedom. It is this episode that featured Judith Jamison in a long white gown holding a huge parasol as she danced (Figure 10-9).

The third section is called "Move, Members, Move," with the episodes titled "Sinner Man," "The Day Is Past and Gone," "You May Run Home," and the finale, "Rocka My Soul in the Bosom of Abraham." In this last episode a sense of triumph over suffering is projected, suggesting the redemption of a people by using the same kind of Old Testament imagery and musical material that opened the dance. The entire section takes as its theme the life of people after they have been received into the faith, with the possibilities of straying into sin. It ends with a powerful rocking spiritual that emphasizes forgiveness and the reception of the people (the "members") into the bosom of Abraham, according to the Bible's prediction. This ending again features an enormous amount of ensemble work and is danced by the entire company, with rows of male dancers sliding forward on their outspread knees and then rising all in one sliding gesture, raising their hands high. "Rocka My Soul in the Bosom of Abraham" is powerfully sung again and again until the effect is almost hypnotically religious in its force.

Such a dance as *Revelations* has at times been criticized as being somewhat slick, somewhat reminiscent of show dance more than of serious modern dance. But for all that negative criticism, there has been much praise. The public—even the public that has little or no dance experience—has always loved it.

The subject matter of *Revelations* is in part that of powerful movement, with remarkable ensemble and solo sections. But it is also more obviously that of the struggle of a people as told—on one level—by their music. The dance has the advantage of a powerfully engaging subject matter even before we witness the transmutation of that subject matter. And the way in which the movements of the dance are closely attuned to the "movement" or rhythm of the music tends to give most viewers a very intense participation, since the visual qualities of the dance are so powerfully reinforced by the aural qualities of the music. Not all modern dance is characterized by this, although it is true that most show dance and most dance in filmed musicals encourages a similar closeness of music and movement.

PERCEPTION KEY ALVIN AILEY'S *REVELATIONS*

1. A profitable way of understanding the resources of *Revelations* is to take a well-known black spiritual like "Swing Low, Sweet Chariot," part of which appears on page 309, and supply the movements that it suggests to you. Once you have done so, ask yourself how difficult it was. Is it natural to move to such music?
2. Instead of spirituals, try the same experiment with popular music such as rock that you believe definitely stimulates motion. Can you comment on the kinds of music that do this? What characteristics does such music seem to have that stimulate motion?

MARTHA GRAHAM

Quite different from the Ailey approach, and probably much more influential for the history of dance in modern times, is the so-called "Graham technique," taught in Martha Graham's own school in New York as well as in colleges and universities across the country. Like Ailey, Graham was a virtuoso dancer—she has only recently retired from dancing—and has become better and better known as her company, for which she constructs her dances, has appeared in America and abroad. After Isadora Duncan, Graham must be counted the most powerful influence in modern dance. Today there is a certain amount of rebellion against her technique, as is natural for any powerful influence, but an understanding of the rebellion depends on an understanding of what is being rebelled against.

Graham technique is reminiscent of ballet in its rigor. Dancers learn specific kinds of movements and exercises designed to be used both as preparation for and part of the dance. Graham's contraction, for example, is one of the commonest movements one is likely to see. It is the sudden contraction of the diaphragm with the resultant relaxation of the rest of the body. This builds on Duncan's emphasis on the solar plexus but adds to that concept the natural systolic and diastolic rhythms of heartbeat and pulse. The movement is very effective visually as well as being particularly flexible in depicting feelings. Further, it is a movement unknown in ballet, from which Graham has always wished to remain distinct.

At times Graham's dances have been very literal, with narrative pretexts quite similar to those found in ballet. *Night Journey*, for instance, is an interpretation of *Oedipus Rex* by Sophocles. The lines of emotional force linking Jocasta and her son-husband, Oedipus, are powerfully accentuated by the movements of the dance as well as by

FIGURE 10-10   Martha Graham's *Phaedra*. Photograph by Martha Swope.

certain props on stage, such as ribbons that link the two together at times. In Graham's interpretation, Jocasta becomes much more important than she is in the original drama. This is partly because Graham saw the female figures in Greek drama—such as Phaedra (Figure 10-10)—as much more fully dimensional than we have normally understood them. By means of dancing their roles, she was able to develop complexities in their character. In dances like her *Lamentation*, Graham has experimented with more abstract subject matters such as states of mind. For example, *El Penitente*, which features a male dancer in loose white trousers and tunic moving in slow circles about the stage with a large wooden cross, is a powerful interpretation of penitence.

ALWIN NIKOLAIS DANCE THEATER

The work of Alwin Nikolais is another important influence on modern dance. For several decades Nikolais has been experimenting with a total dance theater that is an assault on all the senses he can reach. He avoids narrative pretexts for his dance, just as he seems to avoid pretexts that refer to states of mind or emotional situations. He uses challenging music of the ultramodern sort, light shows of the kind that used to be popular at rock concerts, and costumes of a kind that would make most futuristic movies look like antiques. Yet he puts all these ingredients together, with imaginative movements that other choreographers and dancers can rarely copy, into an event that delights those with little as well as those with great experience in dance.

Nikolais often gets his inspirations from the natural world—sometimes from the world of insects. Although insects such as butterflies, caterpillars, and crickets have inspired many dancers, few dancers have been attracted, as Nikolais has, to praying mantises. One of his dances, *Imago* (Figure 10-11), employs odd headpieces and mantis-like extensions on hands and feet to achieve an extraordinary suggestiveness of insect life. It is not always clear that this is the subject matter of the dance, since it seems that the abstract movements suggested to Nikolais by his examination of the mantis are what interest him most and what attract our attention. However, there is one section, called "Mantis," which suggests that Nikolais is exploring a literal representation. Normally, however, Nikolais' dances are as abstracted from specific objects and events as he can make them. He has been criticized for this as well as for being too technological, thus losing the human qualities dance should have. But these seem cavils

FIGURE 10-11 Alwin Nikolais' *Imago.* Chimera photo.

when one is in the presence of dances such as *Masks, Props and Mobiles*, which has been produced at the amphitheater in Delphi, Greece, and *Vaudeville of the Elements and Scenario*. Light, props, and movement in conjunction with sound are handled with great sensitivity and a marvelous sense of humor. His influence is likely to remain despite his critics.

TWYLA THARP

One of the strongest new choreographers, Twyla Tharp has developed a style pleasing to both serious critics and dance amateurs alike. A thoughtful student of dance aesthetics, she has been able to include a sense of playfulness that seems appropriately modern and psychologically correct in her dances. She has also taken advantage of the new opportunities for dance on television, particularly the Public Broadcasting Corporation's "Dance in America" series, which has been enormously popular and critically successful. She has been particularly successful in adapting black jazz of the 1920s and 1930s to dance, for example, "Sue's Leg" featuring the music of "Fats" Waller (Figure 10-12). For television production, she used cuts from newsreel films along with her dancers' interpretations of 1930s dances. "Bix Pieces" was inspired by the white cornetist, Bix Beiderbecke, the first romantic, self-destructive young man with a horn. "Eight Jelly Rolls,"

FIGURE 10-12 *Sue's Leg*. Choreography, Twyla Tharp; costumes, Santo Loquasto; lighting, Jennifer Tipton; dancers (l. to r.) Tom Rawe, Twyla Tharp, Rose Marie Wright, Kenneth Rinker. Photograph by Tom Berthiaume.

premiered in 1971, and also televised, is a brilliant series of interpretations of eight songs written by the legendary Jelly Roll Morton, who claimed to have invented jazz. Tharp's interest in sequential dances—"Ocean's Motion," a suite of dances to the music of Chuck Berry; "Raggedy Dances," to ragtime tunes; and "Assorted Quartets," to classical music—shows a virtuoso ability to explore the feeling states engendered by movement in connection with stimulating music.

Television has also attracted Mikhail Baryshnikov, Rudolf Nureyev, Dan Wagoner Dance Company, and the remarkable gymnastic dance group, Pilobolus. The Pilobolus Company evolved from a gymnastics and dance group that began informally among undergraduates at Dartmouth College. Its most interesting innovations involve the articulation of interwoven bodies whose shapes sometimes resemble forms in nature. The future of modern dance in America is probably closely related to America's appetite for dance as it has been stimulated by television.

Summary

The variety of dance available for us in theaters, television, and films is overwhelming. For many, it can be baffling to see people in motion interpreting a pretext we know nothing about. For others, it will be distracting to think about the pretext when it is the movement itself that is most interesting. But for most of us, one hopes, there will be a happy melding of both.

What is important to keep in mind is the fact that dance has the capacity to transform a pretext, whether the pretext is a story or a state of mind or a feeling. Our attention must be drawn into participation with this transformation. The insight we get from the dance experience is dependent on our awareness of this transformation. The first step to the achievement of such revelation is that of perceiving the nature of movement in the dance and the narrative or other subject matter on which it is predicated. Once that perception is achieved, understanding grows and our participation with the work deepens.

Chapter 10 Bibliography

Cohen, Selma Jean, ed. *The Modern Dance*. Middletown, Conn.: Wesleyan University Press, 1965.

———. *Doris Humphrey: An Artist First*. Middletown, Conn.: Wesleyan University Press, 1972.

———. *Dance as a Theatre Art*. New York: Dodd Mead, 1974.

DeMille, Agnes. *Dance to the Piper*. Boston: Houghton Mifflin, 1952.

Duncan, Isadora. *My Life*. New York: Liveright, 1927.

Friedman, James Michael. *Dancer and Spectator: An Aesthetic Distance*. San Francisco: Balletmonographs, 1976.

Horst, Louis. *Modern Dance Forms in Relation to the Other Modern Arts.* New York: Dance Horizons, 1961.

Humphrey, Doris. *The Art of Making Dances,* ed. Barbara Pollack. New York: Grove Press, 1959.

Kirstein, Lincoln et al. *The Classic Ballet.* New York: Knopf, 1969.

McDonagh, Don. *The Rise and Fall and Rise of Modern Dance.* New York: New American Library, 1970.

Migel, Parmenia. *The Ballerinas.* New York: MacMillan, 1972.

Nadel, Myron and Constance Miller, eds. *The Dance Experience.* New York: Universe Books, 1978.

Percival, John. *Modern Ballet.* New York: Dutton, 1970.

Sorell, Walter. *The Dance Through the Ages.* New York: Grossett & Dunlap, 1967.

NOTE: *Dance Films Catalogue* (Sara Menke, 5746 Gabbert Road, Moorpark, CA. 93021) and *Index to 16mm Educational Films* (New York: McGraw-Hill, 1967) list dance films and sources. For *Dance in America* and other series, contact the local PBS TV Station or PBS in Washington, DC. Check *Dance Magazine* (September 1965 and April 1969) 10 Columbus Circle, New York, NY 10019. Also distributors such as Harris Communications, 45 East 66th Street, New York, NY 10021; Encyclopedia Britannica Films, 1150 Wilmette Avenue, Wilmette, IL 60091; Audio Films, 406 Clement Street, San Francisco, CA 94118; and Museum of Modern Art, Dept. of Film, 11 West 53rd Street, New York, NY 10019, all supply dance films.

THE FILM

11 The film more than any of the other arts involves collaborative effort. Most films begin with a script and are planned by a director. Ordinarily, the director does not also claim authorship of the script, although it is common for the director to add dialogue and make many changes. However, even if the director is also the scriptwriter, the film needs camera operators, an editor, artistic designers, researchers, and actors—to name only some of the most important people. Together they create the film. *Auteur* criticism urges us to consider the director as equivalent to the *auteur*, or author, of the film. For the popular moviegoer, the central figure or figures in the film will almost surely not be the director, but the star or stars who appear in the film. Colleen Dewhurst, Robert Redford, Jason Robards, Al Pacino, and Marlon Brando will be more likely to be well regarded by the general audience than will such directors of stature as Woody Allen, Federico Fellini, John Ford, or Lina Wertmüller. Nonetheless, we will adhere to the current view that accepts the director as the film's *auteur*, while noting at the same time the essential importance of all the other people who contribute to the artistic achievement of the film.

Even in the days before the separable functions of director, editor, and camera technician were as clearly understood as they are today, the artistic complexity of the film was intensified by its indebtedness to other media, such as the stage play or vaudeville performance. In the early days of film several giants rose in the industry, both before the cameras, such as Charlie Chaplin and Buster Keaton, and behind them, such as D. W. Griffith and Serge Eisenstein, and they struggled to bring the medium closer to what they realized it could be. They fought the early tendency to make each film a record of a performance on the dramatic stage, or in the style of the dramatic stage, with the words often printed out and shown on the screen in brief interrupting moments. In this subservience to another medium, the resources of the motion picture were not fully exploited. This is occasionally true even today, although not so much as in the earliest phases of film's development.

Another popular early use of motion pictures was for recording magic tricks that could not be realized on an open stage. George Meliés, a French student of the magician Houdini, made a number of films, often in double-exposure situations in which he would be looking at himself. In the silent film, Mary Pickford followed his tradition by creating a number of illusions that still baffle film makers. Other favorite subjects were parades, cavalry charges, dances, and rudimentary travelogues. The motion picture often did little more than duplicate situations that, except in the case of the magicians, could be witnessed in another place at another time.

Griffith and Eisenstein

D. W. Griffith and Serge Eisenstein are unquestionably the great early geniuses of film making. They managed to gain enough control over the production of their works so that they could craft their films into a distinctive rather than a subservient medium. Some of their films are still considered among the finest ever made: *Birth of a Nation* (1916) and *Intolerance* (1918) by Griffith, and *Potemkin* (1925) and *Ivan the Terrible* (1941–1946) by Eisenstein are still being shown and are still influencing contemporary film makers. These men were more than just directors. With many of their films they felt responsible for almost everything: casting, choosing locations, handling the camera, directing, and editing.

Directing and Editing

Directing and editing are probably the most crucial phases of film making. Directors control the acting, and supervise the photography, carried out by skilled technicians who worry about such problems as lighting, camera angles and focusing, as well as the motion of the camera itself (some sequences are shot with a highly mobile camera, while others are shot with a fixed camera). The editor, usually assisted by the director, orders the images or frames after the photography is finished. Pieces of film that represent sequences sometimes shot far apart in time and place are organized into a unity, more or less. The film is usually not shot sequentially, and usually only a small part of the total footage shot is ever shown in a film. The old saying of the bit-part actor—"I was lost on the cutting-room floor"—attests the fact that much footage that was thought of as possibly useful winds up being omitted from a film once the final decisions about editing are made.

The Participative Experience and Film

The question of participation with the film is complex. For one thing, most of us know exactly what it means to lose our sense of place and time in a movie. This loss seems to be achieved rapidly in all but the most awkwardly conceived films. In a film like *Black Orpheus* (1958), shot in Rio, the intensity of tropical colors, Latin American music, and the dynamics of the carnival produce an imaginary reality so intense and vital that actual reality seems dull by comparison. But then there are other films that create the illusion of life itself. Aristotle talked about the ways in which drama imitates life and the ways in which an audience identifies with some of the actors on the stage. Yet the film seems to have these powers to an even greater degree than the stage. See our discussion of Aristotle's *mimesis* in Chapter 8.

PERCEPTION KEY FILM, DRAMA, TELEVISION, AND PARTICIPATION

1. Observe people coming out of a movie theater. Can you usually tell by their behavior whether the film was comic, tragic, melodramatic, a western, etc.? Can you do this as easily with people coming from a drama theater? Or from watching a film on television?
2. Does it make a significant difference whether you experience a film in an empty or a packed theater? Compare your experience of a play in a theater. Have you ever experienced, for instance, a comedy performed in a large theater with only a few people present, and did this have anything to do with your sense of the comic? Is laughter somehow enhanced in a crowd? Yet is the humor of a comic film significantly depressed if you see it alone?
3. Are you as explicitly aware of your spatial location in a film theater as in a drama theater? Does the fact that dramas are usually presented discontinuously—that is, with breaks between acts—make you more aware of your place in a theater? Are you more conscious of other people in the audience when you are experiencing a film or a drama? Why?
4. Compare your experiences of the same film in the theater and on television. Which presentation engages your participation more intensely? Is the difference in the sizes of the screens mainly responsible for any difference in the intensity of participation? Or is it, perhaps, the stronger

darkness that surrounds you in the theater? Or the commercial breaks that accompany most television presentations? What other factors might be involved?

5. Do you think it would be easier to make a television film or a theater film? What would be the basic differences?

6. What kinds of theater film are most adaptable for television? Conversely, what kinds of television film are most adaptable for theater showing? Or are there really no significant differences between the moving images made for the theater as distinct from television?

7. Compare your experience of a drama performed on the stage with your experience of a film version of the same drama made for television. What, if anything, is lost or gained in filming? Make the same comparisons for the dance.

Because of its realism participating with a film can become the chief artistic criterion we apply to our experiences of the film. We are all familiar with the details of realism—they permeate our lives—and we are quick to respond to any appeal made directly to our images of ourselves and others. For instance, in *The Hustler* (1961), Paul Newman plays a character who represents so many young people in the film's audience that it is not difficult to see why the film had a wide appeal. The audience of would-be "comers" sympathizes with the young hustler, "Fast Eddie" Felsen, and sides with him—*becomes* him in crucial moments of the film. They share his respect and awe of Minnesota Fats, played by Jackie Gleason, and his distaste for the mere gambler-banker, played by George C. Scott. The makers of movies are keenly aware of that kind of response and often play for it because it is an easy way to assure themselves of success. The plot of *The Hustler* is a remake of countless westerns where the young fast gun in town measures off against the legendary old fast gun. Possibly, even deeper, it is a remake of the young man's basic psychological masculine need to prove his sexual potency—which might explain the improbable love interests in these films. Most young men share that need and tend to see themselves as the chief characters in films like *The Hustler*. The same situation exists in another Paul Newman film, *The Sting* (1975), one of the most commercially successful films of all time. In that film, two appealing con men, Paul Newman and Robert Redford, put the con on the underworld and get away with it. The circumstances are appealing, the dramatic situation is probably similar to fantasies many individuals have had, and the film invites identification with its heroes. Even the enormously popular *Rocky* (1976), starring Sylvester Stallone as a would-be heavyweight fighter making a comeback to dignity, is an example of the genre. Many people identified with Rocky, adopting his name or theme song. *Rocky* was a psychological success because it invited a special kind of personal fantasizing.

But there are problems with that loss of self which is, in fact, nothing but a veiled appeal to the worship of self. Film can inform us about ourselves, or it can cause a kind of short circuit in which we do not become informed: we simply indulge in hero worship with ourselves as the hero. The other arts may also cause this short circuit, of course, but the temptation is the greatest, perhaps, with film.

There are two kinds of participative experiences in film. One is not principally filmic in nature and is represented by a kind of self-indulgence that depends upon self-justifying fantasies. The other is more specifically caused by the artfulness of the entire film and is unrelated to self-indulgence. It is the feeling of being removed from self-awareness, of being a part of the medium of moving images, whether it is a case of narrative action or simply the dynamism of images and sound. This second kind of participative experience means much more to us ultimately because it is significantly informative.

Just a word more about the first kind of participation. It is usually referred to as "escapism." "Escape" films give us the chance to see ourselves complimented in a movie, thus satisfying our desire for self-importance. Unhappily, escape films often help us avoid doing anything about achieving something that would *really* make us more important to ourselves. In some ways these films rob people of the chance to be something in their own right. Most television depends on this effect for its success. Maybe it is even true that large masses of people need this kind of entertainment in order to avoid the despair that would set in if they had to face up to the reality of their lives. It may be cynical to think so, yet it is strongly possible that many people who make motion pictures feel this to be a justification of what they are doing.

The fact that film may cause such an intense sense of participation of the wrong kind deadens our perception of the content of the film. We can see a film and know nothing about the finer points of its form and meaning—the nuances that make a film worth experiencing and then pondering over because of its impact on us. As in any medium, there are many mediocre examples of film making that are hardly worth seeing more than once (or *even* once), while there are others that are rightly called classics because of their lasting qualities, their formal excellence, and their humanizing achievement. We want to get a sense of how one appreciates what a film can really achieve as it aspires to being a classic.

Questions of criticism, as we hope we established in Chapter 3, are always implicitly operative when we view a film or any work of art. We want to ensure that our critical faculties will be engaged in heightening our awareness of what the film actually achieves. We are interested in what we do observe in relation to what we can observe. The main purpose of this chapter is to help us be conscious of those qualities that make a film interesting and effective. They are qualities that, for the viewer who has not developed filmic awareness, might not be noticeable at all.

The Moving Image

The starting point in the film is photography, and it is the photography of the image in motion, not the posed or poised image at rest as in still photography. Just as the basically static visual images of still photographs and paintings can move us profoundly by their organization of visual experience, so can the basically dynamic images of film. Indeed, many experts insist that no artistic medium ever created has the power to move us as deeply as the medium of moving images. They base their claim not just on the mass audiences who have been profoundly moved but also on the fact that the moving images of the film are very close to the moving images we perceive in life. We rarely perceive static images except when viewing such things as paintings or photographs. Watching a film closely can help us perceive much more intensely the visual worth of many of the images we experience outside film.

Let us begin with that aspect of the image that is not specifically motion. Many early film makers composed their films by adding single photographs to each other, frame by frame. Movement in motion pictures is caused by the eye's physiological limitations. It cannot perceive the black line between frames when the film strip is moved at a specific speed. All it sees is the succession of frames minus the lines that divide them. The reason the eye is capable of this phenomenon is that it cannot perceive separate images or frames that move faster than $\frac{1}{30}$ second. This is to use the "language" of the camera itself, which can take a picture in much less time than that. Motion picture film is usually projected at a speed of twenty-four frames per second; the persistence of vision merges the images.

Because of this, many film makers, both early and contemporary, attempt to "design" each individual frame as carefully as they might a still photograph. See "Pictorialism" in Chapter 12 (p. 427). Jean Renoir, the famous French film maker, sometimes composed each frame almost like an impressionist painting, as in *The Grand Illusion.* Eisenstein also carefully framed many of his images, notably in *Potemkin.* David Lean, who directed *Bridge Over the River Kwai* (1957), *Lawrence of Arabia* (1962), *Dr. Zhivago* (1965), and *Ryan's Daughter* (1970), also pays very close attention to the composition of individual frames. The effect of this can be powerful, but it is not necessarily the best or the only way to make a strong film. Consider the stills that are reproduced with this chapter for their power as fixed compositions: you will see that many of them are not striking by themselves. Some stills, even from the greatest films, are really not effective except in the context of motion. Thus, the flawlessly composed still image may not be really exploiting the full advantage of the film medium. Evaluate the stills shown in Figures 11-1, 11-2, and 11-3 from the point of view of their composition, and then try to imagine whether their effectiveness would be enhanced in a sequence of motion. All are from remarkable films.

FIGURE 11-1   From Jean Renoir's *Grand Illusion* with Erich von Stroheim, Jean Gabin, and Marcel Dalio. A Continental Distributing, Inc. release.

FIGURE 11-2   From Ingmar Bergman's *Seventh Seal*. Photograph From Janus Films, Inc.

FIGURE 11-3 From *Easy Rider.* Wyatt (Peter Fonda), Stranger (Luke Askew), and Billy (Dennis Hopper) arrive at the commune. Copyright © 1969 by Columbia Pictures. Permission to reproduce this photograph furnished by Columbia Pictures Industries, Inc. All rights reserved.

For some directors, the still moments of the film must be as exactly composed as a painting. The theory is that if the individual moments of the film are each as perfect as can be, then the total film will be a cumulative perfection. This seems to be the case for many films, but it is not so for all. In those films that have long meditative sequences, such as Bergman's *Cries and Whispers* (1972), Orson Welles' *Citizen Kane* (1941, Figure 11-4), or sequences in which characters or images are relatively unmoving for significant periods of time, the carefully composed and formally exciting still image will be of real significance. However, most stills from exciting films will reveal very little of the real power of the entire film all by themselves: it is their sequential movement that brings out their effectiveness.

Paying careful attention to the composition of each frame, nevertheless, may pay off. It may not be essential to do what Josef von Sternberg and Howard Hawks (two directors who paid exceptionally close attention to the still moments of their film) do—that is, retouch frames or carefully adjust the lighting to get the most out of a given composition. But usually some attention to the frames is helpful. Some directors adjust the focus of their lenses so that the composition is seen first with the foreground in focus, then with the background in focus and the foreground out of focus, as in the visually rich *Barry Lyndon* (1975). This can be an effective way of shifting our attention in a static scene without having to move the camera or the actors.

FIGURE 11-4   From *Citizen Kane* (1941) with Orson Welles and Dorothy Comingore.

However it is a technique that, like so many others, is best used in moderation.

From all this, you can see the motion in the motion picture can come from numerous sources. The actors or the subjects can themselves move toward, away from, or across the field of camera vision. When something moves toward the camera it moves with astonishing speed, as we all know from sitting still while the images of a moving locomotive (the favorite vehicle for this technique so far) rush at us and then catapult "over our heads." The effect of the catapult is important because it is characteristic of the film medium and is not quite so characteristic of a real-life situation. When runners approach the camera, they, too, will seem to catapult into motion the closer they get to the focal plane of the film in the camera; runners approaching you in life do not have the same effect because you are not watching them on a flat screen.

We are used to seeing people move before us the way they move before the camera, but the camera (or cameras) can achieve visual things that our unaided eye cannot: showing the same moving action from a number of points of view, for instance, or showing it from a camera angle the eye cannot achieve. The realistic qualities of a film can be threatened, however, by being too sensational, with a profusion of angle shots and views that would be impossible in a real-life situation. Although such virtuoso effects can dazzle us at first, the feeling of being dazzled can degenerate into being dazed.

Another way the film achieves motion is by the movement of the camera itself. In the 1961 John Huston film *The Misfits*, about cowboys rounding up wild mustang horses to sell for dog food, some amazing chase scenes are filmed with the camera mounted on a pickup truck chasing fast-running horses. The motion itself in the round-up scenes is almost overwhelming because Huston combines two kinds of rapid motion—of trucks and horses. Moreover, the motion of these scenes is further increased because of the limiting focus of the camera. Only the camera records the action. Thus, one has the unmistakable feeling that the action, even in that expansive film, is enclosed, that the boundary of the screen on which we see the action excludes vision that might tend to distract or dilute the motion we are permitted to see. The screen in motion pictures always constrains us, always controls our attention, even when we imagine the space beyond the screen that we do not perceive, as in instances in which a character moves off the filmed space. By eliminating the space beyond the images recorded by the camera, by refusing to permit our eye to be distracted by anything not of immediate importance to the action we see, the camera causes our attention to focus sharply and fix. And such attention is bound to enhance the visual qualities, such as the motion of the moving images.

PERCEPTION KEY CAMERA VISION

Make a mask with two oblong rectangles, approximagely ⅜ inch long by ½ inch wide, as shown:

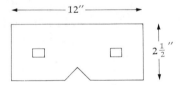

Place the mask so that you can see only out of the slits. This experiment can be conducted almost as effectively by using simple pinholes in place of cutout rectangles. In fact, for those who wear glasses it may be more effective, because the pinholes are actually "lenses" and may permit some people with defective vision to see fairly clearly without their glasses.

1. Does the "framing" with the mask or the pinholes make you unusually sensitive to the way things look?
2. What effect does moving your head have on the composition of the things you see?
3. What are some of the differences between using one eye, then both eyes? Which makes you think more of the camera's way of looking?

4. What do you learn from viewing a scene first with one eye, then the other?
5. One very important feature of this experiment, which ought to be considered, is the analogy with the motion of the camera itself. Be sure that you get a sense of what happens to your visual planes when you move your head in the fashion a camera would move. Moreover, try to consider what kinds of motion you are capable of that the camera does not seem capable of. Are there any?
6. If the camera is the principal tool of the craft of film making, do directors give up artistic control when they have photographers operate the machines for them? Does your experimenting in the questions above suggest there may be a "camera language" that directors should be controlling themselves? Given your experience with film and cameras, how might you define "camera language"?

A final basic way film can achieve motion is by means of the camera lens itself. Even when the camera is fixed, a lens that affords a much wider, narrower, larger, or smaller field of vision than the eye normally supplies will give the illusion of motion, since we instinctively feel the urge to be in the physical position that would supply that field of vision. Zoom lenses, which change their focal length along a smooth range—thus bringing images gradually closer or farther away—are even more effective for suggesting motion, especially for small-screen viewing of movies on television. One of the favorite shots on television is that of a figure walking or moving in some fashion, which looks, at first, as if it were a normal-distance shot but which is actually revealed as a long shot (from a great distance) when the zoom is reversed. Since our own eye cannot imitate the action of the zoom lens, the effect the lens has can be overwhelmingly dramatic—when used creatively. It is something like the effect that slow motion or stop motion has on us. It interrupts our perceptions of something—something that had seemed perfectly natural—in a way that makes us conscious of the film medium itself.

Technique in this sense, then, has an important shortcoming. Too much of it can make us aware of the film as technique and cause us to lose our sense of participative involvement. Slow motion, rapidly changing focus from foreground to background, and zooming in and out repeatedly on scenes can all cause this loss. But more and more the sophisticated and experimental film makers delight in making us do "double takes" that point out to us the fact that we are not participating in an experience on the screen but that we are indeed sitting in a darkened room watching an image on a screen. One very peculiar example of this is in the movie *Tom Jones* (1963), in which Tom, after searching for his wallet everywhere, turns and looks at the audience and asks us directly whether or not we have seen his wallet. The effect of an actor on the screen being aware of the audience as an audience and not as a silent participator in the action is really startling. It unsettles the comfortable relationship we have built up for ourselves and forces us into new awarenesses of the meaning of the images. And although this example is not peculiarly technical in nature, it is representative of what many film makers are now doing.

Technique can sometimes "take over" a film in that it becomes the most interesting and most memorable aspect of the cinematic experience. This seems true, at least to an extent, in the Academy Award winner, *2001: A Space Odyssey* (1968, Figure 11-5), by Stanley Kubrick, in which a computer develops a personality that is comparable in interest to that of one of the film's stars, Keir Dullea. *Star Wars* (1977) and *Close Encounters of the Third Kind* (1977) use similar themes concentrating on space, the future, and fantastic situations that are notable for their technical qualities. The computer-guided cameras that follow the space vehicles of Luke Skywalker and Hans Solo in *Star Wars'* dramatic conclusion are themselves a remarkable technical achievement and produced some of the most extraordinary footage in the modern film (Figure 11-6).

Assuming that the technical aspects of the film do not distract us by making us too consciously aware of them, we may find ourselves participating with the images in motion in a nonescapist way. Then we will be responding to those situations that are unique to the motion

FIGURE 11-5   From Stanley Kubrick's MGM release *2001: A Space Odyssey*. Copyright © 1968 Metro-Goldwin-Mayer, Inc. with Keir Dullea and Gary Lockwood. Dr. Floyd (William Sylvester), one of the scientists from the Clavius moon base, descends the ramp into the TMAi excavation and, for the first time, the visiting scientist from earth has a close look at the strange object, which has been hidden beneath the lunar surface for millions of years.

FIGURE 11-6 *Star Wars.*
© Lucasfilm, Ltd. (LFL),
1980. All rights reserved.

picture: the situations created by showing us images in motion. We become participants through the control of artists who give us a form-content that reveals something significant in our lives. If they fail to do that, assuming our sensitivity, we will come away from their film—as we often do—with a feeling of perplexity, of inconclusiveness, of not being fully sure that what we have seen is worthwhile.

Selectivity in Film

Because it is so easy to shoot a scene in various ways, a good director is constantly choosing the shot that hopefully has the most impact within the total structure. When Luis Buñuel shows us the razoring of a woman's open eyeball in *Un Chien Andalou* (1928), he is counting on our personal horror at actually seeing such an act. The scene is artistically justifiable because of Buñuel's careful handling of the scene and its tight integration into the structure. Since then hundreds of film makers have failed with similar scenes because they show sheer violence simply for its own sake, without any attempt to inform. In Roman Polanski's *Macbeth* (1971), for example, many audiences actually began snickering at the final battle scenes in which Macbeth and Macduff fight—partly because they had already been saturated with blood, gore, murder, and violence since the first appearance of the "bloody sergeant," whose head had been gashed and whose eye had presumably been lost shortly before in battle. The line between the exhibition of horror and the interpretation of horror is sometimes easy to miss. A curious phenomenon about experiencing film is that the audience's imagination, left to its own devices, is sometimes a much more reliable instrument for the interpretation of horror than the fully realized visual scene.

As we have suggested previously, it is fairly easy to evoke stock responses from an audience, and such stock responses as laughter, sorrow, repulsion, horror, and smug security are pretty reliable for keeping an audience's attention. But the more complex responses, some of which are as difficult to control as they are to attain, are usually the aims of the most enduring film makers. When Ingmar Bergman shows us the rape scene in *The Virgin Spring* (1959), he does not then proceed to saturate us with horror. The murder of the rapists by the girl's father is delayed until the final scenes. And we discover that we still have enough emotional reserve to feel the horror in their violent deaths. This probably would not have been true if the film had been filled with violence, because then we would have been emotionally worn out by the end of the film.

In any art, control is absolutely vital. We can become emotionally saturated just as we can become bored. The results are often the same: indifference. In talking about violence portrayed on the screen, we are also talking about timing and repetition. This is to say, we are concerned with the rhythmic strategy that goes into including scenes or omitting them, into showing similar instances frequently or infrequently, into making decisions that may represent restraint on the part of the film maker.

The Question of Sound

Sound has been a staple feature of professionally made films since Al Jolson's *Jazz Singer* (1927), and its introduction had overwhelming impact on the industry. For one thing, it put those actors out of work who were excellent at pantomime or at broad-style acting but who could not deliver dialogue convincingly. But that was a minor problem in film making. More important was the fact that the people writing films then became more than writers of scenarios—the scenes to be shot. They now had to write films that included dialogue, much the way most live dramatic productions include dialogue. Today we take this for granted. What we may not realize is that this change literally revolutionized the entire art. We find in some contemporary films that the entire progress of a film can be given over more to what is said than to what is done on the screen. Numerous films avoid visual possibilities in favor of relatively simple (and sometimes simply dull) solutions with dialogue. Eisenstein feared, and rightly so, that sound might kill the artistic integrity of film. He was afraid that with sound no one would work basically with the images that make film not only effective but specifically filmic, that film would once again become subservient to drama.

Eisenstein knew that images in motion could sustain the kind of dramatic tension that was once thought limited to the dramatic stage. This is a point of consummate importance. First of all, a film is images in motion. Whatever is added by way of speech, music, or anything else is supplemental. Great film makers will not depend on those supplemental elements for the strength of their films. They may exploit them, but they will never make them the basic ingredients. On the other hand, mediocre or poor film makers will do precisely the opposite; they will rely on the narrative line of the film almost exclusively, using the camera to do little more than visually record people talking to one another. This almost invariably results in a film of little importance.

Sound in film implies much more than the addition of dialogue to the visual track. Music had long been a staple ingredient of the silent films, and special portfolios of piano and organ music were available to the accompanist who played in the local theater while watching the film. Such portfolios indicated the kind of feeling that could be produced and sustained by merging specific music with specific kinds of scenes, such as chase scenes, love scenes, or scenes of suspense. D. W. Griffith's *Birth of a Nation* (1916) features a "rescue" charge by the Ku Klux Klan, which was cut to the dynamics of Richard Wagner's *Die Walküre*. Francis Ford Coppola may have had that in mind when he cut the incredible helicopter battle scene in *Apocalypse Now* (1979) to Wagner's "Ride of the Valkyries." *Apocalypse Now*, a film about the Vietnam War, used sound in exceptionally effective ways, especially in battle scenes, and particularly in the skyrocket fireworks battle deep in the jungle (Figure 11-7).

FIGURE 11-7
Apocalypse Now.
Copyright © 1979.
United Artists
Corporation. All rights
reserved.

In almost every silent film theater, the accompanist had music that was designed for the film as much as the sound-track music is designed for today's films. In 1926 the great actor John Barrymore appeared in a major film called *Don Juan*. The sound was provided by recorded discs in a technique known as the Vitaphone process. The event was a gala, with the New York Philharmonic Orchestra, the violinist Mischa Elman, singers from the Metropolitan Opera, and other musical events appearing before the film drama itself in what was called "A Vitaphone Prelude." Although the Vitaphone process lost out in competition with 20th Century Fox's Movietone sound process (recorded on the film itself as in current processes), *Don Juan* ranks as the first film to include synchronized sound effects and music. Today, sound effects play a vital part in films such as *Bullitt* (1974), featuring Steve McQueen in a high-speed car-chase whose snarl of tires provides much of the drama of the film, and *The French Connection* (1975), which also features one of the most dramatic high-speed chases ever filmed. In these films the sounds have profoundly important roles to play in maintaining the feeling, in establishing dramatic value, and in supplying what we have grown to believe is a necessary realism in the film. In many other films, such as Kubrick's *2001: A Space Odyssey* (1968), the music, Richard Strauss' *Thus Sprach Zarathustra* (Thus Spake Zarathustra), was carefully fused with the film's most memorable images. The film's images are likely to be evoked simply by hearing the music.

PERCEPTION KEY SIGHT AND SOUND

1. Analyze carefully the next film you see on television. Examine the frames you see for their power as individual compositions, recalling some of the points made in the chapters on painting and sculpture. Decide how strong you feel the film is from this point of view.
2. Do the size and shape of the television screen inhibit intense visual experience? Is your participation with film stronger with television or in the theater? Why?
3. If you have a color set, experiment with the color control and try to produce more interesting color combinations than are provided by the "normal" setting.
4. Turn off the sound entirely. Can you follow clearly what is going on? Is much of importance lost?
5. Tune out the video portion of the program and listen to the sound only. Can you follow clearly what is going on? Is much of importance lost? When you come right down to it, you may find that in all but the more impressive films not terribly much is lost when the images are eliminated. You may have to wait a long while before you find a film in which this is not true. Show a really successful film in class or in a group, and then try the above "modifications" to see how well the film survives.

These experiments probably indicate to you that most contemporary film is a marriage of sight and sound. Yet we must not forget that film is a medium in which the moving image is preeminent. Were we to consider the value of most films we see on this basis alone, we would soon learn the sad fact that the mass production of films has tended to make film making take the easy way out most of the time. It is rare to see a film that takes seriously its responsibilities to fashion a fine series of moving images. Those that do are memorable.

The Question of Structure

One kind of structure in films is the narrative sequence that orders our experience: a character or characters get into some kinds of difficulties and persist in either worsening their situation or improving it. Such narrative structures seem to have a natural form for most of us. But that form often is, in effect, formula. This is one of the traps—relying on simple formulas that cannot honestly represent the complexities that even the simplest viewer would have to face in life—that Eisenstein always tried to avoid. Yet it is also true that his own films, like *Potemkin*, were themselves narrative in structure. *Potemkin* opens with sailors on a Russian ship (the *Potemkin*) being badly mistreated. They mutiny and take over the ship, restoring justice and humanity. The people of Odessa give them welcome in their harbor. In reaction, the Czar's troops shoot down women and children in Odessa indiscriminately, and gunboats are sent out to sink the *Potemkin*. The Czar's sailors mutiny, however, and will not fire on the *Potemkin*. All this is revealed without audible dialogue. The carefully selected visual aspects of the narrative—the photographed moving images—do the telling economically, without reliance upon formula, and for that reason it is still a powerful film even for those of us who find it difficult to adjust to silent films.

It should be clear that the narrative in this sense is a narrative of outward action: characters performing actions affecting themselves and others. But there are other kinds of narratives. One very popular kind is the narrative of inward or psychological action. Consider, for example, the motorcycle-acid drama, *Easy Rider* (1969, Figure 11-3); we realize that the organizing elements are not those of *Potemkin* or other films like it. There is action, to be sure, but the sequence of events does not have the same close causal order. The structure is what is referred to in literature as episodic or picaresque. Things happen to the protagonists as they go from place to place. What happens to them, how they change and grow because of their adventures, is of principal importance in such structures. Wyatt and Billy are simply motorcycling from coast to coast, from Los Angeles to the East. They are not specifically trying to accomplish anything other than getting their pay-off money from drugs safely away. They realize ultimately, however, that what they have done is wrong. They are struck by the moral consequences of their action, and when they realize what they are Wyatt says drily—"We blew it." You might ask yourself what, among the adventures they had and the exposure they had to people of all sorts, good and bad, caused that change of heart. The form of that film, along with many like it, reveals the characters as altered by their experience. The fact that Wyatt is gunned down by rednecks after his moment of understanding is something of a formula, but within the context of this film it is artistically effective. Once one has begun to truly understand himself, as some pessimistic existentialists claim, there is nothing left—death is a blessing, the only rightful conclusion to that narrative structure that is our life. Such a gloomy understanding is rare in life. But art functions to give us a sense of the various possibilities of self-understanding. Certainly the implications of *Easy Rider*, with its enormous popularity, were understood and valued.

Michael Cimino's portrayal of three hometown men who fight together in Vietnam, *The Deer Hunter* (1979 Figure 11-8), has serious structural problems. Yet it won several Academy Awards and has been proclaimed one of the great antiwar films. Cimino took great risks by dividing the film into three large sections: sequences of life in Clairton, Pennsylvania, with a Russian Orthodox wedding and a last hunting expedition for deer; sequences of war-prisoners and fighting in Vietnam; sequences afterward in Clairton, where only one of the three men, Mike, played by Robert DeNiro, is able to live effectively. Mike finally sets out to get Steven to return from the wheelchair ward of the VA hospital to his wife. Then he sets out to find his best friend, Nick, a heroin addict still in Saigon, playing Russian Roulette for hardened Vietnamese gamblers. Cimino made Russian Roulette a metaphor for the senselessness of war.

Cimino relied in part on the model of Dante's *Divine Comedy*, also divided into three sections—Hell, Purgatory, and Paradise. In *The Deer Hunter* the rivers of molten metal in the steel mills and more obviously, the war scenes, suggest the ghastliness of Hell. The extensive and ecstatic scenes in the Russian Orthodox church suggest Paradise, while life in Clairton represents an in-between, a kind of Purgatory. In one of the most stirring scenes, when he is back in Saigon during the American evacuation looking for Nick, Mike is shown standing up in a small boat negotiating his way through the canals. The scene is a visual echo of Eugene Delacroix's "Dante and Virgil in Hell," a nineteenth-century painting. For anyone who recognizes the allusion to Dante, Cimino's structural techniques become clearer, as do his views of war in general and of Vietnam in particular.

The relationship of photography itself to the form of films like *Easy Rider* and *The Deer Hunter* is sometimes difficult to assess. If we agree that the power of the moving image is central to the effect and to

FIGURE 11-8 Robert DeNiro and Meryl Streep in a scene from *The Deer Hunter*. Copyright © by Universal Pictures, a division of Universal City Studios, Inc. Courtesy of MCA Publishing, a division of MCA, Inc.

the ultimate meaning of the motion picture, we can see that the most important structural qualities of any good film develop from the juxtaposition of different kinds of images—the texture. Some people place this aspect of film under the term "editing," the process that follows after the shooting of the picture. Sometimes many different versions of a single action will be filmed. The editor and the director decide which will be the final mix after they have given thought to each version in relation to the structure they want for the total film. Once they decide on what will be included, the editor does the actual joining of the parts of the film, deciding exactly which frame will end one sequence and which will begin the next. This is a crucial artistic job. The editor usually works very closely with the director because editing decisions have such a powerful impact on the viewer's ultimate responses to the final product.

FIGURE 11-9 *Annie Hall.* Copyright © 1977. United Artists Corporation. All rights reserved.

Woody Allen reduced *Annie Hall* (1977, Figure 11-9) from the original rough cut of three hours down to the final cut of 93 minutes. The film is rambling and episodic, meant to parallel important moments in the lives of the characters, Alvy Singer (Woody Allen) and Annie Hall (Diane Keaton). The film is about the difficulties people have in sustaining romantic relationships for more than brief periods of time. The editing was complicated because the narrative was based on the genuine romance of Allen and Keaton, who separated shortly before the picture was released. The structure of Alvy and Annie coming together, parting, coming together, and parting was meant to help us understand the tensions such romances develop. Cutting the film down to manageable size was a special challenge to Allen, particularly in face of the personal implications of the narrative.

Editing: Montage

The editor's work gives meaning to the film just as surely as the scriptwriter's and the photographer's. Consider, for instance, the final scenes in Eisenstein's *Potemkin*. The *Potemkin* is steaming to a confrontation with the fleet. Eisenstein rapidly cuts from the inside of the ship to the outside: showing a view of powerfully moving engine pistons, then the ship cutting deeply into the water, then rapidly back and forth, showing occasional anxiety-ridden faces, all designed to raise the emotional pitch of anyone watching the movie. This kind of cutting was used by Alfred Hitchcock in the murder scene of the 1960 horror thriller, *Psycho*. He demonstrated that the technique could be used to develop an immense amount of tension and terror, even though no explicit murderous actions were shown on screen. This kind of editing is called montage. It gives a clear meaning to the film itself as film. The tension is being portrayed by the moving images—it is being shown to us, not told.

The editing stage of film making can easily be abused. But when it is handled well, it can be profoundly effective because it is impossible for us in real-life experience to achieve what the film editor achieves. By eliminating the more or less irrelevant, good editing accents the relevant. We cannot "cut" instantly from an airport, where we were watching a hired assassin from Chicago landing at Los Angeles, to the office of the political candidate he has come to kill. Film can do this with ease. The connection or montage—the showing of the psychologically connected but somewhat physically disconnected second scene immediately after the first—can be made without a single word of dialogue. You can undoubtedly recall innumerable instances of this kind of "cutting" and montage work. When done well, this tying together of images that could not possibly be together in real-life experience enhances the meaning of the images we see.

1. Study the next film you see carefully for its use of editing techniques, principally its effort to give meaning to what you see by the conjunction or the disjunction of image sequences.
2. Decide whether the film you are watching is very original in its use of cuts and montages. Or is the editor relying on well-worn clichés?
3. In conversation with others interested in this question, try to see if you can come to an agreement about what is intended by the editing you observe.

Content

The question of meaning is no less complicated in the film than it is in any artistic medium. The fact that we cannot translate filmic meaning into language, any more than we can translate musical meaning into language, should not deter us from trying to understand what meanings are revealed by the technical moves employed by the film maker. In some cases we will be able to approximate a "translation" by describing the connections—emotional, narrative, or whatever—implied by the sequence of images. But there are aspects of that sequence that defy the meanings of language, such as the psychological impact of the juxtapositions. Sensitive participants are especially interested in films which explore this kind of "meaning."

When we watch the overturning coffin in Bergman's *Wild Strawberries* (1957) we are surprised to find that the figure in the coffin has the same face as Professor Borg, the protagonist, who is himself a witness to what we see. That there is very significant meaning implied seems quite clear. Yet we cannot translate this scene into language, although we can do a great deal of profitable talking about the power of the scene and its implications for the entire film. The scene, and others like it, achieves full meaning in relation to other dramatic moments in the film. The scene has a certain amount of tension and impact all its own, and yet it is apparent that the full meaning depends on the context of the whole film in which it appears. The relation of part to context exists in every art, of course, but that relation in its nuances often may be more easily missed in our experiences of the film. For one thing, we are not accustomed to permitting images to build their own meanings apart from the meanings we already associate with them. We tend to resist that process. Second, we do not always observe the way one movement or gesture will mean one thing in one context while it will mean an entirely different thing in another context or in isolation —that is, insofar as *any* movement or gesture can exist in isolation.

The film maker is the master controller of contexts, just as is the dramatist. In Eric Rohmer's film *Claire's Knee* (1970), a totally absurd gesture, the caressing of an indifferent and relatively insensitive girl's knee, becomes the fundamental focus of the film. This gesture is loaded with meaning throughout the entire film, but loaded only for the main masculine character and us. The girl is totally unaware of what her knee has come to mean to the man. This is absurd, in a way, yet plausible. It is absurd in the strict sense in that the meaning of the gesture is unimportant—except as the gesture is understood in context. It is plausible, however, in that such fixations can occur, even in normal people. But this film is not concerned solely with plausiblity; it is mainly concerned with gestures in context that reveal what is unclear in real-life experience. And this is done primarily through skillful photography and editing rather than through a spoken narrative plot line.

PERCEPTION KEY CONTEXTS

1. Examine the next film you watch for its power to give meaning to gesture through the contexts which are established for it.
2. To what extent do the gestures in this film tie the images together?
3. To what extent is this film meaningful because of its contextual relationship to the world we ourselves inhabit?
4. Compare the gestures in film with the gestures of sculpture. How do they differ?

All meanings, linguistic or nonlinguistic, are within some kind of context. Most first-rate films exist in many contexts simultaneously, and it is our job as sensitive viewers of film to be able to decide which are the most important for us. Film, like every art, has a history, and this history is one of the most significant of the contexts in which every film takes place. In order to make that historical context fruitful in our filmic experiences, we must do more than just read about that history. We must accumulate in our experience a historical sense of film by seeing films that have been important to the development of the medium. Most of us have a very rich personal backlog in film; we have seen a great many films, some of which are memorable and most of which have been influenced by landmark films. Furthermore, film exists in a context that is meaningful for the life work of a director and, in turn, for us. When we talk about the films of Orson Welles, Ingmar Bergman, or Federico Fellini, we are talking about the achievements of artists just as much as when we talk about the paintings of Van Gogh or Rembrandt. Today we watch carefully for films by Francois Truffaut, Francis Ford Coppola, Michelangelo Antonioni, Michael Cimino, Stanley Kubrick, Robert Altman, Sidney Lumet, Martin Scorsese, and Lina Wertmüller—to name only a few of the most active current directors—because their work has shown a steady development and because they,

FIGURE 11-10 From Sidney Lumet's *Equus* (1977) with Peter Firth and Jenny Agutter. Courtesy of United Artists Corporation.

in relation to the history of the film, have shown themselves in possession of a vision that is transforming the medium. In other words, they are altering the history of film in significant ways. In turn, we should be interested in knowing what they are doing because they are providing new contexts for increasing our understanding of film.

But these are only a few contexts in which films exist. Every film exists in a social context, in relation to the social system it springs from, portrays, or criticizes. We do not usually judge films specifically on the basis of their ability to make social comment, but if we lived in Russia or China we would probably take it for granted that we judge a film on the basis of its ability to make a positive contribution to the building of a new society. Obviously, the context of the society would then outweigh any context of internal parts: the relation of texture to structure and the meaning of the structure. You can see that our concerns in this book have not been exclusively with one or another kind of context, although we have assumed that the internal context of a work of art is necessarily of first importance to begin with. But no work can be properly understood without resorting to some external contextual examination. A visual image, a contemporary gesture, even a colloquial expression will sometimes show up in a film and need explication in order to be fully understood. Just as we sometimes have to look up a word in a dictionary—which exists outside a poem, for instance—we sometimes have to look outside a film for hints about meaning. Even Terence Young's James Bond thriller movies need such explication, although we rarely think about that. If someone failed to understand the assumptions about Russia and China that such films make, he or she would not fully understand what was going on. Of course, political conflict is something of a constant the world over, and even if we do not fully understand the nature of the political rivalry of East and West (and it changes all the time), we can still comprehend the struggles we witness in nonpolitical terms.

Experimentation

Because of the vast technical problems involved in film making, a great deal of experimentation has occurred in the film from its earliest days. The fact that many of the original people involved with the medium had technical interests or technical training probably helps account for this experimentation. Today the experimental work is less technical, perhaps, and more a "trying out" of the technical advances. We think of Andy Warhol, originally a painter and sculptor, who has done some interesting work in extending the limits of realism. For example, many of us seem to prefer the starkly realistic film to the improbable or unlikely fantasy film. At least many of us say we do, and we undoubtedly think we do. But when Andy Warhol places a figure in front of a camera to sleep for a full eight hours' rest, we may begin to get the message as we watch this monotonous reality: we want a transformation of reality that gives us insight into reality, not reality itself. The difference is really much more important than it may seem because it is the difference between reality and art. We all have reality in front of us most of the time. We have art much less frequently. Realistic art is a selection of elements which conveys the illusion of reality. When we see Warhol's almost direct transcription of reality on film, we see clearly that the value of selecting—through directing and editing—may be greater than we had thought. The power of most striking films is often in their ability to condense experience, to take a year's time, for example, and select its most intense ninety minutes. This condensation is precisely what Marcel Proust, one of the greatest of novelists, expected from the novel:

> Every emotion is multiplied ten-fold, into which this book comes to disturb us as might a dream, but a dream more lucid, and of a more lasting impression, than those which come to us in sleep; why, then, for a space of an hour he sets free within us all the joys and sorrows in the world, a few of which, only, we should have to spend years of our actual life in getting to know, and the keenest, the most intense of which would never have been revealed to us because the slow course of their development stops our perception of them. It is the same in life; the heart changes . . . but we learn of it only from reading or by imagination; for in reality its alteration . . . is so gradual that . . . we are still spared the actual sensation of change.[1]

Some interesting modern films have to do with the question of the film's creation of reality. Antonioni's *Blow Up* (1966), for example, had the thread of a narrative holding it together: a possible murder and the efforts of a magazine photographer, through the medium of his own enlargements, to establish the reality of that murder. But anyone who saw the film would know that the continuity of the narrative was not the most important part of the film. The basic content came out of what were essentially disconnected "moments": a party, some driving around London in a convertible Rolls-Royce, and some unusual tennis played without a ball. What seemed most important was the role of the film itself in creating certain "realities." In a sense the murder was a reality only after the film uncovered it. Is it possible that Antonioni is saying something similar about the reality that surrounds the very film he is creating? There is a reality, but where? Is *Blow Up* more concerned with film images as reality than it is with reality outside the film? If you have a chance to see this film, be sure you ask that puzzling question.

Some more extreme experimenters remove the narrative frame entirely and simply present successions of images, almost in the manner of a nightmare or a drug experience. The images themselves,

[1]Marcel Proust, *Swann's Way*, C. K. Scott Moncrieff (trans.), The Modern Library, Random House, Inc., New York, 1928, p. 119.

like an abstract painting, are capable of establishing their own meaningfulness. Or so the experimenters feel. The fact that we have very little abstract film art may have several explanations. Part of the power of abstract painting seems to depend on its "all-at-onceness' (see Chapter 4), precisely what is missing from film. Another reason may be tied in, again, with the popular nature of the medium: masses of people do not prefer abstraction. There may well be other reasons for the small amount of abstract film making. A recent invention in the field of moving images is Thomas Wilfred's *Lumia*, an installation that displays shifting patterns of light and color which are totally abstract and always in motion. There is not only no narrative line but also no relevant way of adding one, since the moving images are not those of people, places, or things. The success of *Lumia* has been limited, although Wilfred's *Lumia Suite, Opus 158*, which was opened to the public in 1964 in The Museum of Modern Art in New York City, apparently has become a permanent installation. Most visitors, however, rarely extend their viewings for more than a few minutes. Apparently the public is generally convinced that film, like drama and literature, must have characters, themes, and narrative lines. Thus even filmic cartoons are rarely abstract, although they are not photographs but drawings.

Narrative and Film

It is important to consider, finally, why narrative elements seem so crucial to the film medium. What alternatives can you see for affording meaningfulness to film? Are there any? How excited can you get about them?

PERCEPTION KEY MAKE A FILM

1. For some of you it may be possible to experiment with making a film or videotape. Take the opportunity seriously. Try to invent new ways to give a meaningful unity to the succession of images you photograph. Try substituting another organizing principle for the usual one of narrative. For example, take a musical composition that is especially interesting to you, and then fuse moving images with the music.
2. Assuming you do not want to abandon narrative as an organizing principle, try to use narrative "lines" that you do not usually find in films. We all know the normal plot for a western, for instance. Can you free yourself to some extent from preconceptions about such plots and invent a new narrative principle?
3. Short of making a film, try some editing by finding and clipping from twenty to thirty "stills" from magazines, brochures, newspapers, or other sources. Choose frames you feel have a coherence and arrange them in such a way as to make a sequence that is meaningful to those who view them. How is your sequence affected by rearrangement? This project will

be much more interesting if you use or make slides for viewing. Then consider adding a "soundtrack" to heighten interest and to clarify the coherence of the sequence.

The experiments of this and some of the other perception keys have been challenging and informative, we hope. Perhaps they may even have stimulated some of you to work in the arts, to become at least amateur artists. They probably have indicated to all of you that making or attempting to make works of art is not an ordinary activity. Artistic creation, for all of its rewards, is usually highly demanding, time-consuming work. But the art that results, we claim, is one of the most powerful of civilizing forces. This is a large claim. For if we are correct, none of the other humanities could achieve very much without the help of the arts.

Summary

The artistic complexity of the film is due largely to the collaboration required among many people who contribute to directing, photographing, and editing the film. The charm of especially important actors contributes importantly to most films as does the expertise and style of the director. The relationship between the film and its subject matter is as complex as we found in the drama and its subject matter. The point of view that can be achieved with the camera is similar to that of the unaided human eye, but because of technical refinements such as the zoom lens, the wide-angle lens, the moving camera, and the use of multiple cameras, the dramatic effect of many films can be intensified. Although in some cases this may reduce the realism of a film, it helps separate the film experience from the experience we have watching a stage play. Because it is usually easy to block out everything irrelevant to the film in a dark theater, we can expect our participative experience to be especially intense. The temptation to identify totally with a given actor or situation in a film may also distort the participative experience by blocking our perception of the more demanding structural and textural qualities of the film. The combination of sound, both dialogue and music (or sound effects), with the moving image makes the film a total experience for most filmgoers. It may also contribute to our sense that the film is not only the most modern of our arts but also the most potentially powerful.

Chapter 11 Bibliography

Arnheim, Rudolf. *Film as Art*. Berkeley: University of California Press, 1966.
Barthes, Roland. *Semiology of the Cinema*. Boston: Beacon Press, n.d.
Bazin, André. *What Is Cinema?* Berkeley: University of California Press, 1967.

Bobker, Lee R. *Elements of Film*, 3d ed. New York: Harcourt Brace Jovanovich, 1981.

Braudy, Leo. *The World in a Frame*. Garden City, N.Y.: Doubleday, 1976.

Dick, Bernard. *Anatomy of Film*. New York: St Martin's Press, 1978.

Eisenstein, Sergei, *Film Form and Film Sense*, trans. Jay Leyda. New York: Harcourt Brace Jovanovich, n.d.

Huss, Roy, and Silverstein, Norman. *The Film Experience*. New York: Harper & Row, 1968.

Kracauer, Siegfried. *Theory of Film*. New York: Oxford University Press, 1960.

Lindgren, Ernest. *The Art of the Film*. London: Allen & Unwin, 1963.

Mast, Gerald. *Film/Cinema/Movie: A Theory of Experience*. New York: Harper & Row, 1977.

———— and Cohen, Marshall, eds. *Film Theory and Criticism*. New York: Oxford University Press, 1974.

Monaco, James. *How to Read a Film*. New York: Oxford University Press, 1981.

Nicoll, Allardyce. *Film and Theatre*. New York: Crowell, 1937.

Pudovkin, V. I. *Film Technique and Film Acting*, ed. and trans, I. Montagu. New York: Grove Press, 1960.

Spottiswode, Ray. *The Film and Its Techniques*. Berkeley: University of California Press, 1951.

Stephenson, Ralph, and Debrix, J. R. *The Cinema as Art*. Baltimore: Penguin Books, 1965.

Weiss, Paul. *Cinematics*. Carbondale: Southern Illinois University Press, 1975.

NOTE: Some distributors of films for classroom use are: Audio-Brandon, 34 MacQuesten Parkway South, Mount Vernon, NY 10550; Contemporary/McGraw-Hill, Princeton Road, Hightstown, NJ 08520; Janus Films, 745 Fifth Avenue, New York, NY 10022; United Artists 16, 729 Seventh Avenue, New York, NY 10019; Universal 16, 445 Park Avenue, New York, NY 10003; Warner Brothers, Inc., Non-Theatrical Division, 4000 Warner Boulevard, Burbank, CA 91522.

PHOTOGRAPHY

12 The excitement being generated in contemporary photography circles has been matched by the interest of museums and collectors in the work of great photographers such as Minor White, Ansel Adams, Cecil Beaton, W. Eugene Smith, Diane Arbus, Dorothea Lange, and many more. Artists working in other graphic media, such as painting and printmaking, have also taken a strong interest in photography. Andy Warhol, Robert Rauschenberg, and many other young painters have been using photography as part of their compositions for years. The effect of painting on photography, a sometimes controversial subject, can easily be matched by a consideration of the effect of photography on painting. Although at first it was considered that the older medium of painting would be indifferent to any developments in photography, it has become clear from recent researches, such as those of Peter Galassi in his book, *Before Photography*, that there has been a longstanding interaction dating even to a period before it was possible to fix a photograph permanently. As Galassi points out, many paintings of the late eighteenth and early nineteenth centuries show an awareness of "photographic vision."

Photographic vision began with the discovery that a box with a lens attached could project an image of whatever it was aimed at. That image was projected in correct perspective and in great detail. When photographs were first available for study, it was not clear that they were anything more than exact replicas of a given scene or subject matter. But it was eventually realized that photographs had the power to transform subject matter and achieve a form-content. Partly through reduction or magnification of size of the subject matter, through the rendering in monochrome black and white (or sepia and white), through distortion of lens, selectivity of framing, and careful attention to the relationship of structure to details within the photograph, it was possible for the photographer to evoke the kinds of participatory experiences possible in other graphic media. Today the capacity of photography to comment on values, to produce a participatory experience, and to have form-content is taken for granted by photographers, many of whom are searching out new subject matter and new means of transformation in order to expand and understand the considerable resources of the medium. In order to understand the direction of the new photographers, it is helpful to look briefly at the history of photography, particularly since the art has progressed a great deal in a short time. In an important sense, the history of photography is a history of discovering the resources of the medium and how they can be used effectively in the transformations implied in form-content.

The Power of Detail

One of photography's first successes was its capacity to reproduce detail accurately. Since that capacity was thought essential to realism in painting, photography's impact on the art of painting was almost instant. Paul Delaroche, a French academic painter (1795–1856), was widely admired for his realistic technique, as in his "Execution of Lady Jane Grey" (Figure 12-1), a massive painting (97" X 117").

When he saw the Daguerreotype process demonstrated in 1839, he declared, "From today painting is dead." He was quite wrong, but he was responding to the clarity of detail Daguerre's instant process (like the modern Polaroid) could extract from nature. It was truly remarkable, and even today clarity remains among the most important resources of the photographic medium.

PERCEPTION KEY "EXECUTION OF LADY JANE GREY"

1. What qualities of Delaroche's style of painting would have made him think of photography as a threat? In what ways is this painting similar to a photograph?
2. Is it surprising to learn that this painting was exhibited five years before Delaroche saw a photograph—actually before photography's invention?
3. Like many painters before him, Delaroche may have used the camera obscura (a light-tight box with a lens and a ground-glass surface for tracing the projected image) to compose his figures and render them exactly as

FIGURE 12-1 Paul Delaroche, "Execution of Lady Jane Grey." Reproduced by courtesy of the trustees, National Gallery, London.

they appeared. Would this painting be less a work of art if he had used such an instrument to assist him?

Four Early Photographers

The capacity of the camera to capture or control details is revealed in many early photographs. Robert Howlett's portrait of Isambard Kingdom Brunel, a builder of steamships (Figure 12-2), uses the power of the lens to isolate Brunel from his surroundings.

PERCEPTION KEY ROBERT HOWLETT, "ISAMBARD KINGDOM BRUNEL"

1. What is the subject matter of this photograph?
2. What is the relationship between structural shapes and details in the photograph? Refer to Figures 3-4 and 3-5 for assistance with this question.
3. What is the difference in sharpness of focus between the foreground and the background of the photograph? How might this difference affect the content of the photograph?

FIGURE 12-2 Robert Howlett, "Isambard Kingdom Brunel." International Museum of Photography at George Eastman House, Rochester.

Howlett set his lens so that only Brunel's body was in focus. The depth of field (range of sharpness of focus) of the lens was, therefore, only about twenty inches or less. The wood pilings in the lower right are in soft focus because they are just out of that depth of field. The pile of anchor chains, which serves as background, is even farther out of focus, thus softening their massive, fascinating pattern. By being out of focus, the chains are rendered subservient to Brunel and establish his mastery as designer of great steamships. The huge chains make this image haunting, but rendering them sharply (which Howlett could

FIGURE 12-3 Julia Margaret Cameron, "Sir John Herschel." International Museum of Photography at George Eastman House, Rochester.

FIGURE 12-4 Étienne Carjat, "Charles Baudelaire." International Museum of Photography at George Eastman House, Rochester.

easily have done) would have weakened the effect of the photograph. In Delaroche's painting everything is in sharp focus, which may simply mean that the Howlett style of selective focus was not part of his repertoire, as it was to become for some later painters.

Brunel's posture is typical of outdoor portraits of the period. We have many examples of men lounging with hands in pockets and cigar in mouth, but few paintings reveal such men. Brunel's posture was already typical of a photograph. Few photographs of any age show us a face quite like Brunel's. It is relaxed, as much as Brunel could relax, but it is also impatient, "bearing with" the photographer. And the eyes are sharp, businessman's eyes. The details of the rumpled clothing and jewelry arrest us, but they do not compete with the sharply rendered face and the expression of the control and power that resides there. Howlett has done, with simple means, what many portrait painters do with much more complex means: reveal the essence of the model.

Julia Margaret Cameron's portrait of Sir John Herschel (1867, Figure 12-3), and Étienne Carjat's portrait of the French poet Charles Baudelaire (1870, Figure 12-4) avoid most of Howlett's problems by ignoring the background entirely. But their approaches are also different from one another.

Cameron, who reports being interested in the way her lens could soften detail, isolates Herschel's face and hair. She drapes his shoulders with a black velvet shawl so that his clothing will not tell us anything about him or distract us from his face. Cameron catches the stubble on his chin and permits his hair to "burn out," so we perceive it as a luminous halo, like the edges of a fog-softened sun. The huge eyes, soft and bulbous with their deep curves of surrounding flesh, and the downward curve of the mouth are remarkable. While we cannot know what he is thinking, we are aware that he is a thinker capable of deep ruminations. He is the chemist who first learned how to permanently fix a photograph.

The portrait of Baudelaire, on the other hand, includes simple, severe clothing. The only concession to fashion is the poet's foulard, tied in a dashing bow. The studio backdrop is set far out of focus so it cannot compete with the face for our attention. Baudelaire's intensity creates the illusion that he sees us, not the camera. Carjat's lens was set for a depth of field of only a few inches. Therefore the eyes are in focus, but not the shoulder. Carjat, working directly on the camera's ground glass under a focusing cloth, had complete control over what was in focus. What he could not control, except by waiting for the right moment to uncover the lens, is the exact expression he would catch. As a studio portrait, this one compares stylistically with many paintings of the period, such as some of Ingres' portraits. This is less true of Cameron's portrait and still less true of Howlett's portrait.

One irony of the Carjat portrait is that Baudelaire, in 1859, had condemned photography's influence on art, declaring it "art's most mortal enemy." He thought photography was adequate for preserving visual records of perishing things, but that it could not reach into "anything whose value depends solely upon the addition of something of a man's soul." John Canaday and Susan Sontag are both close to that view even today. Baudelaire was the champion of imagination and the opponent of realistic art: "Each day art further diminishes its self-respect by bowing down before external reality; each day the painter becomes more and more given to painting not what he dreams but what he sees."[1]

An impressive example of the photograph's capacity to render detail is Timothy O'Sullivan's masterpiece, "Canyon de Chelley, Arizona," made in 1873. Many photographers go back to this scene, but none have treated it quite the way O'Sullivan did, although most, like Ansel Adams (Figure 12-14), pay homage to O'Sullivan.

PERCEPTION KEY TIMOTHY O'SULLIVAN, "CANYON DE CHELLEY, ARIZONA"

1. Which parts of the photograph are most sharply detailed? Which parts are in soft focus?
2. What do the men in each set of buildings contribute to the artistic form and content of the photograph?
3. Refer to the Perception Key following Cézanne's painting, *Mont Sainte Victoire* (pp. 37–38). We identify the subject matter of Cézanne's painting as the mountain, which, we have said, "is clearer in this painting than . . . in the best of photographs." What is the subject matter of O'Sullivan's photograph? Is the stoniness of the rock wall revealed to the same extent that the mountainness of Mont Sainte Victoire is revealed?
4. What is particularly "photographic" about the contrast between the two groups of buildings?

O'Sullivan chose a moment of intense sidelighting, which falls on the rock wall but not on the nearest group of buildings. He waited for that moment when the great rock striations and planes would be most powerfully etched by the sun. The closer group of buildings is marked by strong shadow. Comparing it to the more distant group shows a remarkable negative-positive relationship. The groups of buildings are purposely contrasted in this special photographic way.

The most detailed portions of the photograph are the striations of the rock face, whose tactile qualities are emphasized by the strong sidelighting. The stone buildings in the distance have smoother textures, particularly as they show up against the blackness of the cave. The men standing in the ruins show us that the buildings are only twelve to fifteen feet high at most. Nature dwarfs the works of man.

[1]*The Mirror of Art*, Phaidon, London, 1955, p. 230.

FIGURE 12-5 Timothy O'Sullivan, "Canyon de Chelley." International Museum of Photography at George Eastman House, Rochester.

By framing the canyon wall as he does, and by waiting for the right light, O'Sullivan has done more than create an ordinary "record" photograph. He has concentrated on the subject matter of man's puniness—and softness—in contrast with the huge stoniness of nature in the Canyon de Chelley. The content of the photograph centers on the extraordinary sense of stoniness—accented by the immobility of the great stone formation—both in nature and in man's work, revealed in large part by the capacity of the camera to render detail.

Pictoralism

Pictorialists are photographers who depend on the achievement of painting, particularly realistic painting, in their effort to explore photography's potential as art. The early pictorialists tried to avoid the "head-on" directness of Carjat and Howlett, just as they tried to avoid the amateur's "mistakes" in composition, such as including distracting elements. The pictorialists controlled details by subordinating them to structure, thus producing compositions that often relied on the same underlying formal structures found in many nineteenth-century paintings. See our discussion of Figures 3-4 and 3-5, pp. 62–63. Usually the most important part of the subject matter was centered in the frame. Pictorial lighting, also borrowed from painting, sometimes became Rembrandt-like, with dramatic effects of the sort we associate with the stage.

In his early work, Alfred Stieglitz was a master of the pictorial style. His "Paula" (Figure 12-6), done in 1889, places his subject at the center in the act of writing. The top and bottom of the scene are printed in deep black, while the light falls on the important part of the action with an interesting pattern of light created by the venetian blind. Paula's profile is strong against the dark background partly because Stieglitz has dodged out (removed in the act of printing) one of the strips which would have fallen on her lower face. The candle, ordinarily useless in daylight, is a beacon of light because of its position. The strong vertical lines of the window frames reinforce the verticality of the candle and echo the back of the chair.

A specifically photographic touch is present in the illustrations on the wall: photographs arranged symmetrically in a triangle. Two prints of the same lake-skyscape are on each side of a woman in a white dress and hat. The same photograph of this woman is on the writing table in an oval frame. Is it Paula? The light in the room echoes the oval portrait. The three hearts in the arrangement of photographs are balanced; one heart touches the portrait of a young man. We wonder if Paula is writing to him. The cage on the wall has dominant vertical lines, crossing the lines cast by the venetian blind. Stieglitz may be suggesting that Paula, despite the open window, may be in a cage of her own. Stieglitz has kept most of the photograph in sharp focus because most of the details have something to tell us. If this were a painting of the early nineteenth century, we would expect much the same approach.

Pictorialism is still an ideal of many good photographers, although we associate it mainly with those working at the beginning of the twentieth century. Gertrude Käsebier was among the most successful. She introduces another feature of the approach: a soft focus that was thought to be particularly artistic. The title of her photograph, "Blessed Art Thou Among Women" (Figure 12-7), is clearly sentimental. But

FIGURE 12-6 Alfred
Stieglitz, "Paula."
International Museum of
Photography at George
Eastman House,
Rochester.

sentimentality is fused with powerful form: strong vertical doorposts
with grooved lines, the upright daughter and mother, and the repetition of those shapes in the painting on the wall in the rear. The
verticals have very little competition, but all the lines are softened as a
way of suggesting femininity. The daughter is posed strikingly in dark,
at attention, as if getting her final instructions before passing through
the door of life.

1. Pictorialists are often condemned for their sentimentality. Write down your own definition of sentimentality. Compare it with a dictionary definition. Are there important differences?
2. Are "Paula" and "Blessed Art Thou Among Women" both sentimental? Is their subject matter sentimental, or does their formal treatment make a neutral subject matter sentimental?
3. Is Delaroche's "Execution of Lady Jane Grey" sentimental? Does its sharpness of detail contribute to its sentimentality? Would softened focus make the painting more or less sentimental? Why?
4. Is sentimentality desirable in paintings, photographs, films, plays, novels, or any art form?

FIGURE 12-7 Gertrude Käsebier, "Blessed Art Thou Among Women," © 1900. Platinum print on Japanese tissue, 9⅜ × 5½ inches. Collection, The Museum of Modern Art, New York. Gift of Mrs. Hermine M. Turner.

FIGURE 12-8 Edward Steichen, "John Pierpont Morgan," 1906. Photogravure from *Camera Work*, 8⅛ × 6¼ inches. Collection, The Museum of Modern Art, New York. Gift of A. Conger Goodyear.

It is clear that both paintings and photographs can be sentimental. The severest critics of such works complain that sentimentality falsifies feelings by demanding emotional responses that are cheap or easy to come by. Sentimentality is often an oversimplification of very complex emotional issues. It is also likely to become mawkish and self-indulgent. The case of photography is special because we are accustomed to the camera's harshness. Thus, when the pictorialist finds tenderness, romance, and beauty in everyday occurrences, we become suspicious. We may be more tolerant of painting doing those things, but in fact we should be wary of any such emotional "coloration" in any medium.

The pictorialist approach, when not guilty of sentimentalism, has great strengths. The use of lighting that selectively emphasizes the most important features of the subject matter often is an immense help in creating meaning. Borrowing from the formal structures of painting also may help clarify subject matter. Structural harmony (or disharmony) of the kind we look for in representational painting is possible in photography. Although it is by no means limited to the pictorialist approach, it is clearly fundamental to that approach.

An interesting pictorialist success is the portrait of J. P. Morgan by Edward Steichen (Figure 12-8). The financier was a very busy man and resented losing time sitting for a photographer. Steichen tells us that he suggested a pose that Morgan, visibly ruffled, rejected. However, after being asked to pose himself, Morgan ended up exactly as Steichen had wanted him. Steichen took the photo and said he was done. Morgan, delighted that the entire operation had taken only three minutes, told Steichen that they were going to get along just fine. The result shows tension in Morgan's face. Even the hand clutching the chair (it is not a knife) conveys that instant of unwilling cessation of activity. The pictorialist technique appears in the fact that the lighting emphasizes the face at the expense of everything else. Steichen has driven all the unimportant areas into blackness. We see the hand and sense its power; the grasping of the chair reminds us that Morgan was probably the most powerful chairman in America. The glimpse of gold chain and watch tells us that part of the subject matter of the photograph is wealth and time. Steichen eliminates distracting details even more than Rembrandt does in his *Portrait of Nicolaes Ruts* (Figure 5-16), and juxtaposes face and hand in a long diagonal. The soft focus of the face gives us an overall impression rather than a sequence of details we must ponder.

Three Pictorialists

P. H. Emerson, Chansonetta Emmons, and W. Eugene Smith are all pictorialists to some extent. Emerson photographed life on the marshes of England, often taking his large, unwieldy camera out on boats to make photographs such as "Gathering Waterlilies" (Figure 12-9), 1886. Little is known about the Maine photographer Chansonetta Emmons, but her "Old Table Chair No. 2" (Figure 12-10), 1901, is a strong portrait of the farmer Emery Butts and a way of life. Much the same is true of W. Eugene Smith's "Spinner, 1951" (Figure 12-11), originally shot on assignment for *Life* magazine.

FIGURE 12-9   P. H. Emerson, "Gathering Waterlilies." International Museum of Photography at George Eastman House, Rochester.

FIGURE 12-10
Chansonetta Stanley
Emmons, "Old Table
Chair No. 2," copyright
1977 by Marius B.
Péladeau. From the
Collection of Marius B.
Péladeau and Samuel
Pennington.

PERCEPTION KEY THREE PICTORIALISTS

1. Establish the specific pictorial qualities of these photographs. Consider the questions of structure in relation to detail, lighting, centrality, balance, symmetry, and focus.
2. Do any of these photographs verge on the sentimental? Do they seem to have a clear emotional content? Is the subject matter sentimental, or does the form produce a sentimental content?
3. Which of these photographs most resembles a painting? What qualities lead you to this conclusion? Is one of these photographs unlike a painting? What are your reasons?
4. Which photograph makes the fullest use of the camera's capacity to render detail? Does this rendering of detail distract from its pictorial qualities?

FIGURE 12-11 W. Eugene
Smith, "Spinner, 1951,"
© W. Eugene Smith.

Answers to the questions above will vary with one's experience of painting and photography. The most pictorial of the photographs is, the authors believe, "Gathering Waterlilies." That judgment is supported by Emerson's intention to imitate painting. He simplifies his photograph by placing the boat centrally in the frame, but at a dynamic angle so that the eye moves from one corner of the photograph to the diagonally opposite corner (Steichen often used the same technique). The oars are caught at the moment they produce a relaxed triangular form, which further helps emphasize the movement to the upper-left corner. The boat is in a clear watery space, separated from the lily reeds that form a pleasant, caressing background. All surrounding vegetation is rendered in some detail, but this does not distract from the sharp focus of the woman who is caught at the very moment of taking the lily from the water. Our eye is drawn to that action, and the details of the woman's hat balance the lily, which is beautifully lighted against her shadow. The powerful form lends importance to these humble workers. Emerson made strong claims for a connection between photography and painting. Some of his influences came, possibly, from Impressionists such as Manet and Monet, although he never names them. He specifically celebrates the English painter, John Constable, who painted from nature, and the French painter, Jean Francois Millet, who painted scenes from everyday country life. The composition of "Gathering Waterlilies" would not be surprising in the work of Constable, but it must have been a surprise to see that the organization of boat, oars, people, and lilies could be so completely controlled in a photograph.

Emmons is pictorial in choosing the table chair's powerful round structure against which to position Emery Butts. She places him at a dynamic angle relative to the wall and the frame of the photograph. The repetition of circular shapes is also carefully calculated to control the details, which abound in the photograph. The strong verticals of the wall posts, broom, and table supports fall at rhythmic intervals, stabilizing the composition. The photographic qualities of this work show in the clarity of detail. The striations of the trousers, the straw hat, beard, and wall shingles communicate the rough texture of life as Butts must have lived it. Selective framing—choosing only the important parts of the main figure—is a photographic technique that became part of the repertoire of painters, such as Degas, who were interested in photography. Emerson avoided such framing because he theorized that the main figures should be presented in their entirety, sharply focused, and isolated near the center of the photograph. Emmons, on the other hand, maintains visual interest in a static situation by framing to omit portions of Butt's body and by placing his face slightly off center.

Even in the midst of fast-moving events, W. Eugene Smith aimed at unified formal organizations—often through selective lighting. "Spinner, 1951" was part of a study of a Mediterranean Spanish village. It is less pictorial than the works of Emerson and Emmons partly because the thread maker is less isolated from her environment than the other figures. For instance, Smith could have removed the figure working in the background, but he left her there because she is an essential part of the environment. J. P. Morgan's environment is omitted because he controlled it. The thread maker is literally a product of her environment; thus Smith includes it. Smith contrasts the triangular structure created by her arms with the bulbous shape of her spindle and dress. Nonessential details—the pattern of the rug, the textures of the wall and ground—are in soft focus. Essential details, such as the thread maker and the thread, are in sharp focus, heightened by careful lighting and printing.

These examples of pictorialism are important because they show that the resources of formal organization of painting—particularly late nineteenth-century realism—can be appropriated by the photograph. They also show that sentimentality is not a necessary consequence of such an appropriation. Nonetheless, many subsequent photographers have resented the dominance of painting and its techniques of formal organization over the photograph. It was not long before new approaches to organization were attempted. Combined with a change of subject matter, the new approaches produced a new content.

Straight Photography: Two Schools

Straight photography's reactions to the pictorialist approach have helped shape our sense of what a successful photograph is. Two schools developed from the movement of straight photography pioneered by the late work of Alfred Stieglitz. There is considerable overlap between the first school, the F/64 Group, working in the 1930s, and the second school, the ongoing documentarist tradition which developed in the early twentieth century as a reaction against the influence of painting. Straight photography respected photographic techniques, even photographic limitations. It de-emphasized pictorialism and sentimentality, taking the position that, as Aaron Siskind said later, it "is a kind of dead end, making everything look beautiful." The straight photographer wanted things to look as they do, even at the risk of representing ugliness. The two schools, the F/64 Group and the documentarists, were in agreement with Siskind, although they sometimes sought a deeper beauty of their own. One of the effects of their work has been to help us redefine our concept of what is beautiful.

Straight photography defined excellence in photographic terms, not in terms of painting. Susan Sontag summarizes for us: "For a brief time—say, from Stieglitz through the reign of Weston—it appeared that a solid point of view had been erected with which to evaluate photographs: impeccable lighting, skill of composition, clarity of subject, precision of focus, perfection of print quality."[2] Some of these qualities are shared by pictorialists, but new principles of composition —not derived from painting—and new attitudes toward subject matter helped straight photography reveal the world straight, as it really is.

ALFRED STIEGLITZ: PIONEER OF STRAIGHT PHOTOGRAPHY

One of the most famous straight photographs leading to the F/64 Group was Alfred Stieglitz' "The Steerage," 1907 (Figure 12-12). It was

[2]*On Photography*, Farrar, Straus & Giroux, New York, 1977, p. 136.

FIGURE 12-12 Alfred Stieglitz, "The Steerage," 1907. Photogravure (artist's proof from *Camera Work* No. 36, 1911), 7¾ × 6½ inches. Collection, Museum of Modern Art, New York.

taken under conditions that demanded quick action. It is often considered the most famous of all American photographs.

PERCEPTION KEY ALFRED STIEGLITZ'S "THE STEERAGE"

1. How many of the qualities Susan Sontag lists above can be found in this photograph?
2. What compositional qualities make this photograph different from the pictorialist examples we have discussed? How does the structural organization control the details of the photograph?
3. What is the subject matter of the photograph? Is the subject matter made

to seem beautiful? Should it be? How does the question of beauty affect the content of the photograph?

4. Does the framing cut off important figural elements of the photograph? Does Stieglitz use selective focus? Why?

5. Does the photograph achieve content? Does it have the qualities of perfection of form, insight, and inexhaustibility that characterize works of art at their best?

"The Steerage" portrays poor travelers huddled in the "budget" quarters of the Kaiser Wilhelm II, which is taking this group of failed immigrants back to their native lands. Ironically, the New York Public Library uses this photograph to celebrate the arrival of immigrants to America. Stieglitz wrote that while strolling on deck he was struck by a "round straw hat, the funnel leaning left, the stairway leaning right, the white drawbridge with its railings made of circular chains, white suspenders crossing on the back of a man in the steerage below, round shapes of iron machinery, a mast cutting into the sky, making a triangular shape . . . I saw a picture of shapes and underlying that the feeling I had about life."[3]

"The Steerage" shares much with the pictorialist approach: dramatic lighting and soft focus. But there is much that the pictorialist would probably avoid. For one thing, the framing is selective in that it omits important parts of the funnel, drawbridge, and the nearest people in the lower-right quadrant. The very clutter of people—part of the subject matter of the photograph—might be difficult for the pictorialist to tolerate. Certain focal points have been used by Stieglitz to stablize the composition: the straw hat attracts our eye, but so too does the white shawl of the woman below and the white dress of the child. The bold slashing of the composition by the drawbridge sharpens the idea of separation. On the other hand, the leaning funnel, the angled drawbridge and chains, the angled ladder on the right, and the horizontal boom at the top of the photograph are rhythmically interrelated. This rhythm is peculiarly modern and mechanical. The stark metal structures are in opposition to the softer, more random assortment of the people. Photographs such as this have taught us how to look at and appreciate such formal organizations.

THE F/64 GROUP

The name of the group derives from the small aperture, f/64, which ensures that the foreground, middle ground, and background will be in sharp focus. It was formed as a group which declared its principles through manifestos and shows by Edward Weston, Ansel Adams,

[3]Quoted in Beaumont Newhall, *The History of Photography*, Museum of Modern Art, New York, 1964, p. 111.

Imogen Cunningham, and other members. It continued the fight against pictorialism, adding sharp focus to subject matter of the sort that interested the later Stieglitz. Edward Weston, whose early work was in the soft focus school, developed a special interest in formal organizations. He is famous for his nudes and his "portraits" of vegetables, such as artichokes, eggplants, and green peppers. His nudes rarely show the face, not because of modesty, but because the question of the identity of the model can distract us from contemplating the underlying formal relationships.

Weston's "Nude" (Figure 12-13) shows many of the qualities of the F/64 Group. The figure is isolated and presented for its own sake. The sand is equivalent to a photographer's backdrop. The figure is presented not as a portrait of a given woman (although we know it is his wife, Charis), but rather as a formal study. Weston wanted us to see the relationship between legs and torso, to respond to the rhythms of line in the extended body, and to appreciate the counterpoint of the round, dark head against the long, light linearity of the body. Weston enjoys some notoriety for his studies of peppers because his approach to vegetables was similar to his approach to nudes. We are to appreciate the sensual curve, the counterpoints of line, the reflectivity of skin, the harmonious proportions of parts.

Weston's approach is in direct opposition to the pictorialist's tolerance for sentimentality. Weston demanded objectivity in his photographs. As he said, "I do not wish to impose my personality upon

FIGURE 12-13 Edward Weston, "Nude," 1936. © 1981 Center for Creative Photography, Arizona Board of Regents. Used by permission.

nature (any of life's manifestations), but without prejudice or falsification to become identified with nature, to know things in their very essence, so that what I record is not an interpretation—my ideas of what nature should be—but a revelation."[4] One of Weston's ideals was to capitalize on the camera's capacity to be objective and impersonal, the very qualities that the pictorialists usually fought against.

The work of Ansel Adams establishes another ideal of the F/64 Group: the fine print. In even the best of reproductions it is very difficult to point to the qualities of tonal gradation that constitute the fine print. Only the original can yield the beauties that gradations of silver or platinum can produce. In his "Antelope House Ruin," Adams aimed for a print whose textural subtleties are virtually endless. Unlike O'Sullivan, Adams did not aim for the great structural power of the horizontal striations in contrast with man-made houses. He chose a canyon face and a specific lighting that emphasized the textural gradations that would yield a print of tonal brilliance. In Weston's terms, he renders the essence of the rock and ruin.

PERCEPTION KEY: O'SULLIVAN AND ADAMS

1. Compare Timothy O'Sullivan's photograph of the Canyon de Chelley (Figure 12-5) with Ansel Adams' version (Figure 12-14). Is the subject matter the same in both photographs? What is it?
2. Compare the photographs for their perfection, insight, and inexhaustibility.
3. Is the content of both photographs the same? How do the formal organizations of the photographs differ?

TWO MASTERS OF SYMBOLISM

Aaron Siskind and Harry Callahan were never members of the F/64 Group, but their techniques are close in spirit. They avoid sentimentality and are both masters of the fine print. Further, they are interested in the symbolic meanings their images can evoke. Some critics refer to their images as iconic, meaning that they take on an abstract significance which was not apparent in the objects before they were photographed. The concept is very important: the photograph, by the act of selection or isolation, imparts an abstract significance to the object. We will call such images visual symbols (compare with Literary Symbols, pp. 253–257). Many photographs impart such significance, but Siskind and Callahan, along with Minor White, are important for going beyond the essence of things and pursuing their implied symbolic meanings.

[4]*The Daybooks of Edward Weston*, ed. Nancy Newhall, 2 vols. Aperture, New York, 1966, vol. 2, p. 241.

FIGURE 12-14 Ansel Adams, "Antelope House Ruin, Canyon de Chelley National Monument, Arizona," 1942.

Siskind's image "Gloucester, Massachusetts" (Figure 12-15) is evidence that the camera can invest even very ordinary objects with symbolic power. He tells us that in Gloucester he deliberately sought out everyday objects (like Kurt Schwitters, see pp. 164–165) rather than obviously important subject matter. But the fascinating thing is that the glove—although it had apparently been cast aside or lost—seems to have a living spirit of its own. It takes on the vitality of the hand that, only a while before, animated it. Isolated on the board, the glove

FIGURE 12-15 Aaron Siskind, "Gloucester, Massachusetts," 1944. International Museum of Photography at George Eastman House, Rochester.

becomes a pulsing symbol with a significance that can be felt but not pinned down. The isolation of the glove from its normal environment helps create a significance it would not otherwise have.

The symbolic power of Callahan's "Chicago" (Figure 12-16) depends in part on the low camera angle connecting the nearest woman (and the people behind her) with great architectural forces of the city. Behind her is a black building. It is noon and the light is intense. Near the woman is a sprouting metal lamppost—suggesting a sorry substitute for a tree. The woman reveals strength and determination. Her shape shares uprightness and powerful stability with everything around her. She has taken on Chicago's power and radiates significance; yet it would be difficult to limit that significance to a single meaning. What we see here is a mixture of forces: human, mechanical, architectural, metropolitan. Their interaction is complex and exciting.

PERCEPTION KEY SISKIND AND CALLAHAN

1. Can either photograph by Siskind or Callahan be clearly related to the pictorialist tradition?
2. Which photograph emphasizes detail more than the other? Does either invite a sentimental response?
3. What is the subject matter of these photographs? What is their content? How does using a visual object as a symbol affect the content of the photograph?
4. Symbolic meanings are not limited to photographs, of course, but can be found in paintings. Examine paintings in chapter four or in the first three chapters for their symbolic significance. How are they like or unlike the photographs of Siskind and Callahan? Examine other photographs in this chapter (or in the Film or Drama chapters) for similar kinds of symbolic meanings.

FIGURE 12-16 Harry Callahan, "Chicago," 1961.

THE DOCUMENTARISTS

Time is critical to the documentarist, who is portraying a world that is disappearing so slowly (or quickly) we cannot see it go. Henri Cartier-Bresson used the phrase, "the decisive moment," to define that crucial interaction of shapes formed by people and things that tells him when to snap his shutter. Not all his photographs are "decisive"; they do not all catch the action at its most intense point. But those that do are pure Cartier-Bresson.

Many documentarists agree with Stieglitz's description (p. 435) of the effect of shapes on his own feelings, as when he took "The Steerage." Few contemporary documentarists, however, who are often journalists like Cartier-Bresson, can compose the way Stieglitz could. But the best develop an instinct—nurtured by years of visual education —for the powerful formal statement even in the midst of disaster.

FIGURE 12-17 Eugéne Atget, "Balcony, 17 Rue du Petit Pont," 1913. AP:6014.1.69. 1947. Gold-toned printing-out paper, 9½ × 7⅛ inches. Collection, The Museum of Modern Art, New York. The Abbott-Levy Collection. Partial gift of Shirley C. Burden.

Eugéne Atget spent much of his time photographing in Paris in the early morning (when no one would bother him). The balcony and storefront in Figure 12-17 are shot from a sharp angle, to avoid reflecting himself in the glass. Everything is in sharp focus. The importance of this photograph is not in the way the shapes are organized (Stieglitz), nor in its objectivity (Weston), but because, as Beaumont Newhall has said, this "work has no reference to any graphic medium other than photography."[5] The innocence of this photograph links Atget with the contemporary photographer Gary

[5]Newhall, *History of Photography*, p. 137.

Winogrand, who said, "I photograph to see what something will look like photographed." Atget seems to have felt that way in early twentieth-century France. His work has been inspiring to many photographers trying to break away from the grip of pictorialism. Atget's work did not refer to painting: it created its own photographic reference. We see, in Atget's work, a photograph, not just a thing photographed.

James Van Der Zee worked in a somewhat different tradition from Atget. His studio in Harlem was so prominent that many important black citizens felt it essential that their portrait be taken by him. Like Atget, he was also fascinated with the life in his community and spent a good amount of his time photographing public events and activities, from the turn of the century to the nineteen thirties. His portrait of a "Couple in Racoon Coats" (Figure 12-18) is reminiscent of Robert Howlett as well as of Atget. The soft focus background emphasizes the couple and their brilliant new car. But the interaction of formal elements is so complex that it reminds us of Atget: there has been no reduction of shapes to a simpler geometry. We must take these shapes as they are. The car has been selectively framed front and rear, reminding us that this is, first, a portrait of a couple. Their style and elegance are what Van Der Zee was anxious to capture. Our familiarity with the chief elements in the photograph—brownstones, car, and fur-coated people—help make it possible for him to be direct, avoiding

FIGURE 12-18 James Van Der Zee, "Couple in Racoon Coats," 1932. © All rights reserved by James Van Der Zee.

FIGURE 12-19   Henri Cartier-Bresson, "Lisbon," 1955. Magnum Photos, Inc.

the soothing formal order the pictorialist might have insisted upon. If anything, Van Der Zee is moving toward the snapshot aesthetic that was another generation in the making. Yet his directness of approach shows us that he was in the best of the documentary tradition. The photograph reveals something about the style of Harlem in the 1930s.

Unlike Atget and Van Der Zee, who used large cameras, Cartier-Bresson used the 35mm Leica and specialized in people. He preset his camera in order to work fast and instinctively. His "Lisbon," 1955 (Figure 12-19), shows his instinct for formal organization, with the sharp diagonal of the cannon merging with the diagonal formed by the three aligned men. The umbrella and the right arm of the man holding it are poised at the right place to cap this arrangement. The angle of the stone wall echoes the basic triangulation of the primary figures. This attention to arrangement establishes a clear relationship among all the elements of the composition. The men have been caught in a moment of collective reflection, as if they, like the defunct cannon, are merely parts of Lisbon's ancient history.

The formal relationship of elements in a photograph can produce various kinds of significance or apparent lack of significance. The best documentarists, building in part on both the achievement of the pictorialists and the F/64 Group, search for the strongest relationship of elements while also searching for the decisive moment. That moment is the split-second peak of emotional intensity (as Beaumont Newhall puts it), and it is defined especially in terms of light, action, expression, and organization.

PERCEPTION KEY: ATGET, VAN DER ZEE, AND CARTIER-BRESSON

1. Which of these photographs most completely rejects the pictorialist approach to formal organization? Is it also the least sentimental photograph? Is it the least feelingful?
2. Some critics assert that Atget and Van Der Zee have made interesting social documents, but not works of art. What arguments might support their views? What arguments might contradict their views? As an aid for this entire question, consider how the pictorialist would value these photographs.
3. Contemporary photographers and critics often value the work of Atget very highly because it is "liberated" from the influence of painting. Is this an adequate reason to celebrate such photographs?
4. Which of the three photographs seems to be most clearly successful as a work of art? Refer to the standards of perfection, insight, and inexhaustibility.

Two of America's most renowned documentarists are Walker Evans and Dorothea Lange. They took part in a federal program to give work to photographers during the Depression of the 1930s.

FIGURE 12-20   Walker Evans, "A Graveyard and Steel Mill in Bethlehem, Pennsylvania," 1935. Silver Print, 7⅞ × 9⅝ inches. Collection, the Museum of Modern Art, New York. Gift of the Farm Security Administration.

FIGURE 12-21
Dorothea Lange,
"Migrant Mother," 1936,
Dorothea Lange
Collection, The Oakland
Museum.

PERCEPTION KEY EVANS' "BETHLEHEM, PENNSYLVANIA" AND
LANGE'S "MIGRANT MOTHER"

1. Which photograph is more likely to have been influenced by Atget? Which
   is more likely to have been influenced by Cartier-Bresson and his concept
   of the "decisive moment"?
2. Which photograph is more carefully attentive to the possibilities of
   repetition of shapes? (Consider circles, rectangles, strong vertical and
   horizontal lines.)

3. What is the subject matter of each photograph? What is the content of each photograph?
4. Compare Lange's photograph with the represenations of the Madonna and Child in Chapter 4 (Figure 4-3; 4-4; 4-5). What are the differences in subject matter and content? How does the documentary approach to formal organization contribute to the differences?
5. Is either of these photographs impersonal and objective in the terms that Weston established? Is either sentimental?

Both photographs depend on careful formal organization. Lange stresses centrality and balance by placing the children's heads next to the mother's face, which is all the more compelling because the children's faces do not compete for our attention. The mother's arm leads us inevitably upward to her face, emphasizing the triangularities that Lange captured in several other segments of the photograph. We are drawn to the subject matter, apart from formal considerations, because we respond to such a powerful portrayal of uncertainty and suffering. Within ten minutes, Lange took four other photographs of this woman and her children, but none could achieve the content of this photograph.

Evans' photograph shows us a view of Bethlehem, Pennsylvania, and the powerful shape of the off-center white cross reminds us of what has become of the message of Christ. The vertical lines are accentuated in the cemetery stones, repeated in the telephone lines, porch posts, and finally in the steel mill smokestacks. Evans has chosen to make everything equal in terms of focus and detail. His lens has also compressed the space so that we see the cemetery right on top of the living space, which is immediately adjacent to the steel mills where some of the people who live in the tenements work and where some of those now in the cemetery died. The compression of space reveals a psychological compression of death, life, and work. The aspirations of the dominating verticals are dampened by the powerful horizontals, which, through the low angle of the lens, tend to merge from the cross to the roofs. Once we understand the relationships between the formal elements and their relationship to subject matter our participation with the photograph deepens.

Lange caught the exact moment when the children's faces turned and the mother expressed anxiety. Evans caught the right moment for the light, which intensifies the white cross, and he aligned the verticals and horizontals for their best effect. Both photographers use selective framing, although it is much more evident in the Lange photograph. Lange's lens has mercifully softened its focus on the mother's face, while leaving her shabby clothes in sharp focus. This softness helps humanize our relationship with the woman.

The Modern Eye: Four Photographers

As with all artistic media, the relationship between subject matter and form lies at the heart of the successful photograph. But the art of photography is young, and the mood is often rebellious. The successes of the pictorialist and straight photographic movements have led to reactions which are often like those we have seen in painting, sculpture, and architecture. Some of the rebellion has produced novel attitudes toward subject matter, as in the work of Diane Arbus, who specialized in photographing dwarfs, aberrants, and freaks for their surprise value. Some rebellion has produced novel approaches to the composition of forms, such as the work of Robert Frank, a Swiss documentarist famous for his study of America in 1958. Jerry Uelsmann combines several negatives to make a single print, often with Freudian undertones. Duane Michals' sequences of prints form a narrative that is also sometimes Freudian, contrasting the subconscious with the conscious. In one sense, all four of these photographers approach the same basic subject matter: the nature of reality. All treat it differently.

DIANE ARBUS

Diane Arbus was drawn to people who were outcasts, and her personality permitted her to establish a liason that produced frank and remarkable images. Her photograph of the Jewish giant with his parents (Figure 12-22) is powerful primarily because of the strangeness of the subject matter. Nevertheless, Arbus has organized the elements of the photograph carefully. The giant is standing, bent over against the ceiling. His parents stand beside him looking up in wonderment. The simplicity and ordinariness of this room are significant when we think of how unordinary this scene is. In one way, Arbus is feeding our passion for looking at freaks, but in another way she is showing us that freaks are quite like us. We know this, of course, but Arbus' images make us feel its truth. Arbus brought exceptional sensitivity to her work and a great sympathy for her subjects.

ROBERT FRANK

Although it is not quite accurate to associate Robert Frank with those photographers who began a vogue for the snapshot, his work fits in well with current practice. Janet Malcolm has said, "Photography went modernist not, as has been supposed, when it began to imitate modern abstract art but when it began to study snapshots."[6] John Szarkowski of the Museum of Modern Art has praised the snapshot as one of the great

---

[6]*Diana and Nikon: Essays on the Aesthetics of Photography*, David Godine, Boston, 1980, p. 113.

FIGURE 12-22 Diane Arbus, "A Jewish Giant at Home with His Parents in the Bronx, N.Y." © 1971 by the estate of Diane Arbus.

resources of the medium. Its low technical demands, its unself-consciousness, its potential for cluttered composition, and its refusal to attend to the standards of pictorialism all offered a way to rebel against the photographic establishment. And even though there is no school of photographers to establish a snapshot canon, it is clear that the snapshot is the product of amateurs, while the studied photograph seems the product of professionals. In that sense the snapshot is more primitive—more spontaneous, less planned, more accidental, perhaps even more exciting.

Frank's "Gallup, New Mexico," (Figure 12-23) gives the impression of being unplanned, with little attention to the Weston dogma concerning the fine print (the book it appeared in was wretchedly printed). However, despite its unconventional composition, it achieves content. The light is brutal, befitting a tough, male-dominated environment. The sharp angle of presentation is unsettling and contributes to our lack of ease. The main figure, posed with his hands in his pockets, seems at home in this environment, while the menacing black forms of the men in the foreground shadow us from the scene.

We cannot tell what is going on, but we are given a powerful sense of the "feel" of the place and the people. One of Weston's concerns—for rendering the essence of the scene—is certainly satisfied. However, Weston's concern for objectivity, the impersonal rendering of the subject matter is ignored. Frank is making more of a personal statement, coloring what he sees with his camera angle and apparent disregard for technique. It is possible that these men are at a raffle raising funds for the local hospital; we really do not know. Frank presents them to us as if they are in a barroom with violence lurking just beneath the surface. The harsh light, low camera angle, and selective framing contribute to Frank's personal statement.

FIGURE 12-23 Robert Frank, "Gallup, New Mexico," 1955–1956. Courtesy of Paul Katz, Zebra Corporation, New York.

JERRY UELSMANN

Uelsmann's excursions into the worlds of external and internal reality may be compared with surrealist painters, such as Dali and Max Ernst. Many of his works resemble dreams, with positive and negative images side by side, women "buried" in bushes, and other interesting combinations. "Tiltawheel" (Figure 12-24) seems at first to be a straight photograph of a becurtained amusement park ride. But closer examination shows that the two sides of the photograph have been skillfully reversed and joined, while the foreground bends down to us in an unearthly fashion. This is a disturbing image partly because we could

FIGURE 12-24 Jerry Uelsmann, "Tiltawheel," 1968.

not see it in real life—we need the mediation of Uelsmann's technique. This image makes us think of otherworldly objects, of very strange things, even if they are slightly anthropomorphic. "Tiltawheel" does not give us the usual comfort of the amusement park. The figures are hooded, as if their power derived from the nightmare images that sometimes threaten us. They are vague, despite the sharpness of detail, and ambiguous despite our knowledge that they are instruments of entertainment. Uelsmann achieves the symbolic technique of Siskind and Callahan, but he abandons straight photography in doing so.

DUANE MICHALS

Duane Michals adds a narrative element to the surrealism of Uelsmann. "Alice's Mirror," 1974 (Figure 12-25), like many of his sequences, informs us in an amusing fashion about how we see. The first frame shows us something that is revealed in a totally different scale in the second frame. This image is then compressed in a series of mirrors until the composition is finally smashed and discarded. No one of these images has the power of formal structure that would interest the pictorialists, nor the quality of objectivity of print values that would interest the straight photographer of the Weston camp. Taken together they make a sequence that constitutes an exploration of how we see. This is a series not about an armchair and glasses, nor about mirrors. It is about how we see those things and the ambiguities in the medium of photography, whose essence, for the general audience, is in its *lack* of ambiguity. Michals' revelation is both startling and emotionally convincing.

Summary

Photography's capacity to record reality faithfully is both a virtue and a fault. It makes many viewers of photographs concerned only with what is presented (the subject matter) and leaves them unaware of the way it has been represented (the form). Because of its fidelity of presentation, photography seems to some to have no transformation of subject matter (the content). This did not bother early photographers, who were delighted at the ease with which they could present their subject matter. The pictorialists, on the other hand, relied on nineteenth-century representational painting to guide them in their approach to form in the photograph. Their soft focus, sometimes sentimental and carefully composed images are still valued by many photographers. But the reaction of the straight photographers, who wished to shake off any dependence on painting, began a revolution that was to emphasize the special qualities of the medium: especially the tonal range of the silver or platinum print (and now color print), the impersonality of the sharply defined object (and consequent lack of sentimentality), spatial

FIGURE 12-25 Duane Michals, "Alice's Mirror," 1974.

compression, and selective framing. The revolution has not stopped there, but has pushed on into unexpected areas, such as the exploration of the random snapshot and the rejection of the technical standards of the straight photographers. The contemporary photographer is searching for new ways of photographic seeing.

Chapter 12 Bibliography

Barthes, Roland. *Camera Lucida.* New York: Hill and Wang, 1981.

Bayer, Jonathan. *Reading Photographs: Understanding the Aesthetics of Photography.* New York: Pantheon Books, 1977.

Berger, John, and Jean Mohr. *Another Way of Telling.* New York: Pantheon, 1982.

Doty, Robert. *Photo-Secession.* New York: Dover, 1978.

Galassi, Peter. *Before Photography.* New York: Museum of Modern Art, 1981.

Gernsheim, Helmut. *Creative Photography.* London: Faber and Faber, 1962.

Malcolm, Janet. *Diana and Nikon: Essays on the Aesthetics of Photography.* Boston: David Godine, 1980.

Newhall, Beaumont. *The History of Photography.* New York: Museum of Modern Art, 1964.

————, ed. *Photography: Essays and Images.* New York: Museum of Modern Art, 1980.

Petruck, Peninah R., ed. *The Camera Viewed.* 2 vols. New York: E. P. Dutton, 1979.

Rosenberg, Harold. *The Tradition of the New.* New York: McGraw-Hill, 1965.

Sandler, Martin W. *The Story of American Photography.* Boston: Little Brown, 1979.

Scharf, Aaron. *Art and Photography.* New York: Penguin, 1974.

Time-Life Books. *Life Library of Photography.* New York: Time-Life, 1970–1972, revised, 1980.

THE HUMANITIES:
THEIR INTERRELATIONSHIPS

13 The Arts and their Interrelationship

In the preceding chapters we have emphasized the autonomy of the various arts, how they differ. We have seen how the medium of an art—the material that the work of art is made in, such as colors, tones, words, etc.—makes available certain kinds of subject matter for interpretation. For example—and to oversimplify grossly—the medium of painting is especially adaptable for interpreting the visual appearance of things; sculpture for bringing out the solidity of things; architecture for centralizing spatial contexts; literature for probing the complexities of human character; drama for revealing with extraordinary condensation the comedy and tragedy of human destiny; music for clarifying the nuances of feeling; dance for vivifying states of mind; photography for capturing with exceptional precision the essence of actual objects and events; and, finally, film with its moving images that seem to be able to go almost anywhere has, perhaps, the broadest range of subject matter. At the same time, each art has limitations as determined by its medium. Music, for instance, is extremely limited in interpreting the visual appearance of things. These limitations restrict the combining of the arts. Yet from the earliest times mixed media, such as songs, have flourished. In our time new mixed media—such as sculpto-paintings and happenings—are continually being developed.

Of all the arts, however, opera has taken the meshing of media the farthest, sometimes including all the major media except the film and photography. Indeed, it would not be surprising to see a twentieth-century Wagner even incorporating those arts.

PERCEPTION KEY INTERRELATIONSHIPS AMONG THE ARTS

1. Is a film of an opera such as Ingmar Bergman's film of Mozart's *The Magic Flute* an example of a mixed-media art? As you think about this, note that Bergman made many changes in the traditional staging. It was not simply a matter of placing cameras in the opera house and recording a performance.
2. Of the art media we have studied, which ones do you think most resist being meshed with other media? Which ones most lend themselves to meshing? Are there any media that cannot be meshed?
3. Are there any reasons for thinking that a mixed-media work is of lesser artistic quality—other things being equal—than an unmixed work? Some musical purists, for example, disregard the meaning of the words of songs, listening only to the tonal relationships, believing that program music is a decadent offspring of pure music.

Each artistic medium, despite its distinctiveness, lends itself to some extent to being mixed with some of the other artistic media. There are two basic reasons. In the first place, artistic media are systematically organizable. Some media possess an order of their own, in the sense that the relationships of colors that make up the color wheel are an order that people discover rather than impose. Other media permit the imposing of an order, in the sense that engineering principles impose order upon building materials. If a medium lacked an inherent order, then, in turn, organization of that material by an artistic form would be impossible. That is the basic reason why works of art have not been made out of tastes or smells. An order of tastes or smells, analogous to the scales of music, has not yet been discovered. The order of each artistic medium helps make possible its combination with other media. Order can combine with order much easier than with disorder.

In the second place, every art, unmixed or mixed, interprets some subject matter. All artists, consciously or unconsciously, attempt to organize a medium into a form-content, into a structure that reveals something significant that has never been revealed before. And so they use whatever medium or combination of media that serve their purpose. No angel with a flaming sword stands between them and a choice of media. The choice of mixed media, moreover, is often a challenge that brings out the best in an artist. Great as most of the pure music of Bach is, his Mass in B Minor is surely as great. And to listen to that music without paying any attention to the meaning of the words is to miss much of the power of the tonal relationships. The music and the sound and meaning of the words are an inseparable merger for the most intense participation.

Furthermore, the arts often can thrive in their individuality while in close juxtaposition. Sculpture without architecture is sometimes like furniture without a home. Architecture without sculpture is sometimes a house that is not a home. But because of the powerful autonomy of each of the major arts, the juxtaposition of the arts must be very carefully arranged. Arp's *Growth* (frontispiece and Figure 5-15) commands its surrounding space, and it would be suffocated if placed in a niche. The architectural home of *Growth* must respect its outreaching, which "thickens" the space around with vectors.

PERCEPTION KEY THE JUXTAPOSITION OF THE ARTS

Suppose you were in charge of the installation of an exhibition of painting and sculpture composed of all the eight paintings reproduced in the color plates and the following sculptures: Figures 5-7, 5-8, 5-15, 5-22, 5-23, 5-26, 5-28, and 5-42. Suppose, further, that the space for this exhibition were restricted to the glass pavilion of Philip Johnson's Wiley House and its adjacent patio (Figure 6-31). Where would you arrange and place these sixteen works? Consider such factors as preservation, lighting, privileged positions, access, and spatial conflicts. Obviously it would be much easier to do this on site, but use your imagination.

The arts are a commonwealth. They closely interrelate because all of them, each in its own way, are doing basically the same thing—providing a wealth of immediate or intrinsic values as well as giving insight into what matters most. The arts not only give us delight but also increase our understanding of ourselves and our world. Furthermore, the arts make our perceptions and conceptions more flexible, discriminating, and responsive. The arts cultivate our sense of dignity as human beings in these special ways.

PERCEPTION KEY *DEATH IN VENICE:* THREE VERSIONS

Read Thomas Mann's novella *Death In Venice*, published in 1911. This is a haunting tale—one of the greatest short stories of this century—of a very disciplined, famous writer who, in his fifties, is physically and mentally exhausted. Gustav von Aschenbach seeks rest by means of a vacation, eventually coming to Venice. On the beach there, he becomes obsessed with the beauty of a boy. Despite Aschenbach's knowledge of a developing epidemic of cholera, he remains, and, afraid the boy will be taken away, withholds information about the epidemic from the boy's mother. Casting aside all restraint and shame, Aschenbach even attempts, with the help of a barber, to appear youthful again. Yet Aschenbach, a master of language, never speaks to the boy nor can he find words to articulate the origins of his obsession and love. Collapsing in his chair with a heart attack, he dies as he watches the boy walking off in the sea. Try to see the recent film version, first shown in 1971, directed by Luchino Visconti and starring Dirk Bogarde. Also listen to the operatic version composed in 1973 by Benjamin Britten, with libretto by Myfanwy Piper, as recorded by London Records, New York City, and starring Peter Pears.

1. Which of these three versions do you find most enjoyable and interesting? Why?

2. Does the film reveal insights about Aschenbach (and ourselves) that escaped even Thomas Mann? Does the opera reveal insights that escape both the novella and the film? Be specific. What are the special powers and limitations of these three media?

3. In both the novella and the opera the opening scene has Aschenbach walking by a cemetery in a suburb of Munich. The film opens, however, with shots of Aschenbach coming into Venice in a gondola. Why do you think Visconti did not use Mann's opening? Why, on the other hand, did Britten follow Mann's opening?

4. In the film, Aschenbach is portrayed as a composer rather than a writer. Why?

5. In the opera, unlike the film, the dance plays a major role. Why?

6. The hold of a boy over a mature, sophisticated man such as Aschenbach may seem at first highly improbable and contrived. How does Mann make this improbability seem plausible? Visconti? Britten?

7. Is Britten able to articulate the hidden deeper feelings of Aschenbach more vividly than Mann or Visconti? If so, how? What can music do that these other two arts cannot do in this respect? Note Aschenbach's (Mann's?) thought in the novella: "Language could but extol, not reproduce, the beauties of the sense." Note also that Visconti often uses the music of Gustav Mahler to help give us insight into the depths of Aschenbach's character. But does this music, as it meshes with the moving images, do this as effectively as Britten's music?

8. Do you think that seeing Britten's opera performed would add significantly to your participation? Note that some opera lovers prefer to hear only the music and shut their eyes most of the time in the opera house.

9. Do these three works complement each other? After seeing the film or listening to the opera, does the novella become richer for you? If so, how is this to be explained?

10. In the novella, Socrates tells Phaedrus: "For beauty, my Phaedrus, beauty alone, is lovely and visible at once. For, mark you, it is the sole aspect of the spiritual which we can perceive through our senses, or bear so to perceive." But in the opera, Socrates asks: "Does beauty lead to wisdom, Phaedrus?" Socrates answers his own question: "Yes, but through the senses. . . . And senses lead to passion . . . and passion to the abyss." Why do you think Britten and Piper made such a drastic change in emphasis?

11. What insights about our lives are brought to us by these works? For example, do you have a better understanding of the tragedy of beauty and of the connection between beauty and death?

The Humanities and the Sciences

In the beginning pages of Chapter 1, we referred to the humanities as that broad range of creative activities and studies that are usually contrasted with mathematics and the "hard" sciences, mainly because in the humanities strictly objective or scientific standards do not usually dominate.

CONCEPTION KEY CLASSIFYING SUBJECTS OF STUDY

1. Suppose you have been charged with grouping the courses of study at your or some other school. Is it possible to make reasonably clear and defensible groupings? If so, how would you do it? For example, would you place psychology with the sciences? Where would you place sociology? And what about such studies as education and business administration?
2. It seems obvious that literature, music, and painting belong to the humanities. Is there something strange about putting such studies as history, philosophy, and theology in the same slot as the arts? How would you justify such a grouping?

Most college and university catalogues contain a grouping of courses called the humanities. First, studies such as literature, the visual arts, music, history, philosophy, and theology almost invariably are included. Second, studies such as psychology, anthropology, sociology, political science, economics, business administration, and education may or may not be included. Third, studies such as physics, chemistry, biology, mathematics, and engineering are never included.

The reason the last group is excluded is obvious—strict scientific or objective standards are clearly applicable. With the second group, these "hard" standards are not always so clearly applicable. There is an uncertainty about whether they belong with the sciences or the humanities. For example, most psychologists who experiment with animals apply the scientific method as rigorously as any biologist. But there are also psychologists—C. G. Jung, for instance—who speculate about such phenomena as the "Collective unconscious" and the role of myth. To judge their work strictly by scientific methods is to miss their contributions. Where then should psychology and the subjects in this group be placed? In the case of the first group, finally, the arts are invariably listed under the humanities. But then so are history, philosophy, and theology. Thus, as the title of this book implies, the humanities include subjects other than the arts. Then how are the arts distinguished from the other humanities? And what is the relationship between the arts and these other humanities?

These are broad and complex questions. Concerning the placement of the studies in group two, it is usually best to take each department case by case. If, for example, a department of psychology is dominated by experimentalists, as is most likely in the United States, it would seem most useful to place that department with the sciences. And the same approach can be made to all the studies in group two. In most cases, probably, you will discover that clear-cut placements into the humanities or the sciences are impossible. Furthermore, even the subjects that almost always are grouped within either the humanities or the sciences cannot always be neatly catalogued. Rigorous objective standards may be applied in any of the humanities. Thus, painting can be approached as a science—the historian of medieval painting, for example, who measures, as precisely as any engineer, the evolving sizes of haloes. On the other hand, the beauty of mathematics—its economy and elegance of proof—can excite the lover of mathematics as much as, if not more than, painting. Edna St. Vincent Millay noted that "Euclid alone has looked on beauty bare." And so the separation of the humanities and the sciences should not be observed rigidly. The separation is useful mainly because it indicates the dominance or the subordinance of the strict scientific method in the various disciplines.

The Arts and the other Humanities

Artists differ from the other humanists primarily because they create works that reveal values; that is, they present works that are clearer than nonartistic reality. Artists are sensitive to the important concerns or values of their society. That is their subject matter in the broadest sense. They create artistic forms that clarify these values. That is their content. The other humanists—such as historians, philosophers, and theologians—reflect upon, rather than reveal, values. They study values as given, as they find them. They try to describe and explain values—their causes and consequences. Furthermore, they may judge these values as good or bad. Thus like artists they, too, try to clarify values; but they do this by means of nonartistic forms (see Chapter 2).

CONCEPTION KEY ARTISTS AND OTHER HUMANISTS

1. Explain how the work of an artist might be of significance to the historian, philosopher, and theologian.
2. Select works of art that we have discussed in this book that you think might be of greatest significance respectively to historians, philosophers, and theologians. Ask others to do the same. Then compare and discuss your selections.
3. Can you find any works of art we have discussed that you think would have no significance whatsoever to any of the other humanists? If so, explain.

The other humanists do not transform values in their studies as in artistic revelation. Often they study values independently of the arts, but if they take advantage of the revealing role of the arts, their studies often will be enhanced because, other things being equal, they will have a more penetrating understanding of the values they are studying. This is basically the aid that the artists can give to some of the other humanists. Suppose, for example, a historian is trying to understand the bombing of Guernica by the Fascists in the Spanish Civil War. Suppose he or she has explored all factual resources. Even then something very important may be left out: vivid awareness of the feelings of the noncombatants. To gain insight into those feelings, Picasso's *Guernica* (Figure 1-2) may be a great aid.

CONCEPTION KEY OTHER HUMANISTS AND ARTISTS

---

1. Is there anything that Picasso may have learned from historians that he used in painting *Guernica*?
2. Explain how the work of the other humanists might be of significance to the artist. Be specific.

Other humanists may aid artists by their study of values. For example, in this book we have concerned ourselves in some detail with criticism—the description, interpretation, and evaluation of works of art. Criticism is a humanistic discipline because it studies values—those revealed in works of art—without strictly applying scientific or objective standards. Good critics aid our understanding of works of art. We become more sensitively aware of the revealed values. This deeper understanding brings us into closer rapport with artists, and such rapport helps sustain their confidence in their work.

The arts reveal values; the other humanistic disciplines study values. That does not mean that artists may not study values, but rather that such study, if any, is subordinated to revealing values in an artistic form that attracts our participation. The other humanists, conversely, study values and communicate their findings in nonartistic forms.

Perception and Conception

Another basic difference between the arts and the other humanities is the way perception dominates in the arts whereas conception dominates in the other humanities. Of course, perceiving and conceiving (or thinking) almost always go together. When we are aware of red striking our eyes, we are perceiving, but normally our brain is also conceiving, more or less explicitly, the idea "red." On the other hand, when we conceive the idea "red" with our eyes closed, we almost invariably remember some specific or generalized image of perceptible red. Probably the infant only perceives, and as we are sinking into unconsciousness from illness or a blow on the head it may be that all ideas or concepts are wiped out. It may be, conversely, that conceiving sometimes occurs without any element of perceiving. Descartes, the great seventeenth-century philosopher, thought so. Most philosophers and psychologists believe, however, that even the most abstract thinking of mathematicians, since it still must be done with perceptible signs such as numbers, necessarily includes residues from perception. In any case, the question of the relationships and interdependence of perception and conception, which has been puzzling thinkers from the beginnings of civilization, still remains open.

CONCEPTION KEY PERCEPTION AND CONCEPTION

1. Think of examples in your experience in which percepts dominate concepts, and vice versa. Which kind of experience do you enjoy the most? Does your answer tell you anything about yourself?
2. Is it easily possible for you to shift gears from conceptually dominated thinking to perceptually dominated thinking? For example, if you are studying intensely some theoretical or practical problem, do you find it difficult to begin to "think from" some work or art? Or, conversely, if you have been participating with a work of art, do you find it difficult to begin to "think at" some theoretical or practical problem? Do your answers tell you anything about yourself?
3. Select from the chapter on literature (Chapter 7) that poem that seems to demand the most from your perceptual faculties and the least from your conceptual faculties. Then select that poem that seems to demand the most from your conceptual faculties and the least from your perceptual faculties. Which poem do you like better? Does your answer tell you anything about yourself?
4. Which of the arts that we have studied seems to demand the most from your perceptual faculties? Your conceptual faculties? Why? Which art do you like better? Does your answer tell you anything about yourself?

It seems evident that perception without some conception is little more than a blooming, buzzing confusion. Thus, all our talk about art in the previous chapters has been a conceptualizing that we hope has clarified and intensified your perception of specific works of art. But that is not to suggest that conception ought to dominate perception in your participation with a work of art. In fact, if conception dominates, participation will be weakened or prevented—we will be thinking *at* rather than thinking *from*. If, as we listen to the sonata form, we explicitly identify the exposition, development, and recapitualation sections, we will be lowering the sensitivity of our listening. Yet, if you were to ask trained music lovers *after* their listening, they probably could easily name the sections and tell you where such sections occurred. In other words, to experience the arts most intensely and satisfactorily, conception is indispensable, but perception must remain in the foreground. When we come to the other humanities, however, conception usually comes to the foreground. The other humanities basically *reflect about* values rather than *reveal* values, as in the case of the arts. With the other humanities, therefore, concepts or ideas become more central than percepts.

Values

A value is something we care about, something that matters. A value is an object of an interest. The term "object," however, should be understood as including events or states of affairs. A pie is obviously an object and it may be a value, and the course of action involved in obtaining the pie may also be a value. If we are not interested in something, it is neutral in value or valueless to us. Positive values are those objects of interest that satisfy us or give us pleasure, such as good health. Negative values are those objects of interest that dissatisfy us or give us pain, such as bad health. When the term "value" is used alone, it usually refers to positive values only, but it may also include negative values. In our value decisions, we generally seek to obtain positive values and avoid negative values. But except for the very young child, these decisions usually involve highly complex activities. To have a tooth pulled is painful, a negative value, but doing so leads to the possibility of better health, a positive value. *Intrinsic values* involve the feelings, such as pleasure and pain, we have of some value activity, such as enjoying good food or the nausea of overeating. *Extrinsic values* are the means to intrinsic values, such as making the money that pays for the food. *Intrinsic-extrinsic values* not only evoke immediate feelings but also are means to further values, such as the enjoyable food that leads to future good health. For most people, intrinsic-extrinsic values of the positive kind are the basis of the good life. Certain drugs may have great positive intrinsic value, but then extrinsically they may have powerful negative value, leading to great suffering.

CONCEPTION KEY PARTICIPATION WITH ART AND VALUES

1. Do you think that the value of a participative experience with a work of art is basically intrinsic, extrinsic, or intrinsic-extrinsic? Explain.
2. Many psychiatrists treat their patients by retraining their sensory receptivity. In *Art of Awareness* Dr. J. Samuel Bois cites the example of a surgeon

who came to him for treatment because he was nervous and unsure of himself in performing very delicate operations. Bois discovered that the surgeon conceptualized his operations—that is, as he cut through the layers of tissue and encountered the various parts of the body, he named each one silently to himself—interfering with the nervous and muscular control of his eyes and hands. Bois prescribed remedial exercises resulting in a decrease in the *conceptualizing* and an increase in the *perceptualizing* process of the operation. Instead of identifying each tissue, vein, artery, and organ by name, the surgeon was trained to identify them by more efficient looking and feeling, through greater sensitivity to nuances of color, shape, texture, size, etc. The treatment worked: the surgeon reduced his nervousness and increased his confidence and effectiveness, so that the time involved in operating was cut in half. Do you think that learning to enjoy painting or sculpture more intensely might have been a part of Bois' remedial exercises? Or might any of the other arts have been helpful to the surgeon?

3. Dr Vikor Frankl, a medical doctor and psychiatrist, writes in *The Doctor and the Soul*, "The higher meaning of a given moment in human existence can be fulfilled by the mere intensity with which it is experienced, and independent of any action. If anyone doubts this, let him consider the following situation. Imagine a music lover sitting in the concert hall while the most noble measures of his favorite symphony resound in his ears. He feels that shiver of emotion which we experience in presence of the purest beauty. Suppose now that at such a moment we should ask this person whether his life has meaning. He would have to reply that it had been worthwhile living if only to experience this ecstatic moment."[1] Do you agree with Frankl, or do you consider this an overstatement? Why?

4. It has been variously reported that some of the most sadistic guards and high-ranking officers in the Nazi concentration camps played the music of Bach and Beethoven during or after torturings. Goering was a great lover of excellent paintings. Hitler loved architecture and the music of Wagner. What do you make of this?

Participation with a work of art not only is immediately satisfying but also is usually extrinsically valuable because it leads to deeper satisfactions in the future. To participate with one poem is likely to increase our sensitivity to the next poem. Moreover, by enhancing our sensory receptivity, participation with art can sometimes help in our practical activities, as in the case of the unsure surgeon. But most important of all, the understanding of values we achieve through participating with works of art may be extrinsically very valuable because such understanding helps us face our moral dilemmas with sounder orientation and deeper sympathy for others. And yet again, what about the last question of the last concept key?

[1] Viktor E. Frankl, *The Doctor and the Soul*, Richard and Clara Winston (trans.), Alfred A. Knopf, New York, 1955, p. 49.

1. Select that work of art discussed in this book that is the most valuable to you. Why is it so valuable?
2. Do you believe that value is projected into things by us, or that we discover values in things, or that in some way value originates in the relationship between us and things? Explain.

Values, we propose, involve a valuer and something that excites an interest in that valuer. *Subjectivist theories* of value claim, however, that it is the interest that projects the value on something. The painting, for example, is positively valuable only because it satisfies the interest of someone. Value is in the valuer. If no one is around to project interest, then there are no valuable objects. Value is entirely relative to the valuer. Beauty is in the eye of the beholder. Jane is not really beautifuly. Jane is beautiful only if someone sees her so. *Objectivist theories* of value claim, conversely, that it is the object that excites the interest. Moreover, the painting is positively valuable even if no one has any interest in it. Value is in the object independently of any subject. Jane is beautiful even if no one is aware of her beauty.

The relational theory of value—which is the one we have been presupposing throughout this book—claims that value emerges from the relation between an interest and an object. A good painting that is satisfying no one's interest at the moment possesses only *potential* value. A good painting possesses properties that under proper conditions are likely to stimulate the interests of a valuer. The subjectivist would say that this painting has no value whatsoever until someone projects value on it. The objectivist would say that this painting has actualized value inherent in it whether anyone enjoys it or not. The relationalist would say that this painting has potential value; that when it is experienced under proper conditions, a sensitive, informed participant will actualize the potential value. To describe a painting as "good" is the same as saying that the painting has positive potential value. Furthermore, for the relationalist, value is realized only when objects with potential value connect with the interests of someone.

Values are usually studied with reference to the interaction of various kinds of potential value with human interests. For example, criticism tends to focus on the intrinsic values of works of art; economics focuses on commodities as basically extrinsic values; and ethics focuses on intrinsic-extrinsic values as they are or ought to be chosen by moral agents.

CONCEPTION KEY VALUES AND THE SCIENCES

Since values involve human interests, and these interests are likely to vary from individual to individual, do you think values can be described by the sciences? If so, how?

Values that are described scientifically as they are found, we shall call "value facts." Values that are set forth as norms or ideals or what ought to be, we shall call "normative values." The smoking of marijuana, for instance, is a positive value for many. Much research is being undertaken to provide descriptions of the consequences of the use of marijuana, and rigorous scientific standards are applicable. We would place such research with the sciences. And we would call the values that are described in such research value facts. A scientific report may describe the relevant value facts connected with the use of marijuana, showing, for instance, that people who smoke marijuana generally have such-and-such pleasurable experiences but at the same time incur such-and-such risks. Such a report is describing what *is* the case, not what *ought* to be the case (that is, normative values). When someone argues that marijuana should be prohibited or someone else argues that marijuana should be legalized, we are in a realm beyond the strict application of scientific standards. Appeal is being made not to what "is" or to factual value—this the sciences can handle—but to the "ought" or normative value.

CONCEPTION KEY FACTUAL VALUE AND NORMATIVE VALUE

1. Do you see any possible connection between factual and normative value? For example, will the scientific studies now being made on the use of marijuana have any relevance to your judgment as to whether you should or should not smoke marijuana?
2. Do you think that the artist can reveal anything relevant to your judgment about using marijuana?
3. Do you think humanists other than artists might produce anything relevant to your judgment about the use of marijuana?

There is very close relationship between factual and normative value. If scientists were to assert that anyone who uses marijuana regularly cannot possibly live longer than ten more years, this obviously would influence the arguments about its legalization. Yet the basis for a well-grounded decision about such a complex issue—for it is hardly likely that such a clear-cut fact as death within ten years from using marijuana regularly will be discovered—surely involves more than scientific information. Novels such as Aldous Huxley's *Brave New World* reveal aspects and consequences of drug experiences that escape the nets of scientific investigation. They clarify features of value phenomena which supplement the factual values as discovered by science. After exposure to such literature, we may be in a better position for well-grounded decisions about such problems as the legalization of marijuana.

The arts and the other humanities often have normative relevance. They may clarify the possibilities for value decisions, thus clarifying what ought to be and what we ought to do. And this is an invaluable function, for we are creatures who must constantly choose among various value possibilities. Paradoxically, even not choosing is often a choice. The humanities can help enlighten our choices. Artists help by revealing aspects and consequences of value phenomena that escape scientists. The other humanists help by clarifying aspects and consequences of value phenomena that escape both artists and scientists. For example, the historian might trace the consequences of drug use in past societies. Moreover, the other humanists—especially philosophers—can take account of the whole value field, including the relationships between factual and normative values. This is something we are trying to do, however briefly and oversimply, right here.

CONCEPTION KEY VALUE DECISIONS

1. You probably have made a judgment about whether or not to use marijuana. Was there any kind of evidence—other than the scientific—that was relevant to your decision? Explain.
2. Reflect about the works of art that we have discussed in this book. Have any of them clarified value possibilities for you in a way that might helpfully influence your value decisions? How? Be as specific as possible. Do some arts seem more relevant than others in this respect? If so, why? Discuss with others. Do you find that people differ a great deal with respect to the arts that are most relevant to their value decisions? If so, how is this to be explained?
3. Do you think that in choosing its political leaders a society is likely to be helped if the arts are flourishing? As you think about this, consider the state of the arts in societies that have chosen wise leaders, as well as the state of the arts in societies that have chosen unwise leaders.
4. Do you think that political leaders are more likely to make wise decisions if they are sensitive to the arts? Back up your answer with reference to specific leaders.
5. Do you think there is any correlation between a flourishing state of the arts and a democracy? A tyranny? Back up your answers with reference to specific governments.

Factual values are verified experimentally, put through the tests of the scientific method. Normative values are verified experientially, put through the tests of living. Satisfaction, for ourselves and the others involved, is an experiential test that the normative values we chose in a given instance were probably right. Suffering, for ourselves and the others involved, is an experiential test that the normative values we chose were probably wrong. Experiential testing of normative values involves not only the immediacy of experience but the consequences that follow. If you choose to try heroin, you cannot escape the consequences. And, fortunately, certain works of the humanities—Nelson Algren's *Man with the Golden Arm*, for instance

—can make you vividly aware of those consequences before you have to suffer them. Science can also point out these consequences, of course, but science cannot make them so forcefully clear and present, and thus so thoroughly understandable.

The arts are closely related to the other humanities, especially history, philosophy, and theology. In conclusion, we shall give only a brief sketch of these relationships, for they are enormously complex and require extensive analyses that we can only suggest.

The Arts and History

CONCEPTION KEY HISTORY AND THE ARTS

1. Can works of art be of great significance to the work of a historian? Explain.
2. Suppose an ancient town were being excavated but, aside from architecture, no works of art had been unearthed. And then some paintings, sculpture, a few musical scores, and some poems come to light—all from the local culture. It is likely that the paintings would give the historian information different from that provided by the architecture or the sculpture? Or what might the music reveal that the other arts do not? The poems? As you reflect on these questions, reflect also on the following description by Heidegger of a painting by Van Gogh of a pair of peasant shoes:

"From the dark opening of the worn insides of the shoes the toilsome tread of the worker stares forth. In the stiffly rugged heaviness of the shoes there is the accumulated tenacity of her slow trudge through the far-spreading and ever-uniform furrows of the field swept by a raw wind. On the leather lie the dampness and richness of the soil. Under the soles slides the loneliness of the field-path as evening falls. In the shoes vibrates the silent call of the earth, its quiet gift of the ripening grain and its unexplained self-refusal in the fallow desolation of the wintry field. This equipment is pervaded by uncomplaining anxiety as to the certainty of bread, the wordless joy of having once more withstood want, the trembling before the impending childbed and shivering at the surrounding menace of death. This equipment belongs to the *earth*, and it is protected in the *world* of the peasant woman."[2]

Historians try to discover the *what* and the *why* of the past. Of course, they need as many relevant facts as possible in order to describe and explain the events that happened. Often they may be able to use the scientific method in their gathering and verification of facts. But in attempting to give as full an explanation as possible of why some of the events they are tracing happened, they function as humanists, for here

[2]Martin Heidegger, "The Origin of the Work of Art," in Albert Hofstadter (trans.), *Poetry, Language, Thought,* Harper and Row, New York 1971, pp. 33f.

they need understanding of the normative values or ideals of the society they are studying. Among their main resources are works of art. Often such works will reveal the norms of a people—their views of birth and death, blessing and disaster, victory and disgrace, endurance and decline, themselves and God, fate and what ought to be. Only with the understanding of such values can history become something more than a catalogue of events.

The Arts and Philosophy

Philosophy is, among other things, an attempt to give reasoned answers to fundamental questions that, because of their generality, are not treated by any of the more special disciplines. Ethics, aesthetics, and metaphysics or speculative philosophy, three of the main divisions of philosophy, are very closely related to the arts. Ethics in part is often the inquiry into the presuppositions or principles operative in our moral judgments, and the study of norms or standards for value decisions. If we are correct, an ethic dealing with norms that fails to take advantage of the insights of the arts is inadequate. John Dewey, one of America's foremost philosophers, even argued "that art is more moral than moralities. For the latter either are, or tend to become, consecrations of the *status quo*, reflections of custom, reenforcements of the established order. The moral prophets of humanity have always been poets even though they spoke in free verse or by parable."[3]

CONCEPTION KEY ETHICS AND THE ARTS

1. In the quote above, Dewey might seem to be thinking primarily of poets when he speaks of the contribution of artists to the ethicist. Or do you think he is using the term "poets" to include all artists? In any case, do you think that literature has more to contribute to the ethicist than the other arts? If so, why?
2. Reflect on the works of art which we have discussed in this book. Which ones do you think might have the most relevance to an ethicist? Why?

Throughout this book we have been elaborating an aesthetics or philosophy of art. We have been attempting to account to some extent for the whole range of the phenomena of art—the creative process of the artist, the work of art, the experience of the work of art, criticism, and the role of art in society—from a philosophic standpoint. On occasion we have avoided restricting our analysis to any single area within that group, considering the interrelationships of these areas.

[3]John Dewey, *Art as Experience*, Minton, Balch and Co., New York, 1934, p. 348.

And on the other occasions we have tried to make explicit the basic assumptions of some of the restricted studies. These are typical functions of the aesthetician or philosopher of art. For example, much of our time has been spent doing criticism, analyzing and appraising particular works of art. But at other times, as in Chapter 3, we tried to make explicit the presuppositions or principles of criticism. Critics, of course, may do this themselves, but then they are functioning more as aestheticians than as critics. Furthermore, we have also reflected on how criticism influences artists, the participants, and society. This, too, is a function of the aesthetician.

Finally, the aim of the metaphysicians or speculative philosophers, roughly speaking, is to understand *reality* as a *totality*. Therefore they must take into account the artifacts of the artists as well as the conclusions and reflections of the other humanists and the scientists. Metaphysicians attempt to reflect upon the whole in order to achieve some valid general conclusions concerning the nature of reality and our position and prospects in it. A metaphysician who ignores the arts will have left out some of the most useful insights about value phenomena, which are very much a fundamental part of our reality.

The Arts and Theology

The practice of religion, strictly speaking, is not a humanistic activity or study, for basically it neither creates values in the way of the arts nor studies values in the way of the other humanities. A religion is an institution that brings people together for the purpose of worship. These people share certain religious experiences as well as beliefs about the interpretations of those experiences. Since the beliefs of various people differ as well as their interpretations, it is more accurate to refer to religions than to religion. Nevertheless, there is a common-sense basis, reflected in our ordinary language, for the term "religion." Despite the differences about their beliefs and interpretations, religious people generally agree that their religious values—for example, achieving in some sense participation with God—are ultimate, that is, more important than any other values. They have ultimate concern for these values. Moreover, a common nucleus of experience seems to be shared by all religious people: (1) uneasy awareness of the limitations of human moral and theoretical powers; (2) awe-full awareness of a further reality—beyond or behind or within the world of our sense experience; (3) conviction that participation with this further reality is of supreme importance.

Theology involves the study of religions. As indicated in Chapter 1, the humanities in the Medieval period were studies about humans, whereas theology and related studies were studies about God. But in present times theology, usually broadly conceived, is placed with the humanities. Moreover, for many religious people today, ultimate values or the values of the sacred are not necessarily ensconced in another world "up there." In any case, some works of art reveal ultimate values in ways that are relevant to the contemporary situation. Theologians who ignore these revelations cannot do justice to their study of religions.

CONCEPTION KEY RELIGIOUS VALUES AND THE ARTS

Reflect about the works of art you know best. Have any of them revealed ultimate values to you in a way that is relevant to your situation? How? Are they necessarily contemporary works?

Dietrich Bonhoeffer, in one of his last letters from the Nazi prison of Tegel, noted that "now that it has become of age, the world is more Godless, and perhaps it is for that very reason nearer to God than ever before." Our artists, secular as well as religious, not only reveal our despair but also, in the depths of that darkness, open paths back to the sacred.

At the end of the last century, Matthew Arnold intimated that the aesthetic or participative experience, especially of the arts, would become the religious experience. We do not think this transformation will happen because the participative experience lacks the outward expressions, such as worship, that fulfill and in turn distinguish the religious experience. But Arnold was prophetic, we believe, in sensing that increasingly the arts would provide the most direct access to the sacred. Iris Murdoch, the contemporary Irish novelist, describes such an experience:

> Dora had been in the National Gallery a thousand times and the pictures were almost as familiar to her as her own face. Passing between them now, as through a well-loved grove, she felt a calm descending on her. She wandered a little, watching with compassion the poor visitors armed with guidebooks who were peering anxiously at the masterpieces. Dora did not need to peer. She could look, as one can at last when one knows a great thing very well, confronting it with a dignity which it has itself conferred. She felt that the pictures belonged to her. . . . Vaguely, consoled by the presence of something welcoming and responding in the place, her footsteps took her to various shrines at which she had worshipped so often before.[4]

Such experiences are rare. Most of us still require the guidebooks. But

[4]*The Bell*, by Iris Murdoch, copyright © 1958 by Iris Murdoch. Reprinted by permission of The Viking Press, Inc., New York, and Chatto and Windus Ltd., London, p. 182.

one hopes the time will come when we no longer just peer but participate. And when that times comes, then a guidebook such as this one may have its justification.

Summary

The various arts, despite their autonomy, often interrelate in mixed media for two basic reasons. In the first place, the media of the arts are each subject to systematic ordering, thus lending themselves to mixing. Second, the arts are a commonwealth because they serve the same purpose: to reveal something significant in their form-content that never has been made explicit before. This common purpose, moreover, often allows the arts to be performed and exhibited in close juxtaposition.

The arts and the other humanities are distinguished from the sciences because in the former, generally, strictly objective or scientific standards are irrelevant. In turn, the arts are distinguished from the other humanities because in the arts values are revealed, whereas in the other humanities values are studied. Furthermore, in the arts perception dominates, whereas in the other humanities conception dominates.

In our discussion about values, we distinguish between (1) intrinsic values—activities involving immediacy of feeling, positive or negative, (2) extrinsic values—activities that are means to intrinsic values, and (3) intrinsic-extrinsic values—activities that not only are means to intrinsic values but also involve significant immediacy of feeling. The theory of value presupposed in this book has been *relational;* that is, value emerges from the relation between a human interest and an object or event. Value is not merely subjective— projected by human interest on some object or event—nor is value merely objective—valuable independently of any subject. Values that are described scientifically we call "value facts." Values set forth as norms or ideals or what ought to be we call "normative values." The arts and the other humanities often have normative relevance: by clarifying what ought to be and thus what we ought to do.

Finally, the arts are closely related to the other humanities, especially history, philosophy, and theology. The arts help reveal the normative values of past cultures to the historian. Philosophers attempt to answer questions about values, especially in the fields of ethics, aesthetics, and metaphysics. Some of the most useful insights about value phenomena for the philosopher come from artists. Theology involves the study of religions, and religions are grounded in ultimate concern for values. No human artifacts reveal ultimate values more powerfully to the theologian than works of art.

Chapter 12 Bibliography

Andrews, Michael S. *Creativity and Psychological Health.* Syracuse, N.Y.: Syracuse University Press, 1961.

Fleming, William. *Arts and Ideas.* New York: Holt, Rinehart and Winston, 1974.

Gotshalk, D. W. *Art and the Social Order.* Chicago: University of Chicago Press, 1947.

Greenberg, Clement. *Art and Culture.* Boston: Beacon, 1961.

Hall, James B., and Ulanov, Barry. *Modern Culture and the Arts,* 2d ed. New York: McGraw-Hill, 1972.

Hauser, Arnold. *The Philosophy of Art History.* New York: Knopf, 1959.

Heidegger, Martin. *Poetry, Language, Thought,* trans. Albert Hofstadter. New York: Harper and Row, 1971.

Kepes, György, ed. *Education of Vision,* New York: Braziller, 1965.

Koestler, Arthur. *The Act of Creation.* New York: Macmillan, 1964.

Kroeber, A. L. *Style and Civilization.* Berkeley: University of California Press, 1963.

Martin, F. David. *Art and the Religious Experience.* Lewisburg, Pa.: Bucknell University Press, 1972.

Maslow, Abraham. *New Knowledge in Human Values.* Chicago: Henry Regnery, 1959.

Murdoch, Iris. *The Fire and the Sun: Why Plato Banished the Artists.* New York: Oxford, 1977.

Panofsky, Erwin. *Idea: A Concept in Art.* New York: Harper and Row, 1975.

Porter, Burton F. *Philosophy: A Literary and Conceptual Approach,* 2d ed. New York: Harcourt, Brace, Jovanovich, 1980.

Rader, Melvin, and Jessup, Bertram. *Art and Human Values.* Englewood Cliffs, N.J.: Prentice-Hall, 1976.

Read, Herbert. *Education Through Art,* 3d ed. London: Faber and Faber, 1958.
———. *Icon and Idea.* Cambridge, Mass.: Harvard University Press, 1955.

Sachs, Curt. *The Commonwealth of Art.* New York: Norton, 1946.

Tillich, Paul. *The Courage to Be.* New Haven: Yale University Press, 1952.

Wilson, Robert N. *The Arts in Society.* Englewood Cliffs, N.J.: Prentice-Hall, 1964.

Wolterstorff, Nicholas. *Art in Action.* Grand Rapids, Mich.: William B. Eerdmans, 1980.

GLOSSARY

Abstract painting   painting that has sensa as its primary subject matter. *See also* Representational painting.

Aesthetics   the philosophy of art: the examination of the creative process, the work of art, the aesthetic experience, principles of criticism, and the role of art in society.

Ambiguity   uncertain meaning, a situation in which not one, but several, meanings are implied. At its best, ambiguity can produce richness and significance; as its worst, it produces confusion.

Archetype   a structural pattern often used in literature, drama, dance, film, and occasionally in the other arts. It derives from structures in the human psyche as determined by culture and nature. It is usually a narrative pattern such as the search for the father, the quest for personal identity, the escape into the dream world, or, as in most comedies, the struggle of the young to marry in the face of their disapproving elders. The archetype is associated with the dream state, the unconscious, the deep, often inexpressible desires that people may not admit having. The term comes from Jungian psychology and has been associated by Jung with myth. *See also* Myth.

Aristotle's elements of drama   plot, character, diction, thought, spectacle, and music. In his *Poetics*, Aristotle cites these six ingredients as basic to drama. *See also entries under individual elements.*

Artistic form   the organization of a medium whereby values are separated from irrelevancies. *See also* Decorative form; Work of art.

Artistic medium   the elements or material out of which works of art are made. These elements either have an inherent order, such as colors, or permit an imposed order, such as words; and these orders, in turn, are organizable by artistic form.

Assemblage   the technique of sculpture, such as welding, whereby preformed pieces are attached. *See also* Modeling.

Auteur   in film the idea that a director (usually) is the author of the total film. *Citizen Kane* was written by Joseph L. Mankiewicz, but its *auteur* is generally recognized to be Orson Welles, its star and its director.

Axis mundi   a vertically placed pole used by primitive people to center their world.

Centered space   a site—natural or man-made—that organizes other places around it.

Comedy   a form of drama that is usually light in subject matter and ends happily. Comedy is not necessarily a drama at which one laughs, nor is it necessarily void of seriousness. Underneath its light surface, comedy can make profound statements.

Conception   thinking that focuses on concepts or ideas.

Configurational center   a place of special value, a place to dwell.

Connotation   use of language to suggest ideas or emotional colorations in addition to the explicit or denoted meaning. "Brothers and sisters" denotes relatives, but the words may also connote people united in a common effort or struggle, as in the expressions "Brotherhood of Teamsters" and "Sisterhood is Powerful." *See also* Denotation.

Content   a subject matter detached by means of an artistic form from its accidental or insignificant aspects, vivified and clarified.

Decorative form   the organization of a medium that pleases or distracts or entertains but does not inform about values. *See also* Artistic form.

Denotation   the direct, explicit meaning or reference of a word or words.

Dianoia   Greek word for "thought," one of Aristotle's six elements of drama. *See also* Thought.

Diction   in literature and drama the choice of words with special care for their expressive impact.

Earth-resting architecture   buildings that accent neither the earth nor the sky, using the earth as a platform with the sky as a background.

Earth-rooted architecture   buildings that bring out with special force the earth and its symbolisms. *See also* Sky-oriented architecture.

Earth sculpture   sculpture that makes the earth the medium, site, and subject matter.

Editing   in film the process by which the footage is cut, the best version of each scene chosen, and these versions joined together for optimum effect. *See also* Montage.

Epic   a lengthy narrative poem, usually episodic, with heroic action and great political or cultural scope.

Episodic narrative   a story the separate incidents (or episodes) of which are often tied loosely together by the device of a journey or by the fact that they happen to the same character. *See also* Organic narrative (its opposite)

Flaws in character   personality traits that reveal weaknesses; the tragic flaw in drama is the prominent weakness of character that leads to the protagonist's tragic end: Othello's jealousy, Macbeth's ambition.

Form-content   the fusion of the meaning of a work of art with the form.

Framing   photographic technique whereby important parts of figures or objects in a scene are cut off by the edges of the photograph.

Genre kind; the genres of literature are poetry, the novel, the short story, the essay, drama.

High relief sculpture with a background plane from which the projections are relatively large.

Humanities broad areas of human creativity and study essentially involved with values and generally not using strictly objective or scientific standards.

Imagery use of language to represent objects and events with strong appeal to the senses. Images can be more or less perceptual. T. S. Eliot's famous image of a "a patient etherized upon a table" is strongly perceptual. John Donne's equally famous image of the flea in: "This flea is you and I, and this/Our marriage bed, and marriage temple is" is vastly more conceptual, since, although we can perceive a flea, we must conceive it in its role of bed and temple.

Irony saying the opposite of what one means. Dramatic irony plays on the audience's capacity to perceive the difference between what the characters expect and what they will get.

Low relief sculpture with a background plane from which the projections are relatively small.

Lyric a poem, usually brief and personal, with an emphasis on feeling as part of the subject matter.

Machine sculpture sculpture that reveals the machine and/or its powers.

Metaphor an implied comparison between different things. An example would be William Plomer's line from "In the Snake Park": "Lethargy lay here and there in coils," in which lethargy is compared with a snake without the poet explicitly telling us so.

Mixed media the merger of two or more artistic media.

Modeling the technique of building up a sculpture piece by piece with some plastic or malleable material. *See also* Assemblage.

Montage cutting and joining pieces of film into a coherent unit. As Serge Eisenstein used the term, it means the joining of physically different, but psychologically related scenes, usually for the purpose of building tension. *See also* Editing.

Myth ancient stories that are rooted in primitive experience. Some myths come from primitive peoples, such as the ancient American Indians; some from Greek and Roman antiquity, such as the stories of Ulysses, Venus and Adonis, and Jove. Recurrent patterns in myth have been observed by recent researchers such as James Frazer and Levi-Strauss, and those patterns have suggested that there are archetypal myths that many culturals share. C. G. Jung, the psychologists, suggested that archetypal myths may be the "storehouse" of the unconscious mind. *See also* Archetype.

Narrative the story line of a poem, novel, or play. Film, opera, program music, dance, painting, sculpture, and even, occasionally, architecture can have narrative elements that act as structural patterns. Any work of art that tells a story has a narrative element.

Narrator the person telling the story.

New Comedy   originally developed by Menander and the Greeks and later developed by the Roman playwrights Plautus and Terence. Usually quite polished in style with bright and incisive humor, New Comedy criticizes the manners and mores of society. The intention is to expose society's foibles, sometimes in the hope that it will improve itself.

Normative values   norms or ideals about values; what "ought to be."

Old Comedy   as originally practiced by the Greeks, a comedy that postulated an inherently ridiculous situation or exaggerated conditions, such as women withholding sex from their husbands until the men agree to stop war, and then following that postulate to its conclusion. Old comedy is often raucous, broad, satirical, and filled with slapstick.

Organic narrative   a story the separable elements of which all relate to one another in tight, meaningful ways. No action takes place for its own sake. *See also* Episodic narrative.

Paradox   an apparent contradicition that, upon reflection, may seem reasonable.

Participative experience   "thinking from" something, letting that thing initiate and control everything that comes into awareness.

Perception   the awareness of something stimulating our sense organs.

Picaresque   *See* Episodic narrative.

Plot   the story or narrative line of a work of art; the sequence of actions or events.

Pop art   art that reveals mass-produced articles.

Presentational immediacy   the awareness of something that is presented with an "all-at-onceness," in its entirety.

Pretext   the underlying story or narrative in a ballet or modern dance.

Protagonist   in drama and literature, the chief character.

Representational painting   painting that has specific objects or events as its primary subject matter. *See also* Abstract painting.

Satire   literature that ridicules people or institutions, often with the hope of improving those people or institutions.

Sciences   disciplines that generally use strictly objective standards.

Sculpture in the round   sculpture freed from any background plane.

Sensa   the qualities of objects or events that stimulate our sense organs.

Setting   in literature and drama the time and the placc in which the narrative occurs. The setting is established mainly by means of description in literature and spectacle in drama.

Simile   an explicit comparison between different things, using comparative words such as "like," and "as." For instance, "He was like a tiger."

Sky-oriented architecture   buildings that bring out with special force the sky and its symbolisms. *See also* Earth-oriented architecture.

Space   the power of the positioned interrelationships of things.

Space sculpture   sculpture that emphasizes spatial relationships and thus tends to deemphasize the density of its materials.

Spectacle   the visual ingredients of drama, opera, dance, or any staged event.

Structural details   the elements or parts of a structure.

Structure   general overall pattern or design of a work of art.

Subject matter   what the work of art "is about"; some value *before* any artistic interpretation.

Sunken relief   sculpture made by carving that cuts grooves of various depths into the surface plane of the sculptural material, the surface plane remaining perceptually distinct.

Surface relief   sculpture with a flat surface plane as the basic organizing plane of the composition, but no clear perceptual distinction is visible between the depths behind the surface plane and the projections in front.

Symbol   something concrete and perceptible that stands for something more abstract; for instance, a rose may stand for love and a tiger for wrath.

Tactility   touch sensations both inward and outward.

Technologies   disciplines that apply for practical purposes the theoretical knowledge produced by the sciences.

Texture   the "feel" of a material, such as "smooth" bronze or "rough" concrete.

Theme   in music a melodic line of considerable importance usually because of later repetition or development. In literature, drama, and film a theme is the main idea or general topic.

Thought   the ideas expressed in literature and drama.

Tragedy   drama that treats a serious subject matter and ends unhappily. Tragedies need not end with death, but they must have significant and unfortunate consequences for their protagonists. Often the question of fate, inevitability, and flawed personality are of first importance. *See also* Flaws of character.

Tragic flaw   *See* Flaws of character.

Tragi-comedy   drama that includes both the qualities of tragedy, such as an unhappy ending, the tragic hero, and intensely serious ideas, as well as the qualities of comedy, such as slapstick humor, witty situations, type characters, and satirical comment. *See also* Comedy; Tragedy.

Type character   in drama and literature a predictable character who seems more a stereotype than an indivdiual, such as the stagestruck young girl, the hard-boiled cop with a heart of gold, the snooty rich kid, the ugly American tourist, the stage Irishman.

Value facts   values described scientifically as they are found. *See also* Normative values.

Values   objects and events important to human beings; something we care about.

Work of art   an artifact that informs about values by means of an artistic form. *See also* Artistic form.

INDEX OF TITLES

Titles are listed alphabetically under the following headings: Architecture; Dance; Film; Literature (& Drama); Music; Painting; Photography; and Sculpture. Page numbers in *italic* indicate illustrations.

FILM

LITERATURE (& DRAMA)

MUSIC

PAINTING

PHOTOGRAPHY

SCULPTURE

SUBJECT INDEX

Page numbers in *italic* indicate illustrations.

Jones, Spike, 307
Joplin, Scott, *Treemonisha*, 347
Jung, C. G., 268, 456
"Junk art," 166
Justice, Donald, "Love's Map," 65–67

Kandinsky, Wassily, 93
Käsebier, Gertrude, "Blessed Art Thou Among Women," 427–429
Katharsis, 275–276
Keaton, Buster, 394
Keats, John, 380
  "When I have fears," 241
Keys, piano, 354
Kinetic sculpture, 161–166
Knappe, Karl, 156
Kricke, Norbert, *Space Sculpture*, 153
Kubrick, Stanley, *2001: A Space Odyssey*, 404

Labanotation, 376
Lachaise, Gaston, *Floating Figure*, 137
Lange, Dorothea, "Migrant Mother," 444
Langer, Susanne, 304
Lawrence, D. H., "Piano," 232–233
Lean, David
  Bridge Over the River Kwai, 398
  Dr. Zhivago, 398
  Lawrence of Arabia, 398
  Ryan's Daughter, 398
Le Corbusier (Edward Jeanneret), Notre-Dame-du-Haut, *64, 192*
Lehr, Harold, ecological sculptures, *171*
Lichtenstein, Roy, 38–39
  comic strip panels, 38–45
Light in architecture, 209–213
Li Ho, "The Grave of Little Su," 252
Limón, José
  The Emperor Jones, 383
  The Moor's Pavane, 366, 383
Longfellow, Henry Wadsworth, "A Psalm of Life," 250–251
Low-relief sculpture, 120
Lully, Jean Baptist, *Giselle*, 376
Lumet, Sidney, *Equus*, 415
Luther, Martin, 339
Lye, Len, 169–170
  The Loop, 169
Lyric, 240–248

Machine sculpture, 166–171
McQueen, Steve, 408
Madame Tussaud's Wax Museum, waxworks of Colonel Glenn and John F. Kennedy, *145*
Madeleine, Church of the, *75*
Magdalene Master, 97–99
  Madonna Enthroned, 98
Mahler, Gustave
  Das Lied von der Erde, 344
  Kindertotenlieder, 344
  Symphony No. 8 in E^b major, 344
  Symphony No. 9 in D major, 344
  Symphony of a Thousand, 344
Malcolm, Janet, 446
Malevitch, Kazimir, *Supremacist Composition: White on White, 90*
Malina, Judith, 298
Malraux, Andre, 99
Manet, Edouard, *Olympia, 51*
Manhattan, New York, 225
Mann, Thomas, *Death in Venice*, 454–457
Mathema, 272
Matisse, Henri, 87–88, 90
  Still Life, Pineapple and Anemones, 87–88, Color Plate 6
Meliés, George, 394
Melody, 356
Melville, Herman, *Moby Dick*, 239, 254, 255
Menander, 280–281
Mendelssohn, Felix
  Concerto in E minor for Violin, 60, 342
  Incidental Music for a Midsummer Night's Dream, 342
  Symphony No. 4, the *Italian*, 342
Menotti, Gian-Carlo
  Amahl and the Night Visitors, 347
  The Medium, 347
Metaphor, 250–253
Meyer, Leonard B., 303
Michals, Duane, "Alice's Mirror," 449, *450*
Michelangelo Buonarroti
  David, 139, *140, 143, 148*
  Palazzo Farnese, 215
  Pietà, 128–130
Mies van der Rohe, Ludwig
  Lafayette Park, *219*
  residence of Dr. Edith Farnsworth, *216*
Millay, Edna St. Vicent, 457